CONTEMPORARY SOCIETY: TRIBAL STUDIES

VOLUME THREE
SOCIAL CONCERN

CONTEMPORARY SOCIETY: TRIBAL STUDIES

Edited by
DEEPAK KUMAR BEHERA
AND
GEORG PFEFFER

VOLUME ONE	—	STRUCTURE AND PROCESS
VOLUME TWO	—	DEVELOPMENT ISSUES, TRANSITION AND CHANGE
VOLUME THREE	—	SOCIAL CONCERN
VOLUME FOUR	—	SOCIAL REALITIES

THE EDITORS

Deepak Kumar Behera is Reader in the Department of Anthropology, Sambalpur University, Sambalpur, Orissa (India.)

Georg Pfeffer is Professor and Head of the Department of Ethnology, Freie University of Berlin (Germany).

CONTEMPORARY SOCIETY: TRIBAL STUDIES

VOLUME THREE

SOCIAL CONCERN

Edited by
DEEPAK KUMAR BEHERA
Department of Anthropology
Sambalpur University
Sambalpur - 768 019
Orissa
India

GEORG PFEFFER
Freie Universität Berlin
Institut für Ethnologie
Drosselweg 1-3
D-14195 Berlin
Germany

CONCEPT PUBLISHING COMPANY, NEW DELHI - 110 059

Associate Editors
Sudhansu Shekhar Guru and
Arun Kumar Basa

ISBN 81-7022-640-6 (Series)
ISBN 81-7022-737-2 (Vol. III)

First Published 1999

Published and Printed by
Ashok Kumar Mittal
Concept Publishing Company
A/15-16, Commercial Block, Mohan Garden
New Delhi - 110 059 (India)
Phones: 0091-(0)11-5648039, 5649024
Fax: 0091-(0)11-5648053

ACKNOWLEDGEMENTS

We are grateful to all the contributors to the volume. Their academic generosity has enabled us to complete this work sucessfully. We offer our special thanks to Mr. Ashok Kumar Mohapatra, Dr. Sudhansu Shekar Guru and Mr. Arun Kumar Basa for their untiring help and co-operation at various stages of the project. Without their support the volume would not have seen the light of the day. We also express our deep sense of gratitude to all others who helped us directly or indirectly for the successful completion of the volume. Last but not least, we are thankful to Concept Publishing Company for showing interest to take up the publication project *Contemporary Society: Tribal Studies.*

DEEPAK KUMAR BEHERA
GEORG PFEFFER

CONTENTS

SECTION II

LAND, ENVIRONMENT AND FOREST

SECTION III

GENDER ISSUES

SECTION IV

EDUCATION

SECTION V

HEALTH AND NUTRITION

INTRODUCTION

DEEPAK KUMAR BEHERA AND GEORG PFEFFER

While examining the current literature on tribal societies we notice a curious absence of scientific studies based on intensive fieldwork among a large and important section of the world population. The series *Contemporary Society: Tribal Studies* tries to fill in this gap and thereby attempts to remove our ignorance on many aspects of tribal social reality. The ongoing series has already brought out two earlier volumes, namely, (I) *Structure and Process*, and (II) *Development Issues, Transition and Change*. The first volume, consisting of twenty-five chapters, is devoted to the study of structural and ethnic relations, gender, ecology, and ideology in contemporary tribal societies. The chapters in the second volume, thirty-three in number, deal with development issues, transition and change in various sectors of tribal life.

Titled *Social Concern*, this volume, under the series *Contemporary Society: Tribal Studies*, draws a number of social scientists together into a commonly scholarly quest for the understanding of different aspects of tribal society. The contributors to the volume express their social concern for various such issues that affect the tribal social life. The volume documents the said aspects through the contribution of many eminent social scientists of India and abroad. The papers in this volume have been presented under five sections, viz. (1) Development Issues, (2) Land Environment and Forest, (3) Gender Issues, (4) Education, and (5) Health and Nutrition.

The objects of knowledge do not exist *per se*. Nor is the volume of knowledge self-evident. What is required in the analysis of knowledge is a consensus of the people in a community in defining and using it in terms of common cultural perceptions and goals. Accordingly, it becomes essentials for the social scientist to formulate the necessary perceptive on knowledge and the methodology of its analysis in correspondence with the said communal consensus relating to knowledge. The perspective on knowledge and the analysis of objects of knowledge thus need to be underpinned by social concern. Keeping this in mind this volume works out empirical parameters of knowledge-production and examines their inherent social concern.

In recent times the tribals have been exposed to various external forces and conditions that hamper their growth and development. As more and more tribal dominated pockets are drawn to the process of modernization and the so-called development, there is the less and less social space for the tribals to participate in the processes of decision-making affecting their life. As a result, they have hot been able to protect themselves and preserve their rich cultural heritage. Both their cultural identity and human dignity have been under constant threat. The government policy of "integration not assimilation" is intended to leave an autonomous cultural space for the tribals, while bringing them into political economy of the mainstream. But such a policy has been problematic in its conceptualization and more so in its implementation. Against the backdrop, the contributors to the volume express their social concern for various issues that have effected contemporary tribal society and culture.

The first section, consisting of eight papers, begins with the paper on sustainable development of the tribals by Behera and Erasmus. The authors try to analyze the ongoing process of environmental degradation and its consequences upon the tribal population. The paper critically examines the concept of sustainable development in the context of the rapid process of globalization. By reviewing some existing literature, it highlights the importance of indigenous knowledge in resource conservation. Finally, the paper suggests some strategies for sustainable development of the tribal population.

The last couple of decades have witnessed a phenomenal rise of dystopian images of the futures of tribal peoples of India. At the same time there seems to be a clear decline in the imaging capacity of the social scientists concerned with tribal scenario. Based primarily on informed optimism about the empowerment of tribal peoples, Jaganath Pathy's paper makes a constructive critique of the existing world view of dynamics and urges for imagining a different historical dynamics of the tribal context in the next millennium. The keys to this forward looking temporal context rest in the nature of tribal, national and global human responses to what is desired or feared in the immediate and distant futures.

Jaganath Pathy, in his next article, argues that the intellectual intervention ought to explore whether the diverse and complex tribal world can analytically fall into a more or less common frame of interpretation, and thereby appropriate political action. He believes that the forced imposition of the modern development paradigm has generated institutional and cognitive crises in the tribal milieu.

P. Dash Sharma's paper is a critique of the development programmes in the Chotanagpur region of Bihar, where one finds today an interplay of forces of tradition and modernity among the tribals of the region. He argues that lack of scientific planning jeopardizes the development programmes in the region, resulting in substantial loss of public money and, therefore, bringing negligible benefit to the tribal population. As a remedy, Dash Sharma suggests that an apex co-ordinating body should be formed to synchronize all the activities of the different government departments for the effective implementation, monitoring and intervention at the district and state levels.

S.P. Punalekar writes about the nature and directionality of development in tribal areas and their impact on tribal communities living in the forest and on the plains of South Gujarat. He also addresses the interface, as also its intricacies, between development, both social and non-social, and physical as well as non-physical environments. He shows that this interface is riddled with unease and tension prevailing in most of the tribal communities in four districts of the state. He argues that the development of tribal society must be perceived as ideological within a larger context of growth or development. While "doing" development among the tribals, the underlying premises of growth or development and attendant strategies as well as initiatives need to be scrutinized in terms of the nature of change(s) brought about in a tribal region.

In the wake of rapid development programmes, numerous people from various sections are adversely impacted -- many times losing their live support mechanism. Worst affected in this process are the indigenous people. Hence, the resettlement and rehabilitation of these people have to be undertaken with utmost care. But often their cause is dealt in an *adhoc* manner only to exacerbate their sufferings. The entire rehabilitation procedure is undertaken mechanically. Rehabilitation measures are limited only to the payment of monetary compensation. Hence many times the intervention to rehabilitate the oustees proves more harmful than good. This happens due to the unscientific and lackadaisical approach by the policy formulators. Against the backdrop, Patel and Behera tries to analyze the impact of Upper Indravati Hydro-electricity project on the Peng oustees. Peng is one of the most adversely affected tribal communities of the aforesaid project. The authors also critically evaluate the rehabilitation measures adopted by the project authorities for oustees of that tribal community.

S.M. Patnaik argues that a major component in our national planning is the installation of mega projects in inaccessible tribal areas of our country. Though such projects are envisaged for the welfare of the nation, they severely affect the local population, unleashing devastating consequences for them. He concludes that the government can no longer afford to cater to the needs of the multinationals at the cost of the sufferings of its own tribal people who are already marginalized from the mainstream society and economy.

Tilak Bagchi explains the genesis of applied-action-development anthropology and charts its development, especially in the context of India. He also brings out the scope and relevance of applied anthropological research in our contemporary society. Some of his suggestions in this regard are very practical.

The second section addresses to various issues relating to land, environment and forest. In the first paper under this section Piet Erasmus holds that different systems of land administration are responsible for the forcible separation and resettlement of millions of black people in South Africa over the years. He outlines the legal framework that influenced the tribal community of Thaba 'Nehu and indicates how they actually reacted in this regard. Thaba 'Nehu has a distinctive history. It was the only district in the Orange Free State Republic with a mix of white and black-owned farms under private as well as communal occupation. It was this region that provided Thaba 'Nehu with an identity of its own, which was destroyed by the government in the later years. The *Barôlông bôôSeleka* (Rolong-Seleka, a Tswana tribe) were/are the founders and original residents of Thaba 'Nehu. Erasmus makes a detail discussion of their traditional way of land administration. The author has also critically examined the reaction of the inhabitants of Thaba 'Nehu to the alien systems of land policy introduced in their district. These people felt that the practices of separation and resettlement were essentially destructive. Their reactions eventually helped them to establish a new dispensation within present local government structures.

L.K. Mahapatra states that the tribal people of India had been enjoying customary rights since times immemorial in respect of land-based resources. The Customary Rights in many areas inhered in communal rights over the common property resources, of which the forest was the foremost. Private property in land was not prevalent in tribal areas before the British colonial regime extended their sway to exploit the local resources or administer the areas as never before. With the passage of time there developed numerous institutional systems and administrative strategies to disinherit the tribal people of their customary rights. After independence the development projects in many tribal areas did not compensate the tribal people for their real loss in life-support base on the plea that compensation was given only for the loss of privately owned land and other immovable resources. Against this backdrop, Mahapatra presents the case of tribal situation of Orissa. He feels that the state government has recently taken a historic decision to recognize land ownership rights of the tribal people on the lower slopes and their usufructuary rights on the higher slope beyond 30° gradient. This augurs well for safeguarding the tribal rights to land in India.

Prasad Rao attempts to delineate the exploitative practices of the non-tribals, which have led to the alienation of the tribals from cultivable land. Practices like giving the tribals liberal credit facility for consumer items and edibles, and also maintaining manipulated accounts have become the standard practice of exploitation of the tribals by the non-tribals. Village elders who were most benefited by the non-tribal *sahukars* (traders) now side with the latter. Prasad Rao opines that the tenure systems that are in vogue in tribal areas have also a baneful effect on tribal economy. Exploitation of tribals has become an unending process and it continues in several forms. He also explains as to how various factions of Naxalites use the habitats of the tribals as their hideouts and cause them inconvenience. The author feels this to be yet another form of exploitation of the tribals.

S. Saraf's paper focuses on the theme of forest vis-à-vis tribal folk. It attempts an analysis of man-forest relationship by highlighting the tribal predilections and the non-tribal polemics regarding ecological conservation and/or exploitation respectively. While doing so he advances a Hegelian synthesis for drafting a pragmatic blueprint of our future forest policy in consonance with our philosophy of development and the expectations of the tribals. He argues for a balance between our science that is grossly fragmented and their philosophy that is holistic, organic, systemic and ecological in tone and tenor.

Pasayat and Barik discuss the participation of tribal people in social forestry programme in the state of Orissa. They state that consorted efforts should be made by all the concerned agencies to motive the tribals for voluntary participation and mass involvement in social forestry programme in the state. The authors finally suggest that the future strategy for forest should be a rational one considering the available forest resources, conservation and needs of the indigenous population.

The third section contains three articles dealing with gender issues in tribal India context. Mann and Mann's paper focuses on women and their role in gearing up changes that are so essential to bring about a desirable integration. They present a social scenario of five Scheduled Tribes of Uttar Pradesh who inhabit the central Himalayan region. Getting into the nexus of tribal culture of the region, the authors unfold numerous areas in which women can prove as stimulants to planned development in all sectors of tribal society and economy. And this holds true for major areas of social and economic concerns. They argue that the in-built provisions in traditional tribal cultures can empower women and equip them to play a very positive role in the entire process of developmental change.

Gopal Singh shows how gender has played a significant role in the lives of human beings. In the traditional/tribal societies of western Himalaya, women have to play an important role in interweaving socio-cultural values with the native environment. A gendered division of labour has evolved locally for productive functional use and has prevailed down the generations. It is seen that the status of men and that of women are exclusively dependent upon the culture of the people concerned. In that region women's status, position and authority are, by and large, equal to those of men. The functional role of tribal women is not only important from the viewpoint of socio-economic activities, but also from that of non-economic activities. Despite the harsh and inhospitable geographic and inclement environmental conditions they have moulded themselves into contributing optimally through the productive enterprises in such intricate eco-cultural and social formation. Introduction of the so-called modern technologies, unrestrained commercialization and influx of tourism are the root causes of disordering the delicate, harmonious and symbiotic relationship between environmental set-up and social-cultural values of the region.

Itishree Padhi presents a case study of a group of tribal women of a rehabilitated village in order to assess the impact of development on their life style in the context of social transformation. She states that the adverse impact of development on them has been greater than the benefits accruing to them. It is a pity that the planners and policy makers have remained insensitive to the gender dimension of tribal development.

The next section begins with Suguna Pathy's article. Here she argues that educational standard is the index of the development of a particular society, be it tribal or non-tribal. She shows that the level of education among the tribal communities in India is far below the average. Further, she highlights the status of tribal female education under the prevailing unequal social conditions. She tries to contextualize the question of tribal education in the capitalistic framework of the changing relations of production from a holistic stand of changing social relations of production and development of capitalism.

N.K. Ambasht discusses the problem of tribal identity in the perspective of contemporary tribal education. Tribal education has the values and ethos of the predominant culture deeply entrenched in its course curriculum. As a result it has imposed on them the ideology of the dominant classes. Suggesting a corrective to this trend, he argues that the content and process of tribal education need to be suitably modified so that cultural disequlibrium can be avoided. Also the life and learning styles of the tribal children will have to inform the pedagogic content and process concerning them.

The fifth section deals with health and nutritional of tribal people in India in general and Orissa in particular. In the first article N.K. Behura discusses the cultural aspects of diseases and their treatment in the context of tribal Orissa. Humans everywhere transform the natural milieu of their habitat into a cultural milieu insofar as they modify their natural life to cultural one. Biological needs are common to all humans, and these are satisfied through cultural imperatives. Health and hygiene are a set of biological needs common to all humans, and their satisfaction calls for adoption of organic (health) welfare measures. In traditional societies people continue to follow ethnic healing methods, and depend on their ethnic healers, since modern medical facilities have not yet been made easily available to them, as in the state of Orissa. Behura opines that lack of proper medical facilities provides an opportunity to quacks and medical mafias to operate and thrive on the ignorance and helplessness of the tribal people. He suggests that ethnic healers should be given primary health-care education to be better equipped to serve their own people.

Mishra and Tripathy present a report on the malnutrition and morbidity pattern of a group of tribal women (Munda) living in an urban setting of Sambalpur, Orissa. They discuss the influence of various socio-economic variables on the prevalence of deficiency signs and symptoms among the Munda women. The authors have used different quantitative techniques to make their analysis effective.

In their paper Guru and Pramanik examine the influence of paternal occupation, education, socio-economic status, belief pattern, etc. on infant mortality on the basis of a sample study of 500 families among the Kharia in Sundargarh district of western Orissa. The significance of such influence has been verified statistically.

Roy, Basu, Mukhopodhyay and Ghosh analyze the practice of mother and child care among the Kharias of Similipal region of Orissa. The study is based on anthropometric measurements carried on women and children. Estimation shows that the Kharias live at a bare subsistence level. There is hardly any special health care system available for the pregnant women. Further some food taboos of the community deprive them of valuable nutrients. The well being of a child depends on the joint care of the mother and female relatives in a traditional age-old style. Modern health care has not yet reached the hill Kharias.

The number of papers in this volume is not large enough to provide our readers with comprehensive understanding of various issues of social concern and social reality in our contemporary tribal societies. Nonetheless the empirical depth and analytical rigour of the papers, it is hoped, will be a modest help in this regard. We wish to receive feedback from scholars of tribal studies on the strength and weakness of this volume. As we get on with the preparation of the forthcoming volumes under the *Contemporary Society: Tribal Studies* series, a word of appreciation will encourage as much in the way as constructive criticism would enlighten us.

SECTION I

DEVELOPMENT ISSUES

ONE

ENVIRONMENT, TRIBAL PEOPLE AND DEVELOPMENT: Some Reflections from the Third World

DEEPAK KUMAR BEHERA and PIET A. ERASMUS

Introduction

Relevant literature clearly reflects that until the 1980s "development" was viewed mainly either as a linear process of causes and effects or it was explained by the "logic of capital" in terms of the radical critique associated with neo-Marxism. In the former approach "development" was seen as an effort to fight poverty, to raise standards of living, and to promote some version or other of progress. Usually a top-down approach was followed; the focus was to locate what went "wrong", why, and how it could be fixed. In the latter approach, capitalism was viewed as an obstacle to development as the cause of poverty, because it promoted only the interests of institutions like the World Bank, USAID, etc. Coetzee and Graaf (1996:3) see this approach as not only theoretically more competent, but morally more defensible. Development theory should, they say, spawn policies and research practices that avoid violence to ordinary people's cultures and aspirations, to the environment, and to human dignity and self-esteem.

Authors like Escobar (1995), Ferguson (1990), Fowler (1996) and Leroke (1996) point out that a paradigm shift has recently (after the 1980s) taken place regarding the way "development" is conceptualized. Recent attention in the development discourse, which links up with post-modernism, goes beyond conventional economic growth thinking. Perhaps the single most important theme is the recognition of the complex relationship between planned intervention and strategic outcomes. It is not possible to link specific achievements with specific outcomes; development can namely be crucially influenced by officials' subjective interpretations, it can be politically too controversial, or even "messy" in the methods applied. Development objectives are also not always clear, or in touch with the reality which people live day by day

Other significant dimensions emphasised in this (current) debate are: environmental support capacity and sustainability; equity in terms of entitlement, empowerment and resource use; human resources as a knowledge base and the significance of values and ethics; and the contribution of institutions to needs and demands.

It can thus be concluded that development is more than a rational and positivistic issue; the significance of values and ethics, negotiations and the appropriateness of governance are, *inter alia,* important.

Against this background, this paper tries to analyze the ongoing process of environmental degradation (ED) and its consequences upon the tribal population. It critically examines the concept of sustainable development (SD) in the context of the rapid process of globalization. By reviewing some existing literature, it highlights the importance of indigenous knowledge in resource conservation. Finally the paper suggests some strategies for sustainable development of the tribal population.

Environmental Degradation

Environmental degradation, or ecological decline, usually arises due to a ruthless exploitation of the biosphere by a small clique of greedy people, unmindful of the sufferings of the vast majority of people and of the future. This is possible because a small group controls a disproportionately large part of the biosphere.

The driving force behind the unmindful exploitation of the biosphere is the craze for industrial programmes by consumerist societies. This consumerist materialism has become more acute with the exposure of the tribal people to urban influences. Finally, humankind's violent attempt to subdue or conquer nature has led to some degree of tension within oneself, tension with other members of society, as well as with nature. As a consequence, man's harmony with nature has either been destroyed or at least disturbed. And this imbalance between man and his environment is leading us into an environmental crisis.

Environment and natural resources are often viewed almost exclusively from the ecological or the commercial point of view where the basic concerns of human beings are forgotten. Environment is primarily for the people. It is the human element that gives meaning to ecology and the environmental question becomes relevant to society only to the extent that it is viewed in relation to the people who are affected by it. Hence, the main concern while studying the state of the environment has to be its relationship with the indigenous (mostly tribal people) who depend on it for survival. Based on the understanding of this relationship, it becomes imperative to work for the restoration of a balance between nature and human needs. Such an understanding of the environment for people becomes imperative in the context of the present crisis of natural resources. Realizing this fact, a number of social scientists have already conducted useful studies on the impact of environmental degradation on people.

Developmental and environmental issues go hand in hand. However, scholars and parties across the ideological and political spectrum do not seem to consider environmental issues as central to their analyses. When we refer to environment, we do not consider natural environment alone, but include social and cultural aspects also. Development planning cannot take place in a social vacuum—take for example the influence of the rapid population growth, rising number of people in absolute poverty, increasing urbanisation, widespread ill-health, high level of unemployment and a lack of skilled personnel. The socio economic and cultural environment thus affects developmental planning and its implementation. Changes in the management practices of these environmental aspects (could at least) contribute to sustainable resource use and to the well-being of the population.

There is now an overdue recognition that the economic fortunes of many developing countries are inextricably bound up in the state of their natural environments, particularly with the quality and quantity of soil, water and biomass resources. Over-use of these resources, combined with only limited appreciation of their complex interdependence, has resulted in depletion of what are, in essence, renewable resources. Use rates have been based on non-sustainable practices, i.e. harvest rates have exceeded the sustainable yields of the resources. The results are soil erosion, water pollution and reduced water supplies, deforestation and other biomass loss, and desertification (Pearc, 1998).

Tribal societies' needs are no longer defined only by the local group itself—market exchanges assume increasing importance, while the amount of work undertaken and surplus produced also increase. The pattern of resource exploitation is closely linked to the exchanges, which occur within the wider economic system.

Often tribal people contribute to the further degradation of already poor environments in the course of trying to meet their survival requirements. The significance of natural resource degradation (NRD), for example, correlates directly in terms of inputs with well-being, with reduced woodfuels supply, increased time cost in woodfuel collection and reduced nutritional intake. The proximate causes of resource loss are, then, forest clearance for agricultural land use, non-sustainable woodfuels harvesting, over-intensive rates of animal stocking, farm practices (including choice of inappropriate crops and rotational patterns), exogenous climatic impacts, and population pressure (population growth will in itself force marginalization of many tribal communities.). It is obvious that if the environment deteriorates, so also does the standard of living and the prospects for meeting future needs.

Perhaps the starkest realization of the need to find new patterns and processes of development has come from the improved understanding of the concept "environmental sustainability". All productivity activities make demands on the resource base in terms of the raw materials obtained. In addition, all such activities involve some waste generation - the so-called "externalities of production". Not all of these activities are harmful to the environment. Those, which do endanger human health, termed "pollutants", also harm ecosystems or interfere with other legitimate uses of the environment. In the last 20 years there has been an increasing recognition of a series of environmental problems, which extend across national boundaries and which affect the global community as a whole.

Poverty and environmental destruction are becoming inseparable twins; the numbers of people have grown and the tribal people (who have the least access to investment capital and technology) occupy those kinds of lands that need the most infrastructure, management and external inputs (Leonard, 1989). Figure 1.1 illustrates some of the linkage between poverty and the environment. It shows clearly how poverty can contribute to environmental stress, such as through the cultivation of steep hillsides. However, the relationship between poverty and the environment can be shown to be circular.

Contributing Factors	Rapid population growth	Agricultural modernisation in high potential areas	Inequitable law distribution	
Underlying problem	Tribal population with limited access to productive lands			
Environmental Stress	Urban migration	Rural stagnation in dry areas	Greater exploitation of hillsides	Pressure to open forested frontier areas
Potential Adverse	* Human settlement in ecologically hazards	* Drought condition exacerated * Desertification	* Destruction of vegetative cover	* Large Scale deforestation. * Loss of soil fertility
Ecological Consequences				
Threats to Well-being of Indigenous People	* Diseases from faecal and chemical contamination * Vulnerability to natural diseases	* Fuelwood shortage * Declining land productivity	* Declining productivity * Fuelwood shortage * Down stream flooding and sedimentation	* Declining land productivity * Loss of potential based forest production * Tropical diseases

Figure1.1: Showing the Connection between Poverty and Environment

Source: Leonard, H.T. 1989. *Environment and the Poor: Development strategies for a common Agenda.* Oxford: Transaction Books

The adverse ecological effects associated with people endeavouring to secure their basic needs, in turn threaten the health and survival of those very people. The environmental concerns of the tribal poor are those associated with immediate survival needs such as for fuel or access to productive lands. Furthermore, it is realised that the world's poorest people are resident largely in the world's environmentally most fragile areas. This has been referred to as "the retreat of poverty", whether into geographical areas, remote and ecologically vulnerable rural areas, or the edges of growing towns. For example, when considering just the world's poorest groups (the poorest 20 per cent among the total population of all developing countries), 57 per cent of the rural poor and 76 per cent of the urban poor are resident in areas where ecological destruction and/or severe environmental hazards threaten their well-being (Elliott, 1994). Such inequalities are not only morally wrong, but also threaten the environmental basis for sustainable development.

Sustainable Development

In 1984 the United Nations commissioned an independent group of twenty-two people from member-states, drawn from both the developed and developing worlds, to identify long-term environmental strategies for the international community. In 1987, the World Commission on Environment and Development (WCED), also known as the Brundtland Commission, reported to the UN, calling for a "common endeavour and for new norms of behaviour at all levels and in the interests of all." Global co-operation and mutually supportive actions between countries at different stages of economic development, were central themes within their report entitled *'Our Common Future'* (WCED, 1987). Despite the extent of environmental decay, which the commission reported, they remained optimistic that, given global commitment and co-ordination, a more prosperous, more just and more secure future was possible for all. Although the WCED was not the first group to use the term "sustainable development" they offered perhaps the most straightforward (and certainly the most widely used) definition.

The WCED defined sustainable development as "development which meets the needs of the present without compromising the ability of future generations to meet their own needs". Other definitions can, of course, also be listed. According to Allen (1980), for example, sustainable development is likely to achieve lasting satisfaction of human needs and improvement of the quality of human life; for Redcliff (1987) the term "sustainable development" suggests that the lesson of ecology can, and should, be applied to economic processes; Coomer (1979) sees the sustainable society as one that lives within the self-perpetuating limits of its environment; while Tolba (1987) states that the concept "sustainable development" encompasses the following aspects:

(1) Help for the indigenous poor because they are left with no option other than to destroy their environment;
(2) the idea of self-reliant development, with natural resource constraints;
(3) the idea of cost-effective development (Different economic criteria to the traditional approach, that is to say: development should not degrade environment quality, nor should it reduce productivity in the long run.);
(4) the great issues of health control, appropriate technologies, food, self-reliance, clean water and shelter for all; and
(5) the notion that people-centred initiatives are needed: human beings, in other words, are the resources in the concept.

The core issues and necessary conditions for sustainable development, as identified by the WCED, are highlighted in Figure 1.2.

Core Issues

- ❑ Population and development
- ❑ Food security
- ❑ Species and ecosystem
- ❑ Energy
- ❑ Industry
- ❑ The urban challenges

Pursuit of sustainable Development requires:

- ❑ A political system that secure effective citizen participation in decision-making
- ❑ An economic system that provides for solutions for the tensions arising from disharmonious development
- ❑ A production system that respects the obligation to preserve the ecological base for development
- ❑ A technological system that fosters sustainable patterns of trade and finance
- ❑ An international system that fosters sustainable patterns of trade and finance
- ❑ An administrative system that is flexible and has the capacity for self-correction

---

Figure 1.2: Showing Core Issues and Necessary Conditions for Sustainable Development

Source: World Commission on Environment and Development 1987. *Our Common Future*. Oxford: Oxford University Press.

The challenges of implementing sustainable development in practice are ongoing ones to which many governments, institutions and individuals have addressed themselves. Because the understanding of successful sustainable development is essential for meeting the ongoing challenge of balancing present needs against those of the future, it is important to pay more attention to the characteristics of such sustainable development. In this regard it can be stated that sustainable development:

(1) examines the transformation of the environment in the course of development (It argues that environmental problems need to be looked at internationally in terms of the global economic system, and that the degradation of the environment is not "natural" but an historical process linked to economic and political structures. If we are to understand the course of environment change we need to understand the momentum behind the history of developmental.);
(2) must encompass not only economic and social activities, but also those related to population, the use of natural resources and their resulting impacts on the environment;
(3) will require a commitment to overcoming poverty through a focus on the welfare issues of the poorest sectors of society, particularly in the developing countries (Their environmental concerns and their development needs are associated with securing the most basic levels of economic and social well-being. Only through a global commitment to addressing these interdependent concerns of the poor, will the environment be conserved and the development aspirations of individuals secured. Sustainable development thus encapsulates the realization that to achieve the goals of either conservation or development, the welfare needs of the poorest groups must be addressed.);
(4) is to ensure that relationships (economic, political and social) between elements in the system (people and places) are such that economic growth is achieved, whilst the environment is also conserved;
(5) is a pattern of social and structural economic transformations which optimises the economic and other available societal benefits in the present, without jeopardising the likely potential for similar benefits in future.

From the discussion thus far, it can be concluded that sustainability appears to be the mediating term designed to bridge the gulf between "developers" and "environmentalists". Furthermore, the notion of sustainability applies most conveniently to the replenishable use of renewable resources. The aim is to benefit from the advantages provided by such resources to the point where the rate of "take" equals the rate of renewal, restoration and replenishment. Only economic activities that raise social welfare with the maximum amount of resource conservation and the minimum amount of environmental degradation, allowable within given economic, social and technical constraints, can be considered as sustainable development.

One of the reasons why many development projects amongst tribal populations are not sustainable, is that indigenous knowledge, which cultures have devised for coping with environmental risks, is not utilised for, or linked to planned development strategies. It would be inaccurate to assume that environmental management is the sole prerogative of technically trained people from developed countries. Many tribal communities possess namely a source of information on the environment that enables them to manage their environments in ways that are sustainable in the long term. However, the experience of these people is rarely incorporated in formal structures for development and/or environmental planning. The next section deals with this topic in more detail. Our basic argument is that indigenous and scientific knowledge are complementary in their strengths and weaknesses and that combined, they may achieve what neither would alone.

The Importance of Indigenous Knowledge and Worldviews

For tribal people environmental conservation is not a new concept. Historically, the protection of nature and wiidlife is an ardent article of faith that reflects in their daily lives. It is also enshrined in myths, folklore, religion, art and culture. For example, each tribe inhabiting a particular geographical area in India has designed a cultural device known to ethnography as "totemism" to safeguard the flora and fauna of its immediate environment (Ratha and Behera, 1990). The tribal people have a belief system, which states that this universe is the creation of supreme power meant for the benefit of all his creations. Each individual must, therefore, learn to enjoy its benefit by forming a part of the system in close relation with other species. Let not any one species encroach upon the other's rights. Thus they have lot of respect for nature and its objects.

Sustainable practices are important for tribal people because it was traditionally the only guarantee for their survival. Denevan *et al.* (1982), for example, have shown that strategies which involve a combination of annual crops, perennial tree crops and natural forest regrowth, constitute a sustainable management system for the Bora Indians of the Peruvian Amazon. Under this system, shifting cultivation swiddens are almost never completely abandoned, but held in a transitional stage. In effect they are systems of agroforestry, designed and managed by the indigenous people themselves. They provide the guarantee that both food crops and perennial cash crop will continue to be cultivated without doing irreparable harm to the environment.

Studies in ethnobotany reveal that people in societies characterised by simple technologies are aware of differences in nature which are invisible to specialists from outside. In the course of development, indigenous environmental knowledge is often lost, because it becomes less relevant to the new situation, or because the process of specialisation around competitive production for the market systematically devalues it. It should be remembered that most indigenous groups whose livelihoods are not dependent on commodity production for the market, have neither the internal tendency towards maximization of profits, nor towards creation of an economic surplus.

Traditional environmental knowledge is not only devalued by development institutions; it is also largely overlooked in the literature on environmental management, as Norgaard (1985) points out. This is partly because of the way such knowledge is recorded in the cultures of tribal peoples. Without knowledge of such a culture, it is unlikely to be aware of, or to identify any knowledge on the environment. The corollary is that, if we want to know how ecological practices can be designed which are more compatible with social systems, we need to embrace the epistemologies of indigenous peoples, including the ways of organizing their knowledge of the environment. Although outsiders can frequently appreciate that indigenous practices make sense, the epistemology employed in arriving at these practices is culturally coded and often "obscure" to outsiders. Norgaard (1985: 876) states that indigenous knowledge is location specific and can only been arrived at "through a unique co-evolution between specific social and ecological systems". He argues in this regard that indigenous knowledge is not easy to incorporate into "scientific" knowledge, since experiential learning requires an evolutionary rationale that is different from that of bureaucratically managed planning institutions.

Tribal peoples "see" the cosmos differently, precisely because they acknowledge its centrality within a long-term time horizon (*cf.* McNeely and Pitt, 1985). According to Mbiti (1969:27) Africans', for example, experience of the cosmos refers to the natural, the supernatural and the social dimension of their existence, and in addition has an emotional, a mythical and a magical element. Given this way of experience/understanding of the cosmos, it is not advisable to interfere with culturally rooted views and practices in the interest of management strategies. Hecht, Anderson and May (1985), for example, point out that extractive activities have rarely been given recognition in tropical areas of developing countries, when these activities are in the hands of local, native, tribal peoples. Hecht, *et al.* (1985) demonstrate that small-scale extractive activities are an important source of income, particularly for women, who are usually denied access to other ways of earning cash income. The low visibility of these livelihood activities to development planners is, as Redcliff (1987) points out, closely related to the fact that the activities are performed by women and children.

What is important regarding the above-mentioned discussion is that development planners, in order to widen their views, need to be aware of not only epistemological aspects, but also of cosmologies. Incorporating the former in development planning implies incorporating cultures and cultural perspectives. The cultural categories that people use to classify and understand their environment should therefore be important to all those interested in its management. Lett (1985: 264-67) writes in this regard that the traditional practices of pre-capitalist societies can serve as a starting point for the implementation of more efficient modes of management under the principle of preserving its basic ecological structures and the cultural integrity of the people.

The above discussions (on environmental degradation, sustainable development and the importance of indigenous knowledge and worldviews) bring us to the central issue of this paper, namely to propose strategies for sustainable development. Before we suggest certain, specific strategies, we would like to identify some broad, general parameters.

Strategies for Sustainable Development

It can be argued that if development is to have any meaning, it can only be done within the framework of the people concerned. To the extent that this is lacking, development can be regressive and even dehumanising. An approach to sustainable development requires that the people constitute the key component —without which development is meaningless. Due to the lack of this dimension, in its truest form, many development schemes turn out to be fragmentary and at times even cross-purposive. The large-scale environmental degradation resulting from these kinds of so-called developmental projects is a matter of serious concern. If the present state of environmental degradation is allowed to continue, it is feared that in the next few decades it will threaten the very basis of life on this planet (Ratha and Behera, 1985).

By "people" we mean not the microscopic minority who are rich and powerful, who own or control or manipulate the means of production, the members of the "upper class" who indulge in conspicuous consumption and vulgar display of their possessions, but those vast majority of people who are socially oppressed, economically exploited and culturally suppressed, those who are dispossessed and hopelessly divided. They are the tribal people in many contemporary societies. Tribal people displaced from their habitat due to so-called development projects are pushed out of their traditional homes and are forced to migrate to the urban centres in search of work—any job that can keep their body and soul together. They are the slum dwellers of the major cities. As a corollary genuine development should mean the removal of these dehumanising processes which are the consequences of such so-called development.

Development cannot be conceived in general terms for the third world countries as if it is a homogeneous and indivisible whole. These countries are multicultural, multiethnic, multireligious and multilingual. They comprise not a single social reality but multiple realities of various groups and communities. Therefore, any genuine developmental programme in these countries should address itself to the specific needs of the situation, to the needs of the local people and the local communities. The tribal communities should have fundamental and inalienable right and access over their environment and natural resources. Any development activity should cater to the legitimate needs of the local people.

Development activities should be aimed at reversing the existing exploitative relations so that tribal people are not objects of development but subjects of their own destiny. In short, real development would be one that is ecologically sustainable and pro-people. Any development that brings environmental degradation is anti-development. Therefore, the path and pace of development must be determined by the people living in the locality or region or in the social environment. The pace of development may be slow or fast; the path or direction may not be spectacular but the decision-making must be left to the concerned people.

Against the aforesaid background, the following specific strategies for sustainable development can be proposed:

(1) Emphasise the *a priori* understanding of social organisation and cultural values of the concerned community;
(2) Acknowledge the importance of the qualitative aspects (quality of life) of human development and also advocate an integrated all-round development;
(3) Try to build up the inner strength of the people and create an appropriate socio-cultural infrastructure to withstand the pressure of the new situation;
(4) Emphasise the need to establish a meaningful link between local and national levels of development;
(5) Try to establish a link between the local human and material resources, and the effective measures for their growth and development;
(6) Try to maintain the primordial equilibrium among various components of nature;
(7) Advocate to a cost-benefit analysis and, in so doing, try to ascertain the long-term implications of a project;
(8) Acknowledge the importance of the human factors (awareness, perception, motivation and participation) involved in the processes of development;
(9) Protect the inalienable rights and interests of the tribal people and thereby provide them with their due share of benefits of the development concerned;
(10) Recognize the various socio-cultural constraints;

(11) Suggest that the co-partners in the process of development should be equal partners;
(12) Emphasize a participatory approach, inviting participation of the people not only at the level of the implementing of the programme, but also at the level of designing the same;
(13) Highlight the importance of orthogenetic development vis-a-vis hetrogenetic development;
(14) Emphasise the built-in cultural mechanisms that maintain the stability of the system;
(15) Try to empower tribal people by transferring them to an appropriate level of technology;
(16) Address the specific situation and the needs of the tribal people;
(17) View the concerned people not as "objects" but as "subjects" of development;
(18) Suggest to the programme implementers that they guide the course of a programme rather than control it;
(19) Realize the low degree of absorption capacity of the indigenous people for any development input and thereby maintain strategies accordingly; and finally
(20) Take into account the gender issues associated with the process of development.

Discussion

What masquerades as "development" in the present day world is not always development in true sense of the word. What takes place in western capitalist and also in the front-line "developing" countries in the name of development, can largely be viewed as anti-development. It is only growth-mania, belief in the political economy of profit and commercialisation, vulgar display of consumer materialism and growing militarism. This kind of development has caused irreparable damage to the poor, the dispossessed and the environment. It has caused the tribal people who have been marginalised and pushed to the periphery of society to be made to pay the cost of rich and powerful people's urge and craze for so-called "development". The irony is that the cost is paid by the people who are least able to afford it and who will benefit the least from the fruits of development.

Threats to the sustainable use of resources come as much from inequalities in people's access to resources and the ways in which they use them, as from the sheer numbers of people. The call for sustainable development in the future stems from a basic concern over the relationships between the current and the projected population of the globe and that resource base which must support it. Inequalities in access to resources in many ways threaten the prospects for sustainable development. Primarily these inequalities confine large number of tribal people to poverty that often leaves them with no choice but to degrade and destroy the resource base on which their future livelihoods depend. It is also such inequalities which allow a minority of people globally, within each nation and even at the community level, to use resources in a wasteful manner and in ways which cause environmental damage (such as polluting industries).

So-called "development" has displaced large numbers of tribal people by, for example, acquiring their land for building irrigation dams. In the case of India, major dams might have helped to irrigate large tracts of land belonging mostly to medium and big farmers. But to the tribal people this has only meant the pain of being uprooted from their homeland with little concern for their rehabilitation. The adverse impact of such projects on the ecosystem and the consequent deprivation and disturbance suffered by certain sections of the society are often lightly dismissed as "price for development" (Ratha and Behera, 1990). It is unfortunate that compensation of displaced persons is viewed exclusively from the economic point of view. Human beings cannot be reduced to mere economics. Their culture, their social and psychological links and their needs get shattered when they are displaced. No amount of economic help can remove the pain caused in the process of displacement. At best, government can only help to make the displacement less painful by providing all the facilities conducive to their holistic development. Reducing compensation to mere economics amounts to degrading human "being". In practice, however, not even the economic rehabilitation is taken seriously (Behera, 1996).

During the past decades the overwhelming desire of industry to squeeze out profits from the natural resources and their consequent commercialization have led to the loss of all interest in preserving the ecological equilibrium. Today the trend seems to be one of indiscriminate overexploitation of these resources resulting in environmental degradation. Deforestation has today become almost synonymous with environmental degradation. In addition to the increasing demand for raw material for industrial and commercial purposes, there is also pressure on forests for meeting the revenue requirements of the country. The state perceives forests almost exclusively as a source of revenue without due concern for regeneration. Thus, there has been massive deforestation by the reckless extraction of forest resources by national and international industrial commercial concerns in collusion with the obliging techno-bureaucratic apparatus of the state (Behera, 1993). This deprives the tribal people of the forest regions, of the life system on which they have depended for centuries. When regeneration of forest is attempted, it is more in the shape of monoculture of commercial species from which the tribal people derive little or no benefit. Therefore, deforestation resulting from the combination of commercial, industrial and revenue interests has adverse consequences on the ecology, and more importantly, on the forest dwellers. It has destroyed the source of their fuel, food, fodder, cultural and religious identity and of their social relations. As a result, the tribals have been trapped in the vicious circle of impoverishment, debt, land alienation and bondage. Their community has been weakened and social control mechanism has been destroyed (*cf.* Allen and Barnes, 1985 and Behera, 1996).

True or genuine development aims for quality of life which bring about joy in men and women and which finally gives peace within, peace with neighbours, nature and environment, and not tension among the people. In short, true development believes in a moral economy of provision of needs for the people and ecologically sound programmes. The guiding principle for attaining this quality of life is for man to co-operate and co-exist with nature, to live and develop in harmony with nature and not to violently subdue nature.

REFERENCES

Allen, J. and D. Barnes. 1985. "The Causes of Deforestation in Developing Countries," *Annals of the Association of American Geographers,* 75 (2).

Allen, R. 1980. *How to Save the World.* London: Kogan Page.

Behera, D.K. 1993. "Impact of Deforestation on the Life of the Plain Bhuiyans," *Journal of Human Ecology,* 4 (3): 255-60.

—. 1996. "Development, Environment and the People: An Anthropological Perspective," *South Asian Anthropologist,* 17 (2): 95-100.

Coetzee, J.K. and J. Graaff. 1996. "Introduction," in J.K. Coetzee and J. Graaff (eds.), *Reconstruction, Development and People.* Johannesburg: International Thomson Publishing.

Coomer, J. 1979. *Quest for a Sustainable Society.* Oxford: Pergamon.

Denevan, W., J.Treacy, J. Alcorn, C. Padoch, J. Denslow and S. Flores. 1982. "Indigenous Agroforestry in the Peruvian Amazon: Bora Indian Management of Swidden Fallows," in J. Hemmings (ed.), *Change in the Amazon Basin.* Manchester: Manchester University Press.

Elliott, J.A. 1994. *An Introduction to Sustainable Development.* London: Routledge.

Escobar, A. 1995. *Encountering Development: the Making and Unmaking of the Third World.* Princeton: Princeton University Press.

Ferguson, J. 1990. *The Anti-politics Machine. "Development", Depoliticization, and Bureaucratic Power in Lesotho.* Cambridge: Cambridge University Press.

Fowler, A.F. 1996. "Assessing NGO Performance: Difficulties, Dilemmas and the Way Ahead," in M. Edwards and D. Hulme (eds.), *Beyond the Magic Bullet.* New York: Kumarian Press.

Hecht, S., A. Anderson and P. May. 1985. The Subsidy from Nature. Successional Palm Forests and Rural Development. Cornell University, Department of Rural Sociology, Unpublished MS.

Leff, E. 1985. "Ethnobotanics and Anthropology as Tools for a Cultural Conservation Strategy," in J. McNeely and D. Pitt (eds.), *Culture and Conservation: The Human Dimension in Environmental Planning.* London: Croom Helm.

Leonard, J.H. 1989. *Environment and the Poor: Development Strategies for a common Agenda.* Oxford: Transaction Books.

Leroke, W. 1996. "Development as a postmodern condition: Towards postmodern development," in J.K. Coetzee and J. Graaff (eds.), *Reconstruction, Development and People.* Johannesburg: International Thomson Publishing.

Mbiti, J.S. 1969. *African Religions and Philosophy.* London: Heineman.

McNeely, J. and D. Pitt. 1985. *Culture and Conservation: The Human Dimension in Environmental Planning.* London: Croom Helm.

Norgaard, R. 1985. "Environmental Economics: An Evolutionary Critique and a Plea for Pluralism," *Journal of Environmental Economics and Management,* 12 (4).

Pearc, D. 1998. "The Sustainable Use of Natural Resources in Developing Countries," (pp. 102-117) in R.K. Turner (ed.), *Sustainable Environmental Management.* London: Belhaven Press.

Ratha, S.N. and D.K.Behera. 1985. "Man-Nature Relationship: Life in a Kissan Hamlet of Western Orissa," *Man and Life,* 2 (3 & 4): 163-70.

—. 1990. "Displacement and Rehabilitation: Data from the Resettled Colonies around the Steel Plant at Rourkela. Orissa," *Man in Asia,* 3 (1): 17-25.

Redcliff, M. 1987. *Sustainable Development. Exploring the Contradictions.* London: Routledge.

Tolba, M. 1987. *Sustainable Development: Constraints and Opportunities.* London: Butterworth.

World Commission on Environment and Development. 1987. *Our Common Future.* Oxford: Oxford University Press.

TWO

ENVISIONING THE FUTURES OF THE TRIBAL PEOPLES IN THE NEW MILLENNIUM

JAGANATH PATHY

The concerns for the future possibilities of individuals and collectivities have remained an abiding interest for ages for scholars, rulers, administrators, social activists as well as concerned persons and groups. Imaging as a social process has thus a long history in human civilization and the imagining of ideal societies has an honourable past. The basic reasoning is that the human life and potentiality can neither be fully understood nor intervened with only reference to its historical antecedents and existential complexities, rather profoundly demands the lure of the glamour and/or danger of the future. Put simply the matrix of past-present-future in totality entire genuine scholarship and thereby unfold our entire indeterministic world.

Unfortunately however, such grand exercises have become relatively rare in this century. In the past, especially from Thomas More's classic *Utopia* (1516) onwards, several thinkers had imagined a future to overcome the ills of their societies and to create new possibilities. But this century gradually replaced utopian constructions by a range of anti-utopia or dystopian images, mostly guided by the western dominated frame of progress, decay and dissolution. Especially the younger generation tend to nurture very negative values of their own future. It seems the social capacity to imagine new and different futures has clearly declined (Slaughter, 1991: 503). Primary reason for the rise of dystopian images, of cynicism, violence and despair as exemplified by Huxley's *Brave New World* and Orwell's *Nineteen Eighty-four* is the shift of focus to avoidance instead of construction.

Consequently the fact that the construction of the images facilitate not simply planning and sharpening of objectives and goals but also selection of alternatives can discern the wider complexity, is ignored. The dystopian projections and the rise of prophets of doom, cannot be however ridiculed outrightly, for they do provide warnings and outline the destinations to avoid.

In fact the steel and concrete utopian images often conceal many dangers beyond a seemingly harmless facade. In that sense the polar contrasts and false oppositions between optimism and pessimism, utopia and dystopia, order and disorder, centralization and decentralization, state and market, direct and indirect democracy are in fact complementaries. Problem solving demands pluralistic principles of social organizations, transcending the dichotomies.

The apparent exhaustion of imaging capacity is however associated with the rise of loss of confidence in our ability to solve our problems. It is however, possible to reclaim and utilize the so far sidelined human and cultural sources of images and re-evaluation and incorporation of counter-traditions with visionary elements, which breach the bounds of everyday assumptions and practices and thereby provide contextual meaning to the future. Such an enterprise would of course demand adoption of a stewardship ethic, attending to the rights of the future generations and redefining development and nation state. In other words, a reinvention of the culture and worldview and a search for a different historical dynamic is called for.

Images of futures do not gather social support across places and times, and thus have enough scope for re-negotiation, re-conceptualization, re-fashioning and rejection of redundant assumptions and destructive visions. Simple extension of contemporary trends inexorably leads on to a devastated and impoverished world. A compelling vision of future essentially transcends the catastrophic futures endemic to the technocratic scenarios, generated through econometric models, systems analysis, shrinkage techniques, game theories, quantitative protocals, Delphi, probabilistic and other extrapolative models. Envisioning the future is not like making a wish-list and of course no panacea. It involves deep questioning, deep learning with unlearning of the Cartesian and Newtonian paradigm, a shift from an anthropocentric to a biocentric norm of reference, a clear grasp of the common humanity where the local differences are placed in the context of universals, methods are heuristic with balanced use of rationality and intuition, higher motivations, consolidation of methods and institutions to faster growth of consciousness and cultivation of a new sense of value and reality with the assumption that the future is not the domain of knowledge but of action of the conscious participants and is essentially a metaphor of human imagination (Ziegler, 1991: 521-22). Unless we imagine better tomorrow, we cannot try our bit towards creating that desired tomorrow. It is not misplaced idealism but of building the capacity to imagine the other and different futures. The positivistic fields of the behavioural sciences and the quantitative disciplines of forecasting are of little help in practising or understanding envisioning, for envisioning is concerned neither with the probable nor the possible but with the desirable, the imagined and the intended *(ibid:* 516). Let us not bother on the actuality of tomorrow. There would always be surprises.

One cannot however responsibly imagine good futures in dark times without knowing the heights and depths of human experience in the past. There is thus a greater need of in-depth knowledge of human history. Secondly we need to have the cultures and aspirations of the marginalized peoples as focussed imaging for that would connect the future with the present and offer the scope for outlining the strategy of actions (Jungk and Galtung, 1969). Dissatisfaction and concern thus happen to be the starting points envisioning and creating shared visions. Forecasting to be meaningful must not restrict itself simply to extrapolative forecasting rather indulge in long-term strategic orientations of focussing on the needs of the suffering peoples. Here one has to build scenarios on casual models without enough data. Need is to create a bridge between objective and subjective probability with sufficient scope of incorporation of value based judgements. Afterall values tend to integrate knowledge.

In the aforesaid perspective, the notion of an objective observer passively observing an objective real world is of very limited utility. Instead the perspective of quantum physics which holds that things are not what they seem to the human senses, and that probability, randomness, uncertainty and non-equilibrium are more common than the assumed rationality of the discrete units of the structures and processes of the world, appear more rewarding. Indeed the Descartian and Newtonian mind-set and predicability has been challenged by current developments (Capra, 1982: 93-117). The ability to predict performance, behaviour and futures though diminishing, the very need generates conditions for removing the uncertainty of human actions and control of empires, dictatorships and other insensitivities. There is thus urgency of thinking holistically and globally so as to act creatively within the local contexts of climate, culture and place.

Such a critical or interpretive futurism stands against positivism and reductionism of the surface futurists who freely indulge in short-term forecasting. Despite some differences, the surface futurists tend to be technophilic, conservative and diversionary. By taking the existing social relationships as given, they provide unconscious support to *status quo* and construct futures externally via science and technology or attempt to explore solutions at a superficial taken for granted level. Their instrumental rationality covers only the physical layer of the world which can be measured but fail to provide any useful insights into the underlying systems and values.

The kind of futuristic exercise we are suggesting here insists on comparative analysis of assumptions and paradigms of diverse cultural traditions and problematizes sources of problems in worldviews and ways of knowing and seeing the solutions emerging from unpredictable shifts at the epistemological level. Recognizing the partiality of traditions, cognitive frameworks and ways of knowing, easily tends to problematize crucial dimensions of the existing rapacious, self-centered political economy. In this matrix, the interpretive futures study assumes that discourses are not neutral and thus indulges in reflexive orientation of constructing qualitatively different futures marked by unconstrained conditions of life. It also assumes that if there is a way out from the present endemic crisis, it will certainly not be via science and technology as they are constituted now but with the strategies of reestablishment of highest human motives and capacities. In other words, the western culture built on the philosophies of Bacon, Descartes and Newton needs to be drastically altered at the higher ontological level. Besides in order to come to the grips with the existing metaproblem, the cultures have to be consciously edited, and the dynamics of destruction must be replaced with a new dynamic of restoration through the release of the potential within the people. The new anthropology can thus anticipate that humans are self aware part of the Nature with the responsibility of protecting it and furthering the innate ends of life itself with concerns for justice, equity, sustainability and stewardship. Anthropologists can provide a lead to the alleviation of human sufferings by anticipating and articulating problems, defining and redefining concepts, warning and challenging leaders on pressing and foreseeable problems and enhancing peoples capacities to understand the problems.

Be that alone, the heuristic methodologies of forecasting or projecting alternative futures aim at evolving a new paradigm, reflecting a sense of holism, harmonization, decentralization, networking, participatory democracy and multiple options. This would stand in contrast to strict empiricism and cartesian reductionism. It would also emphasize human values like cultural identification, local control, distributive justice, meaningful political participation and scope for self-determination and sustainable development (Galtung, 1980: 30-31). By analyzing the present, the future is not merely presented as probabilities but also possible, preferable and desirable futures with necessary inputs to ensure that our worst predictions will not come about.

Such an imaging transcends the borders of positivistic social science that has little concern for values. Of course some intellectual discipline is essential for both long-term predictive and prescriptive enterprises. Excursion into the future can be done with some explicit theory and explicit values as well as necessary action. Put simply, it is not the question of predicting the future rather to participate in creating it with informed optimism and empowerment of all concerned. Shifting foundations of discourse may reveal fascinating scenarios.

II

The contemporary tribal problematique is essentially a product of alien models of economic growth, savage, impersonal, technocratic and deterministic model of development and the modernization, liberalization and globalization syndrome, epistemological individualism and statist ideology, obscurantist theories of nation state and strategies of nation building, national integration and national security, domination of reactionary forces and incomplete democratization of the Indian state system. Despite crucial differences, the tribal peoples across the country face, more or less, similar problems like recent recolonization of their territories, general economic subjugation, socio-cultural stigmatization and various degrees of ethnocide, as well as lack of political power in the current dominant decision-making process, despite the political reservations. The fundamental asymmetry in the decision-making process and the ideological tenets for expropriation of their resources that existed in the colonial times have not only continued in the post-colonial context but are consolidated and aggressively articulated. In a broad qualitative sense, the criticality of the survival of the tribal peoples with necessary dignity and their social reproduction as collective cultural entities happen to be primarily a post-colonial phenomenon.

Not simply the ideologies of individualism, modernization and nation state have threatened the survival of the tribal peoples but have generated a whole gamut of global problems like ecological disaster through desertification, deforestation, pollution, toxicity, loss of top soil, increase of soil acidity and salinity, depletion of protective ozone shield, and rise of global warming, increased poverty, unemployment, starvation, debt crisis, economic disparities, corruption and consumerism, and aggravated ethno-racial conflicts, religious fundamentalism, street crimes, large scale discontent, terrorism, ethnocide, genocide and widespread subversion of fundamental human rights; and the list can go on.

The models of development and science, and the grandiose vision of technological mastery treating the rest of biosphere as an enemy to be tortured and defeated and the treatment of the whole non-human cosmos as mere experimental subject fit for manipulative intervention, generated the unfathomable crisis. The homocentric and reductionist perspective of natural world, the overall aggressive and dismissive attitude towards biosphere and its valuation only in terms of maximization of profit led to the unprecedented ecological crisis. And simultaneously this perspective and practice has severely eroded the tribal people's holistic and anticipatory conception of nature, and their long practised harmonious equilibrium between nature and culture.

Likewise the so-called ideal nation state model assuming the transiency of cultural, linguistic and religious plurality on the basis of the West European premise that a single nation is the legitimate bearer of national identity, led to the state sponsored process of cultural homogenization, standardization and thus subjugation of ethnic minorities in general and tribal peoples in particular. The institutions and values of the subjugated are severely impaired and stigmatized to the extent that they have become more or less internalized.

Similarly the Western Philosophy of Enlightenment and the epistemological individualism maimed the very basis of tribal people's identity, survival and social reproduction. It may be asserted that among the tribal peoples, the individuals nurture a strong sense of obligation and commitment to their community of origin for their very survival as well as treat this as a defence mechanism to alien encroachments and domination. The all pervasive imposition of individualism and espousing the specific variety of nation building have acted as a subterfuge for the elimination of tribal identities and contributed to the process of ethnocide.

The aforesaid dystopian images have recently received considerable attention. But this is not the whole story. There are several counter trends and motive forces compelling us to look for the recuperation of tribal peoples' collective rights as well as reinstitutionalization and revalidation of their systems of existence and knowledge, albeit in modified forms. The renewed visibility of tribal question as a significant world concern at the present moment is of course due to the collapse of the major economic and political ideologies. An increasing number of concerned scholars and activists in their search for development alternatives have taken a second look at the tribal values, institutions, life styles, and management systems. Slowly but certainly an organizational and conceptual framework is emerging to affirm the cultural diversity and emancipation of the victims of internal colonialism, ethnocide and genocide. Suffice to stress now that the final verdict on the destruction and deculturation of tribal peoples is not yet made.

As the global problems inundate humanity, dystopian images of human futures have gained grounds. The disillusionment is of course not total. In face, it should not be. There are some extraordinary achievements of modern science, technology, development, democracy and human rights. None-the-less, the increasing realization of the inherent ecological and cultural crises in the modern development practices has compelled an increasing number of concerned scholars and activists to learn from the knowledge systems and management practices of the tribal peoples for the very survival of the humankind. The critical recovery of the tribal people's institutions, values, creative potentials, etc. seem no longer like a distant dream. No more their way of life can be scorned, and their blatant subjugation remain unchallenged.

Fortunately, traumatized though by deculturation, acculturation and negative identity, the tribal peoples have largely preserved and refined their identity, values of kinship, institutional reciprocity, corporate control and management of land and landbased resources, heritage of sustainable living and philosophical and cultural potentialities. In fact the crucial institutions and values have become stronger and more accessible than ever before. Of course the reinventions of their cultures and knowledge systems are getting reconceptualized, renegotiated and accommodated or modified.

The formidable tribal struggles geared to recuperate their inalienable corporate rights over land and landbased endowments, do defend their socio-cultural, linguistic, legal and political rights, and to cessation of abuses and subtle forms of discrimination have immensely contributed to the very process of rediscovery of their history, heritage and values. Moreover, their struggles against the transnational sponsored mega hydro-electric, mines and factory projects are increasingly supported by diverse movements and activists with concern for equity and sustainability. Despite various cooptive and repressive measures, the struggle of the tribal peoples for some form of collective internal self-determination within the established state system are increasing in intensity. And of course they cannot be legally and morally denied the freedom to choose their own path of development and appropriate political institutions to manage their lifes, survival resources and cultures.

It is of course not easy to generalize about tribal cultures and peoples, given the wide range of westernization, degree of conversion to patriarchal religions and industrialization. But the significant point is that the tribals are fighting back with non-violent spiritual, cultural and political revivals with a few militant struggles. Autonomy movements against the onslaught of a global monoculture is increasing day after day with greater intensity. The other movements like radical feminists, cultural rights, green movement, deep ecology, wildlife, peace movement, anti-nuclear movement, human rights movement, ethnic movements, labour struggles, youth movements, anti-racist/castist movements, consumer movements and even religious fundamentalist movements extend support to the tribal people's struggles.

Moreover, the international law which so far treated the tribal and indigenous peoples in terms of only economic exploitation, poverty, racial discrimination and individual human rights violation has recently recognized some of their collective social, economic, cultural and distinctive political rights. It is not simply to protect and promote the human rights of the tribal peoples in the matters of land, environment, development, education, health and culture but also some degree of internal self-determination. Afterall self-determination is the prerequisite of achieving freedom, equality, justice and peace, and useful for maintaining ecological balance and sustained development.

Most striking trend has been to critically renegotiate the universal and particular dynamics, both domestically and globally. It has been recognized that narrow universalism which despises all ways of life that deviate from the uncritically universalized western norms and the narrow particularism that demonizes all the others in the name of preserving national or cultural integrity are dated. The need of the hour is to appreciate cultural particularities and indulge in a critical dialogue with other cultures. This means not only a severe opposition to the European model of nation state but also the unilateral assumption of the state as the only mediator between itself and the subjects or citizens. Simply put, the nation state is inherently assimilationist and anti-communitarian which though liberates individuals from the tyranny of narrow communities and guarantees them with personal autonomy, equality, common citizenship and a collectively shared way of life, it derecognizes multi-cultural, multi-religious and multi-ethnic existence. There is thus the need for new models of political universalism which respect deep differences as well as ensure equal citizenship. In other words, a suitable balance between the principles of universalism and particularism cannot remain long unfulfilled. In fact, the UNESCO's world decade for cultural development (1988-1997) begins with the statement that "all men are equal and everyone of them is unique." It decries the continuing globalization tending to uniformity of values and standards for that would eventually impoverish creative cultural and developmental diversities and eventually endanger the long-term survival of human kind. UNESCO thus seeks to promote fruitful exchanges among all cultures without discrimination, save the upholding of universal humanist values, acknowledges cultural dimensions of development and affirms and enhances cultural identities. The exercise is obviously futuristic.

In sum, the plethora of contemporary crises, the search for alternative visions of future, the tenacity of tribal people's cultures, and their widespread struggles against alien onslaughts, the rising concern in the United Nations system, public positive response and support of diverse organizations and activists cumulatively indicate that there is a fertile arena of rediscovery and promotion of tribal conceptions of life and living. Knowledge diversity is as crucial as biological diversity. The focus on recovery does not mean a non-change context. But the tribal peoples themselves should decide if or to what extent their heritage, practices, methods and techniques need to be changed so as to be viable in the fast changing world.

In the final analysis the future of tribal peoples rests on the larger political matrix and the process of devolving power over nature, human resources, cultures and their managements from world system to state and from their to regional and local communities. This would contribute to enhanced democracy, federalism, ecological sustainability, quality of life, dignity and self respect. It is a creative potential and historical imperative.

Nevertheless the future of the tribal peoples is intrinsically entwined with the future of all human beings. It is thus reasonable to expect the rise of a qualitatively distinct philosophy and practice compatible with the interests of all peoples and their cultures and the sustainability of the nature.

REFERENCES

Capra, Fridjof. 1982. *The Turning Point.* New York: Simon and Schuster.

Galtung, Johan. 1980. *The True Worlds: A Transnational Perspective.* New York: The Free Press.

Jungk, Robert and Johan Galtung. 1969. *Mankind 2000.* London: Allen and Unwin.

Slaughter, Richard A. 1991. "Changing Images of Futures in the 20th Century,'' *Futures,* 23(5): 499-515.

Ziegler, Warren. 1991. ''Envisioning the Future," *Futures,* 23(5): 516-527.

THREE

INSTITUTIONAL TRANSFORMATION AND SOCIAL CRITICISM IN THE CONTEMPORARY TRIBAL WORLD

JAGANATH PATHY

Noticeably the very title of the paper solicits critical academic and political scrutiny. Given the variegated history, existence and struggles of over five thousand tribal peoples in the world, how can one articulate a generalized social consciousness. Such a censure is ostensibly well founded within the mainstream dominant social science mould. Put succinctly, one can speak about a tribal people or at best, a group of intimately related tribal peoples but never in universal unimpeachable terms. Besides, such a positivistic and empiricist premise, the support is often sought in terms of cultural relativism and post-modernism that such an exercise violates the very essence of tribal reflections and cognitive practices which are rooted in the multiplicity of knowledge systems.

Certainly one can hardly be oblivious to the structural variations in tribal social formations, geographical dispersion, ecological and occupational interactions, levels of external articulation, linguistic and cultural fragmentation, acculturation, demographic status, heterogeneous classes and ethnic conflicts, overlapping bases, shifting crystallizations, paradoxical consciousness, objectives, strategies and tactics, and so on. Likewise the surface level diversities are significant as matters of details as well as for building appropriate contextual theory and action. None-the-less the assumption of exclusivity and diversity as independent of the general structure of the dominant global political economy and culture alienates the project from the concerned peoples, and thereby, diverts attention from praxis. Neither theory nor practice can ever benefit from such exercise. The intellectual intervention ought to explore whether the diverse and complex tribal world can analytically fall into a more or less common frame of interpretation, and thereby appropriate political action.

Be that alone, let us begin with the prevailing problematique in the tribal world, across the globe. The following statements however may not be applicable equally or in the same measure and indeed mostly vary in terms of degree, intensity and scope. But there is hardly any exception. Of course, the list is neither exhaustive nor in proper order of significance, for that would fluctuate from place to place.

(i) The levels and standards of living of the tribal peoples are conspicuously lower than the national averages of the respective countries. And poverty, malnutrition, mortality and morbidity rates are generally higher among the tribals than among others.

(ii) Very frequently, they are the victims of physical aggression by alien settlers, refugees, landowners, entrepreneurs, transnational corporations and the armed forces.

(iii) Progressively their land and landbased endowments have been despoiled by world capitalism and state policies, and consequently, devastated not only their physical survival base but also the continuity of their collective identities.

(iv) Assimilationist policies and theories of progress have crippled their language, culture and identity, including institutions, values, symbols and social relationships. And unfortunately, sometimes the hegemony is so internalized that sentiments of inferiority and self-hate is institutionalized.

(v) A constant feature of tribal society in relation to the wider polity is its powerlessness, and that is the byproduct of the matrix of colonial, neo-colonial and feudal oppression and exploitation. The current trend further demonstrates accentuation of the process of their being trapped in the unequal global market, leading to some kind of ethnocide and at times, even genocide. In essence, this is the gruesome story of their enslavement, exploitation, expropriation and extermination.

Whereas the aforesaid suggests the existence of a more or less shared problem among the tribal peoples of the world, it does not explore the structural basis of the problematique. None-the-less, before searching the epistemological locale of the crisis, it may be some interest to briefly note the fundamental features of tribal societies and cultures. Though most of the following features still prevail, overtly or covertly, i.e. can be resurrected any time under conducive conditions of essential struggle, and indicate the contrasting principles of organization, knowledge, practice and action, there could be variations, mostly in terms of the levels of articulation of capitalism and neo-colonialsim. Besides there may be several more strikingly different institutions, values and principles but the following emphasize only those which are more or less commonly shared by the tribal peoples of the world:

(i) The fundamental principle of life activities and imaginations in the tribal world is their organization by community. Through synergy and collaboration a greater whole is reproduced. Accordingly, in both speech and thought, there is neither proper terms like "I" and "me" nor contain words of abuse or judgemental concepts, which are crucial to modern linguistic discourse. In the tribal world view, the conception of land is so generic and non-individualistic that no single individual can own it in exclusive sense. It is considered as a Creator's will for the use of living and non-living beings in terms of their past, present and future generations. Such an anticipatory and holistic perspective is completely incongruent with capitalism. Unlike the current ethos of appropriation and possession, the notion of sharing among social and spatial collectivities, non-divisibility of cooperative labour, unified conception of social energy and the non-individualistic view of labour encompass the integrity of tribal peoples' existence. Of course, in the "civilizational" encounter, such humane, democratic and egalitarian principles for an emancipated life do not have space. Moreover, the principle of totality is rooted space not on the coercive power of the state and its institutions but on the effective logic or moral and social relations.

(ii) The expansion of the self into the natural and social surroundings is based upon the principle of reciprocity, redistribution, mutuality and equity indicating ecological and social harmony. In the era of acknowledged ecological crisis and pervasive disruption of human relations, the tribal model of life providing harmony with mother nature and father cosmos, a greater social being is generated for human well-being and peace.

(iii) Both production and social reproduction are based upon communal collective control, institutional regulation of territorial survival resources and temporal usufructuary rights of individuals. And there is flexibility and diversity in production, subject to the overall conditions of balanced interaction with nature and sustainable living.

(iv) The power structure is largely rooted in the heritage, and face to face dialogue and consensual model, wherein authority constitutes only a collective leader(s) to carry out the essential and permanent functions of the society as temporarily delegated by the community. It denotes a socially enduring pursuit of linking thought and action with other beings.

(v) All peoples have methods of coming to knowledge. The epistemological foundation of tribal people is to demonstrate scientific pluralism. But for the present purpose, certain shared common denominators may be generalized. In contrast to the mainstream monocultural scientific paradigm, which stresses global uniformity, insists on objectivity and immediate causality, reduces all values in utilitarian terms, measures reality by breaking down it into smallest parts, controlled by chosen experts, separates from religion and values, propagates positivism and social Darwinism, the tribal sciences insist on wholeness, harmony, wisdom and justice. These are based on community control, ultimate causality, holism including spirituality, interrelationship of facts and values, synthesizes information from the mental, physical and cultural/historical realms. The tribal science has a sacral base and the teachings are grounded in the natural world. It is more qualitative and subjective than quantitative and objective. It assumes its power—the living energy that inhabits and/or composes the universe—and place, the relationship of things to one another. It does collapse time and space and hence, past, present and future exist at any given moment. However, it is still an uncharted and often misunderstood territory, involving both cosmologies and experiences. The point is to blend both sciences so as to promote both of their responsible growth.

Moving on to the structural and epistemological basis of the tribal problematique, the genesis can be located in three inter-related phenomena, namely, epistemological individualism, ideology of nation state, and paradigm of development. Each one of these is exogenous, alien to the tribal world.

The all pervasive imposition of the western nation of individual rights, specially with respect to property ownership as the *sine qua non* of civilization and progress pillaged the tribal peoples' survival. The concept of a direct link between individual rights and the state without any structure of mediation dictate hostility to the existence of social collectivities and the corporate claims. In the tribal context however, no individual can be considered as an absolute unit, severed from the structure and values of social groups to which he or she belongs. Capitalism can hardly expand into the matrix of group rights over land and landbased resources, and hence, derecognized and through several legal provisions, individualism is entrenched.

Colonialism had introduced terms like *terra nullius,* i.e. unoccupied territory in places like Australia, which was inhabitated by at least two million tribals at the time of its annexation. Similarly the principle of "Rule of Discovery" was simply an agreement among the colonial powers that the country first "discovering" a land acquired not only title to that land but also dominion over the natives and their resources. Such blatantly unjust international law was used in America, Australia and New Zealand. The "aboriginal title" that developed from the aforesaid two principles, reluctantly permitted some tribals group titles for their exclusive use and occupancy in smaller territories. Besides, in order to justify the massive alienation, the notion of "trusteeship" was institutionalized in terms of the "White Man's Burden".

In colonized Asia and Africa, the notion of *res nullius,* i.e. if the property is not used by an individual then it is of nobody and thus belongs to the state. Of course, in some places, "usufructuary rights" were acknowledged, wherein the state had the underlying title to the land and thereby, unilaterally terminable by the wishes of the state. Institutionalization of private ownership has led to massive alienation of tribal corporate land and landbased resources.

Not that these legal conceptions belong to history but continue to survive with greater intensity, precisely because extinguishment of group rights happens to be the necessary precondition for the growth of capital, both global and national. The superimposition of the capitalist conception of land as an object of permanent agriculture under the proprietorship of individual has endangered the survival basis of the tribal peoples and endangered their socio-cultural existence. In fact the post-colonial countries have not only denied the corporate usufructuary rights of the food gatherers, swidden cultivators and artisans among others but have also in the name of public purposes, national interests, survey and settlement operations, common property resources, transmigration, nation building, development and the like usurped their resource and territory. This is of such common occurrence all over the world that there is little need to name the countries. The state sponsored transmigration projects of Bangladesh, Indonesia, West Papua, French colonies of the pacific and elsewhere has created unfathomable deterioration of ecology, culture and survival base of the tribals. Likewise the case of alienation of resources in the name of protection of environment, wildlife, development, national security and nation building are so overwhelming that mention of a few countries would underestimate the gravity. The role of transnational corporations and multilateral funding agencies in accentuating the extinguishment of tribal corporate rights over territorial resources demand an emphasis in this context.

In sum, the doctrine of individualism and statist ideology, being crucial to capitalist and neo-colonialist development, the tribal collective identities are severely impaired and stigmatized.

Similarly the forced imposition of the modern development paradigm has generated institutional and cognitive crises in the tribal milieu. To note briefly the basic tenets of the model, it has treated the rest of biosphere as an enemy to be defeated and tortured for immediate maximization of exchange value. Such an anthropocentric and essentially reductionist perspective of natural world has eroded the ecological resource base and destroyed the customary tribal matrix of harmonious, holistic and anticipatory equilibrium between nature and culture. And as the paradigm demands individualization, the tribal collective identities are eroded and their territorial resources, knowledge systems and labour are usurped.

The assumption that parts are ontologically prior to the wholes and the emphasis on uniformity and homogeneity among the objects has generated context free abstraction of knowledge. Similarly, the dominant notion of development as the gradual triumph of reason, rationality and value neutrality has consistently cultivated a contempt for consciousness, values and ethics, and institutionalized the faith that abandoning the tribal institutional and cultural values as the *sine qua non* of development. Moreover, it imposed that the motive forces of development are external and thereby, justified internal colonialism and neo-colonialism.

In sum, the capitalist development that consistently ignored the cultural, historical and ecological complexities prevailing in the tribal region, that believes in mutilation of nature, customary institutions and values, and that imposes individualism, statist ideology and reductionist worldview, cannot but lead to the wreckage of physical, cultural and cognitive survival of the tribal groups. In fact, development has become a label for plunder and violence, a mechanism of triage. The nexus between the dominant development paradigm and tribal imbroglio is obvious.

The commercial extraction of timber, marine produces, mega hydroelectric schemes, mining of gold, uranium, oil and other projects, monocultural plantations, cattle ranching, agribusiness, afforestation programmes, biosphere projects like national parks, reservation of forests, game sanctuaries, debt for nature swaps, highway constructions, forced villagification, refugee settlements, tourism, facilitation of non-tribal settlements in their midst and the like have eventually destroyed their livelihoods and displaced them. The remote tribal regions are also brought under the control of world capitalism, the IMF, World Bank and G-7 countries. In fact the capital investment in the recent past happens to be the highest in tribal regions which has aggravated their misery. The projects are intrinsically related to the predatory activities of giant corporations and other profit seeking agencies, connected with an undercurrent of authoritarian and ethnocentric values and political institutions. The process is nothing short of ethnocide. At stake is the tribal peoples' economic and cultural survival.

The unfathomable gravity of the sufferings of the tribals in terms of collapse of local leadership and political disempowerment, economic pauperization, decline in fertility of survival resources, breakdown of traditional mode of cooperation, development of sexual stratification and nascent class structure, decline of conservation and self-management methods and cultural alienation demand political battles for a rule of law not only in autocratic systems but also in so-called democracies. With regard to rehabilitation of the involuntarily displaced, despite several international instruments like the U.N. Convention on Civil and Political Rights (1966), the U.N. Declaration on Racism and Racial Discrimination (1978), the I.L.O. Conventions No. 107 (1957) and No. 169 (1989), and many others, the displaced never receive just compensation. Moreover, in the name of development, international colonization of the tribal regions is carried out by the multinational corporations, World Bank, IMF, WTO, G-7 countries and others. For instance, World Bank has colonized much of the tribal regions of Amazon, Indonesia, India, Southeast Asia as well as the indigenous territories of the developed North.

More ominous is the increasing militarization of the tribal regions like CHT in Bangladesh, East Timor, Guatemala, Peru, Colombia, Panama, Chile, Paraguay, Ecuador, Brazil, Mexico, Khurdistan, West Papua, Somalia, Ethiopia, Tanzania, Kenya, Sri Lanka (Veddas), Philippines, India, Canadian North, Micronesia and other tribal territories. Similarly the uranium mining as well as nuclear testing have led to unprecedented nuclear pollution and threaten the health of the local tribal peoples. Permission is never sought from the tribals, nor even they are warned. Besides nuclear and other virulently toxic wastes is dumped. And with the increased inter-state violence, the borderland regions, frequently occupied by tribals, lose their own security and survival.

And finally, the process of formation of modern nation state through elimination or absorption of smaller and weaker cultural entities, and overpouring of national myths, common national language, culture and identity have severely threatened the existence of the tribal peoples as viable collective entities. The process may be called ethnocide for it imposes such a gamut of changes that the tribals are unable to reproduce themselves and solve their material and spiritual interests. While adopting the model that all sovereign states are national societies or ought to be so soon, it has been ignored that all states of the world are infact pluricultural. Nevertheless, the attempt has been to assimilate the tribal peoples into the dominant cultural-linguistic mainstream.

Tribals are made to feel inferior, their cultures are degraded and stigmatized, their values are rejected as obscurantist, their beliefs demonized, rites and symbols ridiculed, and religions are treated as superstitions or sorcery. Even they are given fictitious and derogatory exonyms. This simply constitutes elimination of cultural and linguistic diversities. Of course, what is allowed to survive is their opaque signs, parody of ceremonial dances and overwhelmed exoticism during national festivals and as promotion of global tourism. In short, commodification of culture according to alien tastes, an ornamental hoax. The contribution of the social scientists to the creation of this scenario is no less significant.

Not only their cultures, languages, religions, political authority and others degraded but also their just and democratic aspirations and struggles have been brutally repressed in the name of law and order, secession or diabolical international conspiracy. And with so-called liberalization, there is greater dissemination of global dreams which cannot but undermine, debase tribal institutions, values and cultures.

In sum, the institutional transformations and the genesis of the tribal problematique is essentially a product of imposition of the philosophy of individualism, ideology of nation state and capitalist model of development. But this is no final story, for the creative resurgence of the tribal ethics, science, management and institutions is on the agenda. The optimism of creative institutional revival rests on the rising social criticisms against the very premises that has created the tribal problematique. The following outlines the scope:

(a) Despite institutionalization of individual proprietorship, various forms of communal control over resources still continue to prevail, to a greater or lesser extent, among most of the tribal peoples. Though traumatized by deculturation, acculturation and negative identity, they have largely preserved their identities, values of kinship, institutional reciprocity and knowledge of shared history and territorial occupancy, which in the ultimate analysis provide some scope for resistance to the alien forces. In fact, the increasing awareness of their being victims of injustices and inequalities due to colonial and neo-colonial development schemes has contributed to the rise of inter-tribal unity and revival of their institutions and values as a defensive mechanism. There is thus a clear tenacity of tribal systems. In addition, it may be noted that the persistence of communal institutions, and egalitarian values in several forms do not hinder modern corporate enterprises (for e.g. Maoris in New Zealand, Inuits of Arctic, Basques of Spain etc.).

(b) The plethora of contemporary crises—increasing poverty, unemployment, management, ecology, communalism, corruption, consumerism, flagrant abuse of human rights, etc.—have questioned the grandiose vision of the paradigm of development, ideology of homogeneous state and the philosophy of individualism. In this turbulent scenario, there is the rise of dystopian images of human futures. Hence the movements for ecology, peace, human rights, women's rights and others not only feel the urgency to transform the dominant models of the west but seek insights from the tribal and ancient wisdoms to work out alternative visions of development and human futures.

In short, increasing realization of the inherent hazards of human existence in the midst of ecological and identity crisis in the modern practice has compelled activists to learn from the tribals about their institutions, values and practices, which helped them to manage ecological resources in fragile and marginal lands for millennia. Awareness of the technocratic syndrome that devastates the survival bases of the people question the model for its dehumanized practices. But the awareness of the environmental crisis as a sequel to relentless quest for conquering nature has sometimes benefited the profit seekers. For instance, as three quarters of the current prescribed medicinal drugs are derived from plants discovered through tribal knowledge, the pharmaceutical concerns have an eye on their knowledge system. So also agribusiness and other concerns. The elders and shamans have provided greater knowledge of environment with contacts of invisible spirits for world capitalist interests. Even the international bodies like IUCN, WRI, WWF for nature, Conservation International and of course World Bank, though concerned with the loss of biological diversity, ignore the tribal intellectual property rights. Patents under the WTO regime and its IPR and TRIP not merely deny the creativity of tribal peoples' traditional knowledge but also deny the creativity of the nature. Hence this is a double edged weapon. None-the-less, no more tribal ways of life can be scorned, and their subjugation can remain unprotected.

(c) Public awareness of the crisis with respect to the tribal issues and realization that tribal culture and values can hardly survive without their control over territorial resources and self-development and increasing realization of the dehumanizing consequences of the welfare system have together provided a political space for autonomy, self-respect, identity and creativity. Essentially the welfare system is a product of their struggles and represents a *quid pro quo* in exchange for political quiescence. Its aim is to mitigate the extreme manifestations of domination and subjugation, and of course to co-opt a few to strengthen the structure of mediation for further expropriation of surplus. It is not the question of humanitarian concern for the disadvantaged or ethical sensibility for social justice and human rights but an urge to challenge the fundamentals of the civilizational milieu. In any case, there is a progressive erosion of humanist and moral vision of nation towards the tribal peoples. In fact, the state has overtly or covertly, protected the classes that exploit the tribal resources and peoples. There is thus the urgency of demystification of the dominant western models.

(d) The scenario of tribal movements have sprung up as a formidable force. In the 1960s, the organized struggles became active in North America, Scandinavia and Australia. In the 1970s, the struggles for self-determination had spread to the Central and South America. And in the 1980s, it covered Asia, Africa and the Pacific. Today it is flourishing with global coverage, encompassing even the U.N. system. It is not a question of relative deprivation and aspiration to preserve the traditional culture and a share power but to challenge the existing exploitative syndrome.

Their demands are generally directed towards recuperation of their customary rights over land and landbased endowments to defend, maintain and develop their legitimate cultural, social, linguistic and political rights; and to cessation of abuses and subtle forms of discrimination. Such struggles, operating outside the frame of institutional politics, are essentially democratic, federalistic, anti-bureaucratic, anti-feudal and anti-imperialistic. Small wonder, they receive increasing support from diverse activists with concerns for equity.

In essence, the tribal struggles aim at some form of collective internal self-determination, self-management and self-development against paternalism, hegemony and elitism. This is to create same form of interactive structure with the larger socio-political system from a position of strength, which may finally lead to the emergence of multiple co-existing civilizations that respect peoples and nature.

However, tribal demands for sovereignty and internal self-determination are though advanced by the American Indian movement and the National Indian Youth Council, the north American governments have conceded only same form of self-administration of federal government programmes within tribal territories through puppet tribal councils, who manipulate illegal treaties, land transfers and mineral contracts. This is no self-determination. The Inuit circumpolar conference and the Sami Regional conference provide a basis and some hope.

(e) Though rooted in the western individualistic milieu, the U.N. System never recognized positively the socio-cultural collectivities. The only provision in the International Bill of Rights that concerns here is Article 27 of the Covenant on Civil and Political Rights, which again, implicitly speaks for individuals. Only the International Labour Organisation's convention No. 107, although paternalistic and assimilationist in essence, speak of tribal collective rights. However, it is ratified by only 27 countries, many of whom have allegedly violated the provisions with impunity. Its new convention No. 169 of 1989 has been ratified by only seven countries. This convention describes tribals as peoples and emphasises fundamental freedoms that goes with it. Similarly, the U.N. Universal Declaration on the right of indigenous peoples (1993) appear a step forward, but it does not address the questions of neo-colonialism, internal colonialism, eco-predatory transnational politics and historical prerogatives of all peoples. Without going to the details, it is sufficient to say that the tribal question in the recent years has received not only global political attention but also of the international and multilateral bodies.

By way of summation, it may be reiterated that it is high time to rediscover, defend and promote the life styles, management practices, technological and knowledge systems of the tribal peoples developed over centuries of trial and error method for their production and social reproduction as well as sustainable management of resources and harmonious relationship with the neighbours. Such a recovery demands honouring their corporate control over everything-knowledge, culture, heritage, social relationships, customary laws and politics—so as to further invigorate them in terms of the balanced interaction with the present context. This is of course a political question and can only be handled in those terms. It is a creative potential and a historical imperative of our times.

FOUR

WE MUST START FROM SOMEWHERE
Planning the Plans in Tribal Areas

P. DASH SHARMA

In the early years of planning, poverty was perceived as a comprehensive social phenomenon by economists, bureaucrats and the political ruling class of that time. When we are talking about tribal people and the tribal areas we are in fact discussing about the poor, poverty, and the underprivileged rural people of India. Most tribals are synonymous with poverty. Poverty removal *(garibi hatao)* has been the major goal of Indian planning since the Fourth Five Year Plan (1969-74).

The situation prevailing in the tribal areas was reviewed on the eve of the formulation of the Fifth Plan (1974-79), whereupon Tribal Sub-Plan (TPS) strategy came into being. The Sub-Plan envisaged a total picture of development of the tribal areas. It was essentially an attempt to appreciate the problem of tribal development in its totality and the first exercise in this regard was to demarcate the tribal areas based on the concentration of tribal population.

One of the most important features of the Tribal Sub-Plan (TPS) is the development of the tribal areas as an integral part of the total development of the state and the country. Integration in administration in tribal areas has been attempted at the Integrated Tribal Development Project (ITDP) level and there were several programmes in this project from time to time till the Seventh Five Year Plan (1985-90). The projects are many, some of the important ones being Integrated Child Development Services (ICDS), Drought Prone Area Programme (DPAP), Training Rural Youth for Self-Employment (TRYSEM), Integrated Rural Development Project (IRDP), National Rural Employment Programme (NREP), Rural Landless Employment Guarantee Programme (RLEGP), Minimum Need Programme (MNP), etc. Jawahar Rojgar Yojana (JRY) was launched in April 1979. The aim of the programme is to provide employment to at atleast one member of a family living below the poverty line for a period of about 50 to 100 days in a year. The Integrated

Child Development Services (ICDS) which started in 1970 has been given priority in the tribal areas for increasing the rate of survival of children among the families who are found to be the most poor in the area.

It has been admitted in the approach to the Ninth Five Year Plan (1997-2002), "although the macro economy performed reasonably well in the Eighth Five Year Plan, some major weeknesses have also emerged. In particular, the growth pattern has not benefited the poor and the underprivileged." (Five Year Plans: Govt. of India, Planning Commission).

The Eighth Five Year Plan (1992-97) of India had set the following objectives: Full employment, containment of population growth, universalization of elementary education, eradication of illiteracy, provision of safe drinking water and primary health care facilities including immunization, accessibility to all villages and entire population, self-sufficiency in food, and development of infrastructure to support growth process on a sustainable basis. These objectives indicate that the awareness of the situation in India was in the mind of the planners but the problems of the fiscal and budgetary deficits, critical situation in the balance of payments and the high rate of inflation diverted the attention of the government.

During the Ninth Five Year Plan (1997-2002) the focus would be placed on the following seven basic minimum services: drinking water, primary health services, primary education, housing to the shelterless, mid-day meals in primary schools, connectivity of the villages and the public distribution system.

This outline of the Five Year Plans very briefly inform us what our planners have achieved and what they intend to do in near future. It is futile to rule out the statistics of our achievements, as statistics usually do not show the reality as it is primarily based on samples which are in most cases not representing the entire situation. The poor people living in the interior rural areas of Chotanagpur or in the tribal areas of Orissa and Madhya Pradesh, can give you a feeling and realization what they have gained in the last fifty years. It took almost fifty years for our Indian leaders and the planners to think about a scheme for the poor villagers, like the Public Distribution System, for the 80 per cent of the Indians who are living in the villages.

It is, therefore, the time for stock-taking of our achievements and for heart-searching to find flaws which have impeded the progress in the fields of our achievements for developing the rural poors.

It is a well-established fact that with economic development the sectorial share of agriculture falls and that of industries and services rise. While agricultural productivity rises, the percentage of population depending on livelihood based on agriculture declines. The USA and Canada whose agricultural productivity is highest in the world just have 2 to 3 per cent of the population which is economically active in agriculture. In a developing country like India the programmes and priorities of development are vastly different from that of the West. India can become a developed country only if it develops the villages and keep the villagers alive, healthy and vigorously active through agricultural input and distribution system, and sustains the minimum need programme for the 80 per cent of the Indian population who are living in the villages. Our planners must realize that there is intimate relation between culture and development.

Human Development Index and Human Poverty Index

United Nations Development Programme (UNDP) in the Human Development Report has introduced a new yardstick of human progress—The Human Development Index (HDI)—by combining the indicators of real purchasing power, education and health. In the Human Development Report of 1996, India was placed at 135th place among 174 countries. This position was even lower than that of Myanmar and Pakistan and far behind Hong Kong (22), Singapore (34), Thailand (52), Malaysia (53) and Sri Lanka (89). It was also pointed out that there is no automatic link between income and human development. It has also been shown that populations with same income can have different levels of human development. Even a comparatively higher income country may be lower in the scale of human development as compared to a lower income country. In 1993 Human Development Report pointed out that HDI indicators are not the same for all the States of India.

UNDP in 1997 has developed a *Human Poverty Index* based on three indicators: vulnerability to death at an early age, illiteracy and less than decent standard of living due to lack of access to health services, safe drinking water and adequate food. This is a departure from the conventional income based method.

On the basis of experience in developed and developing economies of the world it has now been realized that the real motive force of economic progress is the people. So people's participation in development programme is the need of the hour for sustainable development.

For achieving this goal, the first imperative for us is to make our data base perfectly credible and authentic for all the states of India. Secondly, the human development targets for the region should be set and their implementation should be monitored very carefully, so that the progress is known and such steps as may be necessary are taken in time. Thirdly, for successful implementation of the programmes, the responsibilities should be fixed clearly with minimum chances of buckpassing. Fourthly, suitable incentives for the success of the programme and deterrents for its failure, should be devised and administered impartially on a strict principle.

It is not difficult to achieve our goal of sustainable development in India by involving the local people but the greatest hindrance for this achievement is our ignorance, lack of sincerity, inactivity, apathy, get rich quick attitude of the programme implementers and lack of responsibility and accountability of the authorities.

The present author thinks that the glass is only half-full and not half-empty, and, believes that we can do it, if we are determined to do it by strictly adhering to the four primary points as stated above for achieving our goal.

We Must Start from Somewhere

In our country anthropology has expressed its concern for the tribes and has a charter for the welfare and development of the under-privileged communities. Social anthropologists were probably the first among the social scientists to describe man in his environment and habitat and to highlight their interdependence. Anthropology is relevant to the endogenous process of development. It is now being realized that the development process must have a role to play in executing the schemes meant for their benefit and fashioning their life in the way they like it.

I will limit my discussion with reference to Chotanagpur region of Bihar, a tribal concentrated area. However, the tribal situation is more or less similar in different tribal belts of India, so some generalization can be made.

The economy of the tribals of Chotanagpur revolves round the ecological setting of their homeland. As the districts of Chotanagpur region is largely covered with thick forests, so the collection of the various forest produce plays a great role in their economic life. The major tribal groups of Chotanagpur plateau like Santhal, Munda, Oraon, Ho and others are primarily dependent on agriculture as their traditional mode of occupation. The minor tribes like Asur, Birhor, Birjia, Korwa and a few others are primarily food gathering and hunting tribes but many among them lately have acquired the knowledge of agriculture, particularly those who are close to the other neighbouring agricultural communities, and thus are gradually becoming settled agriculturist. Pastoralism also plays an important role in the economy of the tribes of Chotanagpur. Most tribal people of Chotanagpur keep cows, bullocks, goats, hens, etc. which help them in their economic activities and livelihood to some extent. In addition to their traditional mode of occupation the tribals of Chotanagpur also work as labourers in the forest department and also in the nearby mines and the urban centres. Young tribal youths of Chotanagpur even go as far as to Haryana and Punjab to work as labourers. The socio-economic life of the tribes of Chotanagpur are intimately interrelated, intermingled and interwoven with the forest. The forest provide them with the raw material for their shelter, various household articles, agricultural and other implements, indigenous medicines and abundant source of firewood and is the ready source of market economy. The forest environment satisfy their deep rooted tribal sentiments throughout their life and even after death the dead body is laid to rest in a grave close to the forest by most of the hunting and gathering tribes of Chotanagpur.

However, with the beginning of the industrial urbanity in post-independence period the tranquillity and homogeneity of the tribal life in Chotanagpur started declining which ultimately resulted in the change of the entire canvas and thus we find today an interplay of forces of tradition and modernity among the tribals of Chotanagpur.

Generally we find that the impact of urbanization in a village of Chotanagpur is inversely proportional to the distance of the village from the nearest urban centre. Under this generalization the priorities and programmes of development should vary according to the needs of the villages which are nearer to the urban centre and those which are far away from it. So the first task for development planning is the identification of the blocks and the villages as per the selection criteria evolved for the purpose and according to the priorities and needs of the villages/blocks of the region, for an overall development. If the selection criteria for the villages is based on certain specific parameters like population, village size, socio-economic condition of the people, accessibility to the villages, etc. then things move in the desired direction for the success of the programmes. Usually this is not followed while selecting the block and the villages for development programmes. The villages or the block area to be identified for development programme usually depend largely on the political pressure and has little scientific basis. In our type of democracy, which is very different from the West, scientific criteria have little role to play in development programmes. May be in near future we will find more sensible political leadership in this region who will give due recognition to the scientific planning process.

Research Institutes and Development Programmes

My general inquisitiveness for understanding the tribal situation, the village situation and the activities under tribal development programmes led me several times to the Tribal Welfare and Research Institute of the Government of Bihar at Ranchi in recent past, for discussing with the administrative and research personnel who are involved with the welfare activities of the tribals of the region.

Forty-five years of existence of a research institute working among the tribals of the region is fairly a long period for understanding the continuity and change of tribal culture under the impact of urbanization and industrialization of the region. So one can confidently assume that the government department concerned with the tribal welfare activities must have huge data base on the socio-economic and health aspects of the tribes of Chotanagpur which is so very essential for the development planning of the region and its people. Numerous publications some of which are excellent monographs on the tribes of Chotanagpur and the research reports on the various aspects of the tribes of the area and other evaluation and administrative reports are a testimony of the research activities of the Bihar Tribal Welfare and Research Institute at Ranchi.

But a little probing put the officials of the institute in uncomfortable position because they could not provide readily available data on the population of the different villages in the blocks, ethnic composition, distance of post-office/police station from the villages, primary health centres and sub-centres in the villages or in the blocks, accessibility and communication system to the villages, drinking water facilities, number of tube-wells in working condition in the villages, number of primary/elementary schools in the villages, panchayats and blocks, number of NGOs working in different development programmes in some of the contiguous blocks around Ranchi. There is also no ready information available on the different welfare and development programmes which are being run by different government departments at that particular moment of time in some of the neighbouring blocks around Ranchi.

One has to do quite a lot of digging for collecting information on all these aspects from an institute engaged in research and welfare programmes among the tribals of Chotanagpur, as there is no documentation research or personnel having information in the institute.

The author is certainly not attempting to undermine the credibility of the institute as this situation is more or less prevailing in every research and welfare department of the State Governments in India, which is concerned with the tribes, tribal welfare and development programmes.

There is no cumulative information maintaining system for the data bank in most of the institutes. A simple index card system could have helped to some extent in the storing of cumulative information on every aspects of the tribe and the tribal region which is so imperative for us for any development work to be taken up. Every government department of the state is working virtually in isolation and independently of others, without any collaboration, mutual aid or assistance in the field of education, health, forest and environment, and in various development programmes for the tribals or rural people in different blocks of Chotanagpur, sometimes working in the same region but are little aware of each other's programmes. The rural and tribal development programmes are always being run on a piece-meal basis by the state administration. All these are only jeopardizing the development programmes of the rural areas which are ultimately resulting in much loss of public money, without much benefit to the people for whom the development programmes are being run.

Under this prevailing situation in the 50th year of India's Independence it is imperative that the Tribal Welfare Commissioner, institute of rural development, forest department, welfare department and other government departments concerned with rural and tribal welfare and development, come together to develop an apex co-ordinating body to synchronize all the activities of the different government departments for its effective implementation, monitoring and intervention at the district and state levels.

But will the bureaucrats shed their ego and come forward to work together for the betterment of the rural and tribal people with the zeal of a missionary? Will they start from somewhere planning the plans?

Wait, the future will tell you.

FIVE

DECODING TRIBAL DEVELOPMENT
A Narrative on South Gujarat

S. P. PUNALEKAR

A Problematique

The present paper is about nature and processes of tribal development being unfolded through their life situations. Our focus is on tribal society in Gujarat; particularly on those living in its southern parts comprising four districts, namely, Surat, Bharuch, Valsad and Dangs. Apart from objective situation that is being unfolded within that society, the present essay attempts to capture perceptions and dilemmas faced by the tribal communities, and also modalities of their struggles to cope up with tensions emerging out of the prevailing development processes which seem to critically affect their chances of survival and sense of identity (Desai, 1987; Breman, 1990). Thus this essay briefly touches upon some cultural issues and their dynamics also.

While developing this narrative, we have wilfully chosen to exclude quantitative parameters which are amply available through official and non-official documents. Here the thrust is towards constructing a qualitative profile with focus on human facets now under stress. I wish that a story narrated here is read more as a format with questions meriting urgent attention and redressal. We are free to deliberate whether the questions raised in this essay are indeed social or sociological in nature and import (Webster, 1984). Such a debate is necessary and desirable for advancement of our understanding on a problematique of tribal development. That problematique may also throw light on underlying processes of poverty and marginalization; a theme well argued upon by Dutch scholars working in South Gujarat in 1970s (CCSES, 1976; Pilai and Baks, 1979). Discussion is therefore likely to pose questions for a model(s) of social change we are pursuing for development of the tribals not only in Gujarat but also in other states in Indian union. Debate may also pave the way to look critically into the nature and direction of economic reforms and their effects on the livelihood of the *Dalit* masses including the tribals (Vyasulu, 1996).

The Scheduled Tribes (STs) in Gujarat together make up about one-sixth of state population. They possess distinct socio-economic and cultural identities and historical legacies. In terms of social landscape, i.e. their community organization, cultural milieu and leadership, etc. the tribal communities in Gujarat reveal interesting facets. The studies undertaken so far do reveal differentiating characteristics obtaining among them (Bose, 1981). But there are some similarities among them or a common thread binding them together. This is particularly evident when we consider them in terms of their status as citizens of an open, liberal and democratic society or view them as stakeholders in a larger matrix of political economy of growth or development. This aspect has remained somewhat unaddressed or neglected for long in our academic dialogues (Breman, 1985; Lobo, 1994).

Development of tribal society or "tribal development" must be perceived as an idea or ideology within a larger context and processes of growth, development or modernization (Desai, 1987; Pathy, 1982). While "doing" development among tribals, the underlying growth or development premises and attendant strategies and initiatives need to be scrutinized in terms of nature of changes brought about in tribal region. It is our experience that tribals in Gujarat including South Gujarat do constitute the object of these processes, with advantages in some sectors, and disadvantages in other. They do inhere these ambiguous prospects. It cannot be forgotten that some tribals (as individuals or as a collectivity) are actors and participants in this modernization or "development" experiment (Punalekar, 1987; Patel Priyavandan, 1996). And problems encountered by tribal masses also have their roots in this growth or development paradigm. Burden of our narrative is to address to this dilemma, i.e. to uncover subtle links between growth and pauperization, development and marginalization within the same society (Shah, 1992; Punalekar, 1995b).

This chapter is divided into five sections. We describe some key features of social landscape obtaining among the tribals of Gujarat, with special emphasis on tribal communities in South Gujarat (Section II). In Section III we concentrate on aspects of social stratification and economic marginalization among the tribals. Here we also focus on migration practices among them. Issues of dislocation, rehabilitation and protest (or resistance) are discussed in Section IV. A concluding view is given in Section V.

II

Social Landscape

There are about 30 major tribal groups concentrated in the eastern belt of Gujarat state. The major groups are Bhils, Dublas or Halpatis, Choudharis, Dhobis, Gamits, Nayakas, etc. The eastern belt consists of mountainous terrain and the woodlands. The government has identified 32 talukas in 7 districts and 15 pockets in north-east hilly region as the tribal belt. 14.95 per cent of the state population is that of tribals; and together they cover 15 per cent of the geographical area of the state. South Gujarat region is the home of the majority tribals; some 55 per cent tribals of the state live in this region consisting of four districts, namely, Dangs, Bulsar, Surat and Bharuch. Their respective population percentages are: 94 per cent, 55 per cent, 42 per cent and 45 per cent. 15 out of 25 most backward talukas identified by the I.G. Patel Committee (1983) fall under the Tribal Area Sub-Plan (TASP) (Joshi, 1996a).

According to the survey of the Commissioner, Rural Development (1991-92), some 26 lakh families in rural areas were living below poverty line. Of them, more than one-fourth were tribal households. Some 6.89 lakh tribal families were living below poverty line. In other words, 67.08 per cent of the total tribal families in Gujarat were below poverty line, i.e. 3 out of every 5 tribal families on an average are battling against poverty and economic hardships (Joshi, 1996a). Thus the major issue is to bring them out of poverty syndrome. Of the total cultivators in the state, 11 per cent are the tribals, numbering some 3.85 lakhs.

Together they own some 9.41 lakh hectares of agricultural land. A majority of them (83%) own less than 4 hectares land. In other words, programmes specifically targeted towards amelioration of small and marginal farmers hold critical significance. Such target-specific and viable programmes can bring about decisive improvements in the conditions of majority of Gujarat tribals. Conversely any setback, market-driven or otherwise, may push them into further deprivations and hardships (Gupta, 1977; Breman, 1994b). There is additional handicap encountered by the tribal peasantry. Most of them do not enjoy perennial irrigation facility. Only 10 per cent of the land in tribal areas has assured irrigation as against 25 per cent state average. Due to this, per hectare yield of grains in the tribal areas is between 2.87 to 4.87 quintals as against the state average of 9.32 quintals. Out of some 62 lakh total tribal population in the state, 25.2 lakh are main workers; and among them 9.9 lakh are landless agricultural labourers. Taluks of Valia, Dediapada and Bardoli are the principal centres of concentration of tribal agricultural labourers. Many of them are found engaged in sugarcane harvesting work where the working conditions leave much to be desired (Breman, 1978; Dhuru and Pungalia, 1987).

On literacy front there is some positive change over the years, thanks to the efforts of both the government and voluntary organizations, including the Gandhian institutions (Desai and Pandorm, 1974; Joshi, 1980; Patel, 1996). It must be admitted that there is considerable improvement in tribal literacy rate in last three decades; though they lag behind the literacy of general population. Some 36 per cent tribals were literate in 1991 as against 61 per cent in general population (Punalekar and Ranadive, 1984a). Thirty years ago (in 1961), tribal literacy was only 12 per cent. There are inter-tribe literacy differences with Dhodias leading the rest with as high as 45 per cent literacy (1991). "This tribal group (namely Dhodias) is also one tribal group in the state among whom one finds a rapidly growing class of entrepreneurs", writes Satyakam Joshi (Joshi, 1996b). In literacy achievements, Dhodias are followed by the Choudharis (32% literates). Educational situation of Dublas or Halpatis, Varlis, Bhils, Kotwalias, and other primitive groups is indeed disappointing. One must also note that tribal girls or women are not as much literate as their male counterparts even within the same tribe. "Illiteracy among tribal women is glaring and worrisome" (Joshi, 1996b).

Tribal areas have not remained the same; they are changing in their external context considerably due to policy and programmatic interventions of the state and other socio-economic forces. The tribal areas are recipients of development projects and programmes; initiatives and experiments carried out with special network of development-oriented machinery and sometimes with the help of NGOs. Some of these benefits have reached even the interior forest villages of the Dangs and Dharampur, Tilakwada and Chhota Udepur. Roads, schools, health centres, state transport and many other social infrastructural services are now accessible to some forest dwellers also. But mostly these beneficiary villages are on the roadside *(rastee gamo),* and closely linked with other developed towns like Bardoli, Dahod, Godhra, Rajpipla, Vyara, Valod, etc. (Punalekar, 1980; Desai and Chaudhary, 1977). Because of the presence of these vertical linkages, some of these tribal villages have now become dependent on metropolitan centres like Ahmedabad, Baroda, and Surat for trade, commerce, industry, education and employment.

What is the nature of these forest-rural urban linkages and the dependencies generated through them? Do the tribals gain in concrete material terms due to such enhanced opportunity structures aiding their physical mobility and improving their access to diverse, complex structure of urban-metropolitan economy? There are as yet no concrete data and analysis with reference to these questions (Punalekar, 1987; Das, 1994). These are indeed critical questions worth pursuing for a deeper understanding of change and transformation in a tribal society in Gujarat which is in a flux.

III

Stratification, Underdevelopment and Migration

One Major indication of changing scenario in tribal region relates to process of social division and differentiation among the tribals during last few decades; especially since sixties, i.e after the formation of Gujarat as a separate state and implementation of various growth and development programmes in tribal region. Social stratification is particularly noticeable among the Choudharis, Dhodias and Gamits (Shah, 1984; Bose, 1978; Punalekar, 1983; CSS, 1985; Joshi, 1992). We have already noted how Dhodias and Choudharis have outpaced others in literacy and education. This may perhaps be true in terms of their share in employment in government services: a point that can be studied with a wider data base.

On a minor scale, this process of social differentiation is evident among the Koknas living in the irrigated belt or in the plains *(talat vistar)* of Dharampur taluka in Valsad. Devdas Pillai of University of Bombay and Vyas and his IIM team in 1970s in their studies on Dharampur taluka have brought out these features (Vyas *et al.,* 1977; Pillai and Baks, 1979). Later Manorama Savur in her studies on Bulsar Taluka and Anil Bhatt in his studies on Bansda NGOs have come up with similar observations, namely, relative advancement and prosperity among some tribal groups and poverty among others (Bhatt, 1989; Savur, 1987). Certain tribes like Dublas, Bhils, Varlis and Kathodis are still far away from development mainstream within their own, i.e. tribal society; leave alone wider gamut of non-tribal society. These tribal groups are even today socially and economically homogeneous; which is largely the result of their relative isolation and underdevelopment. Cornering of the gains of development by relatively enlightened and articulate tribes has been a distinct feature in a tribal region in the state (Punalekar, 1990a and 1995a; Patel, 1992).

Some scholars studying tribes in south Gujarat had noticed these trends quite early. I.P. Desai was one among them, and in early 1960s in his inquiry into Vedchhi movement; he had brought to our attention the emergence of elite segments in a tribal community (Desai, 1982) Ghanshayam Shah in his studies on Chaudhary tribes too had come across such trends in the region (Shah, 1979). This tendency gathered further momentum and density in subsequent years, i.e. in 1980's and 1990's (Shah, 1992; Breman, 1993). According to Desai, Shah and others, an absence of enlightened leadership among tribal communities like Dublas, Kathodis, Bhils, Varlis, etc. was a predominant factor in their remaining behind other groups like Dhodias, Gamits, Choudharis, etc. That was indeed a handicap, which other studies too have brought up in respect of Dublas in particular (Punalekar and

Punalekar, 1998; Breman, 1974).

But why such leadership could not develop among them? Why Dublas or Kotwalias remained largely leaderless; while Gamits and Dhodias could march forward? These questions beg answers and merit scrutiny of circumstances which hinder the growth of leadership in certain groups; while others living in the same region and sharing the same geographical space move forward on development path under socially sensitive and committed leadership. Jan Breman in his studies on circuitous migration among tribals has tried to address this question (Breman, 1985; 1984a). But more such studies are needed to gauge the full weight of historical conditions on emergence of progressive, forward looking and dynamic tribal leadership. What are the characteristics of upcoming social strata among the tribals? In these socially advancing tribes, some households have gained considerable status in recent years in social, political and economic spheres. Better irrigation and land productivity have enhanced their economic power and ranking. They are brought nearer the levers of social power and material wealth. There is considerable expansion in the nature and quality of their contacts with other mainstream social groups, i.e non-tribal social strata comprising middle and also upper castes of Gujarat (Punalekar, 1980).

As stated earlier, this has happened principally after Independence, and at more rapid pace after the formation of Gujarat as a separate state in 1960. Creation of Ukai dam and similar other facility structures; emergence and consolidation of cooperative institutions in the field of agriculture, horticulture, milk, credit, marketing, etc. and also expansion of educational institutions in tribal region have contributed decisively to the rise of better-off classes in a tribal society in Gujarat. There is irrefutable evidence on pronounced social stratification among some tribal castes. In studies conducted by the Centre for Social Studies and other scholars, on Choudharis, Gamits, Naikas and Dhodias of South Gujarat region, it is convincingly demonstrated that some of these tribal groups are no longer a homogeneous entity. They are internally stratified and stand apart from others in the same ethnic group in terms of social status and economic ranking. In cultural realm also, this upcoming strata among tribals is trying to assimilate and integrate with similarly situated social groups in Hindu social order. They vigorously participate in religious and secular activities of the sects like Swami Narayan, Mahanubhav, Swadhyay, Kewal Panth, etc. where they have a chance of interacting with other socially advanced groups. Studies by some scholars vindicate these trends vividly (Lal, 1977; Lobo, 1991; Hardiman, 1984). Some among them have already acquired communal consciousness, and harbour deep antipathy towards the Muslims. One research scholar has perceptively noted this newly emerging communal virus among the tribals of Valia and Sagbara talukas in Bharuch district. Some educated tribals refer to Muslims in a derisive expression. They call them "M Factor." Reportedly there was a tense situation in some rural pockets of south Gujarat; tribals were found spearheading the violence against the Muslims. A few tribals from Bharuch district were found to have taken active part in the *Ratha Yatra* and *Ramjanm Bhumi* episode. Why poor tribals are against poor Muslims is a question that needs analysis and answering (Pinto, 1994).

There is another side to this narrative thought. Not all forest dwelling tribals are better off. Some have to encounter considerable difficulties and hardships. Physical infrastructure in their surroundings is poor. Communication with outside world is tardy and oftentimes inaccessible, especially during rainy season. Also they have to suffer inconveniences due to delayed response to their economic and basic infrastructural demands. There are no regular, daily markets in their midst. Many tribal households have still to walk 15-20 kms. to reach weekly markets or *hats* to sell their agricultural or forest produce and to buy their necessities like salt, spices, cooking oil, etc. (Punalekar, 1978, 1984b). They also face difficulties is securing primary health services. Educational facility for their children is not nearby. They have to depend upon the *Ashram* (residential) schools, usually run by the voluntary organizations in this region. Such schools are not too many; and all tribal parents cannot afford to put their wards in these distantly located schools (Joshi, 1985; Punalekar, 1985a and 1985b). Indeed, some concrete steps are being taken to redress these grievances; but even then the severity of problems has not much diminished. Such problems related to their day-to-day existence need urgent attention of both, the administration and the NGOs working among the tribals for their upliftment.

It is reported that some tribal households cultivating forest lands for generations have a grievance that they are denied of the ownership and cultivation rights in these lands. There are conflicting claims and perceptions on ownership of forest lands (VVSS, 1996; Joshi, 1992; Hardiman, 1994; *Eklavya,* 1996). There is a need to sort out these issues and settle the claims amicably. For the tribals, land in the forest is the only sustainable means of livelihood. On the other hand, the forest officials have responsibility to maintain the forest land-mass without any visible depletion. Both these ends are vital, but are not necessarily mutually antagonistic; given the democratic mandate and spirit of the constitution and overall docility and obedience of tribal groups. Participative dialogue can help to realize these goals of complementarity of forest and needs of forest settlers, i.e. the tribals. An experiment like formation of *Van Samitis* may go a long way in smoothening these relations and activating the process of negotiation between the tribals and the state.

There has been in the recent years a pronounced tendency of regular seasonal migration among tribal households in South Gujarat region. Lack of irrigation, uneven agricultural development and uncertain economic prospects have led to migration tendency among the tribals who were traditionally less mobile. This migration stream begins sometime in October (after the monsoon season) and return migration starts some time around April or May every year. This stream is without letup and we learn every year the number of migrants is multiplying. Jan Breman had noted this phenomenon in his studies on agrarian change in South Gujarat. He observed that the tribals from the neighbouring Nawapur and Nandurbar talukas of Maharashtra were regularly migrating to Bardoli, Vyara and Valod talukas of Surat district; some even went as far as Bulsar and Gandevi talukas. They worked as sugarcane cutters, carters or as casual farm hands. He has graphically described their conditions of living and working some 80-90 kms. away from their native village (Breman, 1978). Kapadia and Pillai have also noted migration among the tribals around Vapi-Udwada areas in Bulsar district (Kapadia and Pillai, 1972).

There is seasonal migration of the tribals within the state boundaries also. The Bhils of Panchmahals district within Gujarat move out in substantial number in search of work after the rainy season. They migrate to Nadiad, Anand, Ahmedabad, Bhavnagar, Baroda, Surat, and Bulsar. They return to their village for ploughing and sowing some time in May, i.e. just a fortnight before the onset of monsoon. One study conducted by the ITDP office (1983) surveyed some 65,883 migrants from the Panchmahals district; together they constituted 8 per cent of district population. In terms of sending out migrants, 3 talukas namely Dahod (11.5%), Limkheda (9.5%) and Santrampur (9%) were prominent. Among the migrants, 36,281 were males (55%), and 29,602 females (45%). 12,427 were children (19%) in the age group of 6 to 14 years. The migrants worked in the activities of road building and repairs, laying telephone cables, loading and unloading of goods in the railyards, etc. Some worked as agricultural labourers also. This study observed that the relationship between these labourers and their masters is many times quite stable in the sense that they return to same contractors or farmers every year . . . They (i.e. migrant labourers) do not bother about educating their children in nearby schools even when such facilities exist and even when they have not to shift every now and then as in case of road construction workers" (ITDP, 1983). They further add that the migrant labourers are interested "in getting whatever paltry amount the children can bring in". This betrays the biases of the administrators towards the migrants in general and the tribal migrants in particular.

Another study covering the same theme (tribal migration) in recent years has provided a graphic description on this process and its inner dynamics (Patel and Desai, 1992; Patel and Desai, 1995). According to this study, there are over one lakh migrant workers in the sugarcane harvesting operation in South Gujarat region alone. They include a large number of tribals from

Dangs district; Songadh, Uchchal and Nizar talukas of Surat district (in Gujarat) and from neighbouring Nandurbar, Nawapur, Dhulia regions of Maharashtra. This shows that there are some compelling reasons for the tribals to move out of their native village and seek employment outside. These tribal migrants are found working in sugarcane cutting activities. Some work on daily wages in agricultural farms owned largely by the middle and upper castes like Patidars, Anavils, Rajputs, Voras (Muslims).

The tribals living in the villages have to be in search of diverse occupations due to severe poverty conditions at home. This we had observed in our earlier studies on migrant labourers in Gujarat and Maharashtra (Punalekar, 1998). This is also evident from data and field observations of V.M. Patel who has noted that the migrant tribals are employed in construction, road-laying, road repairs, digging and carrying mud or on the farms. He observes that ". . . Migrants do not get any housing facility and they are obliged to live either in the open, or on the footpaths, or in the slums. No notable increase was found in their incomes. Most of the migrants have confessed that they would not have moved out if they had the means to earn their daily bread nearer home" (quoted in Jobanputra and Bhatt, 1993).

In my own study on casual labourers in the cities of Surat, Billimora, Valsad, Bharuch, Baroda, Anand and Ahmedabad, I had found that a large number of tribals were moving out of their village and standing in these city labour markets at street corners (known as *chakla bazaars* in local parlance) (Punalekar, 1990b). These market squares gave them opportunities of daily wage in construction and other similar labour intensive activities. Some among them bring their wives and children to these markets to seek work and wages for them also. Their economic situation is pitiable, to say the least.

What are their prospects at these *chakla bazaars?* Employment by the contractors or muccadams was uncertain, workload was heavy and arduous, and their bargaining capacity was too weak. And yet they came to the market daily at 6 a.m., with a hope that they could secure some work to stave off hunger and starvation. And number of such city labour spots are increasing year after year, alongside rise in the number of such daily job-seekers. These are migrant tribals in urban centres. We cannot ignore their presence in Gujarat towns and cities; and also we cannot underemphasize the gravity of their urban social and economic situation. Some scholars have already turned their attention on this phenomenon, but more in-depth studies are needed to fathom the depth of their misery and exploitation (Breman, 1994b; Das, 1989).

The situation of those working on the sugarcane fields is depressing and critical. *Naya Marg,* a Gujarati fortnightly published from Ahmedabad, carried out two articles in 1986 on the conditions of sugarcane cutters employed by the sugar factory management. They brought forth the deficiencies in living and working conditions of tribal migrants. Varsha Bhagat has described elsewhere about the severe hardships and disabilities of the canecutting tribal migrants coming from villages in South Gujarat and from Khandesh region, i.e. Dhule, Nashik, Jalgaon districts of Maharashtra (Bhagat Varsha, 1987).

This goes to suggest that more concerted action is needed, firstly on the issues emerging on rural front; and secondly those emerging on the urban front. There seems to be manifest and latent linkages between the rural and urban issues and manner of their manifestations (Breman, 1976). Why do the tribals migrate from their village in such a large number, and at regular intervals? This is because they have no means to sustain in their own native habitat. Their agriculture is unhelpful, due to lack of dependable irrigation and productivity. There are no job opportunities nearer native village. That means their agriculture has to be improved with sustained irrigational and other inputs. Also some definite steps need to be taken to develop agro-based industries (including food processing units) in the rural hinterlands so that, if need arises, they can undertake short-distance migration during slack season. Such opportunities nearer home may also bring in some stability in their domestic life, including some education and enduring parental care for their children.

Also some thinking has to be done about the nature of state interventions in the unorganized sectors of employment in the towns and cities. The migrant tribals (and also others) flock to these sectors which are devoid of basic social security and also amenities (Das, 1992; Punalekar and Patel, 1990). The city planning and implementation units must pay urgent attention to their needs, and provide for their shelter, health and other services. Most of these tribal casual workers live on pavements. They lack water and toilet facilities. Unsanitary conditions in which they live in turn affect the health and sanitation of city's general population; a lesson that we learn during the Plague epidemic in Surat a hard way (Shah, 1997). Also the NGOs working among the tribals have to evolve special strategies and programmes to attend to the problems of the urban tribals living in insecure conditions (Punalekar, 1996).

There is need to evolve a sustaining dialogue and communication with private employers and their associations/organizations. Such a need is extremely urgent, as there is increasing polarization and conflict among the rural haves and have-nots (Parmar, 1978; Breman, 1990; Labo, 1994). This is not a healthy and constructive tendency; and if it gets accentuated, it may result into conflagration and violence. There is special responsibility on the part of those with economic status and power to initiate positive, rights-respecting measures to safeguard the interests of the tribal poor.

There are some instances to prove that local farmers and sugar factory management are somewhat indifferent about the prevailing critical conditions among tribal migrant workers, their wives and children. The management seem to be more worried about economic prospects of their own enterprise. This fact was brought forth in sharper focus by Kokilaben Vyas, a Gandhian worker who was implementing an *Anganwadi* project for the children of migrant workers in South Gujarat villages. She admits that she had to work in a hostile environment. Experiences and eye-witness account of Kokilaben Vyas and Harshaben Joshi on experiment of educating the tribal children reveal the intensity of subterranean tensions in some villages (Setu, 1986). This Gandhian experiment began to be scuttled by some powerful farmers. They began to oppose the *Anganwadi* project, because at that time the migrant labourers had started demanding a daily wage of Rs. 11. Kokilaben Vyas began to receive strange reaction from the villagers when she began to set up the *Anganwadi* camp in the village. "We will not allow this *Anganwadi* to function. You are asking for a daily wage of Rs. 11. The labourers will be conscious *(Jagrut)*. Then we have to make provision for their drinking water, shelter, medical help, etc. All these we cannot afford," said the village farmers (Setu, 1986).

Thus the *Anganwadi* experiment suffered setbacks due to opposition from the farmers in some villages; and from the sugar factory management in some other villages. "Earlier, they were harvesting the cane at the rate of Rs. 22 per tonne. Now they are demanding Rs. 11 per day. Kokilaben is responsible for provoking these tribal cane-cutters", said one Sarpanch who was totally opposed to any welfare measures for the tribal migrant labour (Setu, 1986). This is indeed very retrogressive development. The nation needs literate, self-respecting and enlightened citizens, and not the opposite. Balwadi education for tribal children would go a long way in making them a disciplined and committed labour force. We cannot fritter away such opportunities, for narrow ends of private profit and individual gains.

IV

Displacement, Rehabilitation and Resistance

Now about the dams and rehabilitation. Indeed rapid development in agriculture and industry needed tapping of resources for water and power generation. This was the need of the people and the state. It was a matter of mainstream compulsion, and there was no easy way out except to launch mega projects for water impounding; given the time and other constraints. The Ukai dam near Songadh and Narmada dam near Rajpipla exemplify such experiments in mega projects undertaken to answer the immediate and potential development needs of the state and society. The Ukai dam which came up in late 1960s became a source of perennial water to large tract of South Gujarat region which earlier depended totally on rain waters. Especially the downstream villages in Vyara and Bardoli benefited a great deal due to this impounded water. And that has brought in immense gains to landowners in this territory, including the tribal farmers. Their economy has improved, they have also gained in education and other spheres.

But it has also been noted that the development has been uneven and lopsided. Some stark realities imbued with unease and tensions have been surfacing during last few years. The Ukai dam has affected some 344 villages (either partially or fully) from Songadh, Uchchal, Nizar and Sagbara talukas. In Nizar taluka alone, some 27 villages were completely submerged. The official estimates of the affected population was 80,600 in the year 1960-61. By the end of 1980, this figure has reached 1.5 lakh persons with loss of over 40,000 acres of fertile lands. Complete submergence of agricultural lands meant complete dislocation of the farming households. Such villagers were resettled in different sites. These oustee households faced considerable hardships and other tensions.

The resettlement caused dispersal and also distancing from one another belonging to same village, or caste group. The new sites where they were taken for resettlement were devoid of basic amenities and services. The new agricultural plots they received were less fertile, and demanded more physical labour to clear out weeds and tree-stumps, etc. Some land was rocky and barren (Mankodi, 1982; Mankodi and Gangopadhyay, 1983). Hence their agricultural economy was severely affected. For sheer survival many had to look out for casual work not only outside their native talukas. Migrant tribal labourers in the towns and cities that we have described earlier also included tribals from these Ukai Dam-affected families.

The villages which were partially affected were also not without their woes. In such cases, some families had to go out of the village community and resettle on their own elsewhere, as their own house or agricultural fields came under submergence. That caused, apart from economic hardships, severe social and cultural setbacks. Their ties with native village were mostly snapped. "We are forced into the conditions of slavery," the affected persons began to say. Their basic needs of food, clothing and shelter remained unmet or severely undermined. It is reported that some tribals are yet to be compensated for loss of their lands submerged under Ukai dam. This has given rise to considerable uneasiness and frustrations among the tribals living in Uchchal, Songadh and Nizar areas. In Songadh talukas 16 households from Ekalkhab village had lost their land under Ukai dam. Till December 1994 they were not given any compensation; reported one NGO working among the tribals (Punalekar, 1996). Tukaram Valvi of Laxmikheda village (Nizar Taluka) has been a convener of Ukai Asargrasta Khedut Samiti (UAKS). He has graphically described the unsteady conditions of Ukai dam oustees and their socio-economic and cultural hardships. According to him only 138 out of a total of 170 villages have been resettled. This means 32 villages are yet awaiting their resettlement. Due to displacement, educational prospects of the children have dimmed, he says. There is least participation of the tribals in higher educational stream. "Since 1960 in last three generations of tribals, there has not been a single Class I or Class II tribal from the villages of Uchchal and Nizar talukas" (Valvi, 1976).

Those who are affected by the Dam have certain demands for which they are organizing themselves from time to time. Their outstanding demands are: (i) restoration or redistribution of the surplus lands under the Ukai command as on 7th October 1967; (ii) provision of irrigation facility for the resettled villages/their agricultural lands; (iii) consent to earlier landowners to retain their lands which come under the Ukai reservoir; (iv) lowering of the water level of the Ukai reservoir to avoid the flooding and allow the farmers to cultivate their lands lying closer to dam area; (v) provision of enhanced compensation to the oustees or the Project Affected Persons (PAPs) to help them resettle better; and (vi) provision of 100 per cent subsidy to the oustee cultivators. One of their demands was substantial alteration of the syllabus within Uttar Buniyadi (i.e. post basic) schools to synchronize it with the ground level situations (Valvi, 1976).

The UAKS, the PAP's own organization, has been agitating since the beginning of this project for restoration of their land rights. Their other demands were also equally pressing. These were expressed thus: (1) "Our hunger is for our land," (2) "Give us the surplus lands", (3) "Give us back the lands which are now in the backwaters, but where there is no permanent water storage," and (4) "Renew the policy of Ek Sali," i.e. an yearly lease of land for cultivation. The following statement brings out in sharper focus the hurt expression of the displaced tribals. ". . . we are being looted as second class citizens. We are being exploited . . . during last 25 years, the fertile lands have become barren as the affected people were not given possession of these lands. The lands have become undulating in the absence of Nalla bunding and other levelling efforts. Government facility of credit, seeds, and fertilizers is not available to us. Ek Sali Scheme (which allowed the farmers to plough lands on a year-to-year contracts) has been discontinued. Electric connections for irrigation has also been disconnected. . ." (Valvi, 1976).

With a view to bring pressure on government and to create public opinion in their favour, the Samiti (UAKS) has intensified its struggle in recent times. The affected persons under the leadership of the Samiti staged a demonstration and token hunger strike before the office of the Mamlatdar (TDO). This took place on 26th February 1996. The Samiti has resolved to further intensify their struggle to regain their rights (*Gujarat Mitra,* 1996). As the years passed by there has been some definitive changes in state's approach and policy towards issues of resettlement and rehabilitation arising out of mega-projects (CSS, 1984; Joshi, 1990). There is now awareness and recognition of the negative consequences of large projects on displaced population. Some precautionary steps are now being taken to minimize hardships of those whose lands are submerged or whose livelihood is disturbed. In this context, the Sardar Sarovar Project (SSP) or popularly known as "Narmada Project" being commissioned in Nandod taluka of Bhroach district may be cited as an example. The project oustees include not only the villagers from Gujarat, but also those from the M.P. and Maharashtra. Approach of the project authorities towards the affected people and their problems is somewhat different and qualitatively more liberal and progressive (Joshi, 1991; Patel, 1988).

While implementing the SSP project, the state administration is conscious of displacement implications. They are alert to problems that crop up during dislocation and resettlement. A large segment of state bureaucracy is well informed and responsive to PAP demands. It has also brought into operation an elaborate support network of the NGOs and other social organizations in the state. Their help is being sought at the levels of designing, planning and implementation of development schemes. Additionally there is closer monitoring and evaluation of resettlement and rehabilitation (R&R) inputs. Mid-term corrections deemed desirable for resettled families are carried out earnestly and without much time-loss. Presence of these factors have certainly helped the authorities to achieve perceptible success in resettlement of the oustees of Narmada Dam. As a result, though there are signs of bickering and dissatisfaction in some sections of resettled families, an overall mood among the oustees is positive.

However, some nagging questions have cropped up during the process of resettling the tribal households whose lands/houses have gone under the SSP submergence or have been acquired for canals, dykes, etc. (Punalekar, 1984c). These questions mainly owe their genesis to differing perceptions among the state/its bureaucratic wings on the one hand, and the project affected persons (PAPs) on the other. Their perceptions differ on the meaning, nature and content of rehabilitation (Mankodi, 1982; Joshi, 1987a and 1987b; Patel, 1991). Also further directionality of current rehabilitation efforts is viewed differently by these groups. Some efforts have already been made in mapping out these differences (Punalekar, 1984c). Arjun Patel, a researcher studying rehabilitation process of the SSP project argues that resettlement results into alteration of their (tribals') social and cultural environment." Their socio-cultural life gets disturbed. This is more so when all friends, neighbours and relatives do not settle at one place . . . The oustees, like all migrants, begin their new life with a sense of anxiety and insecurity" (Patel, 1994).

Not that the tribals are unaware of their needs and interests. As early as in 1986, tribal families from Maharashtra which were to be resettled in Gujarat had come together under an organization called *Narmada Dharangrasta Sahayak Samiti* with headquarters at Akkalkuwa and Akrani in Dhule district. They had then drafted a detailed petition which contained some 21 points underscoring their social and economic needs (Setu, 1986). This included suggestions for stress-free rehabilitation without undermining their solidarity and social cohesion. The petition called for measures against imminent indebtedness of the oustees; fair compensation in terms of lands and other assets; provision of school, dispensary etc. Point number 21 of their petition indicates their concern for children's education. It says that ". . . despite the presence of schools in the official records, the teachers do not remain present in any of the schools in affected villages. All schools are closed. These closed schools should be opened forthwith by making the presence of school teachers mandatory . . . " (Setu, 1986, 43). This reflects on the anxiety among tribal parents. They do not want the education of their children to suffer while they are about to move into new settlement sites.

In initial period of dislocation and resettlement, the Gujarat oustees of Narmada Project did have some difficulties. These included cumbersome access to and use of fuel, fodder and other common resources and facilities at new sites; as the host community was somewhat unhelpful and unresponsive to the needs of the "new-comers" or "outsiders". The local residents of Khadgada village were opposed to the incoming PAP tribals because they were being resettled on a village pasture lands; one M&E report noted (Patel, 1991 and 1996). The oustees resettled in Chhindiapura faced the problems of obtaining the grass or fodder, collecting firewood, and finding a suitable place for grazing their cattle. These problems received immediate attention of the state and the NGO's; and were resolved promptly.

More worrying prospects faced by the tribal oustees resettled far from their native habitat related to socio-cultural domain. The tribal communities facing dislocation were deeply anchored into their society, meticulously following a host of social and cultural practices relating to marriage, birth, illness, death, house-building, transplanting, etc. Some of these core practices got disturbed, once they were dislocated from their native village. Arjun Patel has mentioned that the oustees resettled at Tentalao and Ambavadi found difficult to secure the services of priests, cook, helpers in times of marriage in their family at new sites (Patel, 1991). He informs us that earlier the tribals obtained utensils from their own village or Caste Panch. Now that arrangement did not exist in a new site resettled village. The *bhajan mandalis,* another social institution having some cultural meaning for the tribals, have dispersed and disintegrated already. A tribal or caste Panch which used to earlier decide on matters of marriage, divorce, desertion and such other vital family-rooted issues, is now dormant or dissolved. The old structure enveloping social services network had broken down due to dispersal of households across various sites, and new structures have not emerged so far.

It is indeed difficult to replace or reproduce the age-old institutional structures that have provided to them easy access to *dai, bhuva, bhagat,* priest, marriage match-maker, counsellor, etc. in whom they could confide without guilt or reservations. These ties were existent in their old village; while on new sites there is an absence of such helpers or supporters. The chief reason was that entire village community could not be resettled at one place; they were dispersed, and often at long distances. Thus there was fragmentation of the original village community, and that resulted into fragmentation of their social and cultural landscape also.

Such disaggregated resettlements tend to produce their own cultural consequences, including that of loss of social security and solidarity. Then there emerges a critical social and cultural difference between the old and new environment; the difference which may lead to new worries and tensions due to absence of time-honoured traditional institutions and their supportive network. The prospect of its irreplaceability in a limited time-span furthern heightens their anxieties in a new milieu. Such feelings along with their cultural meanings should not be brushed aside in a bureucratic manner; instead they must be appreciated and examined seriously for its full import for rehabilitation goals. Cultural experience and their shared meanings do occupy a significant place in the design of one's living (Punalekar, 1984c). How do we manage to cope up with such cultural dislocation or disjunction, and make their living livable is a big, complex question. All those concerned with a question of successful social rehabilitation must exercise their minds together to find solutions to such vexed issues.

Not all tribals face such dilemmatic situations. Those belonging to middle and upper peasantry have better social and political linkages, and are in a relatively defensible position to solve their personal, familial problems. Also they themselves hold some positions in democratic institutions like Panchayats, Cooperative Societies, etc. (Bose, 1988; Desai, 1979; Joshi, 1987b). That renders them a vital space to sort out their problems or atleast to mitigate its severities. Also they have vertical social and political ties; and through these they can manage to fulfil their needs and demands (Punalekar, 1980).

For the lower classes or the poor tribal peasantry, there are enormous difficulties in their path. Efforts to mobilize and organize the tribals on radical lines do not usually create favourable climate; rather it leads to hostilities and more internal divisions. Recent events in Dangs and Dharampur are uneasy testimonies on this score. Vidyut Joshi, a scholar on tribal society in Gujarat, has written perceptively on these developments. He says; ". . . If the development (among tribals) has moved in this manner and direction (i.e.

supposedly benefiting the tribals), then why there is Gujarat-wide restiveness and agitation among the tribals who were traditionally peaceful, soft or obedient and kind-hearted? Before this restiveness assumes a dimension of fire-like situation, there is need to correctly apprise this issue in its proper perspective. . . " (Joshi, 1996). Vidyut Joshi also refers to some organizations of the tribals in the district of Dangs and underscores that these are democratic institutions with faith in the rule of law and its just applications.

Ramesh K. Pawar, another scholar, describes how the Dangi tribals were increasingly alienated from their traditional rights of cultivation of forest lands and collection of timber and other minor produce. He also mentions about their slowly decreasing access to common property resource. Indeed it is matter of worry that in some parts there is uneasiness and unrest. Ramesh Pawar writes; ". . . The employees of the forest conservation department took steps against the tribals who were cultivating the land reserved under plantations. They damaged the standing crops of the tribals. After this event, the local tribals and the forest department came into direct confrontation. In this the forest department became the target (victim) of the *adivasi* protest and opposition. . . . To suppress this question, the forest department came down heavily on the local tribals. Some incidence of death has also occurred. Due to these developments, the agitation which till then was going at snail's pace, became more fierce and forceful. The tribals openly decided not to cooperate (with the state agencies). Some offices of the forest department in Dangs were burnt down; and since then the tribals began to be labelled as 'Naxalites' " (Pawar, 1996).

Pawar further elaborates that till these events, the local tribals did not know what was Naxalism or tenets of Naxalbari movement. "To such tribals, the name 'Naxalites' was conferred by the forest staff, government and newspaper dailies". Now the agitation in Dangs seem to have petered out. But that may not be true, writes Pawar. He says; "Do the tribals have no rights to raise their voice against injustice and unfairness? Are these *adivasis* not the citizens of this state and nation? . . . even today there is suffocating environment in Dangs around this question. One should not be surprised if it gets explosive some day" (Pawar, 1996). Vidyut Joshi also mentions about the presence of "Bhumihin Kisan Hakka-Saurakshan Samiti," and describes that organization's demands and working style was fully in compliance with our Constitution. So also the demands and functioning of the forest labour cooperatives; he underscores (Joshi Vidyut, 1996).

V

A Concluding View

The description above vividly indicates the points of restiveness and dissatisfaction among the tribals who are face to face with economic and other insecurities (Mehta, 1983; Lobo, 1992; Patel Arjun, 1994) . . . We have also briefly noted the indices of restlessness among tribal peasants including the landless labourers. This is visible through local as well as regional formations. Last year, a rally was organized by the tribals living in the woodlands under the banner of Disha Sansthan. Purpose of this rally was to draw the attention of the GOG on some of their unmet needs and demands. One report on these events stated; ". . . no comprehensive solution could be found to the entire set of problems and demands. The tribals are agitated on these points even today. . . " (SMS, 1994).

It is imperative that solutions are found without loss of previous time. While reaching solutions, one must keep in view the immediacy of social and cultural needs of the tribals, whose contribution to the development of Gujarat is significant. Resource base of their habitat is a key to overall growth and development of state and its economy.

Fortunately there are positive legacies of tribal support to state's social and economic agenda. Their sense of participation is also quite sincere and spontaneous. This relationship must further develop into active partnership, and should help in unleashing their creative energies in building secular and egalitarian society.

It is indeed possible to come together and jointly (tribals and non-tribals) build a modern, secular and rights-respecting Gujarat society. That would need a balanced, humanitarian approach and capacity to discover tribals inner worries and tensions; some of which are the unintended and unimagined consequences of development path and perspectives we have chosen. Sooner we review our performance, discover the snags and rectify them, better it is for everyone desirous of building modern Gujarat. The entire Gujarat society, tribals and non-tribals together, may stand to gain through such enlightened initiatives.

REFERENCES

Bhagat, Varsha. 1987. "Sherdi Kamdarona Shoshanno Charkho," *Setu Patrika*. 4, April.

Bhatt, Anil. 1989. *Development and Social Justice: Micro Action by Weaker Sections*. New Delhi: Sage Publications.

Bose, P.K. 1978. *Stratification among the Scheduled Tribes in Vadodara, Sabarkantha and Dangs Districts*. Surat: Centre for Social Studies.

Bose, P.K. 1981. "Stratification among Tribals of Gujarat," *Economic and Political Weekly*, 16(6): 191-96.

—. 1988. "Political Economy of Irrigation: A note," in Claude Alvares and Ramesh Billory (eds.), *Damming the Narmada*. Penang, Malaysia: Third World Network.

Breman, Jan. 1974. "Mobilization of Landless Labourers: Halpatis of South Gujarat," *Economic and Political Weekly*, 9 (12).

—. 1976. "Seasonal Migration and Co-operative Capitalism: Crushing of Cane and of Labour by Sugar Factories of Bardoli," *Economic and Political Weekly*, 13(31,32, 33).

—. 1985. *Of Peasants, Migrants and Paupers: Rural Labour Circulation and Capitalist Production in West India*. Delhi: Oxford University Press.

—. 1990. "Even Dogs are Better Off: The Ongoing Battle Between Capital and Labour in the Cane Fields of Gujarat," *The Journal of Peasant Studies*, 17(4), July.

—. 1993. *Beyond Patronage and Exploitation: Changing Agrarian Relations in South Gujarat*. Delhi: Oxford University Press.

—. 1994a *Wage Hunters and Gatherers: Search for Work in the Urban and Rural Economy of South Gujarat*. Delhi: Oxford University Press.

—. 1994b. *Labour Nomads in South Gujarat*, I.P. Desai Memorial Lecture, Surat: Centre for Social Studies.

CCSES, 1976. *Modernisation, Stagnation and Steady Decline: Sociological Contributions on Social Change in South Gujarat, India*. Holland: Centre for Comparative Social-Economic Studies, University of Utrecht, Publication No. 1.

Centre for Social Studies (CSS). 1984. *Narmada Yojana: Ek Parichay*, Surat.

Centre for Social Studies (CSS) (ed.) 1985. *Caste, Class and Reservation*. Delhi: Ajanta Books International.

Das, Biswaroop (ed.). 1989. *Migrant Labour in India—Report of a Workshop*. Surat: Centre for Social Studies.

—. 1992. "*Migrant Labour in the Construction Sector*," *Man and Development*, 12(1), March.

—. 1994. "Slums, Migrants, and the Urban Informal Sector," *The Indian Journal of Labour Economics*, 37(3), September.

Desai, A.R. 1987. *Rural Development and Human Rights of Agrarian Poor in Independent India*. I.P. Desai Memorial Lecture Series, Surat: Centre for Social Studies.

Desai, B.D. 1979. *Socio-Economic Study of the Milk Producers of South Gujarat*. Surat: Centre for Social Studies.

Desai, I.P. 1982. *Vedchhi Andolan*. Surat: Centre for Social Studies.

Desai, I.P. and G.A. Pandor. 1974. *A Profile of Education among the Scheduled Tribes in Gujarat*, Surat: Centre for Social Studies.

Desai, I.P and Banwarilal Choudhary. 1977. *History of Rural Development in Modern India*. Vol. II, New Delhi: Impex India.

Dhuru, A. and S. Pungalia. 1987. *Sugar-cane Harvest Cutters in South Gujarat. Bombay:* Tata Institute of Social Sciences, Typescript.

Eklavya. 1996. "Rojamdar Vanmajoorone Kayami Karvano Hukum Supremema Bahal," 3(2), October.

Gujarat Mitra, (Surat), 1996, February 13.

Gupta, Ranjit (ed.) 1977. *Planning for Tribal Development*. New Delhi: Ankur Publishers.

Hardiman, David. 1984. "Adivasi Assertion in South Gujarat: The Devi Movement of 1922-23," in Ranajit Guha (ed.), *Subaltern Studies*. Vol. 3. New Delhi: Oxford University Press.

—. 1994. "Power in the Forest: The Dangs, 1820-1940" in D. Hardiman and D. Arnold (eds.) *Subaltern Studies*. Vol. 8, Delhi: Oxford University Press.

ITDP Office. 1983. *A Note on the Migration Pattern of Tribals of Panchmahals*. Dahod: Project Administrator, October.

Jobanputra, D. and Nanak Bhatt 1993. *The Problems and Prospects of Development of Eastern Belt of Gujarat.* (Seminar Proceedings, Ahmedabad: Sardar Patel Institute of Economic and Social Research.

Joshi, Satyakam. 1992. *Daxin Gujaratni Jangal Kamdar Sahakari Mandalio:* Ek Abhyas. Ph. D. thesis, South Gujarat University, Surat.

—. 1996a. "Rashtriya Adivasi Niti: Prashno ane Padkaro," *Naya Marg,* December 1.

—. 1996b. "Politics of Tribal Autonomy: A Case of South Gujarat Tribals." Paper presented in National Seminar on *Tribal Policy,* organized by Jignashu Tribal Research Centre, New Delhi, December 7-8.

Joshi, Vidyut, 1980. *Ashramshalao: Ek Adhyayan* (in Gujarati), Ahmedabad: Gujarat Samajik Sevamandal.

—. 1985. "A Century of Tribal Education," In Centre for Social Studies (ed.) *Tribal Education in Gujarat.* Delhi: Ajanta Books International.

—. 1987a. "People's Response to Policy and Programmes", in S.P. Punalekar (ed.), *Rural Development for Rural Poor* (Seminar Proceedings), Surat: Centre for Social Studies.

—. 1987b. *Submerging Villages Problems and Prospects.* New Delhi.

—. 1990. "Sardar Sarovar Project: Thesis, Anti-thesis and Synthesis," *Yojana,* June.

—. 1991. *Rehabilitation: A Promise to Keep (A Case of SSP).* Ahmedabad: The Tax Publications.

—. 1996. "Adivasi Samashyanu Swaroop, mimeo.

Kapadia, K.M. and S.D. Pillai. 1972. *Industrialisation and Rural Society: A Study of Atul-Bulsar Region.* Bombay: Popular Prakashan.

Lal, Rash Bihari. 1977. *Socio-Religious Movements among Tribals of South Gujarat.* Ahmedabad: TRTI, Gujarat Vidyapith.

Lobo, Lancy. 1987. *Monitoring and Evaluation Report (No. 5) of Resettlement and Rehabilitation of Oustees of Sardar Sarovar Project, 1987.* Surat: CSS,

—. 1991. *Religious Sectarianism among the Tribals of South Gujarat.* Surat: Centre for Social Studies.

—. 1992. "Ethnocide and Pauperization of Oustees of Large Dams," *New Quest,* 92, March-April.

—. 1994. "Suppression of Valia Tribals and their Assertion," *Economic and Political Weekly,* 29(3), January 15.

Mankodi, Kashyap. 1982. "Ukai Yojana: Parinam ane Padarthpath," *Arthat,* 2(1), October-December.

Mankodi, Kashyap and Tanushri Gangopadhyay. 1983. *Rehabilitation: The Ecological and Economic Costs.* Surat: Centre for Social Studies.

Masavi Mustali, E. 1991. *Adivasioni Paltati Arthik Sthitino Abhyas.* Ahmedabad: Gujarat Vidyapith.

Mehta, D.B. 1983. *Seasonal Migration from Dangs.* Ahmedabad: School of Planning and Technology, Mimeo.

Parmar J.G. 1978. Impact of Sugar Industry on Surat District with Special Reference to Bardoli Taluka. M.A. thesis, South Gujarat University, Surat.

Patel, Arjun. 1988. *Initial Integration of Narmada Oustees* (Report No. 6). Surat: Centre for Social Studies.

—. 1991. *Social, Economic and Psychological Integration of Rehabilitation of Oustees and the Host Community.* (Report No. 13), Surat: Centre for Social Studies.

—. 1994. "Social and Cultural Implications of Displacement: A Case of SSP," paper presented in a seminar on *Development, Displacement and Rehabilitation,* Centre for Social Studies, Surat, May 11-13.

—. 1996. "Socio-Culture: Missing Aspects of Rehabilitation Policy Packages (Case of SSP)," paper presented in National Seminar on *Tribal Policy,* organized by Jignashu Tribal

Research Centre, New Delhi, December, 7-8.

Patel, Arjun and Kiran Desai. 1992. *Gramin Gujartma Shram Sthalantar,* Surat: Centre for Social Studies.

—. 1995. "Migrant Labour and Law,". in Debi S. Saini (ed.), *Labour Law, Work and Development.* New Delhi: Westvill Publishing House.

Patel, Priyavadan. 1992. "Status of Tribal Development in Gujarat: Case of ITDP Dahd," in Buddhadeb Chaudhary (ed.), *Tribal Transformation in India,* Delhi: Inter-India Publications.

—. 1996. "Gujaratma Adivasi Vikasna Pachhis Varshanu Sarvayyu," *Arthat,* 5(1), January-March.

Pathy, Jaganath, 1982. *Agrarian Structure in Tribal Gujarat and Its Implications for the Tribal Policies.* Surat: South Gujarat University.

Pawar, Ramesh K. 1996. *Gujaratna Junglo ane Bhumi-Sambadho Sathe Sankalayela Adivasiona Prashnono Abhyas.* mimeo. Smt. J. A. Patel Mahila College, Morbi.

Pillai, S.D. and C. Baks (eds.). 1979. *Winners and Losers: Styles of Development and Changes in Indian Region.* Bombay: Popular Prakashan.

Pinto, Stany. 1994. "Communalisation of Tribals in South Gujarat," in seminar proceedings on *Communal Violence and Communalism in Western India.* Surat: Centre for Social Studies, 9-11. February.

Punalekar, S.P. and Ranadive Jyoti. (1984a). *Tribal Education: An Inter-state Study.* Surat: Centre for Social Studies.

—. 1984b. "Weekly Market and Tribal Consciousness," *Mainstream,* 23 (9), October 27.

—. 1984c. "Voluntary Agencies and Rehabilitation: A Case of Narmada Dam Oustees," *Indian Journal of Social Work,* 44(4), January.

—. 1985a "Tribal Education in Gujarat," *Mainstream,* 23(39), 25 May.

—. 1985b. "Social Stratification and Educational Inequalities: A Case Study of Tribals from Maharashtra, Gujarat and Rajasthan", in Centre for Social Studies (ed.), *Tribal Education in Gujarat,* Delhi: Ajanta Books International.

—. ed. 1987. *Rural Development for Rural Poor* (Seminar Proceedings), Surat: Centre for Social Studies.

—. 1988. "Rural Poor in Western India: A Case Study," in Getubig and Ledesma (eds.), *The Most Disadvantaged Groups in Asian Agriculture,* Kuala Lumpur, Malaysia: Asian Pacific Development Centre.

—. 1990a. "Land Mobility and Social Status: A Case Study of Tribal Community," *New Quest,* 79(1), January-February.

—. 1995a. "Dhodias of South Gujarat," in Sachhidanand and R.R. Prasad (eds.), *Encyclopedia Profile of Indian Tribes.* New Delhi: Discovery Publishing House.

—. 1995b. "Bypassing the Poor and Powerless: A Study of Some Aspects of Rural Development in Western India", In Manorama Savur and Indra Munshi (eds.), *Contradictions in Indian Society.* Jaipur: Rawat Publications.

—. 1996. *Tribal Society and Socio-Legal Interventions.* Surat: Centre for Social Studies.

Punalekar, S.P. and Arjun Patel. 1990b. *Survival and Struggles of Female Casual Labourers: A Study of Majoor Bazaar in South and Central Gujarat.* Surat: Centre for Social Studies.

Punalekar, S.P. and Devyani Punalekar. 1998. "Margin of Existence: A Case of Landless Labourers", in S. N. Tripathy (ed.), *Tribals in India: The Changing Scenario.* New Delhi: Discovery Publishing House.

Savur, Manorama 1987) "Water Management for Tribal Development by an Industrial House in India," in S. Punalekar (ed.), *Rural Development for Rural Poor* (Seminar Proceedings). Surat: Centre for Social Studies.

Setu, Centre for Social Knowledge and Action. 1986. *Setu Patrika.* Number 2, August, pp. 43-48.

Shah, Ghanashyam. 1979. "Tribal Identity and Class Differentiations," *Economic and Political Weekly* (Annual Number), February.

—. 1984. *Economic Differentiations and Tribal Identity.* Delhi: Ajanta Books International.

—. 1992. "Tribal Issues: Problems and Perspectives," in Buddhadeb Chaudhary (ed.), *Tribal Transformation in India.* Delhi: Inter-India Publications.

—. 1977. *Public Health and Urban Development: The Plague in Surat.* New Delhi: Sage Publications.

Shramik Vikas Sansthan. 1994. *Purva Patti-Adivasi Vistar Vikas Karyakram,* Jawaharnagar Office, Netrang, Taluka Valia, District Bharuch.

Valvi, Tukaram. 1976. *Ame Bhik Nahi, Amaro Hakka Magiye Chhiye.* Laxmikheda, Nizar, Surat District.

Van Vidheyak Samiksha Samanvay (VVSS). 1996. *Forest for the People: Policy and Legislation.* Bombay: VVSS.

Vyas, V.S., T.K. Moulik *et al.* 1977. *Rural Development for Rural Poor: Dharampur Project.* Parts I & II. Ahmedabad: Indian Institute of Management.

Vyasulu, Vinod. 1996. *Crisis and Response: An Assessment of Economic Reforms.* Delhi: Madhyam Books.

Webster, Andrew. 1984. *Introduction to the Sociology of Development.* London: Macmillan.

SIX

DOOMED BY A DAM
The Pengs of Indravati River Valley of Orissa

SRIKANT PATEL and DEEPAK KUMAR BEHERA

Introduction

Till the other day in the world, the concept of development centered round economic growth with little or no concern for the human beings and their environment. The western blocs saw to rampant and massive development by technological augmentation and rapid industrialization thus establishing them as the "developed nation". The so-called "developed nation" laid the examples to be aped by the third world countries. In order to catch up with their developed brethren the third world countries could not find better alternatives but adhere to the path taken up by them, little realizing its long term implications on environment and socio-cultural matrix. Even though the adverse impacts on the people are well known in advance by the developers, those are deliberately underscored during a cost-benefit analysis. While today the proponents of development show some concern for the environmental factors, the human targets are grossly neglected. As a result numerous development programmes mushroom unabated amidst the hue and cry; though the deleterious impacts it makes on mankind are in vogue. Escobar does not mince matters when he says, "in many places there are worlds that development even today and at this moment is bent on destroying" (1995: 226).

In India after independence the developers pursued with a messianic zeal to help her cross the threshold of underdevelopment through exorbitant plans and policies borrowed from the developed nations. Hence, emphasis was given on massive infrastructure development, viz. giant industrial set-up, power generation, mining, water management projects, etc. However, in their attempts to eradicate the problems of underdevelopment, they often exacerbated them or created newer ones. One such excruciating and pathetic problem generated by development projects is the eviction of people from their settled habitat. Forced displacement has been a companion of development indelibly written into the evolution of industrial as well as developed countries (Cernea, 1994: 46). It not only evicts people of their home and hearth but also robs them off their long-standing cultural heritage and elements of sustenance. However, people fail to realize that many times development, either spontaneous or induced, brings not only benefits but also social disruption. Many planners and policy makers find it difficult to recognize this double impact when it matters: when a development programmes is being designed (Cernea, 1985: 188). Even when the adverse impact of these development programmes are well known to the agents of development, its mitigation for the welfare of the oustees is considered secondary by them. Hence E.J. Mishan says "in contrast to the situation in the West, the people of the third world countries struggling to survive in the face of relentless population pressure are collectively more tempted, impelled almost, to ignore the clear signals of what looks like impending economic disasters. They continue to mine the soil, to level the forests, to pollute rivers and lakes and in other ways to undermine their ecological support system" (1993: 97). Due to the construction of development projects large number of indigenous people are displaced leading to their impoverishment through the eight sub-processes, as identified by Cernea. These are landlessness, joblessness, homelessness, marginalization, increased morbidity, food insecurity, loss of access to common property, and social disarticulation (Cernea, 1995: 266-670). The problems that an oustee may encounter need to be properly mitigated in order to ameliorate the pangs of eviction. However, the enthusiasm shown by the policy makers and programme executors is seldom visible at the time of rehabilitating the affected people. While utmost care is taken to construct the development project, the government fails to realize the need of involving experts to comprehend the concerned socio-cultural matrix for designing a meaningful rehabilitation package. Hence most of the rehabilitation packages lack an imaginative anticipation of the possible mayhem that the oustees may encounter due to the implementation of the development project. Like an eyewash the rehabilitation measures are appended to the body of the project blue print. Such an attitude can also be attributed to the over-estimation of the project benefits and under-valuation of the sacrifices made by the people at the altar of "corporate interest" and under the garb of "national interest".

The Magnitude of Displacement

Annually ten million people enter the cycle of forced displacement and relocation in two sectors, namely, dam construction and urban transportation (Cernea, 1995: 264). In India till 1990 there were 213,00,000 displaced people by one or the other development projects (Fernandes, 1994: 24) and there were 14 millions dam related oustees alone (Fernandes, 1991). The working group on development and welfare of scheduled Tribes during the Eighth Five-Year Plan (1990-95) reports that out of 16.94 lakhs of persons displaced by 110 projects studied, 8.14 lakhs (48%) were tribal (Thukral, 1992: 8). Though the tribals constitute only 8 per cent of the total population of India, yet about 50 per cent from among them are called upon to make sacrifices of various kinds for growth and development of the nation. Many more, who are not displaced but are severely impacted by the development projects, never feature in the list of oustees and hence remain uncompensated.

Development Projects: Whose Temple?

While displacement is an ugly byproduct of development having serious implications on the life of all those who come under its ambit, the impacts particularly on the indigenous people are grave and severe. The irony is that people who suffer the mayhem and bear the brunt most are least benefited and seldom share the fruits of development. Both spontaneous and government sponsored settlement on land have increased considerably since World War II (Thayer and Scudder, 1975: 126). In India this has been a typical post-independent scenario. It may be highlighted here that most of the natural resources of our country are located in tribal dominated pockets. Hence majority of the heavy industries, power generation-cum-irrigation projects and mines are found in backward areas inhabited by the tribals (Mahapatra, 1994: 73). Today the scene is much the same and many of the indigenous people lose their homes and hearths to the temples of development. However, it is hard to believe that availability of natural resources is the only criterion that propels the construction of development projects in the remote tribal regions. It is reasonable to hold that there can be other underlying motivational factors encouraging the planners to consider the "land of the tribal people" for the construction of any development project. First of all, the tribal people do not own *patta* lands hence they cannot prove themselves as claimants in the event of land acquisition for the construction of a development project. Hence the project escapes from the burden of paying compensation to these voiceless people for the acquired land. Secondly it is easier to negotiate and strike a deal with the tribal people during eviction, relocation and rehabilitation. Often the allocated compensation is so nominal that the cost incurred by the project authorities in providing the logistics to the skilled workers is much more than that of the cost of relocation of the oustees. Sometimes they are left uncompensated for generations, as has been the case with the Hirakud Dam oustees of Orissa in India (Baboo, 1992). There have been instances of tribal oustees being displaced in Orissa for second and even third time. In India out of a total of 74,10,000 displaced tribal, only 29.4 per cent have been rehabilitated while a staggering 70.6 per cent still awaits rehabilitation (Fernandes, 1991). The tribal people are scarcely aware of the long-term criticality of the impact of development projects. They are mystified with the construction of large structures and deployment of queer heavy machines at the project site. Moreover the wage they earn in the form of hard cash during the course of construction generates project loyalty among them. Above all the historical experience of always being in the losing situation kills the spirit of these people and rarely one finds any anti-project movement among them to fight for their rights. Hence a vast majority of the oustees in India is from various tribal groups. Hence, the proliferation of such development projects in tribal areas as a deliberate attempt by the developers is not always inconsequential (Behera and Patel, 1997: 2).

In India construction of mega dam projects is rationalized on commissariat grounds to keep pace with its relentless population growth, though initially developing irrigation was with a purpose to counter droughts. B.D Dhawan comments that "the rapid increase of production is now an overriding factor for the planners behind irrigation development even at the cost of relegating the issues of sustainability, long term security and equity" (1990: 3). Dams and irrigation projects are invariably located in the hilly terrain and elevated tracts where majority of the tribals has been living for centuries (Barik, 1997: 1). It has been a practice by the planners to plan dams not only for irrigation but also to generate hydro-electricity. The dams have to be large enough to generate electricity. It is then obvious that a large dam would inundate more land hence greater numbers of people are evicted. In India the number of dam related oustees is 14 million and in Orissa there are around 187 lakhs dam oustees (Fernandes, 1991: 250). Behura (1996: 151) reports that about 50 per cent of the oustees in Orissa belong to various tribal groups. Today the liberalized economy of India welcomes various national as well as multinational concerns to infringe upon the territory of the indigenous people. Therefore it is presumed that in due course of time the development related problems would rise in India under her new economic policy. It is high time that the policy makers give due consideration to the cause of the development related oustees, particularly the hapless and naïve indigenous people living in the remote regions away from the humdrum of urban life.

Major Objectives of the Project

The Upper Indravati Hydro-Electricity Project (hereafter UIHEP) is a large multipurpose dam project of Orissa, India. It has come up in the tri-junction of Kalahandi, Koraput and Nabrangpur districts of Orissa. It envisages inter-basin transfer of water from Godavari basin to Mahanadi basin. It has created a reservoir of 110 sq. kms formed by four dams and eight dykes and an extensive irrigation complex. The catchment area of the project is 2,630 sq. kms and the reservoir area is estimated to be about 12,865 hectares. The project is designed keeping in view two basic objectives: (1) to provide irrigation water for 109,300 hectares (later revised in 1994 to 128,000 hectares) of agricultural land in the watershed of Hati barrage in adjacent Mahanadi river basin and (2) to provide 600 megawatt of electric power to be supplied to the grid of the Orissa State Electricity Board (OSEB).

Genesis of the UIHEP

Investigation on the feasibility of UIHEP commenced in 1959. The approval by the Union Planning Commission for execution of the project was delayed with regard to the equitable distribution of water resources until 1977. The Krishna Godavari Commission approved the project in 1978 and the Environmental Appraisal Committee of the Department of Science and Technology provided environmental clearance for the project in 1979. However, full-fledged construction work started only after obtaining assistance from the World Bank in 1985. The construction faced a setback due to a damage caused by heavy flooding in July 1991. A large number of lives (mostly tribal) were lost, the damage to the project was immense and the neighbouring village suffered immeasurably (Das, 1992: 5). A name sake enquiry was conducted and things moved on merrily as before.

In total the project has affected 97 villages – 44 from undivided Koraput and 53 from Kalahandi district. Of these, 31 villages from Koraput and 34 villages from Kalahandi have been directly affected by the impounding of water. The sole purpose of this dam project was to increase the agricultural production and consequently generate employment in service sectors. However, all this was done at the cost of evicting 17000 people (Report of Resettlement and Rehabilitation Unit, Khatiguda, hereafter R.R.U). The Orissa Krushak Mahasangha and Indravati Gana Sangharsha Parishad put the figure of those who are affected by this dam project at 30,000 in the undivided Kalahandi and Koraput districts of Orissa. The total land acquired by the project is 32, 530.87 acres.

The Reality of Evacuation and the Myth of Rehabilitation

In order to make way for the project, the evacuation of the targeted population was undertaken in four annual phases. The first phase of evacuation started in 1989. Some 5477 families were evacuated. Initially efforts were made to resettle the oustees on government land at Sashahandi in Jeypore sub-division and another 300 acres of land were identified in Talejaring in Kalahandi district. However, the oustees for various reasons did not approve the sites identified for relocation and they chose for individual resettlement on their own. As a result some 458 cluster villages of various sizes in 20 blocks of 5 different districts are formed (R.R.U, 1997: 9). The policy of the government has gone several changes during the various phases of displacement. The first phase envisaged 5 acres of non-irrigated or 2.5 acres of reclaimed irrigated land and 0.5 acres homestead land. However, those displaced families who opted to make their own resettlement and rehabilitation were paid cash compensation of Rs.29,575 as rehabilitation assistance. In the second phase, the cash compensation was Rs.20,075 in lieu of land purchase and it was kept in the State Bank account and released in installments for purchase of suitable agricultural or homestead land, free from all encumbrances. In order to qualify for the cash compensation of Rs.20,075, it was made mandatory for the oustees to purchase at least 50 per cent of the total land as prescribed in the policy of the first phase. In the third phase each displaced family was provided with cash equivalent of homestead land of 10 decimal at the rate of Rs.16,000 per acre. For displaced families having lost an area more than 4 acres, the extent of land allotted was equal to 4 acres of non-irrigated or 2 acres of irrigated land. The rate of rehabilitation was fixed at Rs. 8,000 per acre of non-irrigated land or Rs. 16,000 per acre of irrigated land. In case a displaced family has lost land upto 4 acres, the land to be allotted was equal to the extent of land acquired if non-irrigated and 50 per cent if irrigated. A cash compensation of Rs. 17,000 was paid as house building assistance. During the fourth phase each family was given 20 decimals of homestead land at the rate of Rs.16,000 per acre. Each family was given cash equivalent of agricultural land of 2.5 acres non-irrigated or 1.25 acres of irrigated land and it amounted to Rs.20,000. Each family was given house building assistance of Rs. 17,000. Thus, the oustees were provided with total rehabilitation assistance of Rs. 40,200. In addition to this, a maintenance allowance of Rs. 500 per month for one year was given to each displaced family.

Aims and Objectives

The present paper makes a humble attempt to study the impact of this mega development project on the Pengs—a tribal group affected by the project. The study, by adopting both synchronic and diachronic approaches, analyzes the major changes that have taken place in the life style of the sample population as a result of their displacement. It critically examines the long-term implications of the mega dam project on the targeted population. It also shows how the technological transformation has systematically eroded the Pengs' cultural ethos and values and thereby breaking down some of their traditional institutions, which have been so vital for the maintenance of their life support system.

Methodology

Keeping in view the aforesaid objectives, three affected villages and an unaffected village were selected on the basis of purposive sampling method. The affected villages were selected in terms of their relative distance from and accessibility to the nearest urban centre Khatiguda. For the purpose of analytical convenience these three affected villages were classified as exposed, moderately exposed and less exposed in terms of the same criteria. These villages, namely, Bagbeda, Dudungchua and Sanchhatrang are situated at a distance of 5 kms, 18 kms and 25 kms respectively from the nearest urban centre Khatiguda. A fourth village namely Podaauding located at a distance of 8 kms from Khatiguda, wherein the inhabitants did not suffer any displacement, was also selected for the purpose of synchronous comparison. Data were collected both from primary and secondary sources. Interview, case study and observation methods were used for the collection of data. Local NGOs, activists and government officials were interviewed in order to supplement the data.

The Peng Parjas

The Peng Parjas can be broadly divided into Plain Peng Parjas and Dongerla Peng Parjas. The suffix Parja is the antonym of Raja—the ruler or king. Hence all those who are commoner call themselves as Parjas—the ruled. The Dongerla Peng are more primitive and are found on the mountainous terrain of Kalahandi and Koraput districts of Orissa. They call the mountain-pass as *dharam-dooar* (the Gate of Truth) where they have been living since times immemorial. This mountain-pass forms a part of the Eastern Ghat. Scattered in the *dongerla* region numerous small hamlets of the Peng tribe are found near perennial water sources. These mountains have sustained them both materially and spiritually and the Pengs worship the mountains, the growths and the under-growths as gods and goddesses and hold them in high esteem. The Pengs are an endogamous tribe with exogamous clan and *toden* (a group of clans among whom marital exchange is tabooed). It is interesting to note that a village acquires its name according to the clan name of the people living in it, for example, the village inhabited by the *odring* clan is called as Odri and similarly the place occupied by the *chipizoding* clan is called as Chipizod. Hence each clan is proud of its place of residence and considers its ancestral land sacred. It also owes its allegiance and identity to the ancestral land. They believe that their ancestors reside in this land who protect them from the foreseen as well as unforeseen calamities. Village or hamlet is generally uniclan by nature, but multiclan villages/hamlets are not uncommon.

The Pengs have a subsistence economy and they eke out their living by simple technology. They maintain a symbiotic relationship with nature. Each clan takes care of its totemic object, which can be an animal or plant. They are forbidden to harm or kill them. For example the members of *langlabehing* clan never try to harm a *burka* (tiger) and a *zabeing* clan seldom kill a rach (snake). It is tabooed to kill a pregnant deer or pluck the early cobs of maize before it is ripe. However, due to the infiltration of various developmental forces their cultural infrastructure is in under threat. The Pengs are not nomadic by nature. However, those living in the *dongerla* region practice shifting cultivation and thus change the site of settlement along with the site of cultivation. This kind of shifting is restricted to pre-selected sites following a cyclic order.

The advent of the Project in the land of the Pengs has brought in large-scale changes in the life of the indigenous Peng population. It has uprooted sizeable number of this people, diminishing their subsistence resource base and thereby forcing them to make rearrangements for the benefits of someone else. Michael M. Cernea makes a point when he raises the question about social justice. He says that "social justice" and "social injustice" are not concepts frequently employed in the discourse on development. But they should be (Cernea, 1998: 46). In the face of social injustice and inequity only the meek shall bear the brunt—that has been the case with the oustees of the Peng tribal community.

When Rehabilitation is Limited to Disbursement of Compensation

Benign plan turns into horrendous reality if the effort to alleviate the suffering of the oustees is lackadaisical. The process of resettlement and rehabilitation of the UIHEP has been dealt in an *ad hoc* basis. It is of prime importance that the planners and policy makers should be aware of the cultural infrastructure of a community. The long-term implications of the development project on the cultural infrastructure need to be anticipated before planning resettlement and rehabilitation packages for the oustees. Only enumeration of the condemned assets of the oustees will do little good in rehabilitating them. Any given community is endowed with various informal institutions those have survival values for its members. These institutions have survival values for its members only under certain set conditions but it may fail when encountered with new or changed conditions. Under the new circumstances some members may become exploitative and cause moral hazards leading to the failure of the institutions.

It is important to point out here that in India those encroaching revenue land may become its owner after some time, but those encroaching forest land can never become its owner though their ancestors might have been in possession long before the present colonial law came into force (Singh, 1989: 92). The Pengs in particular draw their sustenance from the forestland hence the usufruct right over the land is not recognized by the government. Hence during enumeration the encroached forestland was not included along with the condemned assets. As a result most of them were considered as landless or marginal landholders. This was a gross underestimation of their actual operational land. Moreover a Peng cultivating 2 acres of land in a single year would require at least 10 acres of forestland for his sustenance all through his life. This is because they mostly depend on shifting cultivation and in this type of cultivation the land is left fallow at least for 5 years so that it gets naturally revitalized. Hence it must be remembered that for a tribal the actual space of operation is much more than what it appears which the persons entrusted for the rehabilitation many times fails to realize. Therefore it is argued that the land allocated by the project has fallen short of their requirements.

As a policy matter the oustees were provided land at the command in Sashahandi area but it failed to attract them, as there was a dearth of the basic amenities. The Aide Memoir of 1989 by the World Bank reports that there was not even provision of drinking water in the command area. Hence, people rejected the relocation site, as they preferred to stay in hilly areas traversed with streams (Aide Memoir, 1989: 4).

It needs to be mentioned here that inhabitants of all the affected villages have suffered minimum spatial displacement as they were given an option to relocate themselves in the place of their choice and most of them preferred to stay close to their ancestral land around the fringe of the reservoir.

Moreover irrigation facilities take times to come up in the command area. Irrigation of the command area is possible only after the completion of the dam as well as the construction of the canals, hence for a long time such areas remain as name sake command area. Hence to hold that allocation of land to the oustees in the command area would alleviate their suffering is a myth, there are every possibility that allocation of land even in the command area may lead to impoverishment. They have an intangible environment that makes them feel secure to live in. While efforts are made to reconstruct the tangible environment, the policy makers fail to comprehend the intangible environment. The intangible environment consisting of various unseen forces influences their socio-religious life so much so that they cannot remain outside its orbit. For example the Pengs believe that the village deity and other demi gods protect them from all possible hazards; hence they feel more confident and secured in their ancestral land. As a result they had lot of inhibitions to shift to a strange land devoid of their protectors and decided to relocate themselves nearby the ancestral land. Baboo makes a point when he says "people living in the fertile basin would hardly want to be dislocated, even if they are poor, because of their unwillingness to start life afresh amid uncertainties. They would not like to be cut off from their kinship/caste/village network especially when they are not the direct beneficiaries of irrigation scheme (1991: 288-303).

The Pengs grow most of their crops through *donger-chass* (shifting cultivation) and rely on this type of technology to a larger extent. Through this method they depend on multiple cropping pattern. In this method different kinds of seeds are sown together in a small patch of land preferably on the slopes of the hills. This method of cultivation ensures them against crop failure and at the same time gives a constant supply of different varieties of grains directly from the field for a fixed period of the year. All the merry-making and festivals are observed by the Pengs soon after the harvest and during this time they spend lavishly. Though they lack a long-term vision in terms of accumulating resources, still they regulate their resource use for their survival. For example it is forbidden to eat mangoes or pluck them from the trees before observing the *pidilaiparbhu*[1] ritual. No one in the village can prepare *pej*[2] (gruel) out of the mango kernels without performing *takuhanas*[3] ritual. It directs the Pengs to use a product in "time" when it is ready and not before. The entire calendar year of the Pengs is interspersed with various such rituals and these act as safety catches and thereby prevent the Pengs from misutilization of the resources. They believe that if they disobey the cultural taboos, the tiger in the wild will attack them. The cultural infrastructure helps maintain a wonderful mechanism of resource utilization and prevent them from spending everything at a time.

However, when the compensation was paid to the Pengs in cash it did not remain with them for long. Since they have a long-standing history and experience of celebration after a harvest, during which they spend lavishly, the award of the compensation was treated nothing more than a harvest. They squandered the major portion of this amount in celebration and social functions, as the safety catch did not prevent them from spending the cash compensation. More so, the highest denomination of currency note known to them prior to displacement was that of twenty rupees. During disbursement of the cash compensation they were paid in 100s and 500s denominations. Therefore, the utilization of cash compensation was reckless as they had neither seen so much money at a time nor ever dealt with such higher denominations of note. Hence the received cash compensation could not be retained by them for long and was mostly invested in non-assets items. Lieutenant C. Elliot in his report on Kalahandi writes "no money passes in the country not even cowries and during my tour it has been necessary to pay the coolies in grains (1865: 468). As the Pengs are not acquainted in dealing with large amount of money, it fizzled out from their hands in no time and the project paid compensation for the second time to enable them to buy agricultural land. Thereafter the project did not make any payment of compensation directly to the oustees; rather bank accounts were opened and the money was deposited in their names. The deposited money was only released during the purchase of land and payment was made to the seller of land in the presence of a witness. In order to qualify for the award of the compensation, the project made it mandatory for the oustees of the 2nd, 3rd and 4th phases to buy at least 50 per cent of the prescribed extent of land. However this strategy of making the oustees landed proved a failure and thereby did more harm than good—many of them are today *patta* holders without any land to cultivate.

Traditionally the Pengs maintain ceremonial relationships with the Doms. A person from the Dom caste, a Scheduled Caste group, is well versed with the language with the other caste people. Due to his communicative ability and exposure he shuttles between the *dongerla* (hills) region and the plain. The Dom hamlet is invariably found like a satellite near a Peng village and the Doms are ubiquitous in and around the village of a Peng. The Doms enters into ceremonial relationship with the Pengs by making one one-time investment on a *gamchha* (towel), a chicken and some country liquor. The Dom promises the Peng to be his trusted friend, leader and saviour—the Dom becomes *mulka* and the Peng becomes *thakada.* This traditional institution of *mulka-thakada* has now taken a new form under the changing milieu. The Pengs while operating in the external world heavily rely on the Doms. As the Pengs do not have a wider kinship network, in matters pertaining to tenurial, judicial, revenue, etc. they always seek help of the Doms. In return the Pengs have to pay the Doms in kind, viz. grains, chickens, country liquor etc.

With the advent of the Indravati dam project the *mulka-thakada* complex got metamorphosed into an exploitative device. Taking advantage of their better exposure and communicative skills the Doms could gather information on the project at a much faster rate than their Pengs counterpart. Moreover any information on the project that was passed to the oustees through the publicity department was beyond the comprehension of the Pengs. Hence most of the Peng oustees thought the entire operation to be the construction of a bridge across the river in order to facilitate them to move from one side to the other. Initially they could not imagine that so much of water would be stored in the reservoir. Without realizing that the entire reservoir would be impounded with water they went on cultivating their condemned land until it was finally inundated. Their conviction led them to take their resettlement lightly and the compensation amount as a bonus. It created panic among them soon after the impounding of the reservoir began. The right perspective would have been to make the information available to the Peng oustees structurally at the same level of their comprehension in order to help them make the most out of the compensation and rehabilitation programmes. But on the contrary they were so ill informed on the project and the rehabilitation programmes that they had to depend entirely on the Doms on such matters.

The faulty information delivery system made them dependent on the Doms. At one end of the continuum the Pengs were least informed and at the other the Doms had all required information on rehabilitation packages. Right from enumeration to disbursement of compensation the Pengs sought the help of their respective mulkas—the Doms, as the witness and to count the compensation money, as the Pengs were not acquainted with the higher denomination currency note. Such a selection by the Pengs proved disastrous and led the Doms to commit moral hazards. The Doms swindled a major chunk of the compensation amount awarded to the Pengs. There was also communication gap between the project officials and the Doms. The officials barely knew the region and the people. So they had to depend on the Doms who were well conversant and acquainted with the Pengs. Thus sometimes the exploitation of the Pengs by the Doms took place in collusion with project officials. As a result the actual due share of the Pengs never reached them. Though the Pengs felt cheated, still they could not do much. They continued to depend upon their *mulkas* for matters related to compensation and rehabilitation as they thought that it would be better to be with a known enemy than an unknown friend. Scudder and Colson on the basis of their study on rehabilitation and resettlement observe that rural communities under "relocation theory" are one of "extreme stress". They see socio-cultural systems as closed systems. They cling to familiar people and familiar institutions, changing during the initial years following removal. As the stress is close to critical threshold, radical changes from within (revitalization) and without intervention from outside to change the social organization is rejected (Scudder and Colson, 1979: 264).

The Pengs also had to pay a higher transaction cost to receive the compensation. Transaction cost can be computed by taking into account the main days lost, transportation, cost of information, hiring intermediaries, etc. Hence the actual compensation received by the Pengs should have calculated only after deducting the transaction cost from the allocated compensation.

The innovative policy in UIHEP to see all its oustees landed was another blunder committed by the policy makers. Such a policy by the Project led to forced buying of unsuitable land for the oustees. Agricultural land in the new settlement was not enough for all the oustees. As the project made it mandatory for the oustees to buy at least 50 per cent of the prescribed land in order to qualify for the award of compensation there was a hike in the price of the land. The landlords tried to make the maximum profit by selling minimum land. Hence whatever land was available became unaffordable for the oustees. Therefore the Pengs were forced to buy land far away from their resettlement. As a result of which they could not cultivate it and leased out land to the landlords from whom they bought it. Most of the land purchased by the Peng oustees were made in distress in order to qualify for the total compensation amount. As the purchased lands are located far off from their settlement, their landholding should be computed to half of the land purchased. For example, an oustee buying 2.5 acres of land eventually receives less than half the produce from the leaseholder. Hence in reality he holds 1.25 acres of land instead of 2.5 acres of land in such a situation. Therefore it is argued that the rehabilitation programmes in the UIHEP is nothing but a chimera and it has failed to rehabilitate the Pengs oustees to the required level.

The Pengs: Beneficiaries or Victims?

The right perspective for the development planners is to make the oustees feel as the beneficiary of the development programme. However, attempts to rehabilitate the oustees are most often half-hearted ones, thereby making their future unknown. The forcibly displaced populations, often already poor, end up worse off for a long period (Cernea, 1997: 1570). The rehabilitation of the oustees is dealt mostly by persons without any knowledge of human relations. There is a dearth of application of soft technology (knowledge of anthropology/ sociology) to rehabilitate the oustees. It is unfortunate to note that the suggestions given by anthropologists/sociologists in matters relating to rehabilitation are never given due consideration. In the UIHEP, rehabilitation of the oustees was limited to only disbursement of compensations and those also did not reach them entirely. The project allowed the oustees to relocate near the submerged village but failed to provide them agricultural land near the site of relocation. The oustees were forced to utilize the compensation amount to buy land irrespective of operational convenience. As a result the Peng oustees of Bagbeda bought 10.5 acres, 7 acres and 70 acres of land at a distance of 1 km, 5-10 kms and 10-15 kms respectively. The Peng oustees of Dudungchuan bought 2 acres, 18.45 acres, 9 acres, 20 acres and 26.55 acres of land at distance of 1 km, 1-5 kms, 5-10 kms, 10-15 kms and more than 15 kms respectively. Similarly the Peng oustees of Sanchhatrang bought 9 acres, 5acres, 8.65 acres, 19.63 acres and 68.32 acres of land at a distance of 1 km, 1-5 kms, 5-10 kms and more than 15 kms respectively (Table. 6.1). Since major portion of the agricultural land is located far away from the relocation site, it is now not feasible for many oustees to cultivate the same while staying at home. This may lead to either disintegration of family or a second displacement of the Peng oustees. Before displacement the Peng oustees devoted more time in there own farms but after displacement they spent more time in hiring out non-agricultural labour and collection of timbers (Table 6.2).

Before displacement the Pengs had a multilateral mode of economy. The products from the land were enough to support them for 8 to 9 months in a year and during the lean periods, which last for about three months, they were dependent on the forest and their social network system. They used to raise livestock, collect non-timber forest produce and hire out agricultural labour. The intra-village cohesion was very strong. The social support system was tremendous and no one would ever go hungry in the village. The inter-village relationship used to get reinforced through marriage exchanges and festivals.

TABLE 6.1: Average Family Labour Disposition Pattern in the Village per Year

Activities	Name of the Villages							
	Bagbeda		Dudungchuan		Sanchhatrang		Podauding	
	B.D.	A.D.	B.D.	A.D.	B.D.	A.D.	B.P.	A.P. Till 1998
(A) Forest								
i. Timber	30	60	40	40	40	30	30	60
ii. Non-Timber	90	35	120	60	90	110	90	60
(B) Wage Labour								
i. Agriculture	90	10	90	25	90	30	40	40
ii. Non-Agriculture	30	210	10	150	15	20	30	80
(C) Own Farm and Self Activities	125	50	105	90	130	65	175	125

TABLE 6.2: Agricultural Lands and its Location from the Resettled Villages

Villages	Distance in kms from the site of resettlement					
	0-1 km	1-5 kms	5-10 kms	10-15 kms	More than 15 kms	Total Land in Acres
(Land Purchased in Acres)						
Bagbeda	10.5	0.00	7	70	0.00	87.5
Dudungchean	2	18.45	9	20	26.55	75
Sanchhatrang	9	5	8.65	19.63	68.32	102.5

Both the inter-village and intra-village relationships have undergone drastic changes after the displacement. The cohesive forces have dwindled considerably. The oustees idea of relocating themselves in the nearby area in order to avail of the local natural and social resources did not prove to be useful. The large reservoir of water has now deprived them of more than half of these resources. The villages, with whom the Pengs had kinship ties, either affinal or consanguineal, have been cut off from them permanently.

It is a pity that the social resources are seldom considered by the government as ones having any meaning in the life of the oustees. Hence, during compensation these are never considered as loss incurred by the oustees from the government's point of view. The operational area of the Peng is much wider than what it is now. Now the pressure on the *donger* (hills) in the catchment area due to shifting cultivation has multiplied. There is a marked decrease in the fallow period of lands in these regions as a result of which the produce from the land has gone down dramatically. These even fall short of their bare necessities. When they look at the forest for food they are frustrated to find those empty. One of our respondents said in his local dialect *ran toe jotu hilu enzo khadi pahilu,* (neither there is any game in the forest nor there is any food in the house). Most often these forest dwellers are blamed by the forest officials as the destroyers of the forest wealth. However, the forest dwellers were the actual guardians of the forest wealth. They maintained a symbiotic relationship with the forest and catered to its growth. As large proportions of their forest flora and fauna are engulfed by the development project they have now lost their allegiance to the forest. And their constructive dependence on the forest has now metamorphosed into a destructive one.

The impacts of UIHEP on the Pengs have been adverse and irreparable. The loss of forest has resulted in the weathering away of their age-old practice of shifting cultivation. The hills near the village are not enough to provide space for cultivation as a result the pressure on the *dongers* are high and the fallow period has come down considerably leading to low yield and rapid degeneration of the hills. The idea of propagating settled cultivation on the *dongers* by the Resettlement and Rehabilitation Agency through local NGOs has almost come to an end as the oustees find it highly unreliable. There is limited scope for them to hire out labour in the local market. More number of people now migrate to hire out labour outside their villages. This has led to rise in female-headed households in the affected villages.

As a rehabilitation measure there is plan to develop pisciculture in Indravati reservoir to provide alternative economy to the oustees. However the water in the reservoir has already attracted the more efficient Bangladesh refugees fishermen. Some of them have already started their operation in this region.

The rapid degeneration of the *dongers* in the catchment area poses a threat to the project's life due to heavy siltation. The authority puts the blame on the indigenous population. It will not surprise us if the Pengs are evacuated for a second time on the ground of project's sustainability. There are number of examples of multiple evacuation in India and there is every possibility that some of the Pengs would be part of the ongoing process.

NOTES

1. *Pidilaiparbhu* is the festival of mangoes among the Pengs. In this festival mango is offered to the village deity called as *jhankarmunda.* Prior to this festival plucking of the fruits from the tree is forbidden. This practice allows the fruit to grow and mature.
2. *Pej* is a kind of gruel made out of various minor millets. The Pengs have a fascination to take their food in the gruel form. They relish *mandia-pej* (gruel made out of bottlebrush millet) the most. During the lean seasons when food is scanty the Pengs prepare a kind of gruel out of dried mango kernel called as *takupej.*
3. *Takuhanas* is the festival of the *taku* (mango kernel). This festival is witnessed during the lean period of rain. The mango kernels are cut and offered to the village deity. Only after the festival the villagers are allowed to use *taku* for preparing gruel. This practice prevents the Pengs from using the food items reserved for the lean seasons and thereby assures them of food during the crisis.

REFERENCES

Arturo, Escobar. 1995. *Encountering Development: The Making and Unmaking of the Third World.* Princeton: Princeton University Press.

Baboo, B. 1991. "Big Dams and the Tribals: The Case of the Hirakud Dam Oustees in Orissa," *Social Action,* 41 (3):288-303.

—. 1992. *Technology and Social Transformation: The Case of the Hirakud Multi-purpose Dam Project in Orissa.* New Delhi: Concept Publishing Company.

Barik, B.C. 1997. "Big Dams and Rehabilitation Issues: Who Shares the Sorrow of Oustees," *Journal of Social Sciences,* I (2):103-111

Behura, N.K. 1996. "Environment, Displacement and Development: Case Study from Orissa," *Journal of the Anthropological Society,* 31(2):150-58

Behera, D.K. and S. Patel. 1997. "Trapped in the Development Wrap: Case of the Project Affected Parajas of Upper Indravati Projects, Orissa," *Journal of Social Sciences,* I (2):113-123

Cerne.., M. 1985. "Involuntary, Resettlement Social Research, Policy and Planning, "in M. Carnea (ed.), *Putting People First.* World Bank: Oxford University Press.

—. 1994. "Population, Resettlement & Development," *Finance and Development,* International Monetary Fund and World Bank.

—. 1995. "Understanding and Preventing Impoverishment from displacement Reflections on the State Knowledge," *Social Action,* 45 (3): 261-76.

—. 1997. "The Risk and Reconstruction Model for Resettling Displaced Populations," *World Development,* 25 (10):1569-88.

—. 1998. "Impoverishment or Social Justice? A Model for Planning Resettlement," in Hari Mohan Mathur and David Marsden (eds.), *Development Projects and Impoverishment Risks. Resettling Project-Affected People in India.* Delhi: Oxford University Press.

Das, B.B. 1992. "World Bank Funded Upper Indravati Project—It is a Death Trap for Poor," Orissa Krushak Mahasangha, Indravati Ganasangarsha Parishad.

Dhawan, B.D. 1990. "Introduction," (pp.1-20) in B.D. Dhawan (ed.), *Big Dams Claims and Counter Claims.* New Delhi: Common Wealth Publishers.

Elliot, C. 1856. Reports on Kalahandi. No. 73 in Senapati's Gazetteer on Kalahandi.

Fernandes, W. 1991. "Power and Powerlessness: Development Projects and Displacement of Tribals," *Social Action,* 41(3):243-70.

—. 1994. *Development- Induced Displacement in the Tribal Areas of Eastern India.* New Delhi: Indian Social Institute.

Mahapatra, L.K. 1994. *Tribal Development in India: Myth and Reality.* New Delhi: Vikash Publishers House.

Missan, E.J. 1993. *The Cost of Economic Growth.* London: Orion Publishing Group.

R.R.U. 1997. Brochure on Resettlement and Rehabilitation Activities of UIP, Khatiguda.

Singh, C. 1989. "Rehabilitation and Rights to Property," in Walter Fernandes and Enaksi Ganguly Thukral (eds.), *Development Displacement and Rehabilitation: Issues for National Debate.* New Delhi: Indian Social Institute.

Scudder, Thayer. 1975. *Man-made Lakes and Human Health.* London: Academic Press.

The World Bank. 1989. *Aide Memoir.* Washington.

Thukral, E.G. 1992. *Big Dams, Displaced People: Rivers of Sorrow, Rivers of Change.* New Delhi: Sage Publications.

SEVEN

PROPOSED PROJECTS AND EMERGING PROTESTS

The Case of Alumina Refineries in Rayagada and Kalahandi Districts of Orissa

S. M. PATNAIK

One of the importat components of our national planning involved installation of heavy industries most of which were located in inaccessible tribal areas. These programmes had different target groups and did not favour the local population. Such projects became the symbol of modernization and development primarily due to the advocacy they received from the political leaders. Though these projects were envisaged for the welfare of the entire society, they affected the local population in an adverse way, unleashing devastating consequences for them. Initially, the local people protest against such projects but standing on a precarious platform. This paper discusses one such instance from Orissa.

In early 1990s the Government of Orissa permitted a few private foreign companies to explore and extract bauxite from the interior and inaccessible virgin forest and hill tracts of Kashipur block in Rayagada district and Thuamul-Rampur block in Kalahandi district. The two private sector companies started prospecting and testing in these areas in 1993-94. The otherwise inaccessible areas witnessed constant and rapid inflow of outsiders busy in collecting information setting up drilling rigs and other machineries and taking soil and water samples. One project is being planned in Kucheipadar panchayat of Kashipur block and the other in Kalyansinghpur in Rayagada district.

The Projects

Utkal Aluminium International Pvt. Ltd. Company (UAIP) which is a consortium of Indian Aluminium Company (INDAL), TATA and Hydro-

Alminum of Norway, plans to build an alumina refinery in Kucheipadar of Kashipur block. The initial estimated investment is Rs. 2400 crores. Kucheipadar is located on the bank of Ghodagado river, a tributary of the river of Indravati at a distance of 20 kms. from Kashipur. It is quite near to the Tikri railway station, located on Rayagada-Koraput rail route. The bauxite ore will be transported by conveyor belt from the Baphlamali plateau which is located at a distance of 24 kms from Kucheipadar. This plant, initially of 1 million metric tonnes capacity, is to be subsequently expanded to 3 million metric tonnes capacity. The UAIP factory will release its industrial waste in Ghodagado river which subsequently connects to Indravati river.

Similarly, Larsen and Toubro (hereafter L&T) in collaboration with ALCOA of USA is planning an initial investment of Rs. 1500 crore and proposes to have its refinery in Kalyansinghpur in Rayagada district. This project will process bauxite from Kutrungmali plateau in the bordering Kalahandi district. Other areas like Sijimali are also being prospected. L&T company has established a camp office in Sunger village of Kashipur where nearly 100 workers, mainly from outside Orissa, are staying to do ground work and preliminaries. They are also travelling into the areas of Kashipur in project jeeps, collecting informations and conducting the survey work. The L&T aluminium company will release its industrial waste into the river Nagavali.

The Ecological Price

The proposed projects for mining of bauxite and aluminium are purely export based units along the border area of Rayagada and Kalahandi districts inhabited mainly by the tribal populations. These projects will lead to extensive deforestation and would render the fragile ecosystem more vulnerable. Further, the projects envisage mining of ore from the plateau through open-cast mining. On Baphlamali plateau the bauxite bearing area is estimated to be about 10 sq. kms. Then the ore will be transmitted via a conveyor belt system to the alumina factory. It is estimated that the projects would require atleast another 1,500 ha. of land for the factory, the red mud or the bauxite residue ponds, the ash pond (from the captive power plant), the township and the conveyor belt.

It needs to be mentioned here that in bauxite mining the land and resources for livelihood would be adversely affected within the impact area which extends upto a radius of ten kilometres. The process of bauxite ore extraction produces huge quantities of dust; the subsequent operations of transportation, grinding and granule metric shorting will add to the atmospheric pollution. The water run off from the ore pile carries toxic elements that are likely to mix in surface and ground water. The factory would discharge huge quantities of red mud sludge, which is the waste product of bauxite processing. It is estimated that to produce 1 tonne of alumina at least 7 tonne of waste has to be generated. An area of 250 ha. has been earmarked for the disposal of this waste. Such a huge quantity of red mud will contaminate the ground and surface water. This red mud would be pumped into the ponds dug specially for this purpose. This red mud which is a pollutant has to be kept in especially dug pond for longer time, so that it does not get mixed up with the surroundings. Once these ponds fill up other sites would have to be found out which will lead to deterioration of forest and natural wealth. The UAIP factory will contaminate the river of Indravati and consequently, the Indravati reservoir. The industrial waste would also have adverse effect on the concrete dam of Indravati hydro-electric project. The government has not paid any attention to such a danger. Pollution of the Indravati river will effect the numerous tribal villages located on its bank. Similarly, the L&T project will contaminate the Nagavali river thereby adversely affecting several tribal villages located on its bank in Orissa and Andhra Pradesh.

The evil effects of aluminium projects have become quite perceptible in other areas of the state. For example, the National Aluminium Corporation (hereafter NALCO) in Anugul has created considerable hardship for the local population. The industrial waste has polluted the Nandira and Brahmani rivers to such an extent that the animals suffer painful symptoms including loss of teeth and ultimately death by drinking the polluted water. The local villagers complain that the skin diseases, which were unheard of in the area, have become quite rampant. The groundwater has also become severely contaminated thus making it unusable by the local population. Most of the villages on the bank of Brahmani river were not having any well or pond. They were mainly dependent upon Brahmani river for irrigation and drinking water. Usually, the village women dig a small hole on the sandy banks of the river so that fresh filtered water can be obtained. This is how they used to collect water for drinking and cooking, but after the establishment of NALCO, this traditional method of obtaining filtered water has become redundant. The villagers suffer from gastroentritis, loose motion and other kinds of stomach diseases which has created panic among the villages. In 1994 several villages such as Kaliahata, Sanakamar and Kirtarpur witnessed the spread of such diseases which took away lives of several children. In these villages a new kind of skin disease has come up which were unknown to the villagers. Therefore, the traditional method of curing was not equipped to deal with such kind of diseases. Considering the gravity of the situation, the government and NALCO have arranged portable water to these areas by trucks and tankers. But the question arises that how long can the government supply portable water regularly. And moreover, whether portable water would satisfy everybody's need.

According to metallurgy and chemical experts, generation of aluminium requires enough electricity, bauxite and other chemicals. To generate 1 tonne of aluminium the following items are required:

1.	Electricity	60 MV
2.	Bauxite	5.5 tonne
3.	Coal	1.3 tonne
4.	Anode Carbon	0.6 tonne
5.	Fuel	0.25 tonne
6.	Caustic Soda	0.2 tonne
7.	Fluoride Salt	0.1 tonne
	Total	7.95 tonnes

Out of this 7.95 tonnes, only 1 tonne aluminium will be generated and the rest will go as industrial waste. The most toxic is the red mud which will be nearly 1.2 tonnes. This red mud has to be kept in specially constructed ponds otherwise it will spoil the underground water.

The Rise of Protest Movement

The local tribals remained silent spectators of such activities for almost 2-3 years. According to one source, the first protest by the local people surfaced in Kucheipadar village on 17th February, 1995. The people of Sunger gram panchayat and the neighbouring villages assembled in large number and blocked the traffic by digging a ditch across the road. They took vow not to allow any vehicle on the road until some clarification regarding the project is made. The local activists claimed that even though there was no prior information regarding this protest movement, people from 40 neighbouring villages gathered through the traditional method of communication. In this area drum beating and blowing the trumpet are the methods by which messages can be sent to different villages, urging the people to assemble at one place. The tribal men and women from Sunger gram panchayat, Kerpai and Nakarundi gram panchayat of Thuamul-Rampur block and few NGO activists, assembled together. The tribals have organized the *Anchalika Suraksha Parishad* which was given the responsibility of protecting the whole region. Spontaneous protest from the local people has resulted in destruction of some government machinery. The entire block has come under siege. In the neighbouring areas people have also become suspicious of constant intrusion into their lives by strangers and alien technology. On this day, they prepared a memorandum which was submitted to local tehsildar on 22nd February, 1995. Despite repeated attempts by various officials and elected representatives including the district collector and the local MLA, they refused to budge unless their demands are met. Few representatives of *Anchalika Suraksha Parishad* met the local tehsildar and submitted a memorandum stating the following demands:

1. It is heard that two Alumina plants are being installed with an investment of Rs. 5,000 crore but so far the government has kept all the information quite confidential and has not allowed the people to know its impact on the natural resources and the life styles of the local people. The government must clearly and in no ambiguous terms state what is to be the effect of these projects and the mining on the local area.
2. The government must make public the terms and conditions agreed upon between the companies and itself for the setting up of these projects.
3. Thousands of local tribals have been surviving primarily depending on the natural resources such as forest, land and water of the region. The proposed alumina projects will take away their rights over the natural resources. If the local tribals are going to be evicted what alternatives government has thought of them.
4. The government must clearly inform the benefits that will accrue to the people of Kashipur and Thuamul-Rampur.

On 25th February, 1995 the *Anchalik Suraksha Parishad* organized a protest march against the alumina projects. Nearly 2,000 men and women from Kashipur and Thuamul-Rampur area participated with full enthusiasm. The way in which the local people are organized and participating in such activities leads one to expect a very strong and powerful protest movement to come up against the alumina projects. This has also raised apprehension about the future projects.

In other areas also several activities in form of protest march, meetings, pamphlets and brochure have come up quite rapidly. Recently the villagers once again took to protest action in Kucheipadar village. They stopped the survey work going on in the village Ranibeda. When some of them were arrested and taken to Tikri, more than a thousand men and women gathered outside the police station till the arrested people were released.

The Role of NGO

Due to such protest movements, the companies are losing time and money and government is hard pressed to honour its commitment to them. If the companies lose few months, they are going to be late by one year because it is very difficult to conduct land survey and other preliminary work during monsoon.

The government authorities believe that the protest movements are not spontaneous, rather they are instigated ones with ulterior motives. The Kashipur of Raygada comes under the operational area of an NGO called Agragamee. The Agragamee thinks that if this area becomes developed and prosperous they will have no role to play in this region. Therefore, they are spreading rumours and tension in the mind of the people against the government and local administration. However, such a logic given by the authorities seems to be far fetched from the reality.

According to intelligence report, the Agragamee activists, clad in tribal dresses participate and organize the local protest marches. Even though the Agragamee is directly involved in such instigating exercises, they have never admitted their involvement in this, they always claim that it is a spontaneous reaction, and natural culmination of people's anxiety and apprehension about the proposed alumina projects. The district police sources said that the activities of Agragamee in instigating the local people definitely have an ulterior motive and, therefore, they do not mind in even creating problems of law and order.

According to Agragamee sources, the people of this region especially of Raygada have become aware of their rights. However, no doubt Agragamee has a definite role in bringing out this awareness among people due to its continuous untiring activities for the last decade and that is the role which can be attributed to Agragamee. And, therefore, it is a very indirect association with such movement for which the organization cannot be held responsible. As far as any direct involvement or direct instigation is concerned, Agragamee has no role to play.

Concluding Remarks

The undivided district of Koraput has a history of highly lopsided development. Government, in its every effort to develop this backward district, have ignored or at best paid very scarce attention to the interest of local tribals. In the upper Indravati dam project, which is nearly 50 kms. away from proposed INDAL mining site in Baphlamali, people from 65 villages have been forced to evacuate. Some of them have come to Kashipur Block and are struggling with various problems in new settlement. But unfortunately, they will now have to move again for the alumina refineries. (Das, 1995).

In the NALCO project, (Damanjodi) the blasting of mining severely affected the rehabilitation housing located around 7 km from the mining site. Several streams around NALCO have either dried out or changed their course due to disturbance in the watertable caused by blastings. The story of sufferings of the oustees of the upper Kolab river dam project in Kotpad is also well known (Patnaik, 1996). Thus the development efforts of government have always confined to the corporate interest and thus making the original inhabitants refugees in their own land. The activists of the local NGOs feel that a lot of money seems to be exchanging hands and the local people's representatives who were once with the people in their quest have subsequently changed their stand. The local media also seems to have forsaken people indicating that the resistance of the people is a non-issue. The process is highlighting that impact of mining could be minimal and displacement would be limited to 100 families from 4 villages. The local administration and companies have dismissed the people's protest as sporadic instigation by the local voluntary organization. But the government is not coming up with the information regarding the waterways that would be affected, the land around the mining sites and even the area required for water disposal. Further, it is also difficult to explain why the government has entrusted ALCOA which is one of the big aluminium companies with foreign operations throughout the world, and is facing a series of law suits against its Monopolistic and Restrictive Trade Practices (MRTP). Both the projects under consideration are completely export oriented, targeted at only to feed corporate interest of the elite and the rich in Europe and North America. The government can no longer afford to cater to the needs of multinationals at the cost of the sufferings of its own people who are already marginalized from the mainstream society and economy.

REFERENCES

Das, V. 1995. "Development or Destruction?: New Mining Projects in Orissa," *Economic and Political Weekly*, XXX (22): 1281-1282.

Patnaik, S.M. 1996. *Development, Rehabilitation and Social Change: The Case of the Paraja Highlanders*. New Delhi: Inter-India.

EIGHT

APPLIED RESEARCH IN ANTHROPOLOGY
An Overview

TILAK BAGCHI

The genesis of applied research in anthropology may be traced back to the interests of anthropology in social change, problems of culture contacts and consequent upon the interactions between the western nations and new nations of Asia and Africa (Sachchidananda, 1992 b). This sort of interaction appears to be more marked during second and third decade of this century when anthropological knowledge was utilized to impart aid and guidance to government and other bodies either in controlling or influencing public life *(The New Encyclopaedia Britannica,* Vol. 1, 1974). Though the term "applied anthropology" was first used by Brinton as early as 1875, yet applied research in anthropology was used in full swing only during First World War.

Initially it was believed that the aim of applied research in anthropology concerns with description and change of human relations and isolating principles that control them (Chapple, 1953). Boas as a profounder of "cultural relativism" as early as 1907 observed that the practical use of anthropology concerns with the relativity of value in showing men as they think and in demonstrating that is evolving from nationalism. Malinowski (1929) on the basis of his study on culture contact coined the term "practical anthropology" where anthropological knowledge can be used to diagnose problems and to suggest remedial measures. For example, with the help of practical anthropology Malinowski recommended the administrations to impose indirect rules in Africa through local chieftains and other selected groups of people (Bhowmick, 1990). Radcliffe-Brown (1932) envisaged this discipline as "applied social anthropology" which is more an admixture of the experience of colonial government and the education of the native people in various parts of the world which would make approaches to being an act on the basis of application of discovered law in anthropology. Radcliffe-Brown's notion is due to the fact that beginning form this century social anthropological knowledge has been recognized by the administration. For a good number of years European cadets before taking up their appointment in colonial countries have received instructions in social anthropology initially at Oxford and Cambridge and later on at London (Evans-Pritchard, 1982). Forde (1953) in this regard observed that "applied anthropology" is the application of anthropological knowledge by the government administration with special reference to British Africa in formulation and execution of government policies. Thus applied anthropology has developed as a concomitant of colonial hang but it also applies knowledge concerning of tribal societies for the development of the people (Mair, 1968). Thus in culture change programme, which is a prime concern in applied anthropology, the anthropologists first turn their interests to target groups (Jones, 1971). To Philips Gulliver the term applied anthropology means research specially oriented to administrative and development problems together with some degree of responsible participation in the process of utilization of the result of such research (*cf.* Borkensha, 1966). Thus it is seen that applied anthropology has developed in western world and its colonies mainly accompanying with colonialism in order to assist the administration.

In the United States of America the employment of anthropologists by government may be said to date back to 1934, when at the request of the then Commissioner of the Bureau of Indian Affairs, the unit of applied anthropology was created (Mair, 1968). However, applied anthropology started developing mostly during fifth decade of this century (Tax, 1965) in order to solve acute social problems due to maladjustments in highly industrialized situation (Bhowmick, 1990). Bestide (1973) has observed that the Second World War made position a convergence of British and American applied anthropology removing the latter from pure pathology by giving it prospective tasks. Thus American anthropologists often pointed out the dual role of applied anthropology. Their job is to speak for the natives to the west in one hand and interpreting and filtering the forces of the west down to the natives on the other (Beattie, 1964). Willigen (1986) has stated that applied anthropology in America is a complex related research based on instrumental methods which produce change or stability in specific cultural system through provision of data initiation of direct action and/or formation of policy. This process on the basis of different nature of problems can take many forms. Thus the role of anthropologists vary in motivating value and extent of action involvement. In America development of applied anthropology has undergone five stages, viz. the pre-disciplinary state, the applied ethnology stage, the feudal service stage, the role extension value explicit stage and the policy research stage. Sol Tax (1957) coined a new term action anthropology. Action anthropology is based on the methods which may be called as clinical or experimental. Action anthropologists do not simply observe what would happen naturally but they are willing to make them happen or to help them or at least act as a catalysers. An action anthropologist has no master. He works as a member of the academic community. The community wherein he works is not only his subject of study but also his object. His role is clinical or experimental in the sense that a physician constantly tries to improve his diagnosis with tentative remedies.

The latest development of applied research in anthropology is the emergence of development anthropology. Cochrane (1971) has observed three important milestones in development work, viz. knowledge and clear understanding of a culture in which a researcher intend to work, sophisticated theoretical and empirical knowledge on the basis of study and analysis of other areas and trends covering all aspects of development work which would depict what might be done and a knowledge of how to implement plans.

Applied physical anthropology received the first major recognition as a result of Civil War in the United States of America when the standardized techniques of measurements were developed by physical anthropologists for immediate practical utility. The first application of this sciences was selection, rejection and classification of people for military service (Verma, 1963).

II

In India applied anthropology has developed as a colonial heritage. As early as in 1807, East India Company realized that anthropological knowledge would be of much help to the administration. During nineteenth century Dr. Francis Buchanon was appointed by the then Governor General to enquire about the life and culture of the people of Bengal (Buchanon, 1820). Since then administrators like Dalton (1872), Risely (1891, 1915), Thurston (1909), Gurdon (1914), Russel and Hiralal (1916), Grigson (1944) and others were assigned the additional tasks of preparing the handbooks, gazetteers, monographs, etc. on the tribes and castes of India. The main aim of this kind of study was to look after the interest of colonial administration. For example Gupta (1982) has observed that the major effort of Risley and Ibbetson (both belonged to the Indian Civil Service) in the direction of applied anthropology was the partition of Bengal on the 15th day of October in 1905. The division was made purely on religious and cultural line with a view to spearhead Indian National Movement.

Work of British anthropologists like Radcliffe-Brown (1922) on Andaman Islanders, Rivers (1906) on the Toda and so on have provided useful recommendations for smooth and effective colonial administration. Hutton (1933) has pointed out the evil consequence of contacts with the tribes. He was in favour of self governing in tribal areas with free power of self determination in regard to surrounding or adjacent units. The British government utilized this recommendation for making policies in certain tribal dominated regions of India including tribal pockets of north eastern part of India.

Roy and Roy did extensive field work on several tribes of Chotanagpur plateau and noted how road and railway tract construction under British rule as well as deforestation and restriction mainly imposed by the outsiders to use forest, led slowly but surely to the process of extinction of the forest dwelling and dependent tribal groups, viz. the Birhor, the Korwa, partly from famine and partly from loss of interests in life (Roy and Roy, 1937). The evil consequences of culture contact on the life of the tribal people have been reflected in the writing of Majumdar on the Ho and the Korwa (Majumdar, 1937, 1950) and Aiyappan's account of the Iravas of South India (Aiyappan, 1944). On the basis of the study of the Baiga of the then Central Provinces, Elwin (1939) suggested for the establishment of "National Park" where tribal peoples could live with utmost happiness and freedom with least outside intervention and contacts. By giving them this autonomy, the access of missionaries and exploiters would be restricted. However Ghurey (1960) opposed the view and believed that isolation no longer could solve the problem of the tribals but assimilation of tribal people into larger Hindu fold could only ameliorate the problems of the tribal folk. However, Sachchidananda (1992a) advocated about integration of tribes in Indian society instead of its assimilation.

Scholars like Haimendorf (1944), Chattopadhyay (1953), Dube 1960), Majumdar (1968), Srivastava (1968), Vidyarthi (1968), Roy Burman (1968), Sachchidananda (1968), Mahapatra (1968), Sarkar and Mukherjee (1969), Singh (1975), Bhowmick (1976), Mukherjee (1978) and many others have made significant contribution in the form of conducting problem oriented study and recommending various welfare measures for the development of tribal people.

In Varrier Elwin's *Philosophy of NEFA* Pandit Jawaharlal Nehru, the first Prime Minister of India, has written a foreword where he has emphasized five principles of *Panchaseel* for tribal development. The principles are as follows:

1. People should be allowed to develop on the line of their own genius and nothing should be imposed upon them.
2. Tribals rights in land and forests should be respected.
3. Induction of too many outsiders in tribal areas should be avoided.
4. There should not be over administration on tribal areas and as far as possible work should be done through their own social and cultural institutions.
5. The results should not be judged by the amount of money spent or by statistics but by the quality of human characters that is evolving.

This *Panchaseel* may be regarded as a classic applied anthropological account in the post colonial Indian anthropology.

Besides individual efforts certain organizations also take leading role in applied anthropological study. Anthropological Survey of India after separating out from the Zoological Survey of India in 1945 formed a separate and large anthropological research organization in India. Anthropological Survey of India has undertaken several applied anthropology oriented research projects on Mizo unrest, Jharkhand movement, social mobility movement, bonded labour, carrying capacity of land, impact of industrialization, juvenile delinquency, blood group and its nexus with genetic traits, diet, body build, nutrition (Danda *et al.,* 1986). Various state government Scheduled Castes and Tribal Research Institutes, voluntary agencies, government, non-government organizations and government aided autonomous bodies also have made significant contribution in the direction of applied-action development anthropology.

Vidyarthi (1979) classified Indian applied-cum-action anthropologists into five distinct categories. The first category of applied anthropologists are the regular employees of the administration and usually function under the control of working administration. Anthropologists working in various government organizations are included in this category. The second type generally consists of such outsider anthropologists who act as consultants to the administrator but they are not included in the regular pay role of the government organization. Faculty members working in various teaching departments of universities and colleges, research fellows and research associates working in different universities or government organizations are included in this category. In the third category, researchers and administrators work together as co-administrators. Anthropologists working as project officers in different development projects, viz. ITDP, ICDS and so on and anthropologists working as Special Officer, Tribal Welfare Department, Tribal Welfare Officer, etc. are included in this category since they are working as co-administrator in tribal development activities along with bureaucratic administrators. The fourth category is represented by some voluntary organizations. Here Prof. P.K. Bowmick and his co-workers of the Bidisa experiment meant for the development of the Lodha, needs special mention. In Bidisa with the help of two wings, viz. Samaj Sevak Sangha and Institute of Social Research and Applied Anthropology, Prof. Bhowmick and his team has tried to rehabilitake the Lodhas (Bhowmick, 1990) and to make their cultural articulation with more sophisticated communities (Gupta, 1981) so that they can pick up middle class value system of the surrounding ethnic groups. Efforts were being made by the Ranchi University under the able guidance of late Prof. L.P. Vidyarthi to apply certain concepts of action anthropology in the study of the Birhor (Vidyarthi, 1979).

III

Applied anthropology slowly but surely is extending the horizons of anthropology. In India applied-action-development anthropology is now penetrating into various areas.

In the field of education anthropologists focus their attention on evaluating illiteracy eradication programmes, formulating and imparting appropriate system of education for tribals in particular and underprivileged in general, suggesting remedial measures of education of underprivileged including tribals and so on.

In the field of health applied anthropologists have taken key role in studying social, cultural and behavioural aspects in determination of health and disease. They also study the association of the disease with somatic, anthropometric, physiological, genetic and bio-chemical factors. Their thrust is also on the direction of studying constraints of adaptation of modern health care and delivery system for the underprivileged and imparting communication and motivation for preventive and promotive service. They also pay their attention in studying indigenous health care practices with a view to juxtapose the same to overall health care delivery system in order to make health delivery system economically viable and socially acceptable. A detailed and clear understanding of traditional health care system would be of great help in ameliorating unscientific elements and prejudices in traditional health care system.

In the field of family planning the role of applied anthropology is manifold viz. diagnostic study for improving the family planning programmes, guidance for high flexibility of execution, impart knowledge to increase awareness of family plannings, study traditional birth control methods, people's perception and constraints of imparting family planning and so on.

In the field of applied physical anthropology studies have been done with respect to role of anthropometry in garment making, occupational health, seat design, nutritional status and subjects, risk with respect to acute and chronic illness, problems and physiological aspects of the sportsman and so on. Study of serology also helps in blood transfusion. Physical anthropologists with the help of human genetics cannot only suggest the pattern of inheritance of genetic diseases but also by genetic counsellings they can reduce the chance of genetic abnoromalities. Study of dermatoglyphics is very important not only for detecting genetic traits or individual identification but is also used for identification of the criminals. Photokits is also used for identification of the criminals. Role of applied physical anthropology is very marked in forensic science.

From the view point of applied anthropology criminal activities and criminal communities deserve special attention and investigation. Similarly dwindle and vanishing communities have also been studied by applied anthropologists on priority basis to save them from the fear of extinction.

Studies on the perception and behavioural responses with regard to agricultural extension are also very useful area of study in applied anthropology.

Study on the impact of industrialization, urbanization, modernization on socio-psychological and cultural milieu of the communities are of utmost importance in urban and industrial planning. Of late anthropologists also take a leading role in communication research.

Studies in respect to the problems and prospects of various categories of labour, viz. labour in organized and unorganized sectors, female and child labour, skilled, unskilled and semi-skilled labour and so on are very useful for formulating any viable plans for labour welfare or to redress labour unrest.

Problems of the underprivileged peoples like Scheduled Castes, Scheduled Tribes, religious minorities, backward communities, women, children and aged have also been studied by anthropologists. Studies on leadership, public administration, voluntary agencies, etc. are very useful study in the field of applied anthropology as these are effective machineries of change and development. In this regard study on customary and statutory law is very useful. Some anthropologists often take active role as social activists by documenting about the violation of human rights or by organizing tribals and other downtroddens against the same and other social vices.

The study of economic, social and political implication of militant organization is another field of growing importance in applied anthropology.

Studies of detecting nutritional status, water supply, environmental sanitation, community and rural development programmes, sports anthropology, adaption with various eco-systems of land, environment management and conservation of bio-diversity, ethnicity, ethnic movement and violence, etc. are some of the areas of special interests in applied anthropology.

IV

In the previous section only certain areas of applied anthropological research have been delineated. But applied anthropologists in India should also initiate certain frontline areas of researches as follows:

Applied anthropologists in India can initiate to study human response to natural disaster with special reference to cyclone, flood, earthquake, famine, etc. for imparting action oriented programmes in disaster management.

They can also explore the clinical efficacy of ethnomedicine and indigenous health care practices by conducting inter-disciplinary researches with bio-medical scientists.

Participatory management in different sectors of development along with monitoring and evaluation of ongoing development programmes should be done by applied anthropologists. Peoples cognition and perception on the development measures should be considered with prime importance in this venture. Peoples resistance to certain infrastructure development measures, viz. construction of dam, industry, etc., by uprooting the physical landscape and cultural setting of the indigenous people, should also be highlighted.

Applied anthropologists should also be involved in certain action programmes, viz. supplying portable water, managements of environment and natural bio-diversity including forests, arranging good environmental sanitation, imparting health and nutrition education, illiteracy eradication, immunization etc. either as consultants or as workers. In this way applied anthropologists can establish their social commitment to the underprivileged who are the main subject matter of enquiry of the anthropologists.

Anthropologists should also study diseases like AIDS, leprosy, etc. and their impact on the society.

The ethnic, tension, unrest, etc. should be studied under the backdrop of legitimate demand on the one hand and underlying unity on the other hand. History of tribal movement should be studied from a new angle of vision where the ethno-history of the downtrodden people could be discussed.

It should be the role of applied anthropologists to portray national integration in the country like India where diversity in every aspect is a stark reality, even after fifty years of our independence. They should try to show the unity in diversity which will be helpful to maintain national integration. This is only possible by identifying common cultural markers of Indianness or *Bhartiyata* which will generate spirit of Indianization. Besides, our rich cultural heritage can be exhibited in the regional and national museums with a view to show our unity amidst diversity.

Applied anthropologists should not only confine themselves in imparting knowledge and wisdom in various applied aspects. Their anthropological knowledge should be utilized for the development and service of mankind, or in other words, they should combine scientific and humanistic approaches. So modern applied anthropology or applied research in anthropology should be synonymous with development anthropology where the effort of anthropology should not be confined to study the manners, customs or in short general ethnography of the people, which may be the means to reach the ends. But their ultimate goal should be service of mankind in general and underprivileged segments of population in particular.

Acknowledgements

The views expressed in the paper are that of the author. Those are in no way connected with the organization to which he belongs. The author is grateful to Dr. Ramesh Chandra, Deputy Director of the Anthropological Survey of India, Udaipur for his valuable suggestions for the paper.

REFERENCES

Aiyappan, A. 1944. *Irava and Culture Change.* Madras: Govt. Printing Press.

Anonymous. 1974. "Applied Anthropology," in *The New Encyclopaedia Britannica.* Vol. -1 Chicago: Encyclopaedia Britannica Inc.

Barnett, H.G. 1956. *Anthropology in Administration.* Evanston: Row Peterson & Co.

Beattie, J.H.M. 1964. *Other Cultures: Aims, Methods and Achievements in Social Anthropology.* New York: Free Press.

Bestide, R. 1973. *Applied Anthropology.* London.

Bhowmick, P.K. 1976. "Role of Social Scientists in Developmental Plans," *Bulletin of Cultural Research Institute,* XII (1&2).

—. 1990. "Development Anthropology," (pp.1-24) in P.K. Bhowmick (ed.), *Applied-Action Development Anthropology.* Calcutta: Institute of Social Research and Applied Anthropology.

Brokensha, D. 1966. *Applied Anthropology in English Speaking. Africa Human Organisation* Monograph No. 8. (Cited by Sachchidananda) 1992 *Tribal India: Past and Present.* Calcutta: ISRAA.

Buchanon, F. 1820. *History, Antiquity, Topography Statistics of Eastern India.* Calcutta: Govt. Printing Press.

Chapple, E.D. 1953. "Applied Anthropology in Industry," (pp. 819-831) in A.L. Kroeber (ed.), *Anthropology Today: An Encyclopedic Inventory Chicago:* University of Chicago Press.

Chattopadhyay, K.P. 1953. "Tribal Education," *Man in India,* 23:1-18.

Cochrane, G. 1971. *Development Anthropology.* New York: Oxford University Press.

Dalton, E.T. 1872: *Descriptive Ethnology of Bengal.* Calcutta: Govt. Printing Press.

Danda, A.K., A. Pal, K.A. Razek and Rekha R. Ghose. 1986: *Catalogue of Research Projects and Publications.* Vol.1, Calcutta: Anthropological Survey of India.

Dube, S.C. 1960. "Approaches to Tribal Problem in India," in L.P. Vidyarthi (ed.), *Indian Anthropology in Action.* Ranchi: Council of Social and Cultural Research.

Elwin, V. 1930. *The Baiga,* London: John Murray.

Evans-Pritchard, E.E. 1982. *Social Anthropology,* London: Routledge and Kegan Paul.

Forde, C.D. 1953. "Applied Anthropology in Government: British Africa," in A.L. Kroeber (ed.), *Anthropology Today: An Encyclopaedia of Inventory,* Chicago. University of Chicago Press.

Ghurey, G.S. 1960. *The Scheduled Tribes.* Bombay: Popular Book Depot.

Grigson, W.V. 1944. *The Aboriginal Problem in the Central Provinces and Bihar.* Nagpur: Govt. Printing

Gupta, R.K. 1981: "Bidisa-Project," in L.P. Vidyarthi (ed.), *Tribal Development and Administration.* New Delhi: Concept Publishing Company.

—. 1982. Pioneers and Followers of Applied Anthropology," *Man and Life,* 8(3&4): 110-132.

Gurdon, P.R.T. 1914. *The Khasis.* London: Macmillan.

Haimendorf, C.V. 1944. "Aboriginal Education in Hyderabad," *Indian Journal of Social Work*, 5 (2).

Hutton, J.H. 1933. *Census of India* 1931. Delhi: Gain (rep in 1986).

Jones, D.J. 1971. "Responsibility and Belief in Basic Research," *Current Anthropology*, 12: 347-349.

Mahapatra, L.K. 1968. "Problems and Welfare of Orissa Tribes," (pp. 362-384). in L.P. Vidyarthi (ed.) *Applied Anthropology in India*. Allahabad: Kitab Mahal (rep. in 1984).

Mair, Lucy 1968. "Applied Anthropology," (pp. 326-330) in D.L. Sills (ed.), *International Encyclopaedia of Social Sciences*, Vol. 1, U.S.A.: The Macmillan Co. & Free Press.

Majumdar, D.N. 1937. *A Tribe in Transition*. London: Longmans Green and Co.

—. 1950. *The Affairs of a Tribe*. Lucknow: Universal Publishers.

—. 1968: "Approach to Tribal Problem," in L.P. Vidyarthi (ed.), *Applied Anthropology in India*. Allahabad: Kitab Mahal (rep in 1984).

Malinowski, B. 1929: "Practical Anthropology," Africa, 2:22-38.

Mukherjee, D.P. 1978. "Action Physical Anthropology for MCH Services among Tribal Populations," in *Souvenir of the Tenth Anniversary of Family Planning Association*. Gomia: Birhor Primitive Tribal Welfare Centre.

Naik, T.B. 1972. "Applied Anthropology in India," in *Survey of Research in Sociology and Social Anthropology*. Bombay: Indian Council of Social Science Research.

Nehru, J. 1959. "Foreword," in V. Elwin (ed), *A Philosophy of NEFA*. Shillong: NEFA.

Radcliffe-Brown, A.R. 1922. *The Andman Islanders: A Study in Social Anthropology*. Glencoe: Free Press.

—. 1952. *Structure and Functions in Primitive Societies*. London: The English Language Book Society.

Risley, H. 1891. *Tribes and Castes of Bengal*. Calcutta: Firma Mukhopadhyay (rep. in 1981).

—. 1915. *The Peoples of India*. Calcutta: Thacker Spink & Co.

Rivers, W.H.R. 1906. *The Todas*. London: Macmillan.

Roy, S.C. and R.C. Roy, 1937. *The Kharia*. Ranchi: Man in India Office.

Roy Burman, B.K. 1968. "Anthropological Concepts on Problems, Planning and Research for Social Development," (pp. 39-57) in L.P. Vidyarthi (ed.), *Applied Anthropology in India*. Allahabad: Kitab Mahal. (rep. in 1984).

Russel, R.V. and Hiralal. 1916. *The Tribes and Castes of Central Provinces of India*. London: Macmillan.

Sachchidananda. 1968. "Community Development and the Tribals," (pp. 213-221) L.P. Vidyarthi (ed.), *Applied Anthropology in India*. Allahabad: Kitab Mahal. (rep. in 1984).

—. 1992a. "Integration of Tribes in Indian Society," (pp 1-12) in Sachchidananda (ed.), *Tribal India: Past and Present*. Calcutta: Institute of Social Research and Applied Anthropology.

—. 1992b. "Planning Development and Applied Anthropology in India," in Sachchidananda (ed.), *Tribal India: Past and Present*, Calcutta: Institute of Social Research and Applied Anthropology.

Sarkar, D. and D.P. Mukherjee. 1969. "Physical Anthropology in Education and Training," *Pop. Sc. & Tech*, 9(2): 91-97.

Sen Gupta, S. 1977. *Applied Anthropology: Meaning and Necessity*. Calcutta: Firma KLM Pvt. Ltd.

Singh, K.S. 1975. *Indian Famine: A Study in Crisis and Change*. New Delhi: People Pub. House.

Srivastva, A.R.N. 1968. "Education for the Tribals", (pp. 252-271) in L.P. Vidyarthi (ed.), *Applied Anthropology in India*. Allahabad: Kitab Mahal. (rep. in 1984).

Tax, S. 1957. "The Fox Project", in P.K. Bhowmick (ed.) *Applied-Action-Development Anthropology*. Calcutta: Institute of Social Research and Applied Anthropology (Originally presented in the symposium "Values in action" at the Chicago meeting of the American Anthropological Association in 1957 and rep. in 1990).

—. 1965. "The Use of Anthropology". in S.Tax (ed.) *Horizons of Anthropology.* London: George Allen & Unwin Ltd. pp. 248-258.

Thurston, E. 1909. *Castes and Tribes of South India.* Madras: Govt. Printing.

Vidyarthi, L.P. 1968. "History of Applied Anthropology in India", in L.P. Vidyarthi (ed.) *Applied Anthropology in India.* Allahabad: Kitab Mahal (rep. in 1984).

—. 1976. "Applied Anthropology in India". in S.C. Sinha (ed.) *Anthropology in India,* Vol. 1. *Cultural Anthropology.* Calcutta: Anthropological Survey of India.

—. 1977: *Rise of Anthropology in India.* Delhi: Concept Publishing Company.

—. 1979. *Trends in World Anthropology.* Delhi: Concept Publishing Company.

Verma, B.K. 1963: "Physical Anthropology Chart Design for Work and Living", in L.P. Vidyarthi and B.K. Verma (eds.), *Some Aspects of Applied Physical Anthropology in India.* Ranchi: Council of Social and Cultural Research.

Willigen, J. 1986. *Applied Anthropology: An Introduction.* Massachusetts: Bergin & Garvey.

SECTION II

LAND, ENVIRONMENT AND FOREST

NINE

THE ROLONG-SELEKA OF THABA 'NCHU
Forced Separation, Resettlement and Reaction

PIET A. ERASMUS

Introduction

For a long time the sustained policy of forcibly separating and removing people was one of the most reviled practices of social engineering of the South Africa state (*cf.* Desmond, 1986; Du Toit, 1982 and O'Regan, 1989). It was applied not in times of need (natural disaster or impending national crisis), because of a policy aimed at bringing about a geographical segregation of ethnic groups. Consequently, these practices have been described and analyzed in an impressive body of literature (Harries, 1987). According to Niehaus (1989:178), a dominant theme in the literature is the comparison of conditions of life prior to and after separation and/or removal and/or resettlement. While this kind of material certainly provides an overview of the structure and pattern of forced separation and resettlement, there is also a growing awareness of the need to have knowledge of people's experiences and reactions (Sharp, 1982:11-12).

The question can rightfully be asked whether the anthropological recording of people's experiences and reactions contributes to the knowledge and understanding of these processes. Experience forms part of the individual's "experimental inside of reality" and cannot necessarily be regarded as a "cultural pattern" or a "pattern of social behaviour". However, according to Barth (1994: 5), any existential human problem "will have found diverse solutions, which must be worth knowing about, thinking about, and comparing". Therefore, when, with due allowance for the context, the analytical outsider (in making generalizations) turns experience into expression, it becomes part of ethnography. In this regard Hastrup and Hervik (1994: 10) are of the opinion that "while the scope of anthropology lies beyond the retelling of local stories, these and their experiential grounding remain the foundation of anthropological knowledge."

Over the years different systems of land administration were responsible for the forcible separation of millions of black people in South Africa. This paper attempts to outline the legal framework that influenced the tribal community of Thaba 'Nchu, and how the people actually reacted in this regard. The strategy followed for this purpose will be to introduce historically the Barôlông bôôSeleka (Rolong-Seleka, a Tswana tribe) who were/are the founders and original residents of Thaba 'Nchu. This will be followed by a discussion of their traditional way of land administration. As the situation in Thaba 'Nchu is a reflection of different Eurocentric methods of land administration in South Africa, these systems will be examined. A chronological classification will be used and the implications of relevant legislation will be explained. Terms such as "Native", "Bantu", "whites", etc. will be used in their historical context and consequently the titles of acts will be used as they were promulgated. In the last section the reactions of the inhabitants of Thaba 'Nchu (based on their experiences) on the land policy will be discussed.

The Thaba 'Nchu Case

A Brief Historical Introduction

Four Rolong groups are found in Southern Africa. Before 1760 they formed a political unit, but after the death of chief *(kgosi)* Tau, they split up under his sons Ratlou, Tshidi, Seleka and Rapulana (*cf.* Kitching, 1984: 40; Murray 1992: 13 and Schüler 1965: 10).

After wandering for some time, mainly as a result of the political violence and uncertainty associated with the difaqane/mfecane (± 1821-1838), three sections of the Rolong (the Seleka under Moroka, the Rratlou under Gontse and the Tshidi under Tawana) settled at Thaba 'Nchu (east of Bloemfontein in the Free State, South Africa) at the end of December 1933 (*cf.* Kitching, 1984: 40-43 and Schüler, 1965: 21-39). The transaction regarding the land around Thaba 'Nchu was concluded on 7 December 1833, and the Rolong area was 355,000 ha in extent (Kitching, 1984: 45). The Rolong under Gontse and Tawana left Thaba 'Nchu in August 1841 to return to Botswana (Schüler, 1965: 47).

In the meantime white farmers had started to settle on part of the land belonging to the Rolong. This state of affairs was unacceptable to the Wesleyan missionaries at Thaba 'Nchu and the British government in the Cape Colony. At the time of the annexation of the Orange River Sovereignty by Britain on 3 February 1848, white farmers living in Moroka's territory were given full property rights under British authority. The subsequent fixing of boundaries reduced the area of Thaba 'Nchu to approximately 200,000 ha (*cf.* Agar-

Hamilton, 1928: 16-17; Kitching, 1984: 49,55; Murray, 1992: 15 and Schüler, 1965: 43).

After the British withdrawal from the Orange River Sovereignty in 1854, Moroka became effectively independent, was recognized as such by the Orange Free State Republic (which then came into existence) and granted farms to several individuals (Kitching, 1984:61 and Murray, 1992: 16).

After Moroka's death (on 8 April 1880) his eldest living son with his main wife, Samuel Lehulere, claimed that he was the legal heir and successor. Because of rumours that he was not Moroka's son, Moroka used to favour and support his adopted son Tshipinare as successor (Kitching, 1984: 72 and Murray, 1992: 22). In July 1880 Samuel Lehulere and Tshipinare requested President Brand (of the Orange Free State Republic) to settle the successor dispute between them, and the President ruled in favour of Tshipinare (Kitching, 1984: 73 and Schüler, 1965: 60). Samuel Lehulere then tried to take over the government of Thaba 'Nchu, although without success, and was banned. Tshipinare was murdered by followers of Samuel Lehulere (assisted by Free State farmers and a number of Sotho chiefs) in 1884 (*cf.* Murray, 1992: 31; Plaatje, 1916: 111 and Schüler, 1965: 61). Tshipinare's councillors refused to accept Samuel Lehulere as chief and appealed to President Brand to settle the matter. The latter ruled that Thaba 'Nchu was without a legal government, and annexed the area on 12 July 1884.

Land Administration

Traditional Way of Settlement and Land Administration

Although the Rolong-Seleka, because of the unstable conditions in the interior of Southern Africa during the eighteenth century, never lived in one place for very long, Schüler (1965: 105) maintains that their way of settlement and their land administration were not much affected by this. They lived in villages *(metse)* which were usually quite far from the cattle posts. The main village *(moshate)* of the *kgosi* consisted of a number of households divided into patrilinear family groups *(lesika)*. The *motse* of an ordinary member consisted of a number of households that were arranged more or less in a circle around the cattle and small stock kraals. In this circle there was, apart from the stock kraals, an open space *(kgotla)* where (usually) the men could gather to discuss matters of general interest.

Specific rules applied to the lay-out of a tribal area. The *kgosi* had to give his permission; he had to choose the place where his *moshate* would be built and his was built first. Subsequently the various districts *(dikgotla)*, and/or wards *(dikgôrô)* and/or subwards *(dikgôrwana)* were allocated after consultation with the headmen *(dikgosana)* *(cf.* Erasmus, 1978: 217-224;

Schapera, 1959: 19 and Van Zyl, 1958: 50-51). The size of the local units was determined by administrative considerations, availability of resources, as well as existing and future needs of male heads of families. Every married man was entitled to a plot on which he could build his *motse,* land for crops *(phatse)* for his wives, as well as to the use of the communal grazing. There was no limit to the size of a building area and if a shortage of building or agricultural land occurred in a *kgôrô,* the *kgosana* had to discuss the allocation of more land with the *kgosi.* However, sufficient land for future extension was often kept in reserve *(cf.* Erasmus, 1978: 220-229 and Jeppe, 1980: 7-17).

Before a man could build his *motse* on the land allocated to him by his father (or his legal successor), it had to be inspected by the *kgosana,* his advisers *(bagakolodi)* and members of the *kgôrô* to ensure that it was part of the land that was allocated to the head of the family. If *kgôrô* members had no objection, the land could be cleared and building could commence. If any one else claimed the land, the matter would be discussed in the *kgotla* and settled by the *kgosana* and his *bagakolodi.*

Once a *motse* had been built, it remained in possession of the family and passed from generation to generation. When a person left a *kgôrô* to live elsewhere, the *kgosana* did not have the right to allocate his plot and *motse* to other persons, as such a person was entitled to return to his original *motse* and repossess it. The same rule applied if a man died without having children and his widow returned to her parental home. Only if a person told the *kgosana* that he was leaving the *kgôrô* permanently could the *kgosana* make the premises available to other applicants. If the original owner returned later, he had to apply to the *kgosana* for another plot *(cf.* Jeppe, 1980: 30 and Schüler, 1965: 113)

Land Administration by the Orange Free State Republic (1884-1910)

The Rolong territory of Thaba 'Nchu was annexed by the Orange Free State Republic during July 1884 as the district of Moroka. Like all other districts in the Orange Free State Republic, it fell under the laws and authority of the Free State Republic. In brief this meant that direct administrative control was exercised by a magistrate who, *inter alia,* was responsible for issuing certificates for plots to residents *(cf.* Brooks, 1974: 97 and Schüler, 1965: 92). At the time of the annexation, the matter of the land allocations made by Moroka and Tshipinare was raised *(cf.* Kitching, 1984: 82 and Murray, 1992: 280). Consequently the Free State President appointed the Prinsloo Commission to investigate land claims in Thaba 'Nchu.

The Commission submitted its report on 16 August 1884. It found that although traditionally individual landownership did not exist among the

Rolong, Moroka and Tshipinare had allocated about two-thirds of Thaba 'Nchu to either individual tribe members or white farmers. Because the area had not been formally surveyed, it was difficult for these people to prove individual property rights.

The House of Assembly of the Orange Free State Republic appointed a Commission to advise it on the report of the Prinsloo Commission. This Commission's viewpoint was that Moroka and Tshipinare did not have the right to give their subjects ownership rights. At the same time the commission recommended that the House of Assembly give full-fledged title-deeds only to the white farmers who had been allocated land. When President Brand intervened, the House of Assembly decided that the question of land claims was to be put before a judge for final decision. Judge Gregorowski submitted a provisional report on 25 May 1885 and a final report on 16 June 1885.

By virtue of Mr. Justice Gregorowski's recommendations, the House of Assembly decided that the land allocated to whites and Natives had to be registered in their names. However, in the case of the latter they were not allowed to sell the land allocated to them for a period of 15 years. After this period the land could be bought by whites only. In terms of Chapter XXXIV of the Orange Free State Statute-book Natives were prohibited from obtaining ownership rights from other Natives or whites. They could sell or lease their properties only to the government or to whites *(cf.* Kitching, 1984: 17)

On 2 June 1887 the House of Assembly revoked the decision regarding the 15-year servitude and the Rolong could sell their land at any time, but still only to the government or to whites. After the inalienability servitude had been revoked, many residents lost their land because they became the prey of land speculators *(cf.* Kitching, 1984: 101-106 and Murray, 1992: 280).

Moroka District existed as such until 1894, after which it became part of the Bloemfontein District and was known as the Moroka Ward. In 1902 the name Moroka Ward was changed to Thaba 'Nchu District (Kitching, 1984: 81-82 and Schüler, 1965: 69).

During the Boer War (1899-1902) many of the residents of Thaba 'Nchu were forced to move off their land. After the Free State Republic had been subjected to British authority in May 1900 (after which it was called the Orange River Colony), all state land became the property of the British government. The 71,105 ha of state land in Thaba 'Nchu was supplemented by additional land purchases until the extent of the Crown land was approximately 120,680 ha. This land was used by the British authorities for their "land settlement" project. In the course of time several British settlers became landowners in Thaba 'Nchu by means of the Crown grant of the Land Settlement Board.

In the period after the Boer War until the unification of South Africa in

1910, the following events were important and deserve mentioning. Firstly, the South African Native Affairs Commission (1903-1905) formulated the principle of territorial partition as the only basis for the development of a South African society and politics. As far as the Commission was concerned, the development of a mixed society was to be avoided (*cf.* Butler, Rotberg and Adams, 1978: 9 and Kitching, 1984: 125).

Secondly the National Convention was held in 1909 with the aim of establishing the Union of South Africa. Legal and civil rights for Natives was one of the more problematic matters that had to be dealt with. Eventually the following was decided:

— That provision would be made for a Union Department of Native Affairs to which all the functions would be assigned which had fallen under the various provinces before unification (Section 14, Zuid-Afrika Act, 1909).
— That the franchise would not be extended to Natives in the Orange Free State (Section 35 en 152).
— That all the laws that had been in force in the four different provinces would remain in force until revoked by the Parliament of the Union of South Africa (determined by Section 135).
— That the management and administration of Native Affairs throughout the Union of South Africa would fall under the Governor-General in Council (Section 147). Legally this meant that the Governor-General would be the paramount chief of the Natives in the Union of South Africa (Transkei areas excluded).

The Legislative Framework of Separatism (1910-1948)

After the unification of South Africa, a select committee was nominated by the Union Parliament to investigate the question of Native landownership. On the basis of the recommendations made, the Natives Land Act, 1913 (Act No. 27/1913) was introduced reserves (the so-called reserved or scheduled areas). These areas consisted of 9 million ha (10.7 million morgen) *(cf.* Olivier, 1975: 10,56; Republic of Bophuthatswana, 1977: 192 and Tatz, 1962: 159-161).

In the schedule to the above-mentioned act, Thaba 'Nchu is defined and its size drastically reduced to 5679 ha (Kitching, 1984: 126-129). Furthermore Act 27/1913 also stipulated that Chapter XXXIV of the Orange Free State Statute-book would remain in force. According to Murray (1992: 282), this placed African landowners in Thaba 'Nchu in a very particular dilemma. The value of their land depended on its potential sale to whites. The result was a decreasing aggregate area, increasing formal subdivision of individual farms and rapidly increasing indebtedness.

A second act with important implications was the Native Affairs Act, 1920 (Act No. 23/1920). This act provided for the introduction of a permanent Native Affairs Commission, as well as Native Councils. These institutions were to establish consultation and liaison with the Africans, among other things to settle deadlocks with regards to the making available of land.

The above-mentioned Native Affairs Commission visited Thaba 'Nchu during 1922 and 1923. The Rolong submitted the question of private Rolong land in Thaba 'Nchu to the Commission, and pointed out that since the annexation of the area in 1884, the Rolong had been forbidden to obtain land in the Orange Free State. They were dissatisfied about the private Rolong farms that had fallen into the hands of whites and asked for legislation that provided for "black" land; if a Native could not buy the land, the state and not a white person had to buy the land so that it could be sold to a Native later on. This would ensure that land occupied by the Rolong could be retained by them (*cf.* Kitching, 1984:143 and Plaatje, 1916: 113).

As a result of these discussions, the Moroka Ward Land Relief Act, 1924 (Act No. 28/1924) was accepted. This Act (which came into effect on 1 March 1925) provided, *inter alia,* that notwithstanding the provisions of any other act, approval was granted to a Native who was a registered owner of land situated in the district of Thaba 'Nchu, with the approval of the Governor-General to sell, lease or convey any right or title to such land to a *bona fide member of the Barolong tribe* (author's emphasis). If this act had not been introduced, the harsh effects of the provisions of Chapter XXXIV of the Orange Free State Statute-book on private landowners in Thaba 'Nchu would have resulted, according to Kitching (1984: 149), in two-thirds of Thaba 'Nchu going to white buyers.

The Native Administration Act, 1927 (Act No. 38/1927) introduced a separate administration system for Natives, and provided for the recognition of tribal chiefs and Native legal systems. From the time of the passing of Act 38/1927 until the system of tribal authorities came into being in 1951, tribal chiefs and ward headmen were officially responsible for the administration of tribal land in their private capacities. Their individual duties and functions were defined and were limited to administrative, judicial and police duties (Jeppe, 1980: 87).

The Native Trust and Land Act 1936 (Act No. 18/1936) envisaged the acquisition of 6. 3 million ha (the "released areas") for Natives, as well as the introduction of the South African Native Trust (SANT), later known as the South African Development Trust. In the areas scheduled to be transferred, whites were compelled to sell land to the Native Trust for inclusion in the reserves. The SANT was an incorporated institution, with the South African State President as the only trustee. The basic principle of the SANT was to use a statutory state institution as trustee of all state land available to natives of the Bantustans/homelands, and to entrust the SANT with the purchase and settlement of additional land. The landownership of the SANT in the Bantustans was confirmed by title deeds registered at the deeds office *(cf.* Butler, Rotberg and Adams, 1978: 11-12, Jeppe, 1980:60, Republic of Bophuthatswana, 1977: 192 and Tatz, 1962: 159).

The released areas in the Thaba 'Nchu district were some 67,543.6 ha in extent (Kitching, 1984: 175). Act 18/1936 imposed no ethnic restrictions on obtaining land in the released areas and as such it was contrary to the provisions of the Moroka Ward Land Relief Act, 1924.

After the passing of Act 18/1936, the acquisition, exercising and alienation of rights to land in Thaba 'Nchu mainly became subject to the stipulations of this act. The legal implication was that in "released areas" only the SANT or a Native could obtain land from another Native [Section 12 (1) (a)]. According to Murray (1992: 284-285), land purchases by the SANT in Thaba 'Nchu significantly undermined private African landownership (all residents of land became subject to settlement under the "communal" regime) and gave rise to a determined official effort to rationalize the terms of settlement (People were allocated individual portions of land of 3 or 6 morgen for arable use, and had access to communal grazing land which was divided into camps.) SANT areas in Thaba 'Nchu were systematically replanned (known as betterment and rehabilitation) during the 1940s/1950s/ 1960s. Forced resettlement of communities in some 40 SANT or rural villages resulted from this process.

The Legislative Framework of Apartheid (1948-1990)

For almost 50 years apartheid legislation was imposed on blacks. For the purpose of this discussion, the following laws are important.

The Bantu Authorities Act, 1951 (Act No. 68/1951) introduced a system of local government founded no traditional institutions (viz. Tribal Authorities and Regional Authorities) which culminated in a Territorial Authority with a measure of legislative and administrative jurisdiction over a Bantustan. Of special importance was the fact that the government of the tribe was entrusted to the tribal chief-in-council. Tribal chiefs had to exercise their control over and execute their other duties with regard to the rights to land and use of land by their subjects in consultation with their respective tribal authorities. *(cf.* Jeppe, 1980: 87; Kitching, 1984: 201; Oliver, 1975: 18; Republic of Bophuthatswana, 1977: 192 and Tatz, 1962: 183-184).

In terms of government Notice 1275, 1953, read together with Proclamation R182,1962, the Barolong Tribal Authority for the Thaba 'Nchu District was established. This body consisted of 10 members who were nominated by the then regent (Maria Moroka) in consultation with traditional councillors (Schüler 1965: 94).

In its report the Tomlinson Commission recommended that existing reserves should be extended even to the point of independence, and that territorial authorities should be appointed on an ethnic basis. It was possible to link an ethnic group to a certain territory by the introduction of the Promotion of Bantu Self-Government Act, 1959 (Act No. 46/1959). This act provided the constitutional machinery for progress towards autonomy as a prelude to full independence.

Within the framework of the above-mentioned legislation, the Tswana Territorial Authority was established on 21 April 1961 (in terms of Government Notice No. 585, 21 April 1961). It was made up of eight regional authorities on a union basis. Until 1968 the Tswana Territorial Authority had no executive functions—it was merely an advisory body. However, in that year it was reconstituted (in terms of Proclamation R140, 1968 and Proclamation R141,1968), and given more powers and functions.

The Homelands Constitution Act, 1971 (Act No. 21/1971) facilitated the process aimed at obtaining self-governing status by providing for a first and second phase of self-government. The first phase of self-government (namely the introduction of a legislative assembly and an executive council) started on 1 May 1971 when the Tswana Territorial Authority was replaced by a Legislative Assembly (Proclamation R87, 30 April 1971). Although there were no changes in terms of composition, the change of name did bring about a change in status, as the body immediately received the authority to introduce legislation across a wide spectrum of subjects. The Barolong Regional Authority, Thaba 'Nchu district, was represented in the Legislative Assembly.

In terms of Section 26(1) of Act 21/1971 the Tswana Homeland (in terms of proclamation R131, 1972) became a self-governing area on 1 June 1972 and the name "Bophuthatswana" was accepted. In terms of the above-mentioned proclamation the Legislative Assembly of Bophuthatswana consisted of 72 members. The Barolong Tribal Authority appointed their chief and three members.

On 7 July 1972 (in terms of Proclamation R163, 1972) the election date was announced (4 October 1972). At that stage there were no political parties in Bophuhtatswana. *Kgosi* T. Pilane, tribal chief of the Kgatla-ba-ga-Kgafela tribe of Saulspoort in the Mankwe District founded the Seoposengwe Party (United Party, SP) on 29 July 1972. On 5 August 1972 *Kgosi* Lucas Mangope founded the Lekobo la Setshaba sa Bophuthatswana (Bophutatswana National Party, BNP). The most important differences between these two parties was the role of the tribal chief in political development (the BNP accepted the chief system as basis for political development), obtaining of land, and future relations between Bophuthatswana and other Bantustans in South Africa. The BNP won 20 of the 24 seats, while urban voters inside and outside Bophuthatswana largely supported the SP *(cf.* Butler, Rotberg and Adams 1978: 50-55, Olivier 1975: 87 and Republic of Bophuthatswana 1977: 202-204 for an exposition of the policies of the different political parties).

Bophuthatswana: From Independence to Incorporation (1977-1994)

Bophuthatswana became independent on 6 December 1977 in terms of the Republic of Bophuthatswana Constitution Act, 1977 (Act 18/1977). The Bophuthatswana Constitution contained, *inter alia,* a Declaration of Fundamental Rights which stated that everyone had the right to own private and communal property [Section 17(1)]. With regard to legal provisions on communal rights, the Bophuthatswana Traditional Authorities Act, 1978 (Act No. 23/1978) stipulated that the President was the authority responsible for tribal and communal authorities, he acknowledged tribal chiefs and appointed them, while the authority and control over all tribal matters rested with him. Act 23/1978 also defined the Constitution, powers, authorities and functions of tribal, community and regional authorities. Land administration was one of the stipulated duties of tribal authorities.

Land in communal use (i.e. tribal land) became Bophuthatswana state land and could be used in any way (leasing, selling or allocation) by government. There were more than 70000 ha of communal land in Thaba 'Nchu. The Barolong Tribal Authority was responsible for land administration and allocation. They handled it as follows: Land was allocated to an individual and not to a family head as had been done traditionally Individuals who applied for permanent settlement addressed their applications via the headmen (who made sure that the site was vacant) to the Barolong Tribal Authority.

Jeppe (1980: 22, 31 and 33) characterized the general practices with regard to land allocations and administration by traditional leaders (as described above) in an independent Bophuthatswana as follows:

- Rights of use to residential plots and fields were sold in a covert way in tribal areas.
- The pattern of land usage became very static in tribal areas. The duties of the persons in authority (tribal chiefs and ward headmen) with regard to land allocation were minimal and did not make many or very complicated demands. From the viewpoint of the persons in authority in tribal areas, the system of land allocation and control had, however, important security value. The political unity and stability of Tswana life depended to a large extent on the determination of rights to land.

February 1990 opened up the probability of the political re-integration of the independent Bantustans into a unitary South African state. Although all homelands ceased to exist in terms of the interim constitution of the "new" South Africa, Lucas Mangope remained committed to the independence of Bophuthatswana. However, the uprising and revolt in March 1994 ousted him, and the Transitional Executive Council set up an administrative structure to run Bophuthatswana during the pre-election period. Since the elections of April 1994, Thaba 'Nchu has once again been part of the Free State.

Discussion

Until approximately the middle of the nineteenth century the Rolong-Seleka to a large extent handled their own affairs. The indigenous concept of land for the Tswana was socio-politically determined, since only tribesmen could obtain rights to land Membership by birth or by formal affiliation was the basic qualification for the acquisition of rights to land. The following traditional Tswana land rights can be distinguished. Every married tribesman had an undisputed natural claim to a residential site, tillable land and the right to use communal areas; no-one was "landless", as all tribesmen had similar rights; no payment was made for land; traditional land use rights could only be taken away in exceptional circumstances; and the lay-out of residential sites and the placing and lay-out of fields did not occur in an arbitrary way.

The concept of territorial segregation was a cornerstone of different governments (Free State Republic, Orange River Colony, Union of South Africa and the Republic of South Africa) and was closely related to the issue of land administration. According to authors such as Butler, Rotberg and Adams (1978: 9-10) and Tatz (1962 17-24), separatism did not result from a desire to produce the territorial basis of a just, if segregated, society in South Africa. Instead, it constituted a response to the expressed need of white farmers for continued access to supplies of low-wage labour. Pre-apartheid legislation intended to minimize competition between Natives and poor whites by forbidding Natives to puchase land or to offer themselves as sharecroppers on white-owned land.

It must be kept in mind that ideological considerations played a role. It was during the lead up to Apartheid and increasing restrictions were being imposed on the Africans by the authorities. In this regard Van der Bank (1993: 358) states that it is significant that these measures were only introduced in those areas where the Africans posed a possible threat to the whites, namely with regard to citizenship, the right to vote, free economic enterprise and ownership of land.

Du Toit (1982: 155) suggests that the more autocratic a government, the more likely it is that decisions regarding population groups will be made without consulting those involved. And that is exactly what happened in Thaba 'Nchu. A system of land administration was imposed upon the inhabitants of Thaba 'Nchu, without their involvement. Until 1991, legislation prevented them from purchasing land in ex-white South Africa. Even an independent Bophuthatswana could not free itself of Dr. Verwoerd's philosophy ("in accordance with their nature, traditions and capabilities)" and the inhabitants had no opportunity to become involved in negotiations or decision-making with respect to land affairs inside Thaba 'Nchu.

As is often the case with forced removals *(cf.* Du Toit, 1982 and Gans, 1991), the systematically and forced resettlement of people in some 40 SANT or rural villages in Thaba 'Nchu did not allow for the transfer of social systems. It must be kept in mind that:

— the decision to resettle was not taken voluntarily, but was forced on the people.

— the objectives of the relocation were formulated and the process conducted by white officials whose cultural frame of reference with regard to the importance and meaning of kinship, the nuclear family, peer-group membership, neighbourhood ties, etc. differed from those of the Thaba 'Nchu residents; and

— as indicated by the Kariba Studies *(cf.* Colson, 1977: 71), kinship is of maximum importance in the period immediately after resettlement, because people need it to restore order to their world and to integrate themselves into their new environment.

The breakdown of social security and structures led to a period of intense manoeuvring and re-structuring where the people in the small communities, for the first time, were feeling their way towards taking responsibility for their own affairs. In this regard many inhabitants saw the Barolong Tribal Authority, which was established in terms of Apartheid legislation and was instrumental in the continuation and administration of resettlements, as co-operating with the Apartheid regime. This invoked large-scale reactions (uprising and revolt) among the residents during the mid 1980s and early 1990s. Their desire to destroy a discriminating dispensation gathered momentum and resulted in the rejection of the long been thoroughly discredited Barolong Tribal Authority and the collapse of local government in Thaba 'Nchu.

Thaba 'Nchu has a distinctive history. It was the only district in the Orange Free State Republic with a mix of white and black-owned farms in private tenure as well as communal land occupied by African communities. It was this universe that provided Thaba 'Nchu with an identity of its own, and which was destroyed by government over the years. The inhabitants of Thaba 'Nchu experienced the practices of separation and resettlement as deconstructive and negative, and their reactions helped to establish a new dispensation with new local government structures.

REFERENCES

Agar-Hamilton, J.A.I 1928. *The Native Policy of the Voortrekkers: 1836-1858.* Cape Town: Maskew Miller.

Bath, F. 1994. *Balinese Worlds.* Chicago: University of Chicago Press.

Brooks, E.H. 1974. *White Rule in South Africa: 1830-1910.* Pietermaritzburg: University of Natal Press.

Butler, J., R.I. Rotberg and J Adams. 1977. *The Black Homelands of South Africa: The Political and Economic Development of Bophuthatswana and Kwazulu.* London: University of California Press.

Colson, E. 1971. *The Social Consequences of Resettlement.* Manchester: The University Press. (Kariba Studies IV)

Desmond, C. 1986. *The Discarded People.* Braamfontein. The Christian Institute of South Africa.

Du Toit, B. M. 1982. "Involuntary Migration and Government Policy: Population Displacement in South Africa", (pp 139-158) in A. Hansen, and A. Oliver-Smith. (eds.), *Involuntary Migration and Resettlement: The Problems and Responses of Dislocated People.* Boulder: Westview Press.

Erasmus, P.A. 1978. *Die Sosiale Organisasie van die Hurutshe ba ga Suping.* Ongepubliseerde M.A.-verhandeling, Universiteit van die Oranje-Vrystaat, Bloemfontein.

Gans. H.J. 1991. *People, Plans and Policies. Essays on Poverty, Racism, and other National Urban Problems.* New York: Columbia University Press.

Harries, P. 1987. "A Forgotten Corner of the Transvaal: Reconstructing the History of a Relocated Community through Oral Testimony and Song," (pp 93-134) in B. Bozzoli (ed.), *Class, Community and Conflict. South African Perspectives.* Johannesburg: Ravan Press.

Hastrup, K. and P. Hervik, 1994. "Introduction", (pp. 1-12) in K. Hastrup and P. Hervik (eds.) *Social Experience and Anthropological Knowledge.* London: Routledge

Jeppe, W.J.O. 1980. *Bophuthatswana Land Tenure and Development.* Stellenbosch: University of Stellenbosch.

Kitching, B.M. 1984. *Die Evolusie van die Thaba 'Nchu-enklave. 'n Polities-geografiese studie.* Ongepubliseerde M.A.-verhandeling, Universiteit van die Oranje-Vrystaat, Bloemfontein.

Murray, C. 1992. *Black Mountain: Land, Class and Power in the Eastern Orange Free State 1880s-1980s.* London: Witwatersrand University Press.

Niehaus, I.A. 1989. "Relocation into Phuthaditjhaba and Tseki. A Comparative Ethnography of Planned and Unplanned Removals," *African Studies,* 48(2): 157-182.

Olivier, W.H. 1975. *Die staatkundige ontwikkeling van Bophutatswana tot 1975.* Ongepubliseerde M.A.-Verhandeling in Staatsleer, Universiteit van Pretoria, Pretoria.

O'Regan, C. 1989. "No More Forced Removals? An Historical Analysis of the Preventing of Illegal Squatting Act," *South African Journal on Human Rights,* 5(3): 361-394.

Plaatje, S.T. 1916. *Native Life in South Africa, Before and Since the European War and the Boer Rebellion.* New York: Negro Universities Press.

Schapera, I. 1959. *A Handbook of Tswana Law and Custom.* London: Oxford University Press.

Schüler, G.M.K. 1965. *Die Barolong van Thaba 'Nchu, O.V.S.: 'n Studie van Kultuurverandering.* Ongepubliseerde D. Phil-Proefskrif, Universiteit van Stellenbosch, Stellenbosch.

Sharp, J. 1982. "Relocation and the Problem of Survival in Qwaqwa: A Report from the Field," *Social Dynamics,* 8 (2): 11-29.

Tatz, C.M. 1962. *Shadow and Substance in South Africa.* Pietermaritzburg: University of Natal Press.

The Republic of Bophuthatswana. 1977. Johannesburg: Chris van Rensburg Publications.

Van der Bank, D.A. 1993. *Die stryd om die behoud van die identiteit van die Afrikaner in die Oranjerivierkolonie, 1902-1910.* Ongepubliseerde D. Phil-proefskrif, Univerisiteit van die Oranje-Vrystaat, Bloemfontein.

Van Zyl, H.J. 1958. *Die Bakgatla van Mosêtla. 'n Volkekundige studie van 'n Bantoestam se ekonomiese lewe en posisie.* Johannesburg: Voortrekkerpers.

TEN

TRIBAL RIGHTS TO LAND AND THE STATE IN ORISSA

L. K. MAHAPATRA

Community, Individual and State Rights in Land

The former Chief Justice of the Supreme Court of India argues that "notions of ownership of goods and chattels were stronger than that of land and the awareness of ownership of land came when particular areas were appropriated for hunting or agriculture and when there was scarcity of well-situated lands for occupation. He also notes that, property in land of the members of a clan or tribe had a dual meaning. While devolution of property was from the community to the individual, the devolution was subject to the control of the community. It could then be said that it belonged simultaneously to the community and the individual either alone or in a family group. According to him, a kind of 'secondary and subordinate ownership' is created when family clears uncultivated or unoccupied land belonging to the village or clan or lineage. The rights of the community were always primary. The British, for the first time, tried to separate the individual from the community against the old traditions. It was Roman Law which distinguished between a natural mode of acquisition' and 'legal mode' " (Hidayatullah, 1983: 25 quoted in Mahapatra, 1983: 87).

Professor Roy Burman notes that "the formal status of ownership may be with an individual or family, but customarily the other members of the lineage or clan or local group may have defined rights to access to, or share of, the resources. On the other hand, while at the ideological level the land may be owned by the community, the decision-making authority and effective possession may pertain to certain categories of individuals and families only. He, therefore, emphasizes that it is more important to examine the pattern of access and possession, the terms and conditions of access and the source of legitimization of access, rather than the formal status of ownership" (Roy Burman 1986: 6 quoted in Mahapatra, 1993: 87).

Professor F.G. Bailey had differentiated tribes from castes in India on the principle that as member of the tribal community (his example was Kondh) each tribesman had equal and inalienable access to land, whereas a member of a caste a man had differential and unequal access to land, as there was an unequal division of land based on social hierarchy: the higher the position in the caste hierarchy, the greater the access to land, the lowest being landless (*cf.* Bailey, 1961: 7-10). In the hills, land was not saleable before the colonial times as Bailey has argued.

Denhez has cogently brought to our notice the fact that "although the colonial powers have largely withdrawn from the scene the independent countries which they left in their wake often resort to the same argument–it is as if they view themselves as successors in title to the claims of the previous colonial powers" (Denhez, 1983: 517-546). This position directly went against the traditional Hindu concept of *kingship,* according to which proprietary right in land of the person who settled on that land and made it fit for cultivation was recognized by the king who claimed only a portion of the produce it yielded as revenue.

Professor Roy Burman very cogently points out that there is some confusion even in the minds of the legal authorities. The Law Research Institute of Guwahati High Court had disregarded the same Court's decision on community rights in the case involving the Manipur Nagas and applied the juristic principle of *res nullius.* This led to the assertion of proprietary right of the state over all lands in Arunachal Pradesh by invoking the theory of abrogation of earlier rights through conquest. The correct juristic principle should have been applied there, namely the principle of *lex loci rei sitae* (the law of the place where the thing is situated), and not the colonial concept of *res nullius* (something which has no real owner or holder unless assigned by the sovereign) *(cf.* Roy Burman, 1992: 37-38).

Predatory role of the state in India may be discussed here. Whether under the colonial state or the welfare state after Independence, the predatory role of the state has struck at the root of the customary rights of the tribal people. While discussing land revenue system of the ex-princely states of Orissa, Cobden-Ramsay (1910) asserts, "ownership in the land rests with the state, but the right of occupancy rests with the actual cultivator, who, so long as he pays his rents, is left in undisturbed possession." This forms the bedrock of the British revenue system, though in ancient Statecraft in India, the king never "owned" lands of the kingdom. Later on, Cobden-Ramsay remarks, with his tongue in his cheek: "The Khonds, Binjhals, Juangs and Bhuiyans claim to be the real owners of the soil and when questioned 'who are you?' the answer invariably given, humble in origin and position as the member of these races may be, is 'I am a Zamindar', or owner of the soil. The wild non-Hinduized Khond has never consented to pay a regular land revenue: this class of Khond is mostly found in Kalahandi; where a nominal fee is paid for the Pada or Jhuming area, and it is paid more as an act of concession than as a rental. The Bhuiyans similarly pay a house-tax.

All the elements of the colonial policy are here: the tribal claim that they are the owners of the land; but actually, the chief is the owner on behalf of the state (princely state); the tribal does not pay any rent, which would have entitled him to possession of the land (for which compensation could be paid); he pays instead some fees (most often collectively; as among the Hill Bhuiyan) and hence no individual rights on land can be determined.

Right in this line of thinking was the practice in one of the largest zamindars of the country, which constituted Koraput district. It was found in 1939 that there were only 745 Raiyatwari villages as against 4,203 Mustajari villages. Mustajar is actually an agent or contractor, mostly from among the affluent and influential families of the village or the region, who is to deliver a specified amount of rent to the Estate owner or Zamindar. "The tenants have no records of their lands and they are entirely at the mercy of the Mustajars. The Mustajars do not grant any receipt for the rents realised from the tenants nor do they keep any accounts. Instead of recording individual tenants, their land and rents paid, 'The Demand Register' commonly known as D.C.B. Register, . . . for a mustajari village shows the demand from the mustajar, for the whole village and purports to show the demands from each individual tenants but does not actually contain the names of a large number of cultivating tenants or their assessments" (Report of the Partially Excluded Areas Enquiry Committee, Orissa, 1940).

No wonder, there was a handy alibi for the officials after Independence not to pay any compensation to the Gadaba and other tribal people, who had not only customary rights but also otherwise valid rights under mustajari system, when they were dispossessed of their lands for development projects in Koraput district, namely, MIG factory at Sunabeda, Balimela Hydro-Electricity Project, and Machkund Hydro-Electricity Project.

Customary Rights on Common Property Resources

The U.N. document of 1966 defines customary rights as the rights to use or dispose of use rights over land which rests neither on the exercise of brute force, nor on evidence of rights guaranteed by government statute, but on the fact that they are recognized as legitimate by the community, the rules governing the acquisition or transmission of these rights being explicit and generally known, though not normally recorded in writing. Professor Roy Burman points out that this definition is rather narrow, as it excludes statutes recognizing customary rights; and also it excludes religious codes (*cf.* Roy Burman, 1986).

Almost everywhere when there are communal rights, individual's rights, and even sub-group rights, are embedded in the communal rights. In the village or clan ownership of land or forest, the persons belonging to a clan or village or such other grouping, have the right to use the resources and even control or manage them. Rights to use under certain conditions or usufruct by the individual members of the sub-group invariably go with communal rights of ownership. Even when the state is the ultimate and absolute owner, as when we speak of the sovereign power of the state, the customary rights may be exercised by the persons of the collectivity concerned in all manners short of claiming absolute rights of ownership.

Common property resources and customary rights hang together, as the resources are things or objects of these rights. This is almost invariably so, as common property resources (CPR) are not statutorily recognized by the state: as belonging to the tribal groups. But invariably the customary rights over CPR are the most substantive part of their style of life. Professor Roy Burman thinks of only those resources to which the members of a culturally defined collectivity have a "right of fair share of access and use" irrespective of who formally owns and/or controls these resources. But it seems this interpretation may be too restrictive. Some varieties of common property resources like stream bed flat land which can be reduced to wet terraces or gently sloping uplands for cultivation near the habitation site of a hill village may be very scarce, hence these may be shared differentially among the first settlers' families to the partial or total exclusion of the later immigrant settlers in the village. This was studied among the Hill Bhuiyan of Bonai ex-princely state.

In Orissa common property resources in land, beds and bunds of water bodies, water courses, irrigation channels, threshing floor, drainage channels, village forest, tanks meant for drinking water, cattle stands, village habitation sites, cremation and burial grounds, public places of worship, festival or recreation site, village market, grazing grounds, village roads and paths, etc. were recorded as *porambok* lands for common use by all villagers in Koraput and Ganjam undivided districts. Under the Madras Estate Act which was applicable in these districts village habitation site as a unit was such communally owned land and it was not assessed for revenue. But in other districts under *Sarbasadharana* (public use) rights all these common property resources are shown, except the village habitation site, which is separately recorded and assessed for land rent for each individual land owner. In Ganjam and Koraput village habitation site did not attract any rent as it was communally used.

If we take the percentage of our population below the poverty line, the tribal people come to the top of them. In India as a whole 58 per cent of the tribal people in rural areas were below the poverty line in 1983-84, whereas the rural Scheduled Castes had 53.10 per cent and all India rural population had 40.40 per cent below the poverty line. When it comes to Orissa the proportion is even more abysmal. More than two-thirds (68.90%) of all the tribal people living in rural areas were in 1983-84 below the poverty line, compared to the all-Orissa population of 44.76 per cent in rural Orissa reeling under gruelling poverty. In rural Orissa the Scheduled Castes had 54.90 per cent of their population below the poverty line, (*cf.* Mahapatra, 1994:14). The agricultural labourers, who are main workers and landless, constitute 38.27 per cent of the total Scheduled Tribes main workers in Orissa, whereas in the country as a whole only 32.69 per cent of that total of main workers are landless agricultural labourers. Thus poverty is writ large in Orissa among the Scheduled Tribe population.

When the tribal people are landless and fall below the poverty line, they can survive only when they have access to common property resource in an equitable manner. This author had estimated in 1994 that out of 94.86 per cent rural tribal population in Orissa State, about 80 per cent of the total Scheduled Tribe population are forest dwellers, that is, those who reside on the fringe or in the vicinity of the forest or within daily walking distance from the forest, apart from a large number residing inside the forest as forest village dweller or revenue village dweller. The revenue villages inside the forest are regularly assessed for land revenue and land owners have *ryotwari patta* or record of rights.

Forest is the foremost common property resource, on which depend not only the subsistence, but also the very existence of the tribal people. We find tribal hunters and food gatherers (at least 4 such Scheduled Tribes, Korwa, Hill Kharia, Malhar and Birhor/Mankidi/Mankidia—as per President's list of Scheduled Tribes 6 such Scheduled Tribes), swidden cultivators (Hill Bhuiyan, Juang, Kondh, Saora, Poroja, Gadaba, Koya, Bhumia, Didayi, Bonda, Bhunjia, Erenga Kolha, Parenga, Pengo etc.), basket and mat makers (all tribal women, more or less, also Mahali and some Juang Scheduled Tribes), and some tribes having large livestock population as wealth (as in western and southern Orissa), depending heavily on the forest resources. This has been going on since times immemorial. But, since the colonial period, the utilization of minor forest produce has been a major means of bare survival by exchanging them for cash, as a sequel to swidden cultivation being gradually but steadily, restricted as more and more commercial uses have been found for the timber and bamboo from the forest. Even the settled agriculturist tribes like Gond, Santal, Munda, Oraon, Kisan, Binjhal and a host of others depend on the forest for maintaining their agricultural economy. The cattle have to get their fodder, the houses require timber and thatch and the plough, its raw material, strong wood. All tribal cooking is done with fuelwood energy. Apart from that, herbal medicine is very important not only for saving on medical expenses, but also for effective remedies. Then there are some tribal groups like *Sahara* or *Shabar,* who earn their daily bread by collecting deadwood or branches off the trees for sale as firewood in the nearby towns and villages. Other tribal groups survived by making charcoal and selling them. This is also the situation in project affected areas on which IPDP is being worked out.

The Hill Bonds of South Orissa require as many as 180 species of plants, shrubs, herbs, bushes timber yielding trees, and various types of grass for securing fruits, flowers, leaves, tubers and yams, resin, timber, etc. as food, drink, narcotics, medicine, house building materials and cottage industry materials.

The Hill Kharia has been catching and selling *mynah* birds (which imitate human voice) even before Dalton saw them in 1870's. Most of the tribal people, catch, trap or net small, game animals, birds, fish, etc. in the forest, when available in the nearby forest or water bodies.

The swidden cultivators cannot grow their whole year's food from the swiddens. They depend heavily on the forest resources, mango, jack fruit, tubers, yams, etc. in their lean season. All the landless among those who practise swidden cultivation have no other go than to grow their crops there along with earning wages as day labourer. In the days of privation, even mango kernels are known to have been eaten by poor tribal people. In the drought affected districts of western Orissa, the forest is the only source of succour in the years of severest drought as during 1969-71.

Dr. Walter Fernandes and his co-investigators have hypothesized that there is additional pressure on swidden cultivation in a degraded forest ecology, because of the decrease in the supply of minor forest (non-timber) produce due to deforestation. In their study on Orissa they found that 13.24 per cent households in their sample had mentioned collection and sale of non-timber forest produce as their main occupation and main source of earning, and 33.82 per cent had mentioned it as their subsidiary occupation. That means, 47.06 per cent of their sample had depended on minor forest produce as either primary or subsidiary occupation. "In an area where job opportunities are few and viable economic alternatives all but non-existent, this dependence is significant, for even subsidiary occupation involves total dependence for survival for at least three lean months in a year" (*cf.* Fernandes *et al.,* 1988). Others have found that displaced persons from Hirakud Dam Project and from other major or medium irrigation projects have taken to selling firewood as their main source of livelihood after displacement and self-sponsored resettlement. Professor Roy Burman reports other studies which confirm at least 35 per cent of the total earning coming from sale of non-timber forest products in other regions of India (*cf.* Roy Burman, 1982).

When collection and sale of non-timber forest produce have been of so much crucial importance for more survival of tribal people in Orissa and elsewhere, the author's earlier studies in two most backward gram panchayats in tribal areas of these forest produce have shown how its purchase through government monopoly has resulted in their greater impoverishment. Usually they are either cheated or offered a price lower than the market price or their produce is simply not purchased due to lack of storing space or lack of funds (*cf.* Mahapatra, 1982-83).

The village commons, village forest and waste lands have always provided fruits, leaves, and other edible tubers etc. in the days of penury, even on daily basis, to not only tribal people, but also to Scheduled Castes and other people below the poverty line. That is why they have survived so long in spite of the meagre earnings through not so frequent source of day labour in the villages. But these waste lands, etc. have now been encroached upon, or otherwise rendered out of reach in the villages. The government of Orissa was, therefore, forced to reserve some portion of the village lands by an executive order of 1961 (as reported above) as communal lands for common use.

Tribal Rights in Orissa in Precolonial/Colonial Periods

Under the ex-princely state regimes the locally dominant tribes, like the Bhuiyan and Juang in Keonjhar, the Bhuiyan in Bonai and Pal Lahara, the Kondh in Kalahandi and the Juang in Dhenkanal had enjoyed certain rights, not recognized by the successor state of India.

The Hill Bhuiyan or Pauri Bhuiyan, a more "primitive tribal group" were granted rights much earlier than the nineteenth century, when such rights were formally reported in colonial records and were standardized through periodic land revenue assessment.

R. K. Ramadhyani, I.C.S. had surveyed the existing Land Tenures and the Revenue System of the Orissa and Chhatisgarh States (princely states) in 1940s. He finds the following situation in Bhuiyan and Juang pirs of Keonjhar district:

"In the Bhuiyan and Juang pirs there has been no settlement of land as such in view of the shifting cultivation but in the Bhuiyan pir a plough tax on agriculturists (six annas per plough) and a house tax of 11 annas on non-agriculturists have been imposed; and in the Juang pir a produce rent is fixed for the village as a whole and the distribution of the rent among the villagers is left to the village headman. The terms of both these arrangements do not coincide with that of the settlement and in the case of the Bhuiyan pir the period is 5 years while in the Juang pir it is 7 years. In addition to plough tax and house tax in the Bhiyan pir a commutation case (3 annas per house with plough and 0-1-6 per house without plough) is levied in lieu of *bethi* and rasad in addition to an education cess (2 annas per house). The village headman of a Bhuiyan village is also bound to supply 2 goats one year, and another six months old, in the month of *Aswin* the pata mentions the value of these as Rs. 2 and Re. 1 respectively. Further 1¼ *pahi* of grain is realised from each household for the Jagannath Thakur temple; the headman keeps ¼ *pahi* out of each *pahi* contribution as his own remuneration. All adult male villagers are bound to supply rope and materials for the preparation of Jagannath's car and help to pull it and do other duties. They are also bound to supply *Inda* wood and rope at the time of the *Inda* festival and carry the *Inda Chatra;* they will be remunerated for this according to prevalent practices. They are also required to attend at *Parbani Parba, Aghira Purnima* festivals and render services; to supply coolies to British officers (for which they are responsible), who are entitled only to food, fuel, straw, branches for huts are to be supplied free. Similar supplies have to be made for the Raja, members of his family and certain officers. If any of these goes outside the state coolies have to be supplied free of charge for 15 days (for longer periods wages will be paid). Attendance of all prominent persons at the headquarters in the month of *Chaitra* (March-April) is obligatory. All these liabilities exist in spite of the alleged commutation of *bethi* and *begari.*

Rents and cesses are paid on the 15th February. In the Juang pir a year old goat has to be given at Dussehra by the headman in addition to the produce rent which is specified in the patta and is payable in February. The patta says that the produce rent has to be deposited in the store-room of the Darbar. In addition to the produce-rent, the patta prescribes in a schedule, in which a manuscript entry is made, other commodities to be supplied; in one such patta examined by me "broom grass" is prescribed to be deposited at the palace. Failure to supply articles prescribed or the produce rent entails attachment of moveable property and sale. As in the Bhiyan pir, 1¼ *pahi* being the collection charge of the headman. The following bethi is prescribed for Ruler: (a) thatching of a pig house and building a *pachari* or wall, (b) supply of coolies, fuel, straw, leaf plates (coolies will get good), and (c) supply of coolies for visits outside the State on food only. For the deity at headquarters two ropes have to be supplied and the car constructed and other articles supplied for another deity, thatching of house, making of fence with material brought by themselves. Supply of coolies on food only, fuel, etc. has to be made for British officers but rasad (rations) is on payment. The naiks, padhans and others have to offer presents to the Raja, Rani, Tikait and the Dewan in Chaitra (March-April) for which they receive food. No cesses seem to be levied.

In the Juang pir I was told that the distribution of the land for cultivation as well as the produce rent was made by the headman and there were no disputes. The distribution of rent was made on the plough and was roughly 15 pais (pai = 2 seers approximately) for one plough and 25 pais for two ploughs. The ryots said that they preferred to pay the rent in kind." (Ramdhyani, 1940: 137-138).

From the government receipts I have found that the Hill Bhuiyan were regularly paying such house tax and plough tax, not individually, and not for any specific plot of land used either as homestead or as cultivable land, but as co-shares of the village habitation and village farming land, at least till 1967. When in the same Pauri Bhuiyan region the state of Orissa gave away the so-called government land under degraded forest to a joint-sector Tea Plantation Company, these rights exercised through centuries by the tribal peoples were not taken into consideration as illegally occupied or unoccupied government land, also sank into oblivion. The people were not compensated at all for their continuing use of the now leased out land either as permanent fields under local upland cultivation system *(guda),* or under "swidden" cultivation system, or under permanent irrigated land system by damming a small hill-stream in this area. (*cf.* Mahapatra, 1994: 58).

Based on his personal field research in 1953-57 in Bonai ex-princely state (now in Sundargarh district), the consultant had come across the same plough tax paid collectively by the villagers of Pauri Bhuiyan (exclusive) hill villages, besides the tribute of a goat and some rice for Dusserah worship at the state capital and the worship of the regional deity, Kanta Kumari, in addition to *bethi* or compulsory labour for visiting officials, Rajas hunting visits or visiting British officials, etc.

In Pal Lahara ex-state no cesses were paid by the Hill Bhuiyan pir in Baburi Pargana where swidden cultivation was prevalent. Only house tax of rupee one and two annas (1/8th of rupee) along with 20 seers (1 seer = 880 gm) or *birri* pulses (phaseolus mungo) worth one rupee and nine annas (9/16th of rupee) were paid per household. All other cultivators in this pargana however paid normal assessment as well as all cesses. There were no sarbarakar (rent collectors) in the Bhuiyan pir, but each village had got a headman (*cf.* Ramdhyani, 1940: 201-202).

In Jeypore ex-estate, which constituted the undivided district of Koraput in Orissa, and which included the areas covered by Badanala M.I. Project in the new district of Rayagada (carved out of Koraput district), the following situation prevailed "Rent was paid either in cash or kind, cash rents being more common on the 3,000 foot plateau (where the crops are mostly dry) and in the Rayagada sub-division than on the 2,000-foot plateau of Jeypore itself where much paddy is raised . . . where cash rents were in force the assessment was usually a certain sum on each plough and hoe used. This varied from rupees 2 to rupees 6 a plough and from annas 4 (anna =1/16 of rupee) to annas 8 a hoe, according to the quality of the soil and the accessibility of the village. Normally a single ryot was assessed on the assumption that he had one plough and a hoe and was permitted to cultivate as much land as he could. . ." (Koraput, Orissa District Gazetteers: 286). There is no record or reference to the effect that the tribal ryots were given any concessions or relief that was not granted in favour of other ryots.

"In Rayagada and Gunupur sub-division both *dongar* (swidden cultivation) and paddy lands were assessed, as the economy depends both on paddy as well as on *dongar* land." (Koraput Major Settlement Report: 74) Wastelands were leased out by mustajars for cultivation in the hills and plains, without reference to the zamindar and with no records of rent collected.

"However, in Nowrangpur sub-division (now Nawarangapur district) under the undivided Koraput district the custom was not to assess the *dongar* lands while in Koraput sub-division, the reverse was the case" (*ibid:* 74).

So far as the rights to trees are concerned the Jeypore estate "assumed that the right to all trees standing on the holding belonged to the Samasthanam (estate) and the ryot was forbidden to exercise the rights over fruit bearing trees, such as mango, tamarind and *mahura,* etc. situated in his holding in the *ryotwari patta* which was granted by the estate" (*ibid:* 78). Even the stick lac grown on Kusum trees were taken (the whole?) by the estate officials. However, in Ganjam estate areas under Madras Estates Land Act of 1908 standing trees on the land of the occupancy ryots (with full rights) belonged to the ryot. But there was no separate mention of trees. Under Orissa Tenancy Act 1938 similar rights were conceded to the ryots in other parts of Orissa province (without the merged ex-states).

In Kalahandi ex-state (now Kalahandi district) cultivation of waste land without permission was not considered to be an encroachment, and encroachment on useless *jalchar* (water bodies for common use) was considered unobjectionable. These encroachments used to be settled on the encroachers on the impositions of a penalty. This situation prevailed, most probably because, as in central provinces the village headman was in complete control of the village lands, waste lands, etc. The ruler was the real proprietor, but the headman was as in Sambalpur district, "virtually a *thicadar* taking lease of the village for the term of the settlement." (Kalahandi Revenue Settlement Report: 23,12). The Board of Revenue made it clear in 1952 January that "land which were encroached upon prior to the 15th December 1947 should not be interfered with unless such lands are necessary for the use of the community or unless otherwise objectionable." Settlement Officers were empowered to settle upto 5 acres of land encroached upon in such cases (*cf. ibid.* 23).

In the Dangaria hill tract consisting of 354 villages the Kondh tribesmen cultivated swiddens with *Kodki* (small hoe) and flat lands with plough. There was summary settlement of these lands every 10 years by rough guesswork: *Nazar Paimas*, since 1894 plough tax was recorded: Rupee one per plough and later similar assessment was done in 1903, 1913, 1923, and 1933 (*ibid.* 23).

In Ganjam and Koraput undivided districts, which were under Madras Presidency upto March 31, 1936, Madras Estates Land Act 1908 (amended 1934) was governing their record of rights to land. In other parts of Orissa the Orissa Tenancy Act 1913 (amended 1938) was operative. "The important difference between the Orissa Tenancy Act and the Madras Estate Land Act with regard to recording encroachment over waste lands is that the person encroaching upon *ryoti* land for a continuous period of 12 years automatically becomes a ryot under the Madras Estate Land Act unless in the mean time the land holder (i.e. Zamindar) institute a suit for eviction, whereas under Section 61 of the Orissa Tenancy Act, a ryot who unauthorizedly occupies waste land for a continuous period of four years, the consent of the land holder (proprietor) is deemed to have been given to the occupation, unless in the mean time he makes an application to the Collector for his ejectment." (Ganjam Major Settlement Report: 21–22). In Ganjam Settlement Operations (1938-1962) 2,345.95 acres were recorded as encroachment on communal lands. The encroacher was liable to eviction if no permission was taken from the collector for encroaching upon communal lands.

The legal situation in regard to rights in land and trees and in regard to encroachments on communal lands and waste lands due to adverse possession was discussed above. Usually members of Scheduled Tribes had no ownership documents, but are legally encroachers on the lands they had occupied for decades on basis of traditional rights. As usually they had not taken any legally valid steps to regularize them, this means that they are not eligible for any compensation in case of land acquisition by the government for development projects.

Current Land Tenure Systems

Even after 1948 merger of the ex-princely (feudatory states) in Orissa, there were multiplicity of land tenure system and of the traditional rights to land enjoyed by the tribal people in ex-princely states and ex-zamindary areas in force. The lands were surveyed and tenures were systematically determined at various times in different districts. In the undivided district of Ganjam the Final Report on the Major Settlement Operation (1938-1962) was made officially available in 1963. The Final Report of the Land Revenue Settlement in the undivided Kalahandi district (1946-56) was officially submitted in 1962. The Final Report of the Major Settlement Operations in Koraput District (1938-64) was officially available in 1965. The Report of the Land Revenue Settlement in Bolangir district was not readily available, though other sources were utilized for the purpose.

What was of crucial importance for the traditional rights of the tribal people in the ex-zamindary (ex-estate) areas was the Orissa Estates Abolition Act 1951, which abolished all kinds of intermediary interests and tenures, and thus demolished the age-old barrier between the state and the *raiyats* (the land holders) especially in the undivided Koraput and Ganjam districts. After the passing of the Orissa Merged States (Laws) Act, 1950, the tenants and *Jagir* (service tenure) holders in the ex-state (feudatory states) area acquired better rights in land. Kalahandi, Patna (now Bolangir district) Sonepur (now Subarnapur district), Talcher, Athmallik and Pal Lahara (now constituted as Anugul district), Dhenkanal and Hindol (now constituted as Dhenkanal district) and Bonai and Gangpur (now constituted as Sundargarh district), Bamra and Rairakhol (now constituted as Deogarh district), and Keonjhar and Mayurbhanj (retained as respective undivided districts) were the ex-princely states or ex-feudatory states, which are relevant for our purpose here. The Orissa Act 15 was passed in 1953, under which the Central Provinces Tenancy Act, 1920 which governed the tenancy system in ex-zamindary of Khariar, was amended to make the rights of occupancy tenants more secure with right to transfer by sale, mortgage, gift, bequest or otherwise a part or whole of his holding to a bonafide agriculturist. In case of Scheduled Tribes, free right of transfer were restricted to Scheduled Tribes only. Again the Act was further amended in 1958 to bestow rights on the occupancy tenants to produce stick lac on trees on his land. "With these amendments, the occupancy tenants of the Nawapara sub-division (of Kalahandi district, now reconstituted as Nawapara district) got all the rights which occupancy raiyats of other areas of the state had been enjoying for a long time. "The Orissa Merged Territories (Village Office Abolition) Act of 1963 extinguished the tenure of land rights as village servants, viz. as village headman (Pradhan, Gountia), Chowkidar-watchman, water carrier *(naria),* village priest *(jhakar), pattidar,* etc."

Under Section 8(1) of the Orissa Estates Abolition Act, 1952, the tenants in the *zamindaries* (estates) became the tenants of the state government and they held the land with the same rights and subject to the same restrictions and liabilities as they were entitled or subject to immediately before the date of vesting. In Koraput the *Mustajari* system has been abolished since July 1955.

During the Revenue Settlement Operations in Koraput district lands transferred by hillmen to non-hillmen in contravention of the Agency Tracts Interest and Land Transfer Act of 1917 were not recorded in favour of the transferees. The record *(Khata)* was made in the name of the tribesmen and illegal possession of the transferee describing the nature of transactions: sale, mortgage, gift etc. was recorded.

In Bolangir-Subarnapur districts, all the earlier tenures like *Bhogra* (with protected status for a period of settlement or an agricultural year), service tenure for village servants, Sikkim Rayat or sub-tenants on *bhogra* land, *Thica* tenants (on lease) were abolished and only occupancy ryot tenure or ryotwari tenure remained in force after regularization of the tenure system.

In the other ex-princely states like Dhenkanal, Talcher, and in Anugul areas other tenures like Adhajama Bajyapti Jagirdari (for invalid prisoners and their successors) or Adhajama Annachatra holding for charity purposes were abolished. Under Administration of Orissa States Order, 1948 many Acts of Orissa were extended to the merged princely states and substantial and far reaching tenancy reforms were enacted giving free rights of transfer, full rights over trees standing on the tenant's holdings, protection against increase of rent and against ejectment of occupancy tenants and sukhabasis (landless) notwithstanding anything contained in the Tenancy Laws of the state. Some of these provisions were repeated in the Merged States Laws Act, 1950.

Lands under swidden cultivation on hill slopes above 10 per cent gradient, or even below it, engaged the attention of revenue officers. Some controversies were raised, but resolved to the detriment of the occupation rights of swidden cultivators in Koraput. It will be necessary to go through the stages of development, as ownership rights have been sought to be obliterated on merely technical, though unviable grounds.

"The hill slopes being cultivable come under the definition of *ryoti* land. So the person who had occupied *ryoti* land for 12 years by the date of vesting had become a ryot by adverse possession. The question whether a piece of land is situated above the 10 per cent slope or below it is not relevant from the legal point of view. The view was held that as the *podu* cultivation is not continuous the cultivating persons cannot acquire ryoti right by prescription. Regarding the manner of recording the *podu* lands the Board of Revenue ordered in their letter No. 434-XXI-57/58-L.R.S., dated the 12th March 1959, as follows:

1. All lands in continuous cultivating possession for 12 years prior to the vesting of Jeypore estate in state government, whether these are situated above or below 10 per cent slopes, may be recorded as ryoti lands in favour of the persons in actual cultivating possession of the same.
2. All lands both below and above 10 per cent slopes which are unoccupied will be recorded as government lands.
3. All lands on hill slopes which are not in continuous possession of 12 years at the time of vesting of Jeypore estate in the state government may be recorded as government lands. But against the concerned plot in the remarks column of the record of rights it may be noted that so and so is in the forcible possession of the lands from such and

such years.

The Board of Revenue further issued clarification in their letter No. 604 L.R.S., dated the 17th March 1960, that continuous cultivation does not include *podu* cultivation of any area. The Board of Revenue further sought for clarification from Government in their letter No. 634-XXI-57/58 L.R.S., dated the 21st March 1962, whether the above view was correct. No clarification from Government seems to have been issued so far. In the same letter the Board of Revenue suggested the following procedure to be adopted in the matter of recording of *podu* lands:

"1. The recording of lands in continuous cultivation will stop at 10 per cent slope line. Lands below 1 to 10 boundary will be settled according to the possession and unoccupied lands will be shown as government lands.

2. Lands above the demarcation of 1 in 10 slope should normally be reserved as government lands. But in the contour-bunding operations in certain areas where the population pressure is high, steps are being taken for contour-bunding the twenty degrees line and allow controlled rotational cultivation in the land between these two boundaries. In such areas with the approval of the collector, the area between these two demarcations will be noted as 'land for temporary settlement under special conditions periodically with the approval of the Collector to the village adivasis of the type who normally are habituated to *podu* cultivation.'

No order of the government seems to have been passed on this suggestion of the Board and in the meantime the settlement operation in the district (of Koraput) has been completed. The records previously prepared showing the persons in cultivating possession of lands above or below the 10 per cent lines as ryots in the record of rights stand as such after final publication" (Koraput Major Settlement Report).

There was no gochar or grazing land reserved as common property resource in some ex-princely states. The Government of Orissa in the Board of Revenue has prescribed uniform procedure with effect from 28.8.1961 for recording gochar, village forests, and other communal lands throughout the State of Orissa. Where land is available 10 per cent of the total cultivated area plus *abadjogva anabadi* (culturable waste) should be reserved for gochar, 20 per cent should be reserved as village forest, 5 per cent for other communal purpose including the area for future expansion of homestead sites. Where due to population pressure cultivating land is limited, 5 per cent of the cultivated land for gochar and 10 per cent for communal and village forest etc. should be considered sufficient.

Under the Panchayati Raj Act as per the new constitutional provision for devolution and decentralization of power and resources, social forestry and farm forestry, minor forest produce, roads, culverts, bridges, ferries, water-ways, markets and fairs, maintenance of community assets are the responsibilities of the panchayati raj institutions. They are empowered to manage them and raise resources by taxing their uses. But waste lands, which were the mainstay of the poorer classes in villages for gleaning or food gathering, even encroachment for cultivation or construction of house (in case of being landless or not owning any homestead plot), have not been left to the panchayat management or control.

Orissa's tribal region is administered under the Fifth Schedule of the Constitution, under which the tribal people's age-old and traditional rights on the common property resources are neither exclusive, nor are there much of the village resources earmarked as common property resources for management, control and utilization by the tribal people, as they do in north-eastern Indian states under the Sixth Schedule.

However, the tribesmen have been protected in their rights to land under the protective laws against land alienation, if land has been transferred to non-tribal people. The Orissa Scheduled Areas Transfer of Immovable Property (by Scheduled Tribes) Regulation, 1956 has been mentioned under the section on Constitutional Protection and Legal Framework. Under this regulation tribal land, when illegally alienated, is restored to the original tribal title holder. In 1993-94, 74,457 cases were instituted against illegal alienation and 35,267.434 acres have been restored to 36,618 tribesmen.

Under the Orissa Prevention of Land Encroachment Act 1972, given retrospective effect since 29th October 1954, the government has the power to grant land ownership to "landless" persons, if the encroached land is "cultivable waste" *(abada yogya anabadi);* in such case it is not an objectionable encroachment. A landless person is one who owns no land excluding homestead land and does not own more than one standard acre of land, taking all the land owned by his family members together. But he should have occupied this land for more than 30 years actually, continuously and without any dispute and the land encroached upon should not have been grazing land *(gochar),* reserved *(rakshit)* or *(sarbasadharan)* land for public good and use.

In view of the fact that the tribal people having customary rights over land and other resources in commonly held territories by the village collectivity, did not or could not, acquire legally valid ownership rights in cultivated land on the hill slopes beyond 10° or 10 per cent gradient, the recent executive decision by the government of Orissa in 1994 in respect of the tribal people Kashipur tehasil of Koraput district (at present included in the reconstituted Rayagada district) is of crucial importance in the absence of the state conceding and recognising rights to land, cultivated or otherwise occupied and used, the tribal people were not entitled to any compensation under the Land Acquisition Act (Amended) 1984. This concession by the state government is still restricted to Kashipur tehsil only. But because of its potential applicability to all tribal areas, where swidden (shifting) cultivation is practised or terraces for cultivation have been constructed, or land has been under permanent fruit trees like orange orchards among the Saora of Gajapati (new) district or among the Dongria Kondh of Rayagada (new) district or forest trees planted and grown, this executive decision can form the spring board for a revolutionary change in the state's affirmative action in favour of the tribal people and in the scenario of compensation and proper rehabilitation of displaced tribal people for the sake of development projects or defence or other government-sponsored projects.

Extract from the letter No. 20321 dt. 10.4.92 from deputy secretary to government, Revenue and Excise Dept. addressed to the director of Land Records and Surveys, Board of Revenue, Orissa Cuttack.

"It has been decided that raiyati right shall be conferred on the tribal who are in cultivating possession of the hill slopes either in form of podu or Kudki up to 30°.

Tribals in cultivating possession of the hill slopes above 30° either in form of Kudki or podu or otherwise shall be recorded as raiyats in respect of such land. Conferment of such right is subject to the provision that the land beyond 30° slope shall only be utilized for raising perennial crops in the form of plantation etc. In the remarks column of the patta to be issued in such case, the condition that the land is meant for raising perennial crops in the form of plantations and in the event of failure to do so the right of conferred in respect of such land shall be revoked, shall be recorded.

"Transfer of any land be settled in the manner indicated in para 2 and 3 above is not permissible except by way of mortgage in favour of any public financial institution for securing a loan granted by such institution for any agricultural purpose. The settlement shall be cancelled for violation of this condition. This condition should be appropriately recorded in the remarks column of the patta" (*cf.* Appendix to Mahapatra, 1994a).

If this legal recognition of proprietary and usufructuary rights, enforcing equity and rectifying the colonial administrative injustice, is followed up elsewhere within Orissa and in India, the tribal people will have won a great battle of life, liberty and dignity.

REFERENCES

Bailey, F.G. 1961. "Tribe and Caste in India", *Contributions to Indian Sociology,* 5: 7-10.

Cobden-Ramsay, L.E.B. 1910. Gazetteer of the Orissa Feudatory states. Calcutta.

Denhez, Marxo. 1983. "Folk Law, National Self-Image and their Impact on Sovereignty of Countries," in H.W. Finkler (ed.), *Papers of the Symposia on Folk Law and Legal Pluralism.* Vancouver.

Fernandes, Walter, Geeta Menon and Philip Viegas. 1988. *Forests, Environment and Tribal Economy.* New Delhi: Indian Social Institute.

Government of Orissa. 1940. Report of the partially Excluded Areas Enquiry Committee. Cuttack: Government of Orissa Press.

—. 1962. Kalahandi Revenue Settlement Report. Cuttack: Government of Orissa Press.

—. 1965. Koraput Major Settlement Operations Report. Cuttack: Government of Orissa Press.

—. 1966. Koraput: Orissa District Gazetteers. Cuttack: Government of Orissa Press.

Hidayatullah, M. 1983. *Right to Property and the Indian Constitution.* New Delhi: Arnold Heineman.

Mahapatra, L.K. 1960: *A Hill Bhuiyan Village: An Empirical Socio-Economic Study.* Hamburg: Hamburg University. (mimeographed).

—. 1982.83. "Barriers to Development in Isolated Tribal Areas: Two Case Studies of Most Backward Gram Panchayats in Orissa," *Manav,* 1(1).

—. 1993. "Customary Rights in Land and Forest and the State," M. Miri (ed.), *Continuity and Change in Tribal Society.* Shimla: Indian Institute of Advanced Study.

—. 1994. "Parameters of Forest Policy for Tribal Development," *Social Action,* 44: 91-104.

—. 1994a. *Tribal Development in India: Myth and Reality.* New Delhi: Vikas Publishing House.

Ramadhyani, R.K. 1940's. Report on Land Tenures and the Revenue System of the Orissa and Chhatisgarh States. Vol. III. Government of India.

Roy Burman, B. K. 1982. Report of the Committee on Forest and Tribals in India. New Delhi: Ministry of Home Affairs.

—. 1986. *Historical Ecology of Land Survey and Settlement in Tribal Areas and Challenges of Development.* New Delhi: Council for Social Development.

—. 1992. "Alternative World-views Concerning Self-Management of Tribal Communities and Implications Theories," in N.K. Behura and K.C. Tripathy (eds.), *Science, Culture and Development.* (L.K. Mahapatra Felicitation Volume). Bhubaneswar: Paragon Publishers.

ELEVEN

EXPLOITATION IN TRIBAL AREAS
With Special Reference to Land Alienation

D. L. PRASADA RAO

During my field-work among Jatapu Dora of Srikakulam District in early sixties, it came to my notice that land belonged to the tribesmen earlier is now under the control of merchants. This situation interested me to investigate how this alienation of tribal land had taken place. The present paper is an attempt to describe the tactics the non-tribals adopted to usurp the tribal land.

The Jatapu Dora are a Kuvvi speaking tribal community, and a branch of Khonds. They share with Khonds similar ideas of corporateness of the kin group, and the villages are inhabited by either a single clan or multiclans. Initially the land around the village Errasamanthavalasa was owned by different lineages in the village, and individual families which were cultivating the lands assumed ownership of the land. The Jatapus said that the land presently owned by the *sahukars* belong to them. The investigations of this transfer of land tell us how the tribesmen get exploited by the non-tribals.

An aged Jatapu told how in those days the villages were not linked by roads and the itinerant merchants who used to visit the villages never stayed in the villages, for fear of Malaria. Even drinking water was also avoided by them. In those days there were many wild stories in circulation about the tribesmen. The tribesmen were considered as sorcerers and dangerous people live amidst wild animals, taming them with their magical powers.

An impoverished *sahukar* (merchant) family visited the village and expressed its desire to settle in the village in late 1920's. The tribesmen were very happy and constructed a house for them by the side of headman's house. Till then the non-tribals were avoiding to stay in their village and this stay of the *sahukar* was regarded by the tribesmen as an honour to their village when compared to the other villages. The entry of the *sahukar* family brought many changes in the village. After settling in the village the *sahukar*, opened a petty shop to sell such items as salt, dry fish, kerosine oil, vegetable oil, matches, etc. Most of the transactions between the *sahukar* and tribesmen were of barter type. The tribesmen used to give minor forest produce for the articles they wanted. Besides the commodities mentioned above the *sahukar* used to sell some edible items prepared with rice powder, jaggery, chilly powder. These edible items became very popular among the tribesmen when compared to their aboriginal food which consisted of bitter roots, tubers, etc. The shop become a centre of attraction and every evening tribesmen used to gather before the shop. The *sahukar* had freely given credit to the tribesmen and used to encourage them to take credit if they could not get forest produce to give or money to buy. The *sahukar* had given an assurance to the tribesmen that they can take any thing on credit without hesitation. He made a note of all purchases and by clever manipulation of accounts many tribal families were shown as debtors to him and demanded payment of money. But the tribesmen were not in a position to pay and when he insisted on payment or charge interest, the tribesmen agreed for the latter on the outstanding amount. After two to three years the principal amount and interest along with the fresh credit ran into hundreds and the *sahukar* pressed for payment of money. The tribesmen were not in a position to pay this time also. The *sahukar* then took the issue to the elders in the village and appealed to their conscience that "If their people do not pay him back the dues, his family will die of starvation and the wrath will fall on them". The village elders who were most benefited already instructed all the tribesmen who were indebted to him should pay him or part with a piece of land they were cultivating to write-off the debt. In their anxiety to ward off the wrath of *sahukar* without realizing its consequences on their future life, the tribesmen come forward to part with their lands. Thus started the first transfer of land from tribal to non-tribal and in course of time about 80 per cent of land has gone into the hands of non-tribals. The transaction made by the first *Sahukar* family encouraged others to give loans and get land from the tribesmen. Similar events have been reported from other areas also. Writing about *adivasis* of Attappady hills in Palghat District of Kerala *(Hindu,* 1991, March 3rd) the writer has narrated how the hoteliers who came to that area could easily dispossess the tribal from his land through "spiced masala dosa, sambar chutney". To quote: "Realising their gullibility many hoteliers provided food on credit. Often to lure the *adivasis,* free food was offered initially. Later as the food bill accumulated to a substantial sum, payment was sought. The adivasi not having any money invariably forfeited his land. Thumb impressions on legal paper formalised the transactions." While writing about Inumanda village in Visakhapatnam District, Rao (1988) states as "the *sahukars* after settling down in the village started engaging themselves in a variety of activities through which they derived huge profits. Due to their illiteracy the tribals are at a disadvantage where ever they took loans".

In the tribal-*sahukar* interaction the latter always presented himself to be gentle, amicable person and exhibited an impression that his actions were always on humanitarian grounds to save the tribal from starvation. It is interesting to note that *sahukars* advanced loans only to those who had lands. They used to give advances of petty amounts also for getting the minor forest produce in seasons at a predetermined rate. It was an agonising experience for the tribesmen to part with their lands towards the loans and when they plead to show mercy on them the *sahukars* assured them in the following manner: "Where will I take your land? It will be here and you cultivate it and give me half the produce and you take other half. The transfer of land is only to write-off the debt". With such assurances the tribals felt happy as the *sahukar* promised to allow them to cultivate the land though they transfer the title. They fail to realize the implications of this transaction due to their ignorance and illiteracy and it finally reduced them to the level of bonded labourers. This will be discussed later.

In another village Erramantivalasa the Jatapus sold away their lands in a different situation. The village is near an irrigational canal of a minor irrigation dam. In the year 1956 the Surapadu minor irrigation dam was opened and the tribesmen instead of getting benefit of the canal had to part with their lands. When the irrigation channel was opened the villagers were asked to convert their dry lands into wet lands and each family was given a loan of Rs. 250 by the government. In their anxiety to reap the benefits from the irrigational facility they took further loans from the *sahukar* and converted their dry lands into wet lands. In the first year the yield was not good as they were not familiar with wet cultivation. This had resulted in accumulation of debt. Further the tribals found that the wet crops were less profitable than dry crops as the market value of paddy is less than any dry crop of the same quantity. In addition to the accumulation of debt, low productivity, and low market value of paddy, they were asked to pay a higher tax for the wet land than what they used to pay for the same extent of dry land. The tribal could evade the payment of loan to the *sahukar* for some time but he could not evade the payment of tax. The *karanam* or village tax collector played his own part in oppressing the tribals. His tactics were different from the *sahukars*, he is a man with power and used his position cleverly to grab the land. In many villages in this area the *karanams* were responsible for the alienation of tribal land to the non-tribals and they played their role in a subtle way. Like the *sahukar* the *karanam* also manipulated the tax accounts and grabbed the tribal land by paying taxes on behalf of the tribals when the latter were due. All these dues were converted into a loan and a promissory note was executed. Printed receipts were never given by the *karanams* and the Jatapu said that "he only scribbled something on a piece of paper". The illiterate tribals could not produce receipts nor could give accounts when demanded. The *karanam* always exaggerated the consequences of non-payment of tax ithin a stipulated period, and threatened to report the matter to *tahsildar* ith an advice to jail the defaulter. In such situation the tribesmen had no lternative than to request the *karanam* to help them. This opened up two lternatives to the *karanam*: either he may pay the tax and ask the tribesmen execute a promissory note for the amount or he may take him to a merchant nd ask him to invest on the land by paying the tax due. As the merchants ere anxious to buy wet lands, the *karanams* were not interested to buy. hus the *sahukars* and *karanams* played a crucial role in the alienation of ibal land. Karuppaiyan (1990) quotes a study of Raghava Rao and Bhaskar as on the alienation of tribal lands in Tamilnadu, wherein it is mentioned at 37 per cent of the households had suffered land alienation. The study urther observed that generally small size tribal holdings were most effected.

An examination of the tenure systems that were in operation in the gency areas tell us how they were beneficial to the non-tribals than the ibal. Some of the tenure systems have virtually reduced the tribals to the tate of bonded labourers. As stated already the non-tribal land owner always etained the erstwhile tribal owner to cultivate the land. This strategy instils a sychological feeling in the latter that he is still cultivating his land. But ehind this play there is a bigger plan to fool him. This plan is operated rough two systems of land tenure which are highly exploitative and are nown as (1) *paalu bhagam*, and (2) *gollamagatha* or share cropping without nvestment.

Under *paalu bhagam* the non-tribal land owner and the tribal cultivator ave to share equally the cost of production. Since the tribal cultivator is npoverished he depends on the land owner for every thing towards his part f contribution. The tribal provides the much needed labour which is highly evalued by the land owner at the time of sharing the produce. During the ield work a share cropping case was taken to examine the share portions. It as found that on one acre of land the estimated yield was 500 measures *kunchan* locally called) of paddy which was divided between the owner and e tenant as per conditions in the following: From the total 500 measures, 0 measures for harvesting and 20 measures for threshing were taken out as ommon expenditure by both the parties. The remaining 460 measures were ivided between the two as 230 measures for each. But from the cultivator's ortion he should give to the owner 30 measures for seeds (three times of the 0 measures he had taken from him) and 60 measures for investment made y the owner to purchase manure and expenses for transplantation which was rorated in terms of grain as 20 measures. Then finally the owner's share as 320 measures or 9 bags and the cultivators share was 140 measures or 4 ags. For the advances the tribal takes for his other expenses at least one or vo bags are taken away. Thus the cultivator who was earlier the owner of e land had to content with a fraction of the produce he gets from his own nd.

In the other tenure system *gollamagatha* the owner does not inves anything on land, but enters into a contract with the tribal cultivator, for fixed quantity of grain. Even if there is a failure of crop the tribal cultivato should give him the grain or must execute a promissory note for an estimate value of the crop. Despite the risk involved in this system of tenure some o the tribesmen agree to this arrangement under the hope that if God favour them they can get more.

It is a vicious circle in which the tribesmen live as their monetar requirements drive them to the merchant-cum-money lender who readil gives them as he can get benefit by the transaction in the form of mino forest produce or land. In Inumanda and the neighbouring village Dhamavaram *sahukars* issue crop advances and *Tirumanamu* or conditione loans. The conditioned loans are given in terms of giving a certain produce t the *sahukar* at a predetermined rate irrespective of the market price.

Many tribal uprisings like the Srikakulam movement of 1970, Adilaba of 1981 had their roots basically in the land question as well as the oppressiv forest regulations. One of the causes very often cited for this state of affair is the indifference of officials at local level to the problems of the tribesmen.

The local leaders also in many cases joined hands with the merchants especially the friendship with merchants helped them to have contacts wit other non-tribal officials. While writing about the situation in Inumanda i Visakhapatnam district Rao (1988) writes without the cooperation of th naidu and peddalu, the *sahukars* could not have settled down in Inumanda nor the shandy could be established: "Those who attempt to challenge th *sahukars* accounts are even admonished by the Peddalu (village elders) fo not being careful in spending money and taking loans" (Rao, 1988). As fa back as 1945 Haimendorf while writing about the Reddies of Bison Hill observed how the merchant who entered into the area became powerful b joining hands with the local leaders. The internal exploitation in triba communities has been noted by earlier anthropologists. Bose (1964) cam out heavily on such internal exploitation in tribal communities and lamente that no attempt has been made to correct. Rao (1988) writes "These leader and rich Valmikis became 'tribal *sahukars*' and they do not possess th disadvantages of *sahukars* as the existing law cannot punish them even i they attach the land of the debtors". The influence of non-tribal land owner in tribal areas is strong that they can get even the protective legislatio repelled as it happened in Andhra Pradesh in 1988.

The interference of non-tribals especially in the local panchayats is known fact. It may be either ideological or personal power politics. Th *sahukars* and teachers who constitute the bulk of non-tribal population ar very active and use the tribals as pawns.

In my study (1983) of Bhadragiri block it has been found that *sahukar* nd teachers emerged as two vital groups in the panchayat which afterwards ulminated into the former aligning with congress and the latter with ommunists. The tribal followers are also divided on these lines. The Naxalite novement in Srikakulam collapsed when the non-tribal communists from lains had swelled into the cadres and the tribals withdrew their support. The hoice of tribal area as hideouts by non-tribals who indulge in unlawful ctivities also can be considered as a type of exploitation by the non-tribals. n these cases the innocent tribals are being used as a shield by the different actional leaders of Naxalites. Thus exploitation of tribals has become a ontinuous process in one form or other. This is because of the backwardness f the people and the location of rich resources in tribal areas. A balanced pproach is necessary to protect the tribesmen and to promote the national nterests.

REFERENCES

Bose, N.K. 1964. "Integration of Tribes of Andhra Pradesh." *Man in India,* 44: 29-30.

Dubey, S.N. and Ratna Murdia (eds.). 1977. *Land Alienation and Restoration in Tribal Communities.* Bombay: Himalaya Pub. House.

'urer-Haimendorf, C.Von. 1945. *The Reddis of Bison Hills—A Study in Acculturation.* London: Macmillan.

'he Hindu. March 3, 1991. Dispossessed-for Idlis and Dosas

Kamala Manohar Rao, P. and D.L. Prasada Rao. 1983. "Tribal Movements in Andhra Pradesh," in K.S. Singh (ed.), *Tribal Movements in India.* Vol. 2, New Delhi: Manohar.

Karuppaiyan, E. 1990. "Alienation of Tribal Lands in Tamil Nadu", *Economic and Political Weekly,* 2 June 1990, pp. 1185-86.

Prasada Rao, D.L. 1970. An Analysis of Kinship, Economy and Religion of Jatapus-A Scheduled Tribe of Andhra Pradesh. Unpublished Ph.D. Thesis, Waltair: Andhra University.

—. 1971. "Shahukar in Tribal Society," *Tribe,* 8 (3&4): 7-13.

Rao, P.V. 1988. *Institutional Framework for Tribal Development.* New Delhi: Inter-India Publications.

TWELVE

PERCEPTION OF *OIKOS, NOMOS* AND *LOGOS*
Tribal Predilections and Non-Tribal Polemics

SAMARENDRA SARA

Dwelling on the creation myth the *Holy Bible* has depicted man as the idyllic creature whom "God created... in his own image"[1] and placed in the sylvan retreat where

> "living together, the first human ancestors—Adam and Eve—roamed all free as air, wrapped in the Garden of Eden bliss and bathed in the eternal charm of youth of vernal green with flowerets blossoming-blooming, spreading soft aroma around.
>
> Here Nature was bounteous-beauteous, arresting and bracing the clime. Abounding in hills and dales and groves and meadows far and wide. Foliage rich, bushes and trees luxuriant, plants and creepers wild laden with buds and flowers and fruits—soft and sweet and ripe.
>
> Eden was filled to the brim with fragrance maddening-enchanting, Hovering like a charmed dream on a fair belle's weary eyes; here nymphs and seraphims cast their spell on the garden air; here sprightly Muses sang their blithe hymns—all serene; here bliss didst gently beat her trumpets in the cataract murmurs"[2].

Countless centuries later, when the great English poet John Milton took up the same grand theme "to cut a colossus from a rock",[3] that is, his epic poem-*Paradise Lost,* as a piece of poesy "unattempted yet in prose or rhyme"[4] and chose "to sing of Time of Eternity (as) the mighty-mouthed ivestor of harmonies (and) the God-gifted organ voice of England",[5] his aim was just to "assert eternal providence and justify the ways of God of men".[6] For, in his majestic blank verse, he retold the saga of seduction of the primeval parents and their falling an easy prey to the lure of the evil one, situating them in the same fateful garden where their "first disobedience"[7] was committed with "the first of that forbidden tree whose mortal taste brought death into the world and all our woe with the loss of Eden".[8]

The creation myth has ever since been rehearsed and the expulsion legend narrated umpteen times through the centuries that rolled by, each rehearsal reinforcing the myth and each narration lending further credence to the legend. And, lo and behold: the Tree of Knowledge has ever served as the symbolic "green altar"[9] that stood as a mute testimony tc man's creation and expulsion, the loss of Eden getting more than recompensed when, after shedding "some natural tears (and) hand in hand with wandering steps and slow through Eden, (Adam and Eve) took their solitary way"[10] seeking their first refuge amid unfamiliar rocks and unfriendly beasts while eking out their earthly existence in the forest wilderness.

The shift of the site thenceforth from the biblical garden to the prehistoric caves and woods market just a very small step but, in the long run, it proved to be a great leap: it came to stand as the "leaf-fringed legend"[11] of the human destiny wedded once and for all to the forest lore—the legend that the palaeobotanists heard as the "tongues in trees"[12] spoke to them or the geologists read in the "book (of) the running brooks"[13] or the archaeologists as the grave-diggers retrieved from the inscriptions they found engraven as the "sermons in stones";[14] the legend that goes to inform us of how the vast stretches of our palaeolithic and mesolithic past had once lasted so long as to spare for our neolithic phase only one-twentieth part of our one million years[15] on the earth.

The time scroll of our stone age era also goes to inform us of how our hunting-gathering forerunners got freed from their pursuits for a precarious subsistence and how they moved onto the primitive hoe culture, how our nomadic precursors came to have their sedentary mode of living and how they bade a fair adieu to their erstwhile philosophy of life of vagrancy that is perhaps best encapsulated (in an altogether different situational context though) in the following phrase from John Milton's elegiac poem--"tomorrow to fresh woods and pastures new"[16] and moved on to that of the rural settlements marked by the cultural complex of fields and huts, domestic pets and pasture-lands throbbing with a new content of life and fringed by the forests luxuriant and green. The caveman was transformed into a hut-dweller. The collector of food got turned into a producer of roots and fruits and cereals of different kinds. The hunter had learned the secrets of the animal lore to tame and domesticate some friendly beasts for their flesh and fat and milk hither, for their hide and wool, their horns and hoofs thither.

Cut off from the civilizational mainstream, the primitive men as the heir-apparent of the biblical Adam and Eve or as the bonafide descendants of the "missing link" continued to live in their equally primitive but blessed habitat of hills and dales hither, of forests and deserts thither. Every continent was bestrewn with their populations sizeable; every archipelago hosted them on its native soil; every island registered their presence as its proud autochthones too. While living in jungles "as free as nature first made (them), wild in woods the noble savage ran"[17]. And, while so running amok hither and thither, the primitive hunter-gatherer got thoroughly familiar with every nook and corner of his sylvan environ. and, while tending his flocks of sheep, "the shepherd. . . grew at last acquainted with love, and found him a native of the rocks"[18]—the aged rooks where, many a century later, the first lawgiver-prophet of the Hebrew-speaking people of yore had come to receive the Ten Commandments from the Almighty;[19] the solitary rocks where, in some solemn moment, God didst appear to Moses in the burning bus there, just to reveal his name and identity as "I am";[20] the rocks where the Saviour of mankind had ever preached his "sermon on the mount".[21]

Several changes got ushered in as time rolled on; in their festive moods the primitive folk congregated every New Year Dawn to

"Ring out the old bells, ring in the new,
Ring, happy bells, across the snow;
Ring in the nobler modes of life,
With sweeter manners, purer laws.
Ring out the want, the care, the sin,
The faithless coldness of the times;
Ring out false pride in blood and place,
The civic slander and the spite.
Ring out the thousand years of old,
Ring in the thousand years of peace".[22]

For centuries unnumbered and millennia unremembered the primitive continued to ring out every year the bells betokening their age-old hostilities and strife while ringing in their hopes and expectations for several thousand years of peace in the same vein in which the vedic seers had ever chanted their *santipatha*[23], thus: *oṁ dyauḥ śāntirantarikṣa śāntiḥ pṛithivīśāntirāpaḥ Śāntiroṣadhyaḥ, Śāntiḥ, vanaspatayaḥ, śāntirvisvedevāḥ śāntiḥ brahmaśāntih sarvaṁ śāntiḥ śāntirevaśāntiḥ,* which expresses a vitalistic and organic view enlivened by an interdependence between the macrocosm and the microcosm, a harmony and a concordance between the votary and the world, and which also goes to hint to a symphony that is sought to be rehearsed at the very outset of every ritual performance. So does the atharvavedic seer's "Pṛīthivī Sūkta"[24] go to establish the man-nature relationship in terms of their kindred filiation as *mātā bhūmih putrōham prthivyāh parjanyāh pitāh* and echoes the same organic world view that is reflected in the *sāntipātha* above. Likewise, the Chinese[25] philosophers had long enshrined the father-mother metaphor of the atharvavedic hymn in their male-female conceptualization of the *Yin-Yang* principles and visualized their harmonious functioning on the entire cosmic plane.

Like the Chinese metaphysical constructs of *Yin* and *Yang* were conceptualized the complementary dyads of the Hindu tantrism as Śiva-Śakti[26] or statis-dynamis or the like where their metaphysical complementarity (recall the Nobel Laureate Neils Bohr's principle of complementarity[27] as *contraria sunt complementa*[28]) yields a holism and harmony on the ontological plane. What a world view of organic interdependence is visualized by the vedic seer when he invokes the cosmic forces in the following *ṛca: oṁ payah pṛthivyāṁ payo osadhīsu payodivyantarikṣapayodāḥ pavasvatiḥ pradiśaḥ santu mahyaṁ*[29]? And do not the Baiga and the Kamar predilections and polemics and ethics, when advanced in support of their resolute abstinence from plough cultivation, go to resound a prosaic reiteration of the aforesaid great traditional ethos of the vedic seers in their little traditional tribal settings? Do not the tribal beliefs relating to totemism, animatism and animism go to transform a tree into an organic, vitalistic sanctum sanctorum?[30]

It is so very interesting to recall here what great compliment the renowned Sanskrit poet Panditarāja Jagannātha has paid to the trees:

> "My obeisance to the venerable trees that bear the burden of leaves and flowers and fruits, standing firm in the scorching heat of the sun and enduring the rigours of the chilling winters while sacrificing even their bodies for others' sake".[31]

Likewise, it was none other than the celebrated Roman poet, Virgil, who had echoed the Graeco-Roman myth of the woods as the favourite haunts of the celestial beings, while composing his *Ecologue* in his highly spirited moods, thus:

> "You teach the woods to echo back the charms of Amaryllis. Whom do you flee, madman? Even gods have lived in the woods".[32]

And it was the Nature-poet William Wordsworth who had perceived the woods as the teachers of moral philosophy *par excellence:*

> "One impulse from a vernal wood
> May teach you more of man,
> Of moral evil and of good,
> Than all the sages can".[33]

And while invoking his readers to join him for a stroll in his "Woodland Peace", George Meredith has found "the enchanted woods (of Westermain where) sweet as Eden (was) the air and Eden sweet the ray".[34] So had the

TRIBAL CULTURES AND THEIR SYLVAN EXTENSIONS

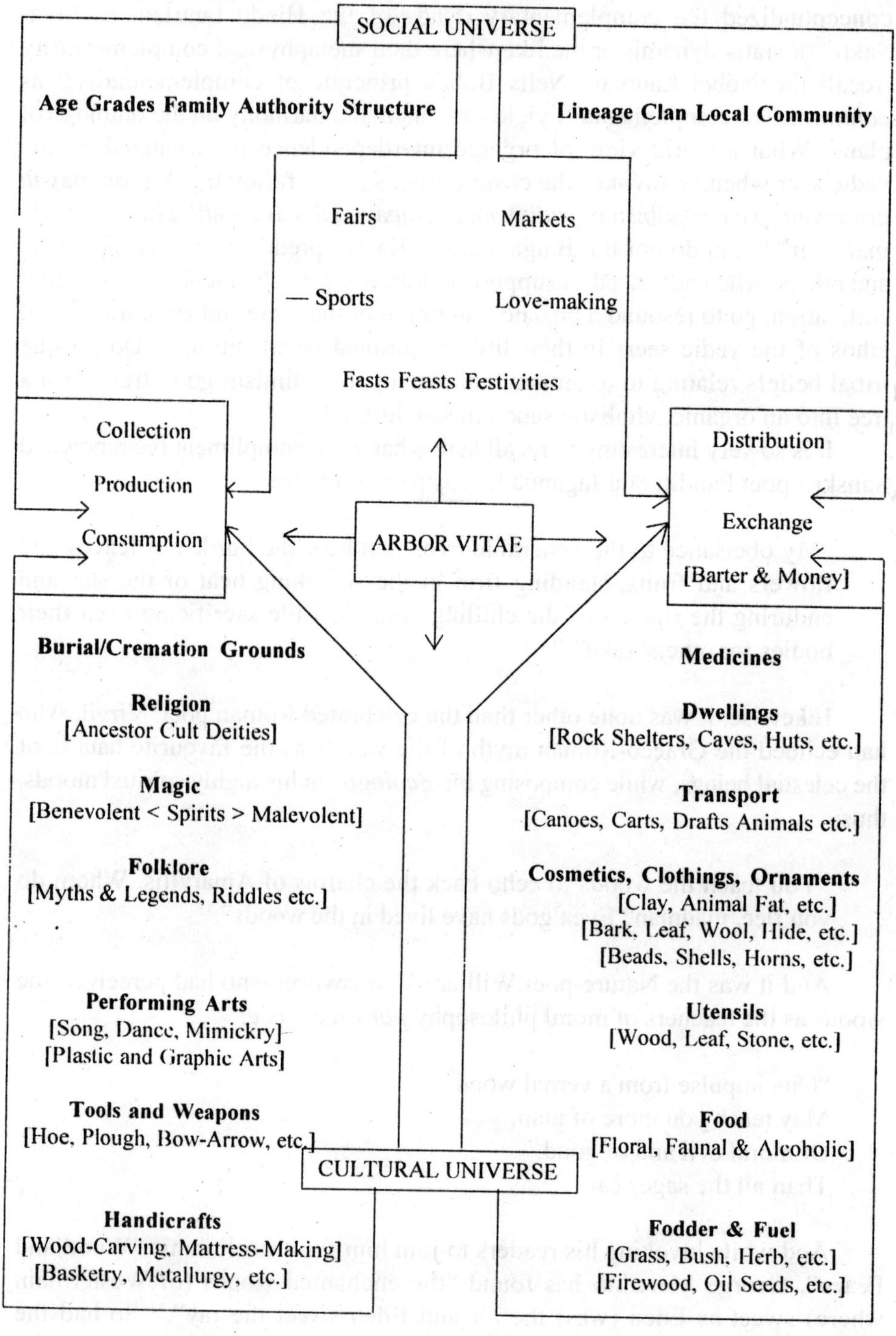

tribals their own cultural perceptions of their *oikos* and *nomos* and *logos* and invested their forests therewithal with a semantic new or "a local habitation and a name" for their *arbor vitae,* as the accompanying diagram displays.

From the matrix of the tribal people's chauvinistic/jingoistic filiation got begotten the nostalgia in which forests stood for them as their life-blood or their mainstay; and the total habitat came to symbolize to them what the wizard of the north, Sir Walter Scott, had characterized in his patriotic zeal and poetic fervour as "this is my own, my native land". Forests provided them their home and hearth, their food as roots and fruits and edible foliage along with the wild game of different species—aquatic, avian or terrestrial; they stood for the centre of their economic pursuits of collection, production, consumption, distribution and exchange; and all these activities held them together in a natural bond of piety, as it were. Forests gave them the arena for their games and sports hither, the favourite haunts and hideouts for their amorous trysts in the youthful dormitories thither. Forest yielded them the raw material for their genius to express itself in their artistic-aesthetic creations as wood-carvings, basketry and clay-modelling, let alone their ornaments and apparels, the tools and implements of their trade, the whole gamut of their musical instruments that made up their orchestral inventories, and their primitive garrisons of bows and arrows, boomerangs and clubs, spears and spear-throwers that constituted their offence and defence mechanism and strategies.

Forests marked the chosen places where their prayers and incantations of secret mystical formulas resounded, where their sacrificial rites involves a fowl here, a cattle there, occasionally a human being elsewhere were solemnized with great zeal and zest. Here places were demarcated for their mortuaries and crematoriums where their heart-rending bewailments were raised to the heavens. Here stood their *sanctum sanctorum* where their magico-religious rites were performed, where the sanctuaries for their clan totems and patron deities were enclosed with many a golden bough.

It was here in the forest thicknesses that there stood their "little woodland lake of Nemi–'Diana's mirror', as it was called by the ancients"[37]—the lake surrounded by "the sacred grove and the sanctuary of (their) Diana Nemorensis and (their) Rex Nemorensis or King of the Wood". Here some mighty priest personated himself as Diana's lover:

> "In his character of the founder of the sacred grove and first king of Nemi (he) is clearly the mythical predecessor of the archetype of the line of priests who came, like him, to a violent end. . .
> . . . the mortal King of the wood (who) had for his queen the woodland Diana herself--Diana . . . revered as the goddess of woodlands and of wild creatures, probably also of domestic cattle and of the fruits of the earth; that she was believed to bless men and women with offspring and

to aid mothers in child-bed; that her holy fire tended by chaste virgins, burned perpetually in a round temple within the precinct; that associated with her was a water-nymph Egeria who discharged one of Diana's own functions by succouring women in travail, and who was popularly supposed to have mated with an old Roman king in the sacred grove".[38]

What sir James George Frazer had written in his "gold and purple style"[39] while attempting his prosaic portrayal of forests and gardens of the Graeco-Roman myths, Samuel Taylor Coleridge attempted in his poetic depiction in his unfinished poem--"Kubla Khan," thus:

" . . . there were gardens bright with sinuous rills,
Where blossomed many an incense-bearing tree;
And here were forests ancient as the hills,
Enfolding sunny spots of greenery.
A savage place! As holy and enchanted
As ever beneath a wining moon was haunted
By Woman wailing for her demon lover".[40]

And it was again their forests that offered them the stage for their performing arts—the open-air stadium for the public recitals of their folk songs hither, for the performance of their folk dances and operas thither. They served as the venue for their colourful annual fairs, marking the rounds of fasts, feasts and festivities in honour of the tribal deities here, those of higgle-haggle at the market places there. Forests stood as a veritable complex, indeed.

"Until the base laws of servitude began", the tribal way of life stood as the virgin cultures so much so that they could have been characterized in the same figurative vein in which John Keats had addressed the Grecian Urn:

"Thou still unravished bride of quietness,
Thou foster-child of silence and slow time![41]

But the tribal precincts have changed past imagination; and so have changed their ecology and economy, their science and technology--indigenous, their social networks and cultural moorings, their norms and value orientation, and what not. How the forests in the tribal scenario came to witness some very radical transformation can perhaps best be understood by sitting in retrospection for a fresh and dispassionate survey of the past few centuries of our scientific and industrial advancement that have made a deep impact on the human psyche by bequeathing to the world at large the legacy of a cumulative knowledge, rational in tone albeit partisan in spirit. It is this tradition of scientific knowledge that has made its determined strides and marked its all-too-confident, all-too-spectacular and all-too-triumphant march towards one pole, as it has augmented "all our woe" of the post-scientific, post-industrial and post-information-technology revolutions by heightening the fears of extinction of life and culture at the opposite pole. Severe dents have been caused by the techno-scientific innovations making their deep inroads into the calm and quiet tribal precincts, including their forest reserves and resources.

The entire span of the past few centuries is the saga of some very radical changes, some of them being positive in their outcome, others being negative in their overall impact. The whole span also stands a mute testimony to the embarrassing fact of the ushering in of a *mechanistic world view* in lieu of its age-old counterpart of the *organic world view.*[42] If we recall the Baconian-Cartesian-Newtonian metaphors, their immediate import and their far-reaching, long-term implications, we get to the inevitable conclusion which the historians of civilizations and the philosophers of science are now arriving at: the inauguration and enshrinement of the mechanistic world view as an *ego-centred way of life*[43] has rustically marched and remorselessly trampled over the organic world view *that was essentially an eco-centred way of life.*[44]

The Baconian dictum *"to torture Nature's secrets from her,* to have her *hounded in her wanderings. . . bound into service* (and) *put in constraints"* (emphases supplied), the Cartesian water-tight compartmentalization of *res extensa* and *res cogitans* as the two distinct and impassable universes, on one hand, and his placement of higher stakes on the former, on the other, and the Newtonian projection of the world as a huge big machine governed by the laws of mechanics—every metaphorical depiction only begot a psyche oriented towards a materialistic, aggressive, competitive, expanding, ego-centric, ethnocentric and exploitative ethos that was grossly hedonistic in its tone and tenor, motivated by an urge for self-aggrandisement, haunted by a Narcissus complex, rooted in the sadism of a peculiar description, untroubled and untortured by any qualms of conscience. It hardly needs to be stressed here that the whole saga of the tribal problems, including thier ecology and economy as revolving around the forest habitat, is to be traced back to the mechanistic world view and the monstrosties of its psyche.

One may well find it further disquieting and distressing, perhaps also equally disenchanting, to run into such occasional characterizations that go to project a one-sided picture or a distorted view of the reality by placing a rather singular and exclusive onus on the head of the tribals for whatever gross depletion of forest resources and whatever indiscriminate exploitation of forest wealth have come about during the post-Independence era in our country. For instance, the *obiter dictum*—"Despite the privileges and concessions for the tribals, they have been guilty of destruction of forest in the forest areas"[47]—is a categorical pronunciamento that is tentamount to an *ex parte* decree (or damnation!). Likewise, whenever it is complainingly alleged that

> "Even several times various commissions and committees have recommended to integrate the forestry programmes with the growth of tribal economy, yet the degree of development has not reached to that extent".[48]

Such biases go to alert the students of the science of man, culture and society in regard to the cartography of the psyche whence they have proceeded. For it is here that any anthropologist is likely to find his shoe pinching.

Frankly speaking, passages like the ones cited above present a lop-sided portrayal of the situation, ignoring the causative factors and forces that have been all-too-diverse and all-too-decisive in their impact as they have been primarily non-tribal or extra-tribal in their origin and identity. Let us simply recall the entire saga of invasion of our tribal precincts by such processes as urbanization, industrialization, proselytization and money economy, to name just a few, that have so radically transformed the tribal canvas as much as they have so drastically vitiated the tribal ethos. Had not the seventeenth century master satirist, John Dryden, sounded a like note of diagnosis in his poem-"The Conquest of Granda"—when he had so very rhetorically complained:

> "I am as free as nature first made man,
> Ere the base laws of servitude began,
> When wild in woods the noble savage ran"?[49]

Had not the eminent poet viewed the entire metamorphosis of "the noble savage" all the world over as a process rooted in what he calls "the base laws of servitude" and what the anthropologists go to characterize as the forces of colonization that inaugurated the era of ruthless exploitation of our tribal ecology and economy here, of rank and gross vitiation of the tribal psyche there?

All our failures, foibles and follies as well as all aspirations and frustrations of our tribal brethren in regard to forest management and development vis-a-vis tribal ecology and economy during the recent past need be re-examined against the total backdrop which is no other than the present-day tribal value orientations, ethos, politics, ethics, education, religion, trade and commerce, to name a few, that have proceeded from the matrix of and are rooted in the compulsions or concomitants of urbanization, industrialization, proselytization, westernization, modernization, secularization and the like—thoroughly nurtured and nourished by the mechanistic orientation of thought that we have smuggled ourselves into the tribal settings. Let us recall Carolyn Merchant's carping note that voices it fairly, vocally and rhetorically, thus:

> "*The image of the earth as a living organism and nurturing mother served as a cultural constraint restricting the actions of human beings. One does not readily slay a mother, dig into her entrails for gold, or mutilate her body . . . As long as the earth was considered to be alive and sensitive, it could be considered a breach of human ethical behaviour to carry out destructive acts against her*" (emphases supplied).

Indeed, merchant has paid a very eloquent tribute to the organic world view that it merits. It does not go to condemn the Cartesian-Newtonian world view nor does it deride the spectacular strides and the indisputable successes that it has made in the direction of our material affluence and comforts. None would deny that science and technology have opened the portals to the domain of an unprecedented knowledge from the infra-microscopic world to the supra-telescopic universe, that they have generated new hopes and invested a new meaning and content to life. What Merchant's passage does is to bring into sharp focus the overall changes that have been wrought in our psyche and our approach to reality—our approach that has become more fragmented than holistic, more mechanistic than organic, exploitative than conservative, competitive than cooperative, exclusive than inclusive, ego-centred than eco-centred, and so on.

When we sit to reflect on what we have lost due to our mechanistic world view, we painfully discover that the sylvan hinterland which once celebrated its vernal moods of ecstasies, inspiring the poets of yore to sing of "the blushful Hippocrene"[51] hither, of the "flora and the country green, dance, and provencal song, and sunburnt mirth"[52] thither, of the "woods that wave o'er Delphi's steep"[53] elsewhere, has long lost its native fun and frolic, its brimming gaiety and wild ecstasy. Today, the forests in the tribal areas stand as "the woods that have no voice but the voice of complaining".[54] The tribals who once moved hopefully "tomorrow to fresh woods and pastures new" or ran wild in the woods, now find vast expanses of what the Nobel Laureate, T.S. Eliot, has called "the waste land".[55] Today, we are virtually forced to recall how the scientific revolution has turn us farther away from Nature evermore and to confess like a complaining and lamenting William Wordsworth, thus:

> "The world is too much with us; late and soon,
> Getting and spending, we lay waste our powers;
> Little do we see in Nature that is ours;
> We have given our hearts away, a sordid boon;
> The sea that bares her bosom to the moon;
> The winds that will be howling all the hours,

And are up-gathered now like sleeping flowers.
For this, for everything, we are out of tune".[56]

When we turn our attention to the cultures of the East, the Far-East and the indigenous folk, we stand face-to-face with their organic world view in which these people once lived (as some of them still continue to live) in small and close-knit, wellnigh self-contained and self-sufficient communities, experiencing Nature in terms of organic relations, where the material forces and phenomena were conceived in communion and comunication with the spiritual forces and phenomena, where Body-Mind, Matter-Spirit split was never visualized. In other words, the organic world view has been human, conservative, inclusive, and collectivistic in its character as against the mechanistic world view which has been ruthlessly a-human (or may we go to characterize it as inhuman?), exploitative, exclusive and individualistic.

Moreover, the indigenous folk see no cleavage between Matter and Mind, Body and Spirit, *res extensa* and *res cogitans;* but, in their organic world view, they treat these polar opposites in their continuous, coextensive and complementary interplay. Such situation renders it all the more imperative that, whatever be our recommendations for forest development *vis-à-vis* tribal economy, the blueprint thereof needs must be drawn in terms of an organic-systemic world view that is as much familiar and native to the tribal psyche as it is congenial and conducive to them. Moreover, it also stands in tune (also to reason) with the emerging awareness of the ecologic, holistic, systemic, relativistic world view that is preparing itself to bid an adieu, for good, to the Cartesian-Newtonian legacy of the world view egologic, fragmented, non-systematic and absolutistic in its code and content, also in its orientation and perspective. May we, therefore, go to reiterate that, rather than blame the tribals for forest destruction, we had better go self-searching and inward-looking, probing deeper into our own psyche, our ethics, our laws, our polity, our economy and our exploits. In sum, we have to look afresh and anew at our own Narcissus complex and our egocentrism or, may we call it, our megalomania.

There is no gainsaying the fact that, by forcing the penetration of our science and technology, our economy and polity, our ideology and ethics, we have not only invaded the sleepy tribal precincts of land and forest but also deprived the tribals by and by of their rights thereto, on one hand, but, by imposing our mechanistic world view on them we have also wrought "the loss of their nerve",[57] tearing them adrift from their indigenous moorings and rending them asunder from their native genius that once made them find "tongues in trees, books in the running brooks, sermons in stones, and good in everything", on the other. During the colonial phase, the imposition of the forest policy and the blows of its rigours made them forget their pastoral gaiety, their native spontaneity, their innocence and simplicity about which the celebrated dramatist of the Elizabethan period had once sung in his full-throated ease, thus:

"Under the greenwood tree
Who loves to lie with me,
And turn his merry note
Unto the sweet bird's throat,
Come hither, come hither, come hither:
Here shall he see
No enemy
But winter and rough weather".[58]

Furthermore, the Cartesian-Newtonian perceptions and projections have ignored the truism that man is not merely a Body but also a Mind, not only matter but also Spirit, not only *jada* (insensate) but also *cetana* (sensate), not only a *res extensa* or an automaton like a robot having sophisticated mechanico-electronic gadgetry and performing miraculous tasks and feats but also a *res cogitans* throbbing with what the Czech playwright Karel Capek[59] has characterized as "the little bit of madness" which relates him to ethics and aesthetics and spirituality here, philosophy and rationality there; that man does not simply eke out his existence as a microcosm in the pysical universe but also relates himself as an integral part and parcel of the macrocosm; that he is not merely bound by the immutable laws of biology but also by the inexorable and decisive role of ecology (including the socio-cultural factors, forces and phenomena); that he is both genetics and environment (as that Galileo of Biology, Charles Darwin, had it) insofar as the genetic processes give him life and the environmental processes sustain and shape the content thereof, that man is not merely an *ego-system* but also an *eco-system;* that only a harmonious blending of the polar opposite dyads is the real holistic view.

Such conceptualizations have ushered in a new awareness and brought about a revolutionary change in our outlook. This new perception is the child begotten by the post-Einsteinian world view, partly rooted in the relativistic frame (unlike that of Descartes and Newton which is absolutistic and reductionist in its character) and partly embedded in the emerging systemic view of the phenomenal world. What Arthur Koestler has conceptualized in his coinage of "holon"[60] and what we have called holistic, organic world view is something that comes closest to the overall ethos of the tribals.

A new intellectual climate had started to set in, bringing in new ideas, new formulations and new theoretical insights, immensely consequential in their magnitude and mighty original and challenging and redoubtable in their impact. An arm-chair theorist in the domain of mathematics and physics appeared with his revolutionary theorizing and dared cross the seventeenth century celebrity of a great scientists whom Alexander Pope had paid perhaps the richest tribute:

> "Nature and Nature's laws lay hid in night:
> God said: 'Let Newton be!' and all was light".[61]

Impulses of intellectual agitation began to be felt when there dawned on the horizons of the positive sciences many a disturbing recognition or realization of the truism: what incalculable harm has been done and what monstrosities have been fostered by the Cartesian dichotomy; how a fragmented world view has led us adrift evermore from a holistic view of life and the universe; how the body has been cared for, while neglecting its in-dwelling spirit; how the pleasures of the body have been augmented at the expenses of the bliss of the soul. Such realization speeded up new modes of research in a new scientific temper. The task of piecing the fragments together into an organic unity got initiated with the meteoric appearance of Albert Einstein on the firmament of the physical sciences—his appearance warming up the field of what John Keats had once called the "cold philosophy". For the Newtonian conceptualization of material absolutism and determinism was being subjected to the acid test of the theory of relativity.[62]

Animated discussions ensued and enlivened the scientific forums all the world over, when Newtonian physics was begun to be bombarded along its weakest flank. Furthermore, it generated some furore when, in his relativist frame of mind, Albert Einstein made his bold and provocative utterance, an unprecedented pronunciamento that ever came from a scientist: "Science without religion is lame and religion without science is blind".[63] Had not Einstein echoed the Samkhyan ontology when he employed the metaphorical tool of the *andha-paṅgu-nyāya*[64] that brings the principles of *Purusa* (mind) and *Prakrti* (matter) into a happy communion or consummation for the phenomenal world to proceed? Likewise, does not Neils Bohr's *principle of complementarity*[65] aim at a like reconciliation as contraria sunt complementa,[66] obliquely and impliedly, between mind and matter as the two fundamental realities that are usually thought of as mutually exclusive and polar opposite of each other?

Likewise, when Heisenberg propounded his *principle of indeterminacy* (popularly known as the *Principle of Uncertainty),* did it not revive and resurrect the ancient riddle of the philosophers—"a certain freedom in the realm of natural phenomena"[67]—as the only plausible explanation for the otherwise erratic behaviour of the sub-atomic particles? It is equally fruitful to recall; when Maharsi Dayananda talked about the polar opposite aspects of the vedic culture as *mṛṇmaya* (material) and *cinmaya* (spiritual or mental)[68] or the renowned physicist of our time, Daulat Singh Kothari, dwelt on the dichotomy of the levels of existence as the "I" (Internal) World and the "E"

(External) World,[69] they were also harping on the same Cartesian string of *res extensa* and *res cogitans*, although they parted Descartes' company in their unequivocal emphasis on the synthesis and mutual inter-relatedness rather than exclusiveness and impassability of the two, or in the placement of any higher premium on the one at the cost of the other. Likewise, the tantric philosopher had placed his singular emphasis on the cardinal principles of binary opposition when he conceptualized his ontological realities into a mutually inclusive complementarity and therewithal worked out their fundamental unity similar to that of the Advaita Vedantins, while epitomizing and anthropomorphizing the principles of Siva and Sakti in lieu of Brahman and Maya as the *statis* and the *dynamis* respectively. And, thus, the prestigious notion of holism, begotten in all-too-diverse ways in the equally diverse disciplines, soon started gaining ground and currency in the natural and physical sciences, and the one-time "cold philosophy" started getting all the while warmer too.[71]

Parallel to the awakening in the domains of the natural/physical and biological sciences, there asserted a similar realization which forced itself up in the field of technology here, the humanities there and the social sciences elsewhere. Let us recall the technological myth of the Statue of Golem whose ever-increasing monstrous proportions made its benign architect, the Rabbi of Prague, feel mortally scared and resolve to arrest the growth of the Golem[72] hither; and how the man-made machines, when starting to rival and rebel against man, virtually compelled the technological thither to cry out in utter despair or desperado just to hail, willy-nilly though, our Robot Adams and our Robot Eves[73] as the inheritors of the globe. Had not the Nature poet long complained of it, when he wrote:

"A fingering slave,
One that would peep and botanize
Upon his mother's grave!
Sweet is the love which Nature brings;
Our meddling intellect
Misshapes the beauteous forms of things:
We murder to dissect"?[74]

And had not the youngest poet of beauty and sensuous delight long censured the so-called "cold philosophy", when he uttered his strong complaining note, thus:

"Do not all charms fly
At the mere touch of cold philosophy?
There was an awful rainbow once in heaven,
We knew her woof, her texture; she is given

In dull catalogue of common things:
Philosophy will clip an angel's wings"?[75]

In sum, the moral lesson that emerges from the foregoing silent speech and loud thinking about tribal ecology and economy, cutting across the tribal predilections and the non-tribal polemics, is that the most rational and pragmatic blueprint for the preservation and perpetuation of their *arbor vitae* needs to be drawn up by invoking a holistic view and by following a systemic approach

Acknowledgement

The author places on record his note of thanks to his erstwhile colleague Dr. Jawahar Lal Jain, Professor of Geography in Dr. Hari Singh Gour Vishwavidyalaya, Saugor, who played the patient listener during the sessions of monologue and acted as a passionate sceptic in the situations of dialogue, his reactions exemplifying how even a silent nod of dissent becomes more meaningfully eloquent than what many a loud and laudable note of assent ever does.

NOTES

1. "Genesis" *The Holy Bible*.
2. Quoted from the author's yet unfinished long poem—*The New found land.*
3. Samuel Johnson in Boswell's *Life of Johnson* (13 June 1784).
4. John Milton—*Paradise Lost* Book I, Line 16
5. Alfred, Lord Tennyson—"Milton, Alcaics.
6. John Milton, *op. cit.* Book I, Line 22.
7. *Ibid.,* Line 1.
8. *Ibid.,* Lines 1-5.
9. John Keats—"Ode on a Grecian Urn"-iv.
10. John Milton, *op. cit.* Book X
11. John Keats, *op. cit.* - i
12. William Shakespeare—*As you like It II.* i.
13. *Ibid.*
14. *Ibid.*
15. Movius Jr. 1966: 50; Bates 1958: 105-11.
16. John Milton—"Lycidas" Line 192.
17. John Dryden—"The Conquest of Granada" Part I, I. i.
18. Samuel Johnson—"Letter to Lord Chesterfield."
19. The cardinal summar of the divine law, given by God to Moses on Mt. Sinai.
20. The legend told in the biblical books—"Exodus", "Leviticus", "Numbers", etc.
21. "St. Matthew"—*The Holy Bible.*
22. Alfred, Lord Tennyson—"In Memorium"—cvi.
23. Rendering of the śāntipātha: "May there be peace in the sky and in all directions; may earth and water, medicinal herbs and the vernal green and Visvedevas dwell in peace, may peace dwell in peace".

24. Rednering of the quote: "The earth is my Mother and I am her Son and the Cloud is my Father".
25. Bharati, 1970; Capra, 1982.
26. Saraf, 1974.
27. Patrick, 1935:191ff
28. Kothari, 1985.
29. Rendering of the quote: "May nectar dwell on the earth, in the medicinal herbs and in the sky, including all directions and sub-directions that bring nectar for us".
30. Durkheim, 1964. Eliade, 1960.
31. *"dhatte bharam kusumapatraphalāvalīnāṁ dharmavyathāṁ vahati śītabhava . . . vadānyagurva tarave namo'stute."*
32. Virgil—"Ecologue" I. 5 & II. 60.
33. William Wordsworth—*"The Tables Turned"*
34. George Meredeith—"Woodland Peace" and "The Woods of Westermain".
35. William Shakespeare—*A Midsummer Night's Dream* V.i.
36. Sir Walter Scott—*The Lay of the Last Minstrel* VI. i.
37. Frazer, 1957: 10-11. Saraf, 1990: 156-57
38. *Ibid.*
39. Douglas, 1960: 24
40. Samuel Taylor Coleridge—*Kubla Khan.*
41. John Keats—*Ode on a Grecian Urn*–i.
42. Capra, 1982: 93-117.
43. *Ibid.*
44. *Ibid.*
45. *Ibid.*, 40-1
46. *Ibid.*, 47
47. "I do not recognize any difference between the machine made by craftsmen and those nature alone composes . . . I consider the human body as a machine . . . " said Descartes.
48. Circular D.O.IIFM/DD/NW/94/8243 of November 14, 1994 announcing a National Workshop on "Forest Development *vis-a-vis* Tribal Economy" hosted by the Indian Institute of Forest Management, Bhopal.
49. See 17 above.
50. Merchant, 1980:3.
51. John Keats—*Ode to a Nightingale*–ii.
52. *Ibid.*
53. Thomas Gray—*The Progress of Poesy* II. iii.
54. William Morris—*"Love is Enough".*
55. Saraf, 1990, 152 ff.
56. William Wordsworth—"Miscellaneous Sonnets"-I. 33
57. Saraf, 1982; Saraf, 1986.
58. William Shakespeare—*As you like It* II. v.
59. Capek 1970.
60. Capra 1982: 27 & 303.
61. Alexander Pope—"Epitaph intended for Sir Isaac Newton".
62. Patrick, 1935: 74ff & 88ff.
63. Bergman, 1981; Macdonald, 1992.
64. This alludes to the metaphorical depiction of Purusa and Prakrti as lame and blind respectively, the latter mounting the former on her back.
65. Patrick, *op. cit.*
66. Kothari, 1985.

67. Patrick *op. cit.*, "It may after all turn out that Nature is not a monstrous machine grinding away for ever under the rule of necessity without end or purpose—and that there is still something to be said for freedom."
68. It is the most pivotal and recurring theme in the Vedas and Upanisads.
69. Kothari, 1985 & 1989.
70. Saraf, 1998a; Capra, 1982 and 1988.
71. Capra, 1988
72. Saraf, 1998: 45
73. Capek, 1990-Rossum's Universal Robots.
74. William Wordsworth-Quoted in Chandrasekhar 1992: 55.
75. John Keats—Quoted in Chandrasekhar 1992: 55.

REFERENCES

Bates, Marston, 1958. *Man in Nature.* New Delhi: Prentice-Hall of India.

Bergman, Sonja (ed.). 1981. *Ideas and Opinions-Albert Einstein.* Calcutta: Rupa & Co.

Bharati, Agehananda. 1970. *The Tantric Tradition.* New York: Doubleday & Co.

Capra, Fritjof. 1977. *The Tao of Physics.* New York: Bantam Books.

—. 1982. *The Turning Point.* London: Harper Collins Publishers.

—. 1988. *Uncommon Wisdom.* London: Fontana Paperbacks.

Chandrasekhar, S. 1992. *Truth and Beauty—Aesthetics and Motivations in Science.* New York: Penguin Books.

Doughlas, Mary. 1966. *Purity and Danger: An Analysis of Concepts Pollution and Taboo.* London: Routledge & Kegan Paul.

Durkheim, Emile. 1964. *The Elementary Forms of the Religious Life.* London: George Allen & Unwin.

Eliade, Mircea. 1958. *Yoga: Immortality and Freedom.* London. Routledge & Kegan Paul.

—. 1960. The Sacred and the Profans. London.

Frazer, Sir James George. 1957. *The Golden Bough,* New York: Christian Books.

Kothari, Daulat Singh. 1980. "Atom and Self", in Proceedings of Indian National Science Academy. Part A, Vol. 46. No. 1

—. 1985. "The Complementarity Principle and Eastern Philosophy". in *Neils Bohr-Centenary Volumes.* Cambridge: Harvard University Press.

—. 1989. "Complementarity Principle: Physics and Beyond", *National Physical Laboratory Bulletin,* (Special Issue) No. 14.

Macdonald, Fiona. 1992. *Albert Einstein.* Mumbai: Orient Longman.

Merchant, Carolyn. 1980. *The Death of Nature.* New York: Harper & Row.

Movius Jr., H.L. 1966. "Palaeolithic Period", Harry L Shapiro (ed.), *Man, Culture and Society.* London: Oxford University Press.

Patrick, G.T.W. 1935. *Introduction to Philosophy.* New York: Houghton Migflin.

Saraf, Samarendra. 1974. "The Tantric Tradition", *The Eastern Anthropologist,* 27 (2).

—. 1976. Hindu Ritual Idiom: Cosmic Perspective and Basic Orientations," in Agehananda Bharati (ed.) *The Realm of the Extra-Human: Ideas and Actions.* The Hague: Mouton Publishers.

—. 1986. Hindu Caste System and the Ritual Idiom. Delhi: Mittal Publications.

—. 1990. "Eliot Through an Anthropolgist's Eyes" in R.S. Pathak. New Delhi: Northern Book Centre.

—. 1997. "Keats and the Cult of Shakespeares", in R.S. Pathak (ed.), *John Keats–Poetry and Poetics.* New Delhi: Creative Books.

—. 1998. "Destiny of Man in Modern Society: Polemics of Theology, Philosophy, Science and Technology," inV.K. Pachauri (ed.) *Social Panorama*—Festschrift of Professor Rajeshwar Prasad. Agra. Y.K. Publishers.

—. 1998. A New Medico-Spiritual Strategy for Health Care and Cure-Ayurveda Re-Examined. (Unpublished).

—. 1982. "Research Idiom for Contemporary Tribal Context", in Buddhadeb Chaudhuri. (ed.), *Tribal Development in India.* Delhi: Inter-India Publications.

—. 1986. "Tribal Development and the Role of Tribals," in M.K. Raha (ed.), *Tribal Problems and Tribal Development in India.* Calcutta: Institute of Social Research and Applied Anthropology.

THIRTEEN

TRIBAL PEOPLE AND SOCIAL FORESTRY IN ORISSA

CHITRASEN PASAYAT and MANAS RANJAN BARIK

Traditionally, tribal people inhabit in jungle or areas outskirting the jungle. They depend largely on jungle. Generally, tribal economy has a symbiotic relationship with the jungle. So tribal people cannot visualize a life without jungle that provides them food, fodder and fruits satisfies their deep-rooted sentiments and socio-cultural needs (Jha and Sen, 1991). The forest area in Orissa during 1993-94 was 57, 184 sq. kms. which accounts for 36.7 per cent of the total geographical area of the state. *(Economic Survey of Orissa, 1994-95).* It has registered a marginal increase of 0.7 per cent over 1992-93. Notably, forest covers nearly 80 per cent of the area of inland region which roughly comprises of nine undivided districts, namely, Koraput, Mayurbhanj, Sundargarh, Sambalpur, Kendujhar, Kalahandi, Phulbani, Bolangir and Dhenkanal. The mountainous and forested inland region of Orissa has been ideally suited to tribal inhabitations for centuries. As per 1991 census, the inland region covers nearly three-fourth of total geographical area and nearly 90 per cent of tribal population of the state (Pasayat, 1993: 21-24).

In view of this it may be suggested here that tribal people have tremendous potential and capacity to participate actively in various activities of the social forestry programmes in the state of Orissa. Since the main thrust given under the forest sector during the Eighth Plan is to conserve forests by intensifying productive measures and enlisting people's involvement to check illegal felling and removal of trees and other forests products and raising plantations through application of quality seeds, there is a need to realize and understand the relationship between tribal people and jungle. We may also think of the recognition and restoration of their rights on jungle. The ongoing activities for tribal development in the sphere of social forestry may easily be accelerated by arousing enthusiasm among them.

As per 1971 census, tribal population in Orissa was nearly 38.02 lakhs which rose to 59.15 lakhs in 1981 and further increased to 70.32 lakhs in

1991. The growth rate during 1981-91 estimated at 18.89 was higher than the previous decade (1971-81) of 16.82 per cent. Assuming the same growth rate of the decade 1981-91, at present, tribal population in Orissa may be estimated to be between 75 to 76 lakhs. It means, every fifth men in Orissa is a tribal. Understandably, though a small state, Orissa has comparatively more tribal people than many states and union territories of India (Pasayat, 1993: 21-24; Pasayat, 1995a: 29). The land area of the state being fixed, increased population coupled with various developmental activities has necessitated the diversion of forest land towards non-forest areas. All these days, we have been cutting trees unhesitatingly to make money. As a result of this the forest cover is vanishing at an alarming rate. In 1975 total forest area in Orissa was 48,383 sq. kms. which reduced to 39,425 sq. kms. in 1982. Decline in forest area in just seven years was thus estimated to be 8958 sq. kms. It means nearly 23 per cent of the forest cover had been depleted within a short span of time. Needless to say that it was a significant change. The dwindling of forest base at an alarming rate in the state of Orissa is indeed a matter of deep concern. Of course, considerable depletion of forest cover was also reported in other states and union territories in India also (Pasayat, 1994: 15).

The tribal people of Orissa had the per capita forest of 1.33 ha. The per capita tribal forest is a simple measure of the resources available to the tribal community. The critical ratio of per capita forest (0.2576 ha.) and per tribal capita forest (1.33 ha.) of Orissa was 0.194 which revealed that the tribal culture was facing a serious challenge to its survival in Orissa. The tribal people living in Orissa are extremely poor. They have lost their major economic base, forests, which have been destroyed. There is now migration of tribal people to other areas also. In other words, the overall pressure on the forest resources and the forest dwellers is very high (Jha and Sen, 1991: 128-32). In view of growing population and shrinking forest areas, social forestry appears to be important way to meet the ever-increasing demand for firewood, leaves, small timber and a variety of tree-based products for rural cottage industries and domestic consumption.

The large-scale commercial exploitation and massive encroachment of forest land occurred in the tribal area of Orissa particularly after the merger of princely states and before the Forest Department established its firm control on forest resources. The ruthless destruction of forests has not only put pressure on the forest resources and the forest dwellers but also disturbed the ecological balance. Uncontrolled exploitation of forest resources has severely affected our environment disturbing the natural cycle which has adverse effects on the health and life of tribal people in particular. The central and the state government are promoting the cause of forest conservation and protection by organizing various programmes directly and through non-governmental voluntary organizations so that ecological balance can be restored and the living condition of tribal people can also be improved. Forests are a renewable source and have a major role in enhancing quality of environment. They also contribute substantially to economic development. A programme with twin objectives of conservation and recreation of forests cover through social forestry programme is considered to be most important to solve the problem of environment as well as growing requirements of forest goods. The efforts of the government have been to develop the tribals economically and socially and bring them into the national mainstream (Pasayat, 1994: 16).

Under external assistance from Swedish International Development Authority (SIDA), massive social forestry programme was commenced in Orissa during 1983-84 with the basic objective of averting the fuel-wood and fodder crisis, maintaining ecological balance and creating employment opportunities. Under this project, a number of schemes, namely, village wood-lot, reforestation, rehabilitation of degraded forest, forest farming for rural poor, farm forestry, etc. were implemented. In the first phase, the Social Forestry Project (1983-88) covered 5000 villages and took up 33,590 hects. of plantation. In the second phase (1988-93), 7500 villages were covered with plantation over 55,311.8 hects. During 1993-94, the project has taken up 10,370 hects. of plantation against the target of 10,345 hects. with the financial involvement of Rs. 786.61 lakhs. In the financing pattern of this scheme for the betterment of the tribal people, average cost of plantation comes to Rs. 7585.00 per hect. The project rehabilitated 5542 hects. of land and distributed 300 lakh seedlings during 1993-94 with a financial involvement of Rs. 122.88 lakh *(Economic Survey of Orissa,* 1994-95).

Forest Protection Committees were set-up with active involvement and participation of people for protection and conservation of forest resources. The Report on the Activities of the Forest and Environment Department, 1992-93 revealed that the forest coverage of Orissa was 57,183 sq. kms. with vegetation coverage of only 27,349 sq. kms. In order to check the denudation of forest, felling of trees has been banned in Orissa since November 1992 and large scale plantation programmes has been undertaken for restoration of degraded forests and maintenance of ecological balance (Mohanty, 1993: 17-20). Nonetheless, the success of the programme depends mainly on active involvement and participation of the common people in general and tribal people in particular. But there are several hindrances like mass illiteracy, poverty, ignorance, conservatism, exploitation by outsiders and the like which prevent tribal people from participating actively in most of the development programmes of social forestry.

Although economic and material progress is taking place, there seems to be growing poverty among tribal people in particular. A large number of tribal people are below the poverty line. They are simple, ignorant and, moreover, possess a spirit of contentment. It may be noted here that as per 1991 census, 91.70 per cent of tribal women and 72.08 per cent of tribal men in the state of Orissa are illiterates (Pasayat, 1995b: 64). Facilities for education, drinking water, transport and communication, institutional credit, etc. are comparatively poor in tribal areas. The tribal people also do not get a remunerative price for their products of social forestry like fruits, fuel, food grains, fodder, honey, silk, cocoons, etc. due to absence of an organized marketing system. Processing of their products most likely generates higher income. But the processing work is hardly performed in the tribal villages. Intermediaries often take undue advantage of this situation and exploit them in the pursuit of high profit. They purchase items from tribal people at very low prices and tribal people hardly get any incentive.

A large number of tribal people possess inadequate land and are helpless to participate meaningfully in various social forestry programmes. Majority of them do not possess ownership rights on land. The trees growing under the scheme is subjected to the vagaries of nature such as good monsoon one year and perhaps a drought the following year. There is also no provision which would ensure adequate water supply for the purpose. Allegedly, tribal people are sometimes harassed by the implementing agency of the scheme. At times, greasing the palms of such staff becomes necessary. All these create barriers in the mass involvement of tribal people in various social forestry programmes. Majority of the extension staff in the tribal areas are reported to be non-tribal people. They are generally regarded as outsiders and members of the exploiting class. It does not encourage the tribal people to involve in social forestry programmes. People also feel that many cases of transfer are on account of political reasons and personal rivalry with the local leaders. Such transfers adversely affect the execution of social forestry programmes in tribal areas (Pasayat, 1994:16).

From economic point of view social forestry may be a gainful programme to raise the economic standard of tribal people. But liquor consumption rampant among them has its bearing on their socio-economic life. On account of this habit, they take loans from private money-lenders at an exorbitant rate of interest which ultimately trap them in the vicious circle of poverty. Today, liquor consumption among tribal people is not merely a tradition but a result of frustration generated among them. Frustration may be due to lack of infrastructure, inadequate institutional credit and support, exploitation by outsiders and intermediaries, harassment by other staff and institutions, lack of market facilities and the like. Tribal people feel helpless to solve these problems which directly or indirectly affect the social forestry programme.

In view of the above hurdles it is expected that more attention would be paid to improve communication and extension strategy package and material for dissemination of information on social forestry programme through available mass media like print media, audio-video, television, radio, theatre and the like. It will enhance the content of people's participation in the programme which ensure equitable and sustainable sharing of benefits from the programme.

Tribal people may plant trees in their marginal and sub-marginal lands. They may be allowed to plant trees in the degraded forest areas lying their homesteads and villages to meet the growing needs of fuel wood, fodder, fruits, foodgrains, fibres, small timbers, etc. and to promote fuel wood conservation and substitution. Further, tribal people can play a significant role in tassar culture, lac culture, api culture, herbal medicine and the like for internal consumption as well as for export. Today India earns foreign exchange by exporting tassar silk. Api culture is also gainful. The tribal people ought to be encouraged and trained properly to plant trees to yield nectar and pollen throughout the year. Other gains like fruits, fuel, fodder, small timber will also be available from these trees to them. India is one of the world's twelve leading biodiversity centres with the presence of over 45,000 different plant species. Nowadays, researchers are eyeing a potential market on herbal medicine. The role of tribal people in the prospects of herbal medicines is enormous. All these require regular supervision by the experts, timely availability of cheap inputs and credit, facilities for marketing at a reasonable rate and the like. Very likely, these incentives will generate popular enthusiasm amongst them.

There is a need of area-wise study to understand the socio-economic conditions of tribal people in Orissa. All possible efforts are to be made to ensure the improvement of infrastructure like facilities for education, drinking water, transport and communication, institutional credit, etc. in the tribal areas. For a regular discussion of the problem of soical forestry at the grass-root level, camps should be organized to meet individual tribals and to motivate them to adopt agro forestry so that they can meet their requirements and thereby increase their income too. The extent of tribal participation depends largely on the nature of motivation provided to them by the extension staff, educated and conscious people, leaders of tribal communities, social workers, voluntary organizations and the like who enjoy respectability in the respective tribal community/area. Moreover, panchayat samiti needs to be strengthened in the tribal areas of Orissa in order to involve those in the social forestry programmes and thereby to attract tribal people and to promote their voluntary participation.

It is required to free tribal people from the clutches of intermediaries so that various objectives of social forestry programme may be obtained in a balanced way. Stress would be laid on the setting up of processing units in the tribal belts providing adequate marketing networks for their products. Various non-governmental organizations may actively associate themselves in this field. They have to assume an active responsibility in ensuring that this does not happen. Thus, the production, consumption and utilization processes can be improved, remunerative livelihood through social forestry programmes to tribal people can be secured and additional employment and income generating activities can be created. Government has to provide the degraded forest land and wasteland to each landless tribal household. Reportedly, the government has provided each tribal family with 2 ha. of such land in West Bengal (Jha and Sen, 1991: 136). There is a need to ensure right quantity of water through drip irrigation, manure, weeding, etc. in modern method. It would also be necessary to build reservoirs to ensure availability of water throughout the year. There is a need to identify suitable watersheds to be covered under the scheme. In the process of identification and selection of such watersheds, gram panchayats or other village level bodies will be consulted and involved actively.

Not only the government but also the social workers, educated tribals, tribal leader, various non-government organizations who give them guidance, ought to carry a special responsibility and play a positive role in this field. They should try for the enforcement of law, planning and development of programme for the prevention and control of liquor consumption and private money-lending, dissemination of information relating to various tribal beneficiary oriented schemes sponsored by both government and non-government organizations. It is very important that they should occasionally meet, sit together and get acquainted on a personal level. They can discuss them freely and intervene quickly. It is important to get to know one another because their personal relationships have a great bearing on the discussions they make. Establishment of such personal relations based on a close personal acquaintance is of profound significance in building up awareness of the need of social forestry programmes for improving immediate and long-term needs.

The non-tribal people have to prove their clean image. Understandably, success of any developmental plan rests on mutual trust, faith, understanding and cooperation among various sections of the society. Once these are eroded, it is very difficult to restore them. Besides, attempts should be made to recruit considerable number of tribal people in the extension staff who will work dedicatedly in the tribal areas. Further, the non-tribal extension staff working in a particular tribal area have to learn and understand the prevailing tribal language, culture and society. A vigilance cell should be formed at the district, block, tehsil and village levels in tribal areas, so that tribal people may avail themselves of the timely benefits granted by the government. Such staff must free themselves from the habit of bribe taking. Any member of the staff found corrupt, guilty or dereliction of duty has to face punishment. Notably, honest and efficient staff will promote social forestry programmes rapidly in tribal areas of Orissa. Nevertheless, frequent transfer of officers and staff who direct social forestry programmes in the tribal areas should be checked. They must be given comparatively better emoluments, promotional avenues, housing, conveyance facilities, etc. (Jha and Sen, 1991: 131).

A support cadre of all-India tribal service and state tribal service may be created for the all-round development of the tribal areas not only in Orissa but also in other tribal dominated states and union territories of India. Special training and knowledge on tribal culture, language, economy, polity, religions and society should be imparted to the selected candidates who may discharge their duties with dedication and sincerity to promote tribal welfare. In the context, the role of the Academy of Tribal Dialects and Culture, Bhubaneswar and Tribal and Harijan Research-cum-Training Institute, Bhubaneswar is important. Nowadays, plantations are like any other business venture. There is a sudden spurt in private companies promising money by investing on trees. This is altogether a different type of public participation. Glossy folders, pictures of jungle and waterfalls and the schemes give the feel of money growing on trees. To grow trees to make money looks a bit out of place. Because we are not habituated with it. Nevertheless, it is the high time to think how far it is relevant for our society, environment and ecology.

We should have to emphasize the forest recreation strategies as much as forest conservation. Conservation means more efficient use of forest resources as well as changing our habits in such a way that we use less forest resources. Social Forestry Programmes in tribal areas of Orissa are likely to solve the growing requirements of the country in general and tribal society in particular. We cannot further afford to neglect the tribals. Because they are already neglected, exploited and deprived of their rights. Furthermore, they constitute a sizeable section of Orissan society. Concerted efforts are to be made by all the concerned agencies—government as well as non-government—to enthuse the tribals and those who work for their welfare for voluntary participation and mass involvement in Social Forestry Programmes in the State. Moreover, every sensible human being has a duty to affirm this commitment in active and positive ways. Even though a poor state like Orissa has a number of problems, if a majority of the people work for a cause, despite the efforts of a few selfish and malicious elements, Social Forestry Programmes will be successful. This will benefit everyone. Nonetheless, the future strategy for forest should be a rational one considering available forest resources and conservation, environmental protection and needs of economic growth.

REFERENCES

Economic Survey of Orissa. 1994-95. Government of Orissa.

India 1992 A Reference Annual. Publications Division, Ministry of Information and Broadcasting, Government of India.

Jha, L.K. and P.P. Sen. 1991. *Social Forestry,* Bombay: Himalaya Publishing House.

Mohanty, P.C. 1993. "Environmental Pollution: Policies and Management", *Orissa Review,* L(1): 17-20.

Pasayat, C. 1993. "Distribution of Tribal Population in Orissa", *Orissa Review,* L(1): 21-24.

—. 1994. "Tribals and social Forestry Programme: Reassessment in Orissa", *Kurukshetra,* XLII (6): 15-17, 34.

—. 1995a. "Literacy in Tribal Women", *Social Welfare,* 41(10): 29-32.

—. 1995b. "Low Literacy of Tribal Women in Orissa", *Kurukshetra,* XLIII (10): 64-66.

Report on the Activities of Forest and Environment (Forest) Department, 1992-93.

Report on the Activities of Forest and Environment Department (Environment), 1992-93.

SECTION III

GENDER ISSUES

FOURTEEN

CENTRAL HIMALAYAN TRIBAL WOMEN, DEVELOPMENT AND INTEGRATION

R. S. MANN and K. MANN

Whether it is in tribal India or the non-tribal one, represented by the rural folks, the women still lag far behind in comparison to men. Empirically this is evident from parameters like literacy, education, nutrition, health status, employment opportunities, political participation, ritual status, economic freedom, etc. In addition the mounting restrictions, restraints, taboos, discrimination, underestimation, ritual impurity, segregation, etc. continue to mark women world unabated. Some of the latter are more prominent in caste society than the tribal matrix. Women world-view is more limited, chiefly confined to the immediate surroundings. This is comparatively more valid and exhaustive in case of tribals where isolation, both physical and social, is relatively of high order. Indian women, by and large, are at a disadvantageous position. This holds true in traditional framework, as also in contemporary situation. Least involved remain the females in the processes of planned development and transformation. While the men get into many such processes the women generally remain ignorant and unaware. This is characterized by rural India in general and tribal habitation in particular. General efforts for mobilization of females and campaign for their awareness are neither elaborate nor effective. Our assertion is that unless the women are actively and at large scale involved in the processes and programmes of development the intended aim of bringing the Scheduled Tribes at par with main stream people would not be achieved in stipulated time and at the anticipated level. And if it remains so the policy and approach of integration of tribals will forfeit their claim at the level of achievement. In the descriptions and explanations that follow in this paper the areas of strength and weakness in the focal theme under discussion are highlighted importing substantivism from the Scheduled Tribes of Uttar Pradesh, the most populous and one of the largest states of India.

Uttar Pradesh, with a total population of 139,112,287 (1991 Census) has probably the least, in terms of percentage of total state population, Scheduled Tribe population in the country. According to 1991 Census the Scheduled Tribe population of Uttar Pradesh is 287,901 forming only 0.21 per cent of total state population. Nearly 72.89 per cent of these tribals live in hilly region and the rest inhabit in terrai and other rural and urban areas. Out of the total Scheduled Tribes of the State, the Tharus form the biggest (41%) tribe, followed in order by the Jaunsaris (22%), Bhoksa (14%), Bhotia (8%) and the Raji (0.17%). The Rajis form one of the endangered tribes of India. Whereas the Bhotias are reported inhabiting four districts of Pithoragarh, Uttarkashi, Chamoli and Almora, the Jaunsaris live in Kalsi and Chakrata development blocks of Dehradun district. Rajis are concentrated in Pithoragarh district. Nainital district houses the Tharus. The Bhoksas are widely scattered in the districts of Bijnore, Hardwar, Dehradun and Nainital.

Except Rajis the rest of the four Scheduled Tribes bear a long history of culture contact. Certain sections of Bhotia and Bhoksa have imbibed many culture traits of upper caste Hindus. Instances of similar influence are reported from upper social categories of Jaunsaris. But even then the continuity of tribal culture is imposingly reported. Cultural customs and practices like the polyandry, bride price, marriage by elopement, capture, exchange and the custom of *ghar betha* or *tekwa* (keeping servant husband) are still in vogue. The element of change is visible in economic and trade transactions too. As a very prominent landmark the Bhotia trade across international border has been stopped from sixties of current century. To some extent the Rajis have given up hunting and gathering. This applies more to colonized families. Horticulture has gained popularity among the Jaunsaris. Many Bhoksa and some Tharus have started taking advantage of improved and approved agriculture practices including use of seeds, pesticides, chemical fertilizers, implements, etc. Agents and agencies of planned programmes of change and development have spread a big network in the area. New communication channels have made their own impact. Many schemes in innovative perspective were introduced to pave way to social and economic well-being of the people. These are inclusive of special schemes meant for the tribals of the last row.

In the Scheduled Tribes population the proportion of women is slightly less than 50 per cent. Jaunsaris, however, do not strictly fall in this ratio. The women folk among these groups are involved in almost all the socio-economic pursuits. They participate in agricultural activities like clearing the fields, sowing, weeding, harvesting and storing the grain. Most of the day they are seen braving the rough weather of their physical environment. They are taken as economic asset because of the labour they furnish for the activities they perform. Besides agriculture they are equal partner in hunting and food-gathering among the Rajis who still resort to some extent, to these age-old occupations of theirs. Jaunsaris, Bhoksha and Tharus are mainly agriculturists and animal husbandry people. Jaunsaris have taken to horticulture and vegetable growing also. Every well-to-do family in Jaunsar area owns fruit orchards of varying number. They supply vegetables to the nearby marketing places. But this venture is taken up only by those villagers whose settlements are in the near vicinity of towns. In other places people grow for subsistence purpose only. The Bhotias have also switched over to agriculture since the trade across the border between India and Tibet has come to halt since fifties. The Bhotia women participate, on equal footing, in pursuits of wool gathering, preparing of useful items and selling them in the neighbouring markets. They are equally enthusiastic about their agricultural pursuits as is also true for Raji women who are also gradually getting used to agriculture and sedantry life.

The importance of women as active participants in economic pursuits puts them on a higher status plane. As a girl also she is treated with equal care and love, no discrimination is shown on the basis of sex. A girl is accorded great freedom in her movement when she reaches adolescence. She becomes rightful incumbent of normally heavy bride-price because of her involvement in economic activities. The girls are free to choose their life partners in Bhotia, Raji and Bhoksha groups. Among Jaunsari a girl has limited choice as she has to marry the boy or boys after the parental wishes. In general she is married off as a child only. Though a Jaunsari girl has limited say in the choice of her husband/husbands she enjoys considerable command in favouring her co-husbands if they are there. Even when a strict code of conduct and complete chastity is expected of the wife as a *rayanti* she is extended a fair amount of laxity in her parental village as a *dhayanti*. She is given a good deal of freedom and even her extra marital relationships, if any, are ignored. This anomalous behaviour provision regarding Jaunsari woman has, of late, undergone considerable change due to shift in marriage structure (they are now preferring monogamy instead of polyandry), unpalatable criticism and ill effects on the health of women. The women, among these groups, freely participate in fairs, dances and other social and religious gatherings. They add colour to the functions which are characterized by great pomp and show. Though the women participate in religious festivals yet worship is performed by menfolk alone. Among Bhokshas some women practice black magic for which they are punished. Jaunsari women are said to evoke the spirits of Pandavas and some women practice witchcraft under male priest (Majumdar, 1962). Among the Tharus, who came in deep contact with the caste Hindu culture traits the age for marriage of girls has been drastically curtailed; hence the girl has no say in choosing her life-partner.

In spite of some influence of Sanskritic ways all the five groups accord great freedom to women in divorce and widow marriage. A woman can divorce her husband on the pretext of incompatibility. A Raji woman is pampered to the extent that her husband tolerates even her extra-marital relations. Though the reason to this kind of behaviour is due to exorbitantly high bride-price but it tells of the upper hand of women among the Rajis. A wife is always looked after well in terms of food, clothings and jewellery among the Jaunsaris. High bride-price on one hand reminds husband to behave properly and on the other the importance of women in these communities. After divorce a woman is free to marry anyone. Divorce system is simple. The husband is to be compensated of his bride-price by the new paramour. The children are father's liability and woman can start her new life. There is no social stigma attached to remarriage either after divorce or widowhood which speaks high of women among these communities. Except Jaunsaris where the customary mode of marriage has been polyandry, the other tribes including Bhotia, Bhokshas, Tharu and Raji show favour towards monogamy. The traditional perspective of status of women among these groups is of higher accordance. As they are also influenced by the culture contact, some of the unwanted elements have crept in their social system which has lowered down the status of women among Bhotias for instance. Some of them have imposed *purdah* (veiling) system on their women-folk. Instead of bride-price many have switched over to dowry system and imposed restriction on widow-marriage. They are emulating the so-called higher customs and spade of impositions have fallen on the status of women in the first place. As the status of women among twice-born castes is of a very low scale, the Bhotias have begun to subscribe to the same for a better placement in caste hierarchy. How far this dream of theirs has been fulfilled is anybody's guess. The loss is of the tribals. The overall status of women among these groups is still at an advantageous plane in comparison to their caste counterparts.

As the social set-up among all the five tribals is patriarchal, patrilocal and patrilineal, the authority, leadership, decision-making, descent, succession, inheritance and residence are in male line on family, village as well as on a bigger plane. A woman, in normal circumstance, does not inherit parental property including land, house, cattle and orchards. Though she can inherit mother's jewellery among Bhotias. A wife has to join her husband after marriage and adjust to the new atmosphere which itself is quite demanding on her part. Family, clan or any other headship is always in male line as authority and decision-making are vested in males only. Though a woman has say in family matters and petty economic transactions but the major decisions are taken by elderly males only. She is taken as less informative about the outside world. A Bhotia couple can keep a daughter and her husband as *ghar jawain* if they have no son. Among Bhoksha a poor daughter can be given some share of property if her brothers agree to such an appeal.

The membership and headship of traditional village council are the male prerogative only. Though women are free to place their case before the council where they are given due hearing. The final decision-making rests with the male head only. Male chauvinism has its own assertion. It can curb or encourage any trend among the villagers and females as well. Clan name also runs in male line among all these groups. Although the male child is preferred to a female, a girl is also welcome as she fetches bride-price and is more helpful and hard working than a male.

Widowhood among all the five groups of Jaunsari, Bhotia, Bhoksha, Tharu and Raji is not a matter of much concern as the widows are free to go in for remarriage if they like. Due to polyandry Jaunsari woman does not have to face the situation of widowhood. She is taken care of by the other husbands and life leaps up with the daily chores without much worries for the wife. But if a woman becomes widow she can remarry without any guilt. Her price is enhanced if she has proved her fecundity and is able to produce more children. Though Bhotia have started putting some curb on the freedom of women, due to the impact of culture contact with other higher castes, to remarry but most of others advocate for this freedom in their respective tribal group. Widowhood and remarriage are very common and no stigma is attached to this situation. The children born out of such wedlock also enjoy the same privileges as the other children. A woman's consent is always sought in the matter of remarriage. A Tharu woman can keep a *ghar-baitha/tekwa* (husband servant) after the death of her husband. At the same time she inherits her deceased husband's lands and other property. An issueless widow can have right over her deceased husband's property among the Raji. She is free even to sell a part of it for her benefit. A widow sister, in case of Bhoksha, is allowed to stay in her natal home and her brothers ensure her subsistence.

Among Rajis adult marriage is the practice. Marriage age, on an average, for boy and girl is approximately 24 and 18 years respectively. Elopement, exchange, intrusion and negotiation are commonly used ways to acquire mates where female has an equal say. Forced marriage is not acceptable to a Raji woman. Traditional social status of Raji women is higher than other Kumaonis. Even when culture contact is increasing and some changes are visible it has not enabled to put much impact on Raji women. For instance the Raji women have started emulating neighbouring Kumaoni women in some respects, say wearing of *bulaki* (big nose ring). It shows their inclination for prevailing fashion around and possession of expensive (gold) jewellery. A girl child is accorded great care and affection right from birth as she is equal participant in agriculture activities and forest produce gathering. These days forest produce is gathered mainly by the women. Due to this aspect of economic importance, the women fetch heavy bride-price among Rajis.

The role of women has also undergone change with switching over to sedantry life from the one of nomadic hunter-gatherer. The Rajis are lured to start agriculture and are also provided milch cows by the government. Women have a substantial part to play. Some Raji women received training in tailoring under special development programme for them. Acceptance of new programmes by the women itself speaks of their encouraging attitude and positive world-view. They are making use of public distribution system and get substantial food requirement for their families from ration shops. Road communication has also improved which has brought them in contact with the other Kumaoni population. The Raji are to be secured from evil effects of blind culture contact. Raji women still lag behind in the education field as much attention is not paid to women's education. Though schools are intentively attended by boys the girls are withheld at home for household work. In local world-view education for girls is not as important as the household work and labour in field and forest. Education does not show instant monetary result and as the people are economically hard pressed, they cannot afford to lose the girl's labour in field, forest and household.

Village gram sabha and mahila sabha are main constituents of Bhotia villages. Without approval of mahila sabha no action can be taken up even if approved by gram sabha. All the married females are the members of mahila sabha as are the married men of gram sabha. It establishes women's say in decision-making and her higher social status. Mahila sabha actively shows hospitality to outsiders and manages to organize functions for them. They have been having youth club called *Rang-Bhang* where males and females of above 15 years age join and mix freely with each other. In this youth club or dormitory *(Rang-Bhang)* the youth learn their social and cultural traits and get training for future life by their senior counterpart. Some of the marriage matches are made here and they prove very successful. Birth of a girl child is considered welcome as the females are treated as very hard working. The girl and boy can choose each other for marriage and start living together even without marriage. Sometimes, if the parents cannot perform their marriage their children celebrate this ceremony.

Under Integrated Rural Development Programme (IRDP), the Bhotias have been benefited. Women also involve in development activities like weaving, knitting, sheep, cow and goat rearing for which they are provided loans. Under National Rural Employment Programme (NREP) they get employment in construction work. Education is also attracting these people and women are also coming forward in this area. They need better road communication and market facilities to sell their finished products, besides taking care that they are not exploited by unscrupulous non-tribal people. Care must be taken that they develop according to their own genius.

Womenfolk among Tharus enjoy considerable freedom but normally marriages are negotiated and arranged. In some sections of Tharus child marriage is preferred to discourage elopement which is very common among them. To discourage elopement the marriage age has been drastically curtailed and choice of a girl is hampered. *Mangani* (betrothal) ceremony is performed among Rana Tharus (one of the section) even while the girl and boy are below five years of age. Although marriage takes place after they attain puberty but freedom of choice is cut here. *Mangani* is to be performed in childhood otherwise no match for marriage will be available, for boy and girl, in the later stage. This hampers the freedom of choice in mate selection in certain sections of the Tharus. Separation and divorce can be taken by any party and widow marriage is allowed to facilitate the woman to rehabilitate with respect.

Village council or traditional Panchayat is there to resolve any dispute. Panchayat's resolutions are binding and forceful. Traditionally, the women cannot become its member. Tharu economy, which was mainly based on agriculture, forest and animal husbandry has shaken a great deal due to some problems. They suffer from land alienation and have been reduced to marginal farmers or even as landless labourers. Due to the forest policy of the government they cannot collect wood, timber, fuel, fodder as they used to do earlier. It has minimized their source of income and fodder for their cattle which is secondary source of income to them. Their cattle are of poor quality with minimal yield though number of animals is quite large in every Tharu family. It is important to mention that in almost all these economic pursuits, that is, agriculture, forest produce collection and animal husbandry, the womenfolk put in their labour on a larger scale than even the menfolk. When the economy suffers the womenfolk are more to feel the pinch of it. They get even meagre share of this limited yield. I.T.D.P. is in operation among Tharus of Kheri since 1976 and a Tharu Development Scheme (TDS) is functioning in Gonda since 1980 but their forest problems are not solved any way. Dudwa National Park and Project Tiger have further been made instrumental in denying their rights. No proper employment scheme in forest areas is in operation for Tharus. The development programmes have not given significant results to them. Women can be brought under these schemes for their betterment and development if wise planning is made. It requires greater efficiency on the part of official machinery to chalk out the proper programmes to minimize tribal problems rather than escalating them.

Though a male child is preferred among Jaunsaris the female child is also treated with love and care as she is equal partner and hard worker in most of the agricultural activities. The girls are a constant drain on family income according to the local view-point. The girls will ultimately go to their husbands house and serve there. Moreover, they will be gifted time to time, monetarily. The failure of women's welfare has been because they are not taken as important as men in Jaunsar area. Polyandrous society poses its own problems. Status of women has much to say in the women welfare and development scheme. As a girl is married off at an early age she cannot get formal education. Moreover, education is not considered as an important feature as it is not going to serve any instant purpose in Jaunsari agricultural economy. According to local view-point the educated girls lose interest in agriculture work whereas only the hard-working girls are of immense economic importance. But change is now visible in the outlook of these people. Accordingly though female education is very low and child marriage is prevalent in interior areas the modern influence from plains has attracted people towards educating girls.

In the traditional role and status perspective the tribal women of these five tribal communities enjoy a better deal. How far they fair in the changed perspective is the next important arena to be explored. In the change arena can be included change through culture contact and the development programmes started by the government for the welfare of these people. Change through culture contact and its short and long-term implications are of varied nature. Sanskritization has played its ill effect on these people in differential degree. The social differentiation among Jaunsaris does not allow the lower castes to develop accordingly. Hence the Kolta (low caste) women are not as free to develop as the higher castes (Rajput and Brahmins). The lower social status of Kolta women hampers their development in almost all the fields in spite of the governments strong thrust. All the efforts go futile in the absence of social approval. Imposition of *purdah* system among Bhotias (Johari), dowry system and child marriage are other ill effects of the culture contact with the larger caste Hindu social organization. These practices have drastically lowered the status of women but interestingly majority of the tribal women are still not touched by these disadvantages.

The development policies of the government aim at development and welfare of the tribal people in a way which does not go contrary to their indigenous traditional social-cultural institutions. The tribal people are to be brought at par with others in social and economic fields so that they may ultimately integrate into the national main stream. To achieve this goal of welfare and development many special projects are put on the anvil and field. Though these projects are meant for the overall development of the tribals in general but there are some specific programmes meant for tribal women exclusively and the same aim to insert self-confidence among them. To develop women folk is to develop the community in general, as developed women are more helpful in this gigantic task. The women are to be made aware of the benefits of the welfare schemes and the new statutory provisions to impart justice and implement the programmes.

The main aim of welfare and development hinges around the schemes of socio-economic nature. It carries forward in the fields of health and nutrition, literacy, justice to get the desired results according to the fifth schedule of the Constitution of India. How far women are aware of these welfare programmes and their involvement thereof will only show the change impact on their status and their socio-economic development. Studies have revealed that most of the women are not aware of their rights and privileges officially granted to them. Large scale ignorance of tribal women in the fields of growing socio-political provisions is rather disappointing. The tribal women in Uttar Pradesh are not aware of certain new political provisions and processes, and even if some of them are, they hardly avail of the opportunity to be a part of the new system at their instance. For example the tribal woman has been officially given a right to be elected as a member of the statutory Panchayati Raj bodies. But one hardly comes across women elected to such bodies. The latest provision of 30 per cent reservation of women in these bodies is going to give what type of fruitful result is anyone's guess. Non-participation of this nature is a hindrance to the fair deal to the women folks at the village level and beyond. Traditionally and customarily the women are not allowed to be member or head of village council as these positions are earmarked for men only. The same holds true for traditional councils beyond village, wherever they are reported. Within the traditional framework, defined for the womanhood the women themselves are not keen to hold such responsible position due to the fear of public criticism which they may invite by such involvement. "Woman's work is to run the house not panchayat, if women start passing judgement what will the men do?" is the common cynic remark for this participation. Because of such a complex, they withdraw themselves from participation even in the statutory body what to talk of positions at the state or central level.

The problem of tribal development cannot be solved and we cannot achieve the desired fruits of the schemes unless people participate in them and participation of womenfolk is an essential part of it. The women have, of late, become aware of certain important items. One of the forceful assertions by the women is in the field of forest policy of the government. The tribals were prohibited to go inside the forest and collect their legitimate share of wood, fodder, medicine and herbs due to them since times immemorial. On the other hand the government contractors started felling trees indiscriminately for their profit. It was in this challenging situation that women got stuck (Chipko) to one tree each and did not allow the contractors to do the evil designed work. The tribals who are part and parcel of the nature cannot survive without the eco-balance which was threatened to be imbalanced by the unscrupulous designs (tree felling). The tribal women made the headlines here and made the government think over the policy and amend to the benefit of the local people who are tribals. This is a firy example of women's concern for their eco-development which has direct link to their survival, welfare and development. People's involvement in the projects, meant for them, makes them confident enough to get into the national mainstream.

Some of the Jaunsari women, as others, were given training in tailoring, knitting and child care. Their response was very enthusiastic. Even the girls were persuaded to attend school. But the main drawback of these training and literacy programmes was that only the women and girls of upper strata could attend these and the lower stratum women were deprived of it because of many socio-economic factors. Poverty is one of them. The girl child remains absent from the school because she cannot be spared for formal schooling as she has to attend to household chores in absence of her mother who works in field and forest. Moreover, they do not find any immediate return of education as such. This tribal apathy should be overcome by the agents of tribal development at any cost as it hinders the way of tribal involvement in the larger national interest in the long run and their own interest in the first place.

Another field of gross concern is land alienation among the tribals. Many tribals who depended on agriculture have become landless as the outsiders have encroached upon their land through unfair means. The tribals have become dependent on the mercy of outsiders in all respects and the benefits of schemes of agriculture development does not reach them. On the other hand some of the tribes who were dependent on forest produce only, like the Raji, are forced to leave their age-old profession and made to settle at one place to cultivate the uneconomical patch of land. The sendentary life poses lots of problems to these people who had been nomads till recently and who still have a fondness for it. The development programmes have to look into all this. Though the policy of settled agriculturists is very promising but implementation of the same can bear fruits only if it is in the best interest of the tribals.

The Rajis who are forced to abandon the forest due to governmental policy have been asked to cultivate the uneconomical patches of land far away from the jungles which they claimed to own earlier. Consequently most of them have become labourers for others. As this opportunity is not available throughout the year the poor tribals remain unemployed and it is very difficult for them to meet both ends squarely. The situation demands for better employment opportunities for the people in the near vicinity of their habitat. For the Bhotias, who were traditionally traders, dilemma awaits in the form of stoppage of trade on the one hand and not finding a reasonable market for their indigenous produce such as knitted woollen clothes on the other. The simple tribals are being cheated by the non-tribals. It may be remembered that most of the wool-work is done by the Bhotia womenfolk who do not get their due share in this transaction. Such a plight can lead to failure of the tribal development programmes in this area. The apathy on the part of officials may also be responsible for the troubles of the tribals. Instead of isolating the tribal women in specific and the group in general the necessary infrastructure should be facilitated to bring them in the national mainstream through their socio-economic development. They should be provided all possible facilities to carry their age-old occupation where women can contribute better and are not ignored by more sophisticated infrastructure.

The three approaches to tribal development, that is, isolation, assimilation and integration have failed to yield desirable results because they have been grossly misconceived. Practically social policy has not evolved in the welfare states due to the lack of political will as well as appreciation of socio-economic tribal institutions and ethos which are deeply rooted in their habitat. Eco-developmental approach to tribal problems is advocated which hinges around a symbiotic relationship and envisages that place (environment/habitat) determines the pattern of work (economic activity/organization) which in turn conditions folk policy/social structure and that in the space-time continuum habitat is not static but a dynamic product of ecosystem that evolves due to environmental impact, human economy and social polity. This view helps in delineating the direction and pattern of planned development which is essentially concerned with the development of local resources within the limitations of the local environment and with a view of optimum development of the local people. This approach aims at improving the quality of environment, quality of life and well-being, free from deleterious effects of external interference.

Eco-developmental approach may be very effective in the tribal areas where Uttar Pradesh tribal population is inhabiting. The basic postulates of this approach are development of the people aiming at improvement of quality of life and well-being; promotion of self-reliance and establishment of true symbiosis between man and his environment, leading to lasting human achievements and development. The state government has taken several measures for ameliorating the tribals, socio-economic conditions since their constitutional recognition as Scheduled Tribes since 1967. The Integrated Tribal Development Plan (ITDP) for the Tharus of Nighasan Tehsil (Kheri) was formulated in 1974-75 under the guidance of the Planning Commission and was launched in 1976-77. Next came the Pocket Plan under the Marginal Area Development Approach (MADA) for the Tharus. A micro plan for the Rajis has also been launched under the Seventh Five Year Plan. But other Scheduled Tribes are yet to be covered under the ITDP. The total positive impact of the foretold approaches can be felt only if they are in tune with the eco-development approach and with involvement of the local population. In this connection it would be relevant to mention the importance of women population at every step of these approaches for tribal development. Though there is no denying from the fact that the tribal population of Uttar Pradesh cannot be developed without direct participation of womenfolk, they are mostly overlooked by the development agents. It is the tribal women who feel the pinch of economic, social and ecological imbalance. They have asserted to some extent but need more encouragement from law-makers and policy implementors.

It may be cited with great fun-fare the infrastructure of communication which brings most of the tribal population on road map. The mass-media blares and boasts of reaching upto the interior-most pockets for the benefit of all the people to bind them as one nation state. The womenfolk with their involvement and participation in economic, social, ritual and some new development schemes are well integrated in the national main stream. But they need better planning and implementation infrastructure which in reality improves upon the quality of life of the people. The women are to be made more aware of the importance of their role in this herculean task. Women who are the weakest and the poorest of social category are to be mobilized to achieve the equal status in all fields and then only the country can expect the true development which will ultimately lead to their integration with the rest of the people.

Though there are many problems which hinder the path of social and economic development in the Hill areas of Uttar Pradesh but some are very prominent ones and have direct impact on the social and economic status of tribal women therein. One of such problems is of youth exodus from native villages. It is a well-known fact that most of the able-bodied men come down to the plains of Bhabhar and Tarai to as far as Delhi, Kanpur and Ludhiana in search of employment which leaves behind mostly the females, children and aged people to attend to hill economy with its never ending problems. It is the women then who do most of the agriculture work. Except ploughing the field (though in some cases they do even ploughing), they work hard from preparing the field to storing the grain in the stores. The women go to the steep slopes and hard-terrain to bring fodder for their cattle whose health does not improve enough to supplement their economy any way. These hardy women travel these difficult distances to bring drinking water for the family. The potable water is not accessible within comfortable reach. During summers they have to traverse a longer distance for the same. After dredging for these chores she spends her short time in looking after her children and old persons. In the absence of help from men she has to strive very hard, which tells heavily on her health. The men migrate to the plains because in hills they do not get enough to pull on economically. Most of the tribals are heavily indebted to the local money-lenders. To repay this debt they mortgage their land and migrate to the plains for earning. The appalling poverty makes some of the young girls and women go in for extra and undesirable sex relations in order to raise money for their families.

Polyandry and uninhibited attitude of women of Jaunsar, Garhwal, Nainital, Uttarkashi have thrown some poor tribal women into sex trade.

Though it has helped in improving their families economic status to a considerable extent but not without consequences of ill-health. Trafficking in women makes them cheap commodity which should be curtailed at any cost by providing them substitute for the same. In plains the migratory youths are rather cheated as they do not work in organized sector but mainly as cheap casual labourers. The simple people are ill-treated on both the ends. At the home-front they drag their women-folk to extremely hard labour and here they work for little remuneration. This migration of labour from hill to the plains speaks of lack of social and economic infrastructure available in the hill areas. Due to lack of sufficient employment the youths are attracted towards the plains and their families suffer on this count. This takes a heavy toll on the health of women-folk. They have to work round the clock. Due to ill economy most of the women are under-nourished and suffer from diseases, which makes them poor performers. Most of the women and children are anaemic. This is a sheer wastage of human resource which could be utilized in the development programmes meant for their welfare. Besides poor quality of human resource the official machinery of the development programme are also apathetic to their problems. Most of them do not contact the women who are the actual participants in every economic pursuit in the hills. The functionaries fail to achieve the intended and demarcated goals due to non-cooperation of tribal women-folk in this field as no economic venture can be fulfilled without women here. This lacunae on the part of the officials at planning and implementation levels again leaves the tribal people in loss which is shared the maximum by the women-folk.

Besides nutrition and lack of coordination in plan implementation one big factor hindering the development programme is illiteracy among tribal women. Though people have come out of their reverses to recognize the importance of education the schools for girls are not within convenient reach. More of schools for girls are found to be 8 kms. far from the villages in Pithoragarh, Almora and Nainital districts. These distances are formidable barriers in the pursuits of girl's education. When this is the condition of primary educational institutions the girls cannot even think of higher studies. Mere figures on papers are not sufficient to develop the area. The educated women can only educate family and society of next generation which seems a far cry in these areas.

Hospitals and maternity homes are also given the same treatment in the hills of Uttar Pradesh. "Service of allopathic hospitals can be obtained in rural areas of the Almora district after crossing mountainous tract of above 5 kms. in more than 77 per cent villages. A similar distance has to be covered reaching a maternity centre. In district Pithoragarh the condition is more difficult" (Pande, 1988: 162). Looking to the above situation of health services to women and binding health due to overwork and lack of nutrition consequent to poor economy the women have to suffer physically as well as mentally. Socially they are already handicapped as property inheritance is in male line which does not allow women to take advantage of procuring improved variety of seeds, fertilizer and other modern techniques. These can be obtained, in most of the cases, by the owner of land which leaves women in suffering corner. All these hurdles do not allow women to take advantage of programmes implemented under IRDP, which makes all the developmental policies mainly a farce. To relieve women of some of their burden by supplying tap water and electricity would go a long way in their development. The education is to be not three Rs. only but a common sense affiliated to solving their day-to-day problems. Literacy should provide the right blend of self-motivation, understanding and desire for personal improvement within the limitations set by the local environment, patterns of mutual inter-relationship and finally the accepted societal goals. The I.L.O. training programme for women states that training programme for women aims at both their economic and social development. Vocational training, in this perspective, is one of the fundamental elements for the advancement of women as well as for improving the conditions of their families. It provides for participation in economic life by giving them the skills needed for employment thereby providing economic independence that should both increase the self-confidence and status of women within the family and society.

Women in the hill areas should be given priorities in programmes. They should be given opportunities in existing training system preferably in horticulture and agriculture which must be flexible to suit their local needs. A programme of functional literacy and non-formal education providing day-care facilities and lastly measures for reducing household drudgery would help improve their lot. Involving a large number of women in the propogation and management of programmes which are of great national value, that is, afforestation and preservation of the delicate ecological balance of this very sensitive region will bring women into national mainstream directly. It was found that in village Nandgaon of Pauri block, women were totally responsible for all the activities of the van panchayats. This positive trend should be encouraged and helped to assume extensive and intensive dimensions in other areas. Mahila mandals can mobilize women to participate in the relevant developmental programmes for women within their sphere of influence. Vocational guidance with available resources should be given to promote self-employment. Cottage industries can help in self-sufficiency in women.

Though Uttar Pradesh hill woman enjoys a higher social status it is indeed her involvement in the new schemes of development which makes way for her future development and open new thresholds and horizons for integration in the national mainstream. It is also important to note that the prevailing development programmes have a direct bearing on the status of tribal women hence it is imperative to take into account the specific problems of womenfolk so that they can develop, and through development prove as a part of the national mainstream. To avoid human resource wastage, as also for proper use of it, the traditional higher status of tribal women and freedom should be used to the maximum for their benefit with sincerity on everyone's part. This freedom in almost all the walks of tribal women's life can be usefully channelized into their overall development and bridge the wide gap between have-nots and the national mainstream through integration.

Though the mainstream is not officially or formally defined, but if we take a broader view of Indian society then its component of Hindu social organization sounds most conspicuous and prominent. It is chiefly constituted by the caste people. And the sociologists and social anthropologists are well aware of the fact that caste women are highly under-privileged and suffer from many socio-economic and socio-religious disabilities. Making of such a stream as positive reference model would simply be suicidal for tribal women who are, in many respects, better placed than the caste women and the stream to which they are affiliated. Under the circumstances, the greatest challenge to the agents of planned change, and consequent integration, is to manage for avoidance of all ill-effects emanating from caste social order. Else the integration may assume the form of disintegration. It may be mentioned that the signs of this trend are already visible in case of certain bigger tribes of India including Gond, Bhil, Santhal, Mina etc. Thus, getting into process of development for women is necessary but they should not then make themselves as second rate copy of others who themselves suffer from various forms of deprivations.

Though the substantivism in this paper seeks supports from tribal women of central Himalayas, its wider implications cannot be ruled out. The tribal women, in general, are extremely hardworking and involve themselves in all kinds of traditional economic pursuits. There is no conventional inhibition which debars them from such involvements. Freedom in many walks of life is a common feature in the world of tribal women. Such provisions in the traditional social structures of tribes are positive indicators of better treatment of tribal women. But what would happen when they get exposed, in the process of integration, to alien world-view? Will it be adversely affected? Here is a delicate juncture where the best in and best for tribal women are to be protected so that they do not express regret for their falling in the process of induced development. And if they are properly guided they can certainly overcome the fear of such kind in the course of development proposed from outside. By and large the tribal women in India are intelligent and assertive over their men-folk, and in the event of their being guided properly, they can certainly prevail upon men to agree to decisions needed for planned development and integration of tribes. Need still is to incorporate them to the desired level in a guided manner taking care of in-built provisions of tribal social structures.

Simultaneously the women are to be sufficiently empowered, in formal sense of the context proposed from outside, to grab the innovations. By now most of the procedures proposed under planned development empower men considering that men alone owns land and other property and holds the family leadership with all powers of decision-making. This is true in most of the situations. As an instance the loan provisions are predominantly for men only. As head of the family they enjoy many privileges in the course of development. But when the place of woman is so important in development, the corresponding powers, privileges and facilities should also be provided to her. These may even be brought at par with men. Unfortunately even the proposed amendments and new recommendations in respect of Panchayati Raj have not been implemented and made effective in the background in which they were initiated at ideas level. Somehow the women sector, at this front, remained ignored. And the women themselves are never asserted under certain impositions of conventional framework. Even with modest empowerment the tribal women can do wonders in gearing up development and integration as traditions do not curtail their freedom in many walks of life.

REFERENCES

Majumdar, D.N. 1962. *Himalayan Polyandry.* Bombay: Asia Publishing House.

Pande, G.C. 1988. "Role and Status of Women in Kumaun", in *K.S. Valdiya (ed.) Kumaun: Land and People.* Nainital: Gynodaya Prakashan

FIFTEEN

TRIBAL WOMEN OF WESTERN HIMALAYA
A Socio-Cultural Interpretation

GOPAL S. SINGH

Introduction

Western Himalaya covers about 2 per cent of the country's area and about 11 per cent of Himalaya landmass accommodating nearly 92 per cent people in villages with subsistence farming livelihood. Like other parts of Himalayan region (Ramakrishnan, 1992; Rao and Saxena, 1994), western Himalaya, in general, is characterized by inaccessibility, fragility, marginality, landscape heterogeneity, geoclimatic variability coupled with socio-cultural, economic and political flexibility. In such diverse conditions, the marginal people have developed dynamic ways of living. During the course of civilization, people mainly have been concerned with a productive interaction with nature, that surrounds him to ensure a comfortable existence. In this process, men and women have acquired expertise in different fields for a variety of works. For instance, women, traditionally, have been more skilled in domestic chores and sendentary activities while men have usually got more expertise to engage in strenuous work. On-farm produce is the major source of economy of the majority of the people. Agricultural practices are intensively performed by the women (Singh, 1997). Women's role in western Himalaya is exceptionally greater though it has not been practically evaluated in the realistic perspectives. Though enough literatures are available focussing to the importance of Indian women (Sen Gupta, 1969; Desai and Krishnaraj, 1987; Ghosh, 1984; Sahai, 1985; Pokhriyal, 1985, Biswas, 1990; Samal, 1993), yet information regarding the role of women in western Himalayan region is lacking (Singh, 1997) in terms of its totalitarian orientation. However, position and status of women vary from society to society and place to place depending upon culture and customs they have been born and brought up. To understand the nature of women-folk in any society, it is essential to focus currently on the cultural expression concerned. The pivotal of this paper is, therefore, to analyze the culture of tribal women/people on account of its effective functioning in terms of rights and privileges they enjoy in a tuned indigenous society of Sangla valley of Himachal Himalaya.

Landscape and the People: An Interlinked History

The landscape of Sangla valley is located in remote and inaccessible area of Kinnaur district. There are 11 villages scattered all along the Sangla valley. The houses are two storeyed which are built up by stones and woods, cemented with mud. Houses are either slated or flat roofed and are usually white washed. The ground floor is used for cattle shed, while the upper storey for living purpose. It is considered that people are from the Aryan stock, but a significant trace of mongoloid feature has also been noticed in them. The inhabitants are generally of dark brown complexion but good looking with a well built muscular stature. They are frank, active, generous, hospitable and highly honourable in their dealings. Two principal castes—Rajput Kanets and Scheduled Castes are common. Apart from Hinduism, people mostly follow the tenets of Buddhism. Sheep and goat rearing is very common. The people believe in swearing of the deity(ies) very much. The practice of polyandry is common. The people are mostly dressed in woollen clothes. Their clothing is well suited to the climate and culture. Women wrap a woollen shawl like garments locally known as *dohru* in a slightly different way than the *saree.*

The traditions of the people of Himachal Himalaya date back to the dawn of human civilization. Pre-historically, the Aryan settled down in the lower hills following the fertile valley of the higher Himalaya. Gradually, they fused with the indigenous tribes already inhabiting in area. In the cold desert to Lahaul, Spiti, Kinnaur and Pooh, settlers came from Tibet who were primarily of mongoloid origin. People restricted at the upper hills merged with the settlers. Ultimately, they settled with the harmonious use of variety of locally available resources.

Study Technique: A Participatory Rapid Appraisal Approach

The preliminary survey was conducted in entire Sangla valley. After reconnaissance of the area, three villages namely Batsery/Bosering, Rakchham and Chhitkul at different elevation were finally selected in Sangla valley for a thorough study. While selecting the villages it was ensured that these villages would represent all the characteristics of the valley. Equal representation was given to each village and a total of 75 per cent families were selected at random and were interviewed thoroughly. All informations particularly about the involvement of men and women in a variety of works including agriculture fields, domestic chores, animal rearing and forested area was collected through interview, discussions and filling up questionnaires during the year 1997. Most of the interviewees belong to small and medium size farm-holdings. Women were given equal preference at the time of filling the questionnaires. The role of in-depth rooted culture in eco-development and management programmes was also noted from individuals and was put then altogether into ecological, social and economic development context. Mean value of three villages is presented here. Problem for which no really satisfactory solutions were found was related to children's activities. Therefore, all the activities of men and women aged 12 years or more were recorded.

Social Stratification: A Complex Village Structure

The majority of the population comprises of Hindus. The two distinct and dominant castes, Rajput caste (higher section of the society) and Scheduled Caste (weaker section of the society) were recorded. Scheduled Castes are considered untouchables. Even today, caste factor determines the profession, status, life-style, social and cultural mobility and socio-economic behaviour of the people. Untouchability, one can find ignored at the common service points near water source, working in farming activities and sell-purchase. The notion of untouchability is also found rooted among children. Literacy rate is very poor because of lack of awareness regarding education and non-availability of education facility. However, girls are not sent to school as they are needed at home to look after the children, domestic and agricultural works. There is a general feeling among parents that girls even after study, have to engage themselves in domestic chores. Therefore, they are not in favour of giving education to girls. Such tendency leads to gender stratification. Hence, there is a strong need to promote equal education so that girls will get more benefit of it. Moreover, for changing the attitude of parents, education of adults is primarily needed.

As Table 15.1 reveals that the total population of the sample villages is 2150 comprising of 350 families. The female population is relatively higher than the male population. Therefore, the sex ratio (number of females per thousand males) is relatively higher (1026) from district (885) and state (973) averages. Total literacy rate (30 per cent) is much lower than the district (36 per cent) and the state level (42 per cent) (Anonymous, 1981). As mentioned above, girls are not sent to schools as they are needed at home to look after the small children, domestic and agricultural works. The details of traditional knowledge based practices of the people have been listed in Table 15.2.

TABLE 15.1: Demographic Profile of the Study Villages

Parameters	
Number of Households	350
Number of Human Population	2150
Male	775
Female	797
Children (<12 Years)	580
Sex Ratio	1026
Literacy Rate (percentage)	
Male	40
Female	24
Total	30

TABLE 15.2: Existence of Traditional Knowledge Based Practices in the Study Area

Traditional Practices	
Existence of traditional houses	Common
Existence of skilled person (mason, blacksmith, etc.)	Exist
Hydropower operated watermills	Exist
Hydropower operated sawmills	Exist
Use of wild edibles	High
Use of medicinal plants	High
Cultivation of traditional crops	High
Operation of organic farming practices	High
Operation of traditional breeding patterns	High
Preparation of handicraft objects	Common
Wearing of traditional dresses	Common
Existence of Informal village committee/institutions	Strong
Beliefs in local deity	Strong
Conservation of biodiversity through religious faith	Exist
Use of traditional implements/tools	Common
Participation in fairs and festivals	Good
Domestication of wild animals and its breeds	Exist
Practice of traditional technique and technology	Strong
Honey and liquor preparation	Common
Existence of agricultural crop diversity	High

Work Participation of Men and Women: Asymmetry Distribution

The human way of life is characteristically the thinking patterns of males, though females constitute half of the total population in a community. The beginning of the world historic defeat of the female sex is in dichotomization of the subsistence activities and establishment of the culturally defined division of labour that creates two genders-men and women. Gender virtually creates outer and inner spaces. This creates two genders men and women which leads to a gender asymmetry society. With the advent of the concept of private property, men attempt to control women's labour by engaging themselves farming activities. Significant economic contribution by men and secondary contribution like child care by women place way for the inner and outer spaces in the gender relations.

Agriculture is the primary occupation and major economic source of the majority of the people. Staple food crops like amaranths, chenopodium, chinochloa, hordeum, fagopyrum and vigna are commonly grown by subsistence farmers. Introduction of high yielding variety of food and fruit crops (wheat, apple and pear) is a very recent phenomena. Inherent geoclimatic features did not favour the growth of introduced crops in Chhitkul and Rakchham villages which are located at the higher elevation; the area is prone to heavy snow fall/precipitation. However, the cultivation of local crops is still dominating in the area.

Table 15.3 depicts that men usually undertake arduous and rigorous work like preparation of farm fields, terraces, sowing of seeds and application of chemical fertilizers while, women usually performed light work like weeding and tilling, carrying and spreading of organic manure and harvesting and threshing of food crops. During peak season (crop showing and harvesting, collection of leaf litter for organic manure preparation and storing of fuelwood for lean period), women exceptionally work even up to 17-18 hours per day; working 12-16 hours per day is routine phenomenon. Precarious and

TABLE 15.3: Work-Sharing rate (%) of men and women in Agriculture Sector

Activities	Men	Women
Land preparation before sowing	92.0	8.0
Carrying and spreading of organic manure	8.7	91.3
Use of inorganic fertilizers	100	—
Sowing of grains	100	—
Weeding and tilling	—	100
Harvesting of crops	16.7	83.3
Threshing of crops	23.0	76.9
Horticultural work	85.0	15.0

unpredictable environmental conditions favour such hard work of women. Bhandari (1991) claimed that women in hills have a work schedule stretching between 12 and 19 hours a day. Apple tree plantation is a recently introduced scheme in the area. In apple/horticulture field, men relatively performed major work than women. Marketing and packing of apples and carrying packed boxes near roadhead require the help of men, who are skilled in doing the work outside the village boundary. Therefore, changing agricultural land use and practices has started converting women oriented work to men dominated activity. Such kind of shifting pattern would certainly imperils the sustainability of the area and the people too. It, therefore, requires greater attention for rejuvenation of old practices otherwise women participation in agricultural activity will be neglected. Traditional food crop cultivation favour autonomy to the females.

Domestic chores are usually performed by women (Table 15.4). Food preparation is almost the job of women. Occasionally, when women are busy in some other works then food is cooked by men. Girls are, by virtue, trained by their mothers from an early age to sweep and clean the houses, child caring, clothes and kitchen utensils cleaning and other similar domestic activities. Usually, women of the weaker sections of the society are engaged to prepare handicraft items for subsistence economic generation. The handicraft items were sold either in village and/or in local market. House caring is the entire job of women except some major repairing which is done by men.

TABLE 15.4 : Work Sharing Rate (%) of Men and Women in Domestic Sector

Attributes	Men	Women
Food Preparation	2.0	98.0
Child Rearing	4.5	95.5
Handicraft Preparation	39.4	60.6
House Caring	2.0	98.0

Similarly, women also play very active role in collection of day-to-day required forest based resources such as fuelwood, fodder, and litter collection. Men are, however, relatively more engaged in seasonal collection of minor forest produce, particularly medicinal plant resource (Table 15.5) The collection of medicinal plants requires strenuous and courageous work from inhospitable forested areas. Along with brining fruits and flowers form the forest, women also depend on forest for water, bamboo based articles, herbs, grazing purpose, fuelwood, leaf for organic manure preparation. That is why they maintain a symbiotic relationship with trees of the forest. If forests are destroyed there is also destruction of knowledge which women have been empirically gathering since generations. That is why the whole of society does not have the same relationship with nature that women have. Therefore, forests are source of

TABLE 15.5: Work-Sharing Rate (%) of Men and Women in Forest Sector

Activities	Men	Women
Animal Rearing	22.6	77.4
Forest Litter, Fodder Collection	10.0	90.0
Fuelwood Collection	28.6	71.4
Minor Forest Produce Collection	61.5	38.5

the life for them. On the other hand, men's relationship with trees is primarily lifting the axe at them. Environmental imbalance caused by cutting of natural resources cannot only destroy the life of women but also threaten the loss of knowledge. Women of the area also acquire knowledge of herbs and ability to recognize a variety of medicinal herbs which can cure a number of illnesses. This knowledge has been transmitted from mothers to their daughters through generations. With destruction of natural resources this special knowledge of the girls is also being destroyed. Apart from the women, men sometimes have greater knowledge relating to use of biological resources: in certain cases, men harbour more knowledge about resources because of their contact with the outside world. Distribution/occurrence of biological resources close to inhospitable geographical area is another factor that favours men's knowledge building process because in such area only men can go, collect and use those resources.

Status of Women: A Socio-Cultural Variability

There are many societies, particularly in plains, where women face very lowly status, their indispensable activities do not receive any categorical recognition. At the same time, there are other societies representing remote areas (hilly areas) where women receive some honour and prestige and their roles in society are properly highlighted and governed through different norms, traditions, and ethos. Status of women and their importance differ from society to society, community to community and even place to place. In study area, the status of different sexes are not uniform due to diversified communities. It is exclusively governed by the cultural traditions of the people concerned. The women are, therefore, shaped according to the cultural patterns. The role and status of women are the outcome of the age long traditions of the cultural groups where they are born and brought up. Thus, to understand the nature of women folk in any society, particularly traditional society, the concerned cultural patterns are needed to be focussed accurately. Thus, the status of women is dependent on nature of function in social organization. If socio-economic functions of women are high their status is naturally higher. But, if her economic functions are not very important she does not enjoy a high social standing in the community. In the prevailing social matrix, the tribal women of western Himalaya enjoy considerable freedom of movement compared to their non-tribal counterpart.

The status of women in the different communities can be understood more in the context of the socio-cultural spectrum of the concerned society (ies). It has been found that economy, ecology and ethnic environment make conspicuous differentiation on cultural features. Culture is the product of human sentiment and which is principally guided by environment situation. The status of women in any society is, therefore, the result of multiple factors and it can never be assessed in the background of a single feature of action. In spite of the work variability one can portray that women in hill, in general, spend their time more for productive work than the women in plain. In stead of their hard work, they love to enjoy their culture. Women, particularly from their work distribution point of view, enjoy even high status than men. They freely take the decision of work, what to do and what not to do. Therefore, the social status enjoyed by women of western Himalaya is considered higher in comparison to plain areas. A woman has equal right with her husband in policy and decision-making system. Women enjoy complete freedom to choose their life partner(s). Details of other socio-cultural practices are being discussed here separately.

Polyandry: A Productive Socio-Cultural Institution

Polyandry as a social and cultural institution has often been connotated as a cultural oddity in the evolution of family. In certain parts of Lahaul and Spiti, Kinnaurs, Sirmaur, Jammu & Kashmir, and Ladakhis in western Himalaya, Jaunsaries in central Himalaya and Gallongs, Failobos, Tangamas, Hill Miris and Wanchoos in eastern Himalaya, the practice of polyandry is the singular manifestation of value attitude system, inherent in culture as a most suitable adaptation to sustain the community through checks and controls. The practice of this old institution is still operating in the study areas/villages. Inhospitable geo-climatic condition has resulted polyandry as a suitable cultural institution to maximize the scarce resources available at their disposal for sustenance. Since, it evolved as an appropriate adaptation that upkept economic conditions in conformity with the prevailing ecological and environmental factors, it was made a cultural complex sanction of social codes and conducts. Polyandry favours a number of markers of sustainability which include demographic advantages, economic advantages, and old age security through prevalence of joint family structure. Such a system favours no concept of widow until youngest brother (of the husband) is alive. A girl has the right to select/choose her prospective husband and decide that should she marry him alone and remain his exclusive wife or be wife to his brothers also. In other words, practice of polyandry depends on the willingness of women. There is a tale in this region that a woman is never widow.

Fairs and Festivals: A Interlinked Cultural Practices

Fairs and festivals are indispensable part of cultural life of the people of Himachal Himalaya. Every fair and festival has legendary origin which acts as governing factor in each of such gatherings. It has educational, social as well as religious character. It fulfills the need of social equity from both economic and cultural perspectives. The season plays a major role in shaping the festivals; every season has its own appropriate festival(s). Thus, the arrival of winter is celebrated by the festival of the bonfire and the summer by the festival of flowers. Each season is marked by an appropriate festival in which the ceremonies and celebrations are influenced by the climatic needs or other characteristics of the season. Some festivals are also related to moon, agriculture, gods and goddess. This is also an occasion for mass feasting, drinking and dancing.

The concept of fair is quite different from what it is in other parts of the country. The community gods and their devotees create the atmosphere of fair. The gods with their devotees participate on such an occasion whose sanctity is preserved. Some are commercial and some are agricultural fairs, most of these help in get together, a style unique to the hills. People are very much in love with their traditional style. Fairs as a media of mass recreation, are very popular in these traditional societies. They may be divided into seasonal fairs, mythical fairs, trade and agricultural fairs, and fairs connected with festivals. All the groups/classes of men, women and children are found singing and dancing on local instruments along with local deity(ies). People also sale their agricultural produce, bamboo items, traditional items, and forest resources including medicinal plants at the fairs. Such operations have intricate link with nature-livestock-agriculture sector with social-cultural sector. It contributes immensely to social sustainability. During such instances people visit to their relatives and strengthen their social linkages.

Handicraft Industry: A Traditional Skilled Technique

Traditional techniques for producing a variety of handicraft articles are found to be rich among the marginal people. Techniques of preparation of these items are professionally interwoven among people of different castes. Men are more skilled for preparation of pottery, basketry, metal and wood works than women and this skill is a source of subsistence economy. However, in weaving and embroidery works, women are more expert. Similarly, a variety of woolen items are also prepared by women. Women have, overall, expertise in knitting and weaving. Knowledge pertaining to the preparation of woollen items are found in all the social groups. However, people in lower income groups and weaker sections of the society depend more on such hand-made items. Sheep and goat breedings and rearing are so common to meet their own requirements. Each family has small quality of wool to meet its own needs. In winter when their is no field work, women and even children spin the wool with spinning wheel *takli.*

Most basketry objects are made for purely practical purpose. As compared to the female these items are exclusively interwoven by males; females do help in clearing the bamboo and making small pieces. Weaker sections of the society are oftenly engaged in such traditional products. With the passage of time, handicraft industry has developed its root in day-to-day life of the people and ultimately the industry becomes an inherited occupation. Interwoven with their life, these crafts have provided perpetual inspiration to the folk masses. Details of different items prepared by these people have been discussed by Singh *et al.,* (1996) elsewhere.

Factors Imperil the Culture of Tribal Women

Influx of tourism and growth of unplanned infrastructural facilities and introduction of high yielding varied of food and fruit crops has started distorting the sustainability of the area. Resulting to this, the culture of the tribal society, in general, and women, in particular, is under immense threat. Penetration of market oriented articles is also replacing the traditional values. Modernization has brought up men dominated ideology and technology. Distortion of traditional values and ethos for the sake of modernization is the major factor in widening the gap between old and new values. Change in land use patterns, from traditional food crop cultivation to cash crops and fruit bearing trees, has imperiled the overall tribal culture. Giving more priority to the indigenous knowledge based practices could narrow down the gaps incurred in old values. All the alien factors, introduced in the area, are merely responsible for deteriorating the women status at alarming rate.

Revival of Tribal Women Culture through Participatory Approach

Sustainable priorities are required to revive the indigenous practices that have evolved locally and have been inheriting since generations. Socio-cultural imbalances, widely arose due to introduction of exogenous forces, need to be rejuvenated through capitalizing on old social values. Evolving an empowering curriculum and teaching methodologies for women such as to speak freely, to question without fear, to trust in oneself, to have faith in others, to be empathetic—all call for a level of self awarness and confidence building, which not many people (least of all women) have. The development of these life skills not only facilitate the aquisition of literacy skills but also enhance the quality of skills acquired. The neglect of women's participation in issues of development is also cause of destruction of women-nature relationship. Hence, there is a great need to evolve participatory approach for empowering and capacity building of men, women and nature. To understand the relationship between men, women and nature, it is necessary to know the reality of the specific forms of their relationship and interlinkages. In society, there is division of labour based on sex and class (caste/race). The relationship between people and nature is based on the structure of sex and class relations. In the study area, work sharing in different sub-systems is the result of interlinked relationship between men and women and their environment. Finally, new alternatives must be based on a greater knowledge of these tribal people by taking into account the traditional practices and empirical knowledge of the local community. A broad participatory socio-cultural management could be evolved by applying interlinked scientific knowledge on men-women-forest-animal-agriculture on one hand and in government's developmental priorities on the other.

Summary

Since the dawn of civilization, gender has played a significant role in the lives of human beings. In the traditional/tribal societies of western Himalaya women have an important integrated role interwoven with socio-cultural values with environment. The distinct distribution of work of men and women has evolved locally for productive functional use and has been inheriting since generations. It is seen that the status of different sexes are exclusively dependent upon culture of the people concerned. The women's status, position and authority are, by and large, equal to men. The functional role of tribal women is also important from the point of socio-economic activities as well. On-farm produce is the backbone of economic activities in the area. Women's work is more valuable than that of men in the case of prevailing subsistence intensive farming practices. Women work 15-16 hours a day and enjoy their life in their interwoven socio-cultural set-up tuned to the region. They never feel bore in harsh and inhospitable geographic and incertitude environmental conditions but have moulded themselves to contribute optimally through the productive and conducive enterprises in such intricate eco-cultural and social set-up. Organizing frequent fairs and festivals is one of the ways of their enjoyment since age old times. Women have full right and freedom to do whatsoever they wish. Introduced modern on-farm technologies, infrastructural facilities, mushrooming commercialization and in-flux of tourism are the root causes of disordering the delicate harmonious relationship between tuned ecological-environment set-up and social-cultural values of society. As response to this, it has imposed tumultuous threat to the traditional knowledge of men and women. Lack of government developmental policies focusing on cultural domain is endangering the indigenous knowledge system of the region. Developmental approach should be centered around the traditional knowledge oriented packages rather than introduced alien packages. A planned participatory development policy/programme is required to upgrade the status of tribal women in western Himalaya.

Acknowledgement

Sincere thanks are extended to Dr. Gulab Singh for giving critical suggestions and encouragement while writing the paper.

REFERENCES

Anonymous. 1981. *Census of India, Himachal Pradesh District Census Handbook,* Kinnaur District (Series 7), Director of Census Operations, Himachal Pradesh.

Bhandari, D.K. 1991. "Women and Planning in the Hills", *Himalaya Today,* 111,2

Biswas, B. 1990. "On Being Woman in the Himalaya", in S. K. Biswas (ed.), *Strategy of Development in the Himalaya: A Profile of Socio-Economic Change.* Calcutta: Institute of Social Research and Applied Anthropology.

Desai, N. and M. Krishnaraj. 1987. *Women and Society in India. Delhi:* Ajanta Publication.

Ghosh, S. K. 1984. *Women in Changing Society.* New Delhi: Ashis Publication

Pokhriyal, H.C. 1985. *Woman Power Planning in Himalayan Region.* Bombay: Khadigramodyog, Gramodaya.

Ramakrishnan, P. S. 1992. *Shifting Agriculture and Sustainable Development: An Interdisciplinary Study from North Eastern India.* MAB Series Vol. 10 UNESCO and Carnforth (UK): Parthenon Publishing Group.

Rao, K. S. and K.G. Saxena. 1994. *Sustainable Development of Rehabilitation of Degraded Village Lands in Himalaya.* Dehradun: Bishen Singh Mahendra Pal Singh.

Sahai, S.N. 1985. *Women in Changing Society.* Delhi: Mittal Publication.

Sen Gupta, S. (ed.). 1969. *Women in Indian Folklore: Linguistic and Religious Study, A Short Survey of their Social Status and Position.* Calcutta: Indian Publication Folklore Publication Series 15.

Samal, P.K. 1993. "The Status of Women in Central Himalaya: A Cultural Interpretation," *Man in India,* 73: 87-95.

Singh, G.S., K. G. Saxena, K. S. Rao and S.C. Ram. 1996. "Traditional Knowledge and Threat of its Extinction in Chhakinal Watershed in North Western Himalaya," *Man in India,* 76:1-17.

—. 1997. "Work Participation and Social Status of Women: A Case Study of Kullu Valley," *Man and Development,* 19: 97-108.

SIXTEEN

DEVELOPMENT, DISPLACEMENT, REHABILITATION AND THE AFTERMATH

An Impact Study on Tribal Women

ITISHREE PADHI

In spite of the increased number of studies on women pouring in during the past few years, intensive studies on tribal women remain few and far between. Experience of tribal women, their perspectives on social events have rarely been reflected by the social scientists. Consciously or unconsciously we have cared a little to perceive and analyze the perceptions of tribal women from their socio-economic, politico-religious and developmental point of view.

Things change with time; so also the awareness of tribal women. In the passing years government concerns, growing activism of tribal organizations as well as research have started focussing attention on the changing position of tribal women. While traditionally the status of tribal women was high, colonial policy, sanskritisation, modernization and directed developmental measures have brought conspicuous change in their life-style. Whether this change in status of tribal women is a boon or ban still remains unanswered.

Development and modernization through building of new infrastructures in tribal belts cause displacement of age-old tribal set-ups. Further, rehabilitation measures taken up by government throw the tribal people many a time into completely alien lands. New developmental programmes start in the rehabilitated area both by government and non-governmental sectors, directly or indirectly, bring change in the life style of the tribals in the new set-up. Surprisingly, majority of the developmental measures executed so far are in favour of men-folk. Developmental policies are seen mainly male-oriented; a few of them are sensitive and supportive to the needs of tribal women. Thus, a large majority of tribal women remains poor, resourceless, illiterate and hence exploited.

Agrarian reforms along with industrial mechanization have failed to retain the important role successfully played by the tribal women in their age old traditional occupation of subsistence agriculture. The organized sector offers little scope for women to prove their efficiency. Even under the rehabilitation programmes for the tribal people, opportunities for wage labour, higher paying jobs and training for skilled supervisory positions are mostly availed by men. Tribal females are relegated either to the status of marginal labourers or left behind in non-competitive shrinking traditional sectors.

Realizing the above anomalies in the present system and keeping in view the tribals in general and the tribal women in particular, the present study attempts to conduct a micro-level study on tribal women of a rehabilitated village to assess the impact of development on their life style in the changing social milieu.

Review of Literature

Displacement is believed to be the consequence of the path to development that has been pursued in our country. This can also be seen as a consequence of the struggle for natural resources such as land, forest, water, mineral and other forest products. Whatever may be the reason, displacement brings untold misery to the displaced persons and his family. Pattnaik (1991) shows in his work that the public purpose for which land is acquired is of paramount importance to the government and therefore the individual interests of uprooted families do not enter into the calculation of state policy. The existing policy has no socio-psychological orientation and does not take into cognizance its unequal impact on different groups of displaced people. Vidyarthy's (1976) study of displaced tribals of Hatia Industrial complex in Chotanagpur region of Bihar shows that each compensation cannot be a permanent solution for them. Most of his sample respondents felt that installation of industrial complex in the area had been more beneficial to the aliens and it was hazardous to the local people.

Muthayya and Mathur (1977) give similar statement in their study of oustees of Ramchandrapuram of Medar district of Andhra Pradesh. Displacement of people is not coupled with properly envisaged programme of rehabilitation. The rehabilitation policy is not enough to encompass the intensity of various groups of people displaced. A wide gulf exists between the objective of the planning and its actual implementation. Planning is done in all seriousness but since the cultural factors are not cogently considered some loopholes may exist in it. At the level of implementation the problem becomes accentuated and hence development is not able to yield all that is expected of it. Mention may be made of Behura (1989), Mishra (1982) and Roy Burman (1968) who have also made some important contribution in this regard.

From the above literature it could be known that though a number of studies have been conducted on various aspects of displaced and resettled people, very little effort has been made to focus on the changing conditions of the tribal women who have been displaced and resettled along with their families. Realizing this potential significance involved in such studies, an attempt has been made here to study the impact of development programmes on the Juang women of a rehabilitated village (Kathagada). Data were collected from 21 heads of the households and their wives through a month long field-work using interview and observation methods. Relevant secondary data, wherever available, were collected in order to supplement our analysis.

II

The Juang is one of the aboriginal Mundari speaking scheduled tribes of Orissa, distributed in the districts of Ķeonjhar and Dhenkanal, though more in Keonjhar district. The Gandhamardan range of mountain in Orissa is the original abode of Juang since centuries. History says that Juang tribals are primarily food gatherers and shifting cultivators. They are also engaged in the barter of minor forest produces with local population in order to generate a supplementary income. Shifting cultivation is not only the chief source of income, but it also associates the local people with their social organization, rites and rituals along with political and economic activities. But the practice of shifting cultivation has come to a stand still thereby disrupting their life style when the government puts a ban on the above process. Juangs of Kathagada, having being displaced from the village Pahalada in the district Dhenkanal were forced to change their traditional pattern of cultivation. They now engage themselves in cultivable lands given by the state government. Here begins the plight of women folk of this community. They are found to be the worst sufferens in the process of rehabilitation and resettlement. Traditionally these women were supposed to stay at home in order to take care of their household activities and extend their helping hands in cultivation to their male counterparts. On the other hand men used to engage themselves mostly in different types of economic activities in order to earn their livelihood. But at present, it is found that after rehabilitation the Juang men have lost interest in the traditional economic activities thereby shifting the family responsibilities to the women. The empirical study on the position of the women of this community in Kathagada village provides enough evidence of the above fact.

Table 16.1: Economic Activities and Non-economic Activities

	Male	Female	Both	Total
Economic Activities				
(i) Cultivation and wage earnings	10	11	—	21
(ii) Wood and leaf collection from the forest	03	16	02	21
(iii) Selling leaf plates and wood pieces	—	21	—	21
Non-economic Activities				
(i) Cooking	—	21	—	21
(ii) Child rearing	01	20	—	21
(iii) Cleaning of utensils	—	21	—	21
(iv) Washing of clothes	—	06	15	21
(v) Sweeping	—	21	—	21
(vi) Fetching of Water	—	21	—	21
(vii) Buying food stuff	02	17	02	21
(viii) Taking major family decision	—	10	11	21

In order to assess the role of women in the present study, the activities of the Juang people have been divided into two parts namely economic activities and non-economic activities (Table 16.1). The economic activities include cultivation and leaf stitching which are primary sources of their income. The secondary sources of income is selling of wood and part-time labour work. The non-economic activities include all other works except those relating to economy. Table 16.1 reveals that in 11 out of 21 families, women are directly involved in cultivation of land. According to the opinion of these people till date the government has not provided them ownership right on land *(patta)* after rehabilitation. There is always a sense of insecurity among these people relating to the possession of land. The men of this community hardly contribute labour for the improvement of land thereby conferring this hazardous task on women. Besides this, as the table indicates, even in the activities like wood and leaf collection the participation of women is much more than that of men. The Juang females not only collect leaves from the forest but also stitch them in order to make Leaf plates and sell them in the local market. Also it is the females who bear the responsibility of household management. Not only this, the percentage of male participation in non-economic activities is very negligible. Thus, Juang women of Kathagada are doubly burdened due to lack of support from their male counterparts in running the house. Juang men do not participate in cooking, cleaning utensils, sweeping home and other household activities although most of the time they spend without any other engagement. It is the women who has to look after the child and to take care of each and every member of the family. Interestingly enough in more than 50 per cent houses, major decisions in the family are taken mutually. In ten out of twenty-one houses female opinion gets priority in major decision-making processes. Thus the small population of Juang community of this village gives enough evidence of the misery of these women who by and large single-handedly bear the entire responsibility of the house.

III

After government's ban on clearing forest area, Juang people of Kathagada have been facing scarcity of lands and forest products. As studied from the village itself, economic backwardness of these people has put them at a bare subsistence level. In order to bring them into the national mainstream, government has adopted a number of developmental measures. Among them, mention may be made of NADA (Notified Area Development Appraisal), IBO (Individual Benefit Orientation Scheme), CBO (Commercial Benefit Oriented Scheme), CDP (Community Development Programme) and many more loan schemes and training programmes. Though all these are taken up by government for the betterment of the Juang people, majority of them have failed to reach at the goal and only a few of them are coming into sight. Besides there is no such programme which is specifically meant for the eradication of women's problem. Women are in no way positively affected by these schemes and programmes. Only the widows get a sum of Rs. 100 per month under widow pension scheme and that too not on a regular basis. Further, women are reported to be exploited sexually by the middlemen who come to their village in order to implement the developmental programmes. The traditional way of health practice by women no longer prevails as they are legally forbidden to collect forest products by cleaning forest area. In spite of so many plans and programmes, both from government and non-government sectors, there is no change in the living standard of women who have been settled at Kathagada village after rehabilitation.

IV

Today, these tribal women stand at the cross roads. The adverse impact of development on them has been higher as compared to the benefits of the developmental programmes and modernization process. Loss of identity, loss of traditional knowledge, such as that of indigenous medicine, health practices, etc., have led to the erosion of self-esteem and the overall status of tribal women. Policy makers and planners have remained insensitive to the gender dimensions of tribal development. Now it is the high time to improve the situation so that the needs of the tribal women can be identified and taken into consideration in formulating policies and programmes. Also it should become mandatory to sensitize all concerned about the adverse impact of gender based development on tribal women so as to arrest the present trend.

REFERENCES

Behura, M.K. 1989. "Socio-economic Problems and Social Change among the Velocates of Rengali Dam: A Case Study". *Man and Life,* 15 (1&2): 1-22.

Mishra, Gitanjali. 1982. "Impact of Developmental Schemes on a Hill Juang Village of Orissa", *Journal of Indian Anthropology,* 17: 119-127.

Muthaya, B.C. and J.S. Mathur. 1977. *Rehabilitation of Displaced Villagers: A socio-economic and Attitudinal Study in an Agro-Industrial Complex in Rural Andhra Pradesh.* Hyderabad: National Institute of Rural Development.

Pattnaik, Soumendra Mohan. 1991. "River Dam Projects: Rehabilitation Policies and Social change: A Case of Upper Kolab River Project of Orissa," *The Eastern Anthropologist,* 42 (4): 390-410.

Roy Burman, B.K. 1968. *Social Process in the Industrialisation of Rourkela with Reference to Displacement and Rehabilitation of Tribal and other Backward People.* Census of India 1961. Vol-1. Monograph Series, Part XI E.

Vidyarthi, L.P. and B.K. Roy. 1976. *Tribal Culture in India.* New Delhi: Concept Publishing Company.

SECTION IV

EDUCATION

SEVENTEEN

TRIBAL EDUCATION AND SOCIAL CONCERN
Some Reflections

SUGUNA PATHY

Generally speaking the level of education in a society reflects the prevailing conditions of its political economy, be it tribal or non-tribal formations. With regards to the literacy level of general population India's performance is far from satisfactory. This is notwithstanding the inter and intra-state and regional disparities. Deducing from the general educational development the tribal education scenario cuts a sorry figure. The position of female tribal education requires to be analyzed from this background. The female literacy rate in the tribal population speaks very extreme end of unequal and unjust social relations. Notwithstanding the slight variation between male and female literacy rates in tribal population the conditions, the context and the problems are similar to both. Accordingly it is essential to analyze the tribal education from a holistic point of view in the context of changing social organization of production and development of capitalism. The present paper moves in this direction.

It is shocking to learn from the human research development programme's annual report, United Nations, that India is at the bottom of 180 countries only a bit ahead of Afghanistan, Bangladesh and sub-Saharan countries. However, there is nothing to be consoled here precisely, as all these countries are characterized by continuous civil war and other external political turmoils while India is free from such political stirs. It is significant to note that the education sector in India receives only four per cent of its share from the GDP out of which a larger part is catered to the needs of higher education while only a fifth of its total educational outlay is diverted towards primary education. The state of social sector in India is alarming in the current space age epoch. On the other side there is a wide gap between the North and

* Paper prepared for the Seminar "Tribal Women and Education" in the Department of Anthropology, Delhi University, Delhi, 6-7 May, 1997.

South countries and thus it is important to note that the developing processes we envisage are in the context of unequal social orders—both internal and external unequal contexts. We are trapped in the net of eugenistic utopia of technological civilization with a few natural resources while people are being displaced by the dams, zoological parks, missile testing range, dumping sites, etc. Mostly tribal people are the victims of this developmental onslaught. Today everyone is concerned of future social organization, the flora and the fauna besides the availability of natural resources. The concern is natural as well as desirable in the context of rapid denudation of the natural resources under the rubric of capitalist development. The impact of development resulting profit oriented economy on tribal women needs a special attention who are the victims of the depletion of natural resources.

Since the last five decades various plans and programmes, not to mention the countless academic exercises, have been at work to raise and improve the educational levels among the tribal people. Unfortunately the picture is grim as the results are far from satisfactory. It is a truism that education has an important role in social development. Thus it is assumed that the formal education would enable the tribal people to meet the present and future confrontations specially in the market and consumer cultural milieu while eventually integrating them in the national mainstream. But this could not be resulted given the unequal social conditioning.

The issue of tribal education invariably draws our attention to the tribal question and the related tribal development policies. The less said is much better while the scope of the present paper do not permit us to go in for details. Besides we are aware of the inherent lacunae as well as the inadequacies of the policies. In 1960 the Scheduled Areas and Scheduled Tribes Commission was set up with the aim of integrating the people into the mainstream. Undoubtedly mainstream in this regard refers to the dominating indeologies and cultures which suppress "other" cultures. Till the Second Plan the development programmes were confined to community level in the tribal areas. By the Third Plan this was shifted under sub-plan sector coming under welfare of Backward Classes resulting in Tribal Development Blocks (TDB). In addition Tribal Development Agencies (TDA) were set up during the Fourth Plan period in Andhra Pradesh, Bihar, Madhya Pradesh and Orissa in a bit to cover up the agrarian movement in these areas comprising a comprehensive development schemes like protective measures, economic development and social services. Tribal Sub-plan (TSP) was established during the Fifth Plan with the objective of channelising the flow of benefits arising out of plan outlays from the general sector at the state and central level for the welfare of the Scheduled Tribes. While in the Sixth Plan about 249 pockets outside Integrated Tribal Development Programme (ITDP) with the population of 5000 out of 10,000 in each pocket were identified under

Modified Area Development Approach (MADA). In addition to this 74 primitive tribal groups also were marked during the Sixth Plan for comprehensive development. The results of TSP strategy was a big mess, not to speak of any achievement. Subsequently the Seventh Plan envisaged for overall improvement of social and economic development of the people.

Meanwhile it is acknowledged by the government that only 17 per cent of the tribal sub-plan outlay in the state was catered to family oriented programmes while the bulk was diverted to the infrastructural development (Government of India, 1984: 4). In addition to the financial outlay, the tribal sub-plan is expected to cover issues like (i) raising the productivity levels of the tribal people in production so as to alleviate them from poverty; (ii) developing human resources and improving education; (iii) arresting exploitation of tribal people with special reference to land, usury, indebtedness, trade, excise and forest and (iv) developing of adequate infrastructure *(ibid:* 9). The Seventh Plan document regarding tribal development observes that majority of the tribal areas remained indebted and backward; the tribal areas are characterized by socio-economic exploitation by non-tribals; integrated tribal development programmes do not take into cognition of other programmes and so on. In this connection it is worth to note that "for want of adequate knowledge on the part of the planning personnel, it is possible that by taking a wrong decision, the development process makes no headway at all. To avoid this phased programme codification of customary laws relating to property (particularly land) inheritance, family and kinship, *traditional institutions and traditional village officials* will be necessary" (cited in Roy Burman, 1997: 53). According to the report of the Working Group with regard to Scheduled Tribes in the Seventh Plan, it is observed that despite all measures 85 per cent of the total tribal families live below the poverty line as compared to the 38 per cent at the national level (Report of the Working Group on Development of Scheduled Tribes during Seventh Five Year Plan (1985-1990). If this is the level of economic conditioning after a series of plans and programmes, the level of education of the tribal people is anybody's guess. This is so because of the unilinear mode of development approach to the tribal question. Precisely as tribal development is a complex network of structural factors consisting economic and cultural indicators, strategies, schemes and priorities demanding a holistic approach. Therefore, given the nature of diversities alternate measures need to be context specific.

At the outset education is only a means but not an end in itself, the objective being to impart knowledge to pass on from generation to generation. On the other side informal education is taken care of by different social constituents. Formal education has a major role in the present complex social organization which is expected to equip the future citizens for better tomorrow through schooling and teaching. Thus it goes without saying that it is necessary to perceive education from the wider context, but not in isolation. It is true that education is a convenient tool of state in imparting dominant ideologies and cultures. At the same time this is also true that education brings changes in social and economic spheres. In either ways education is conditioned and accordingly steered by the prevailing political economy. Accordingly education is a social product and changes as per the demands of social dynamics and is not independent agent of transmission of knowledge, ideas and values.

To begin with, education among the tribal communities (right from 1880) was launched to civilize the "wild tribes"—a colonial perception of the people. For the colonial government appointed the Indian Education Commission (1882) emphasizing the need to educate the tribal people (Government of Bombay, 1958. *Review of Education in Bombay State, 1855-1955).* The issue of tribal education is one of the most unresolved item in India despite all the efforts, measures and provisions since fifty years. However, this is not to deny a few changes in tribal literacy rates (Table 17.1). On the whole literacy among STs' is bleak with high dropout rate (wastage) particularly at the elementary stage which requires the attention of the policy.

TABLE 17.1: Level of education among the Tribal Peoples

S.No.	Year	% of total literacy	% of ST literacy
1.	1931	7.5	0.75
2.	1961	28.29	8.54
3.	1971	34.50	11.29
4.	1981	36.70	16.35
5.	1991	38.50	18.32

Source: Government of India, 1994. Report of the Working Group on Development of Scheduled Tribe's Literacy, New Delhi.

In addition not only there is a wide disparity between the tribal people and non-tribal people but also among various states and among different tribal communities. This trend clearly signals that a uniform education policy for all the communities cannot be formulated. For, provision of just a school in the tribal regions is not enough in itself. Be that as it may, the variation of literacy rate in different tribal regions is vast as well as complex. According to an estimate of the Fourth All India Education Survey by NCERT, literacy rate is high in north-eastern region. For this matter Mizoram tops in tribal literacy while Arunachal Pradesh exhibits lowest literacy in the region (Mishra, 1991). The prevalent literacy differentials are due to the unequal levels of development in different regions, states and communities.

More often the assumption with regard to tribal education is to develop them, enlarge their world ethos and also to enable them to face the changing social conditions. This way it is assumed that formal education of the tribal people would eventually lead them to participate in the national stream. In other words the objectives of education is to reduce the gap between the tribal and non-tribal people (Pathy, 1996). So far so good. But the reality is that the cultural cognition of the people is lost somewhere in the course of national integration. What is this integration about? It was aptly observed that "The wider society is making more forceful impact on the Adivasi society than in the past" (Desai, 1977: 144). Does it denote camouflaging their specific identities or stressing their identities in the totality? This needs to be reconsidered at the policy level. For cultures are not static and undergo change according to the changes in the organization of production and it is the reflection of their social and ecological environment. Thus there is a need for identifying, defining and reconfigurating cultural categories. Notable in this context is the handicrafts of the tribal people. It may be mentioned that their handicrafts are the inseparable components of the integrated traditions, where painting, sculpture, pottery and so on are very much related deeply with the annual cycle of festivals, fairs, mythology, folklore, song, dance, ritual practices and oral traditions. In this way the people maintain their eternal rhythm. The significant point is that art for tribal people does not connote individualism but a unique collective expression, spontaneity and an internalized outlook which can be integrated with the education pattern in the tribal context. This can be adopted without changing the ethical and aesthetic expressions. It is disturbing to note that the development of the tribal people through education sometimes takes over their ritual and artistic expression by giving them only commercial direction.

The tribal people in India is a mosaic representing concerned ecological, ethical and production dimensions. They adopt suitable and related changes accordingly and these processes vary according to different levels of development among different communities and in different regions. The point we have been emphasizing in that tribal education needs to focus on community specificities. This diversity has been acknowledged by Kothari Education Commission (1964-68) while National Policy on Education (1986) and the Revised Policy (1992) also reiterated this aspect at micro level. To be precise education for tribal people needs to be contextualized with regard to diverse patterns of the people numbering 67.8 million (8%).

Central and state governments adopt legislative and executive measures for protesting the rights of the tribal communities. These measures are enframed in the Directive Principles of state policy in Article 46 of the Constitution. Despite various protective measures the expansion of formal education in the tribal areas is not uniform and correlates with the striking intra and inter-regional desparities. Thus for instance low literacy rate prevails in the states of Andhra Pradesh, Madhya Pradesh, Orissa, Rajasthan, etc. while it is satisfactory in Gujarat and Maharashtra. The disparities are not merely spatial but also inter-communal as well. Many studies on tribal education have observed that the efforts to raise the level of education of the tribal people at the national level has remained very far (Patel, 1983; Sachchidananda, 1982). In the interim the uniform development policies of the state have been accrued by some sections of the tribal communities. Though enrolment of tribal children on the whole has increased substantially it neither reflects improvement in education nor active participation. While more children between 6 to 11 years of age enrol in Class I and Class II the number drops down in higher classes and finally ends up in high drop-out rate and stagnation.

There are four dimensions with regard to tribal education, viz. the taught, the teacher, the educational institution and more importantly the specificity of the area concerned. These components and their application evidently will contribute a lot in the context of tribal education while arresting stagnation and wastage gradually. For this is the major problem of education in tribal regions as the students take more time than required in a particular class (Srivastava, 1971). Studies have shown that the main reason for stagnation is economic constraint as it is found that there is a close relationship between the level of education and land holding pattern. Concurrently the respective educational benefits are closely related with the respective class positions (Sachchidananda, 1982). Subsequently educational benefits are unevenly distributed. Other reasons for poor educational presence in the tribal regions are manifold like the absence of committed teachers, lack of boarding facilities, no guarantee of employment, alien medium of instruction and indifferent curriculum. Above all is the alienation of the taught as the curricula do not incorporate the cultural ethos of the tribal milieu resulting in increasing marginalization. Besides more often than not educational programmes are targeted to quantitative expansion over qualitative output. It has been observed that often literacy programmes and the educational pattern in tribal areas do not cognize the eco-sociological angle, the specificities and their unique survival strategies in the modern technocratic age as "there is little on ethnic philosophy, ethnic epistemology, ethnic cultural dynamics, ontological bases of community rights, external encroachments and impact of world system" (Pathy, 1996:6). Furthermore the low level of education is also the result of zero access to school, slow enrolment, poor quality of teaching due to lack of infrastructure. On the whole the educational constraints are due to morphological factors like ecological, economic and cultural; anatomical factors like alienation and marginalization processes, non-suitable school calendar and a variety of related factors. In addition the slow education process in tribal areas is further complicated by the gap between the educated tribals and the non-literate tribal people and also between male and female literates. In this connection, very often the needs of women are explicitly or implicitly ignored on the recentric assumption that what is good for men in equally good for women. This bias undermines the potential of women-centred educational development programmes. Specially as education in tribal areas is very closely related with economic activities and in particular with tribal women in collection of forest produce, fuel wood and fodder. In this context it needs to be mentioned that capitalism creates new needs resulting in unprecedented consumption, a regular feature of the modern societies. In this connection often the consumer policies of the third world countries take priority over the needs of the people. For an instance the forest policy in tribal areas which affects women directly is a case in point. When one toils for hours to meet their survival needs where is the time to go or even a thought of going to school? It seems a distant dream under the given structural conditions. The state goes for increasing denudation of forests for industries to supply raw materials. The pro-market bias is visible in converting the protected forests into Reserved Forests. Even in Social Forestry Programme the stance is no better either as the people are supplied with commercial species. Accordingly we hold that on the whole female tribal literacy is a neglected aspect of tribal education. For example the 1991 census data display an alarming picture of tribal literacy rate in Orissa in general and females in particular. As per 1991 census tribal population in Orissa is about 71 lakhs with about 35 lakhs males and an equal number of females. The percentage of tribal literacy is 18.10 per cent in the state out of which male tribal literacy is 27.92 per cent while the female literacy rate is as low as 8.30 per cent speaks volumes (Pasayat, 1994). Among Juang, one of the aboriginal tribes of Orissa concentrated in Keonjhar and Dhenkanal districts followed by Koraput and Mayurbhanj, the illiteracy is as high as 91 per cent among male, and 99 per cent among females which is shocking after fifty years of independence. Lack of communication network in tribal areas has miserably failed to produce desirable results. Even if students want to attend the school, infrastructural facilities are not accessible to them. Besides a major portion of the welfare fund is diverted to concessional provisions with almost nothing left for the development of tribal languages and cultures (Study by Agragami, 1994; an NGO in Kashipur, Orissa). Hardly there is any effort to standardize and consolidate tribal languages, not to speak of callous negligence of their cultures and traditions in the curricula. It has been observed that the "language and the contents of the text-book at the primary stage never attract tribal students, because the language is alien and the curricula are not related to their actual life and culture" (Reddy, 1997: 220).

As mentioned in the beginning of this paper the tribal question and their education needs to be perceived in the present context of globalization.

Precisely as the extent of globalization has been more pervasive and has become a fact of life through revolution in electronic communication. In the present satellite era flow of capital knows no geographical boundaries and the related fact is that the inherent nature of capital is profit maximization through any means. Here it may be noted that concurrently the nation-state evolved "at a time when the capitalist system started growing, the idea was in fact actively prompted by the owners of capital" (Ghosh, 1997: 683). Accordingly capitalism and nation-state evolved together by reinforcing each other. In course of time history and historical realities determine the constitution of nation-state which connotes people with by and large a common heritage, common history and as well as common interests. However, this does not deny diversities when we mention commonness. In other words there are certain interests which are common to all communities despite their specificities where history, geography, traditions and cultures play a vital role. This way the notion of "being together" evolves over a span of time. Perhaps the feeling of commonness/commonality is crucial today to struggle in this unequal world. Theoretically knowledge and science do not have any boundaries; however in actuality there are clear demarcations. In this regard there are no better instances than the Trade Related Intellectual Property Rights (TRIPS) and Trade Related Investment Measures (TRIMS) which are tactfully drafted by the north countries through WTO to restrict the south countries. For, information is controlled unilaterally and takes place all under globalization. Mention may be made here that globalization is not a new phenomenon as it has been there in the past too. However, it changes its strategies acquiring new forms according to specific historical contexts. The so-called "common heritage" issue or for that matter sustainable development is yet another facet of globalization to perpetuate inequality and hegemony of the north. For the backlash of globalization is calamitous.

Nation-state is not a static entity but a conglomeration of values/ideas which are in a constant move. It is a socio-political category with a complex assemble of spatio-cultural identities reflecting "crystallization of symbols of identity" and historical conditioning (Roy Burman, 1996). There is a continuous interaction between the people and the state institutions in the context of production process. In other words the state has major role in the present development context than in the past. Thus the state intervention is crucial to disburse the development programmes and policies effectively towards sustainable development. Otherwise polarization and imbalance will surface assuming the form of ethnic tensions. Precisely these stresses are the outcome of dehumanization process at the behest of consumer capitalism. Here comes the role of state with regards to welfare as it is democratic in orientation and interventionist in implementation which is expected to render economic security while managing capitalism. The question before us is that how far the state is able to deliver the welfare services to the people? The fact under the present circumstances is the people are reduced to more numbers in a specific territory interacting within a pre-framed set of values in line with the expanding capitalist system. The notions of individualism, impact of modernization processes and the attitude of nation-state cumulatively pose a threat to the survival of ethnic peoples. So much so people internalize the imposed values as the "epistemological individualism maimed the very basis of indigenous people's identity, survival and social reproduction" (Pathy, 1997: 37).

In the current political economy the demanding issues for the tribal people in India is the land question, i.e. the right to land and land based resources besides right to culturo-political determination. These major issues are yet to be resolved. It is prerogative of the state to cognize the customary corporate rights vis-a-vis the individual rights. For the undermining of customary rights have negatively effected the survival rights of the people. Put simply the net result of tribal development policies over fifty years in India is nothing but an "imposition of an uncritically borrowed conception of land rights, the so-called development projects of the state have encroached upon the tribal land resources and further eroded their survival support" (Pathy, 1989: 19).

Thus viewing from the above structural conditioning of the tribal people one point emerges clearly is that the education is required to suit the specific needs of the children in tribal areas if it has to be effective. Apparently this needs to integrate the cognitive and aesthetic notions of the people which ultimately assures them their identities and significance. For, tribal people's approach to the physical environment is ontological and ethno-philosophical. At the ontological level they perceive their surroundings as the extension of the self. Thus the idea is that the cosmos is the span of one's existence, while there is a continuous negation and anti-nagation between the self consciousness and the cosmic consciousness (*Note* from the Faculty of Indira Gandhi Rashtriya Sangrahalaya, 1993). Accordingly different educational strategies are sought to different regions and tribes depending on the level of productive forces, conscientization, proximity to urban areas and the like. In short education in tribal areas cannot be tailored uniformly. Secondly, it is equally essential to involve the local leaders, activists and NGOs along with academics at every step of policy making with regard to tribal education. Thirdly, more emphasis needs to be given to female literacy in tribal areas. Therefore, it is crucial to identify the specific cognitive and creative potentials of the people by combining with science and technology. Besides it is desirable to give more weightage for the less advanced communities. For better results educational programmes must be diversified while formulating special schemes for school drop-outs and adults. It is advantageous to introduce female teachers by taking the adult tribal girls to encourage female education. Special efforts are called for enrolment of girls in tribal areas. Indeed it is disturbing to note that "till now education has not received due importance in the scheme of tribal development . . . " (Sachchidananda, 1993: 344). Ethnic people are increasingly feeling alienated as they are not perceived as equal partners in development. Often they are viewed as passive receivers. Evolving peoples' initiative is a precondition for successful formulation and implementation of meaningful strategies for educational development in tribal areas. Besides the issue of education, other urgent needs in the social sector are, streamlining the Public Distribution System, health care and employment facilities. The state of primary health care is almost at the brink. We can no longer be complacent. The foregoing pages are only suggestive but not exhaustive. For, the question of education in tribal areas is very intricate. Be that as it may knowledge is power and education empowers the people.

REFERENCES

Desai, I.P. 1977. "Vedchhi Movement", *in History of Rural Development in India,* Vol. III; New Delhi: Impex India.

Ghosh, A. 1997. "Capitalism, Nation State and Development in a Globalised World", *Economic and Political Weekly,* XXXII, (14), April 5-11.

Government of India. 1984. *Report of the Working Group on Seventh Five Year Plan for Tribals,* New Delhi: Home Ministry.

Indira Gandhi Rashtriya Manav Sangrahalaya (IGRMS). 1993. "Eco-Ethics versus Market Friendly Ecological Pragmatism," A Note from the Faculty.

Mishra, B.C. 1991. "Tribal Literacy in India: A Case Study of Orissa", *Vision,* Vol. II, No. 1-2.

Pasayat, C. 1994. "The State of Female Literacy among Tribal People in Orissa", *Orissa Review,* 1(3): 4-8.

Patel, T. 1982: *Education among Tribal Women in Gujarat.* Ahmedabad: Gujarat University (Mimeo).

Pathy, J. 1996. "Tribal Education: Intervention, Realities, Challenges and Tasks—Some Reflections. Paper presented in a National Seminar", Research on Tribal Education, at NIEPA, New Delhi.

—. 1997. "Destruction and Creation: Dialectics of Indigenous Imbroglio", in Pfeffer and D.K. Behera (eds.), *Contemporary Scoiety--Tribal Studies: Development Issues,* Vol. II, New Delhi: Concept.

Reddy, V.R. 1997. "Problems and Perspectives of Tribal Education in India", in G. Pfeffer and D.K. Behera (eds.), op.cit.

Rout, S.B. 1970. *Hand Book on the Juang.* Bhubaneswar: Tribal Research Bureau.

Roy Burman, B.K. 1996. "Transformation of Tribes, and Analogous Social Formations," *Economic and Political Weekly,* XVIII (27) 1172-1174 (July 2).

—. 1997. "Critical Issues Relating to Tribal Development During the Eighth Plan" in G. Pfeffer and D.K. Behera (eds.), *op. cit.*

Sachchidananda. 1982. "Structural Constraints in the Education of STs and SCs", in B. Chaudhari (ed.), *Tribal Development in India.* New Delhi: Inter-India Publications.

—. 1993. "Tribal Development: Challenges in the Nineties," in Mrinal Miri (ed.), *Continuity and Change in Tribal Society.* Simla, IIAS.

Srivastava, L.R.N. 1971. *Identification of Education Problems of the Sauras of Orissa,* New Delhi: NCERT.

EIGHTEEN

TRIBAL EDUCATION AND FADING TRIBAL IDENTITY

N. K. AMBASHT

Education, as it is unalienably intertwined with schools and schooling processes in modern world, and particularly India, has raised issues of acculturation by dominant societies. Smaller cultures have faced the problem of withering identity in which education has undesirably, played a role of steam rolling. It has taken the values and culture of predominant culture in its basic fabric of curriculum—content and processes—and unwittingly imposed them on smaller cultures or tribal cultures in a multicultural societies like India. It is mainly because of the unintentional process of curriculum development, born more out of ignorance than by design, undertaken by curriculum planners and absence of decentralized curriculum development structure.

To create a new thought power by a new combination of truths, we must strengthen all the elements of our culture to accept and assimilate other cultures to gain a mastry over it. If we assimilate other cultures in the midst of our own culture, we must provide for co-ordinated study of different cultures. Unfortunately, in Indian context, the process has been unidirectional, that is, from the dominant culture to smaller culture and not the other way round. Very few of our school textbooks have any ethnographic account of any of the tribal societies in our midst resulting in total non-appreciation of the strengths of their cultures and values. Thus the process is leading to fading tribal identity, particularly among those who undergo the process of schooling. Understanding of tribal ethos and strengths of tribal culture and values has remained confined to the postgraduate classrooms of social anthropology as an academic exercise and has not percolated down to the Indian populace in general and educated community in particular.

To me, education is a purposive and systematic endeavour to produce an individual, who by knowing the meaning of what he knows, by feeling what others feel and by building within himself a replica of world outside has attained human excellence. The capability of adjustment in society is the basic necessity of an educated man "Is education preparing the tribal child to be able to adjust in his society?" is a question that is intrinsically related to tribal identity. This question has to be seen within the overall perspective of Indian identity. It calls for an extremely fine balance between a national identity and tribal identity. Any imbalance in this equilibrium may result in social disequilibrium. It is also a fact that with the onslaught of media, the impact of school is comparatively regressing. Whatever good is done by the school often spoilt by the street outside. The city fathers teach them to be disorderly, untidy and unclean at every corner. The neighbours impress upon them the joy of being free without any social obligation to society itself. Businessmen teach them how to cheat people and go scot free. Policemen give them practical demonstration how to be rude and vulgar. Publicmen teach them how to gain self publicity and that greatness is to be achieved by means of self propaganda instead of doing real good work. With the ordinary children, if school is against the home, the home will win. If the streets are against the school, the street will win. This is the state of affairs of our schooling in general. If a tribal child rejects such a school, can we blame him? Again the above observation highlights how the schooling has diminishing returns in terms of personality formation. Nonetheless, schooling as a process was conceived to be a single most influential process. It is another matter that external pressures have been gaining ground and cumulatively they are off-setting the influence of the school.

In such circumstances, even if our school does not take care of being culture oriented the picture is likely to be more dismal. The purposive and systematic endeavour needs to be further strengthened to churn out a balanced personality. To a tribal the school is considered as one of those factors which vitiates the child's personality in the context of his own culture. Take the following interview that a Tlinglet Indian in an Alaskan (USA) village gave to me.

Q. Do you think that the "education of your children are getting and doing good to your community?

Ans: "Certainly not. The education that is provided to our children are determined by those in lower 48 (meaning 48 mainland states of USA). They wean away our children from our society. Those who get educated are attracted to jobs in lower 48, leave us and go there and do not contribute to our life either socially or materially. The values that they imbibe during schooling process are diametrically opposite to our values—we are basically community oriented, sharing each others joys and sorrows while they are out and out individualistic and materialistic. With this kind of education I wonder how long shall we be able to retain our identity?"

Q. What, according to you, is wrong in the education that is being imparted?

Ans: "I think it is totally wrong to have an implanted education. Reading and writing—yes. But what goes into our schools are totally alien to our children's experiences. Here a bush-plane and boat are common experience, and not big aircrafts or cars. You may have noticed that in this town, of which I am the Mayor, we have a total 2 kms. of road, with one volks wagan van as Taxi and no cars. If the books that are taught to our children could have our own folk tales, folksongs, our environment, fishing and agriculture as our business, neighbourliness and community life as the core ingredients, they would be more meaningful and acceptable to our society."

The views of the local Tinglet leader speak for themselves. The pinch of losing identity and future citizen is so very apparent.

Compare with the interview of an illiterate Oraon living in a remote village in Ranchi District.

Q. Do you think that the education of your children are getting doing good to your community?

Ans. "My children are not going to school. But the son of my neighbour went to school. The experience of that family deters me from sending my children. My neighbour's child went to a Belangi middle school. After passing the school, he left for Ranchi for some job. He could become a *chaprasi.* He married a Christian Oraon girl and is living there. The family is in great economic trouble as the son is not contributing to family economy and also not helping the parents in the field (agriculture). He also does not like to come and stay with parents as he thinks working in office even as *chaprasi* is better in status than working in his father's paddy field. His income is not even sufficient for him and his wife, so he keeps on making demands on already meagre agricultural produce of his old parents. Instead of becoming a support to old parents he turns out to be a liability. Also he has converted to Christianity to marry a Christian girl. So education has brought only misery than any relief to his family. Our own *dhumkuria,* I feel was better as it did not wean our children from us."

Q. What, according to you, is wrong in the education that is being imparted?

Ans. "Everything. It is making our children learn to read and write no doubt. But at the same time it is not our education. It is your education Babu, you are snatching our children and are making them *diku* (outsider). They start to look down upon us after education. They want to leave everything that is our identity. Are we not human? You do not teach them our language, our culture, our way of life. You are making them aliens in our own homes."

We can see that the pain of being alienated from the roots is universal, whether it is remote Alaska (USA) or Chhotanagpur of Bihar (India.)

One unconverted tribal social worker said:

> "The Christian tribals (for most of them are educated) have grown a fellow feeling with the non-tribals. They have copied their way of life and have been greatly influenced by the foreign missionary teachers. The tribal culture is undergoing a rapid change under the influence of such education. These educated tribals feel themselves culturally alienated from their own brethren. It has reached such an extreme point that one would not find any co-operation between these two sections of tribal population. The non-Christian tribals have with the growth of education developed a national consciousness and national sentiment. The impact of education has made them feel that they are a part of India and have started taking part in the governmental activities and demand effective participation in political life.
>
> The impact of education is felt in high school stage for then a student comes in contact of a number of teachers and many other people and is, therefore, exposed to different ways of life."

How much brain washing does occur in the process of education can be illustrated from the following interviews this author carried out. Our respondent, who himself was a Tlinglet Indian and superintendent of a residential school in Ketchikan, Alaska said,

> "The education that is provided to us has certainly been beneficial. We can go out of our Alaskan environment, get jobs, live in any part of America in the comforts of present day world. What is there is our own culture to be emotional about? Education is progress and one must take it in that way. It is for progress of the individual. Societal development is nothing but the aggregate of the individuals development. Any argument other than this is an effort to keep us backward."

The educated tribals in Ranchi had the following to say:

> "The Christian or non-Christian (tribal) whoever has been educated has advanced, not only materially but also intellectually. The Christian tribals who are educated have even become minister in the state government. The Christian population has been the vanguard of education and changing ways of life. If at all people oppose Christianity, it is only on ground of jealousy for their advancement rather than on theological ground. The impact of education is felt at middle school stage and in high school stage it becomes most apparent."

Further, a Kharia student said:

> "We are finding among us a lot of non-tribals who look down upon our culture. When we put up the slightest of cultural resistance we are regarded as indisciplined. When we try to adjust, we begin losing our own culture. We are in a dilemma."

Another case in point is inter-tribal adjustment. The case of Munda and the Oraon is typical of such an adjustment. They have been living in contiguous area in Ranchi and yet have adjusted very well. One Munda lecturer said:

> "Normally they adjust with the members of other tribes, but it is not so easy with the non-tribals. It is because the non-tribals feel that they are superior and they belong to a superior culture. Moreover, from the very beginning of non-tribal infiltration, the tribals have been exploited and hence the suspicious attitude towards non-tribals has grown to such an extent with the passage of time, that the question of adjustment seems a remote possibility. Of course, there have been exceptions, but too few to correct their attitude."

With this kind of dichotomy, any educational effort with content and processes developed and perfected outside the tribal ethos is viewed with diffidence.

The issue of development is wrought with such a kind of contradicting postures. None of these alternative is correct for reasons so obvious. One cannot be expected to be completely alienated from one's own cultural moorings. Neither can we advocate any *status quo* without providing any educational opportunities to these people. Naturally, it is the content and processes of education that needs to be suitably adjusted so that cultural disequilibrium is avoided. An anthropological approach to education is required in tribal areas. The transition from an illiterate though educated society to a literate society must, therefore, be smooth. Efforts need to be made to develop decentralized curricula, for specific tribes and separately although with same competency levels as that of other non-tribals. Recourse to basing the content on the rich environment, folk-songs, folk-tales and other cultural components will have to be taken. The life style and learning styles of the tribal children will have to find place in the content and processes. For instance, the tribal child does not stay indoors except when he/she is sleeping, confining him to the four walls of unventilated classroom itself is a punishment. Environmental study approach may be a more viable proposition. This is just one example. Similarly punishment, reprimand and rebuke are totally alien to their experience. Any instructional process that uses these are not likely to be appreciated by parents and children alike.

The teachers in such areas are also needed with certain special attributes. These are empathy, if they are from another tribe or are outsiders, but it would be most advantageous if they belong to the same tribe.

A teacher of a Teacher's Training School of Ghiri said:

> "Teachers should be mostly drawn from their own lot and they should have training in anthropology and child psychology. Teachers are so ill-paid that they can hardly devote themselves heart and soul to the betterment of their students. At present the intellectual level of the teachers is not so high as to enable them to do justice in shaping the child's future through education."

Medium of instruction at the initial stage of education—say classes I and II—must necessarily be the tribal language. Unless this is followed meticulously, we shall be increasing the repelling power of the school rather than increasing its attracting power.

These are other connected issues in the area of tribal education, which have been written about by this author in many of his earlier writings and they need not be repeated.

Suffice it to say that education has been contributing to the fading tribal identity and unless some corrective step is taken, the situation is not going to improve.

SECTION V

HEALTH AND NUTRITION

NINETEEN

CULTURAL DIMENSION OF DISEASES AND THEIR TREATMENT

Case Studies from Tribal Societies of Orissa

N. K. BEHURA

Prologue

The foundation of human-life and other forms of life on Earth is the varied bounteous nature itself. Humans transform the natural order of their habitat into a moral order or "natural ecology" to "cultural ecology" by means of their culture. Culture comprizes the integrated sum total of learned behaviour traits characteristic of the members of a society. The manner of coping of the members of a community with their environment is largely dependent on the type of technology they possess and its efficacy. Variability of the physical environment, of course, necessitates differential adaptation. Technology is crucial in man-nature relationship, and thus environment does not fully determine the culture of a human community, although it influences (environmental possibilism rather than determinism) to certain extent.

Biological needs are common to all humans, and these are satisfied through the imperative cultural responses, which are indicative of the type of technology, nature of social structural and ideological endowment of a community. In this regime, technology occupies primary importance.

Paradigm of Man-Nature Relationship

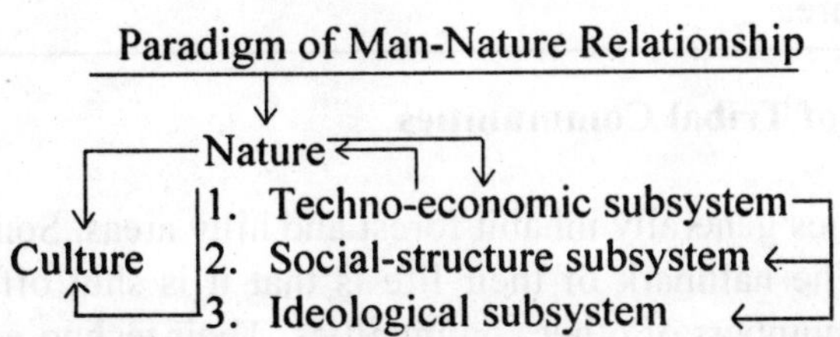

The first determines the second and first and second together determine the third. All the three constitute the domain of human culture, and the latter determines the trend and tenor of articulation with natures as well harmonious continuity of the former two. Culture is the sum total of integrat responses to the basic or biological needs of humans, which are common all, and vary from society to society.

Basic or Biological Needs	Cultural Responses*
1. Metabolism	Food acquisition and arrangement includi production, distribution, processing ar consumption.
2. Reproduction	Regulation of sex through socio-cultur institutions of marriage, family, kinshi juridical machinery and overall politic organization.
3. Bodily comfort	Making provision for shelter, clothing ar covering
4. Safety	Socio-cultural mechanisms for protection ar designing of instruments of law and order.
5. Growth	Mechanism of enculturation, socializatic and training.
6. Movement	Participation in socio-cultural activities defined and delineated by societ Functioning as a member of a society.
7. Health	Adoption of organic welfare measure abiding by culturally defined hygien practices, stead fastly following ethn healing methods of sickness and reposin faith in cultural beliefs regarding health an sickness.
8. Fatigue	Rest and relaxation
9. Fright, Pain & Tension	Riddance of the cause, Equanimity achieved through extrication.
10. Bladder Pressure and Colon Pressure.	Through micturition and defection.

Characteristics of Tribal Communities

Tribal communities generally inhabit forest and hilly areas. Some also live rural interiors. The hallmark of their life is that it is shut off from intens interaction with numbers of other communities. Their techno-economic lev

* Bronislaw Malinowski's formulation, 1931.

ing low and simple they live under marginal and submarginal economic nditions. They depend on more than one economic pursuit. Hunting and thering activities are inalienable components of their economy. Their spective cultures are homogeneous, social structures are segmentary, kinship stems are tempered classificatory, and villages are, by and large, of uni-an composition. Their ideological system centres round supernaturalism, d they are animists and fatalists. They believe that everything is edetermined, and all that happens are inevitable. Gods, goddesses, presiding ities and spirits determine the nature of things that happen to human and ere are specialists who intermediate between the supernatural beings on the e hand and the humans on the other. The levels of their awareness and piration are comparatively lower because they lack education and exposure. fter fifty years of independence, the nation has not been able to achieve tal literacy. "Education for all and health services for all" have remained as llow political slogans. Literacy is not education, and in spite of this the eracy figures are dismal and appalling. As per the 1991 census figures, the e of general literacy in the state of Orissa is 48.55 per cent (population cludes the age group seven and above) with male literacy being 52.5 per nt and female literacy 29.1 per cent, as against the literacy rate of Scheduled ibe Population of the state being 18.10 per cent (male 27.93 per cent and nale 8.29 per cent).

In general the tribal population, which lacks education and material ources, suffers from low nutritional status. The rate of infant mortality is per 1000 among them. Their life expectancy is lower than the national erage of 60 years. As per government record by 1990, about 54 per cent of bal people had access to safe drinking water. But the reality situation in the te of Orissa seems to be different. Most of them live in sub-human physical ndition. They often live in the same house alongwith their livestock which es not have ventilation facility. In many villages both humans and cattle h in the same pond or stream.

Tribal people have adapted to their environments by means of their logical and cultural endowments. Their health and sickness are influenced a combination of biological, cultural and environmental factors.

vironmental Sanitation (Lanjia Saora and Koya)

mans everywhere as per their cultural knowledge, have developed the igenous methods of preventing, diagnosing, alleviating and curing of various eases. In this context environmental sanitation and personal hygiene have erged as important considerations. While growing up humans progressively lize the dialectics between health and sickness, which operationally is endent on certain variables like social circumstances, cultural habits and physical environment. The state of public health can be measured not merel from the incidence of diseases, but from the conditions of life of peopl which encompasses the physical environment, sanitary habits, food patterr and practice of personal hygiene.

A careful review of the literature on cultural dimensions of disease an their treatment" in the context of tribal societies reveals the fact there exis only a few analytical study on this important area. Further it is significant t note that most of the existing literatures are fragmentary by nature and thereb do not appreciably add to our understanding of the problem at hand. Howeve here mention may be made of Ackernecht (1942a, 1942b), Anderson (1958 Behura (1986, 1991), Francis (1959), Gladston (1959), Godelier (1978), Kin Stanley (1963), Lieban (1973, 1977), Mechanic (1968), Roemer (1959), Rose (1963), Scotach (1953, 1960), Suchman (1968), etc. who have done som useful work in the field of medical anthropology.

Tribal people inhabiting forest and hilly areas mostly depend on sma perennial hill streams for their water requirement. As safe drinking water not available in Koya and Saora territory, the state government have installe tube-wells to solve the problem. The tube-wells do not yield adequate wat during summer months, and about 50 per cent of them remain dysfunction always, may be due to improper handling. There are some dug-wells in t Saora and Koya villages, which have been sunk by the state governme agencies to ease the water scarcity problem. The surroundings of the tubewel as well as wells are swampy, dirty and utterly unhygienic as the used wat stagnates and becomes sullage and people throw all sorts of rubbish arou them. People do take bath sometimes, housewives clean utensils and dir linen, and anal washing of children is done after defecation around t tubewells and wells.

The streams are used for bathing of humans and livestock. Dirty cloth are cleaned in the stream water directly. Buffaloes lie down in the strea water most often. Women wash their menstrual linen directly in the strea water. Men and women defecate on either side of the stream and wa directly in the stream water. Besides the stream water always carri decomposed leaves and other vegetative matter, which provide appropria milieu for the breeding of various kinds of parasites. Polluted water sprea water-borne diseases. The Koya and Saora frequently suffer from intestin diseases, like diarrhoea, dysentery and dyspepsia, and polluted water is sa to be the cause of these.

Adult Koya and Saora, both male and female, usually defecate near t stream and in the vacant field surrounding the village habitation. Childr below 7 to 10 years of age defecate within the village settlement, and roami pigs usually eat up the excreta. The excreta of babies are disposed of in t garbage heap located at the backyard of almost every house. The accumulated garbage decomposes, emits foul smell and functions as a favourable receptacle for breeding varieties of parasites.

The environment of tribal villages remains polluted and dirty for a variety of reasons. The village street is littered with animal dung, household refuge, excreta of children and swamps of human and bovine urine. There is no arrangement for the disposal of household sullage water. The water used for such domestic purposes as washing of utensils, cleaning of food materials, occasional washing of clothes, and bathing of children, sick and old persons is released to a pit located outside the house, where it is allowed to soak into the ground or remain stagnant and become a favourable cradle for various types of parasites.

Personal Hygiene

Unlettered tribal people steeped in traditional practices lack an understanding of environmental sanitation and personal hygiene in the context of health and prevention of diseases. When 70.4 per cent tribal people in the country are illiterate, halfed, ill-clothed and mostly live in unhygienic conditions, their attitude towards environmental sanitation and personal hygiene is bound to be archaic.

Educated tribals as well as those who have been converted to Christianity have better sense of personal hygiene. For tradition bound tribal people cleanliness is more a matter of ritual purification. They believe that health is ensured by supernatural entities and factors like regular washing of mouth, regular clipping of nails and toes are not considered as essential from the point of view of good health.

They eject out tobacco saliva everywhere. The inside walls of their houses are littered with saliva. As they lie down on untidy floors and do not regularly wash their bodies most of them suffer from various types of skin diseases.

Food Habits and Food Taboos

In tribal areas of India, the larger part of the diet is obtained from locally available and produced food materials. Religious customs, and local traditions relating to feasts, fasts, and food taboos do have a bearing on the dietary pattern of the people.

There are three major sources of food for the tribal population, these are: (1) their own crop fields, (ii) local forest and water resources, and (iii) local market. There is of course seasonal variation of food for the majority of the tribal people as they cannot ensure steady supply of food materials for the consumption of their family. Their harvest and post-harvest period extends from November to March, during which they depend on the crop-yields of their lands. Hereafter, they become dependent on the nearby forest for food. From April to June they almost completely depend on various types of wild berries, palm fruit and juice, date and datepalm juice, cashew fruits, mangoes, jackfruits, pineapple, orange, banana, papaya, Kendu *(dispyros ambriyopteris),* sago palm juice *(caryotaureus),* etc. And from August to October, the acute lean period for most of them, they depend on seeds of tamarind, mango, jackfruit, palm, bamboo-shoot and wild yarns and tubers. In the past forest was the reservoir of their food materials. They used to gather, hunt and collect materials as and when necessary. Now their entry into forest is considered as an encroachment, and moreover, forest resources have been greatly depleted.

The nutritional value of their food items and the caloric units of their food intake have not been analyzed here. The tribal people eat three times a day when food is available. During morning and mid-day they take millet or rice gruel and eat a simple meal of cereals before dusk. This is the usual pattern.

A detailed list of food materials of the Orissan tribes is furnished below, which are not always available to them. They are aware of these items.

1. Cereals

	Oriya Term	*English Equivalent*
(a)	Dhana	Paddy
(b)	Makka	Maiza
(c)	Mandia	Millet
(d)	Bajra	Spiked millet
(e)	Kangu	Large millet
(f)	Ghantia	Dwarf millet
(g)	Jawar	Oat
(h)	Gahama	Wheat

2. Pulses

(a)	Mugo	Greem gram
(b)	Biri	Black gram
(c)	Harada	Red gram
(d)	Buta	Ground gram
(e)	Bargudi	Dwarf gram
(f)	Kolatha	Horse gram

3. Vegetables

(a)	Baigana	Brinjal
(b)	Kakharu	Pumpkin
(c)	Lau	Gourd
(d)	Kakudi	Cucumber
(e)	Panikakharu	White pumpkin
(f)	Kalara	Bitter gourd
(g)	Bhendi	Lady's finger
(h)	Kandamula	Sweet potato
(i)	Alu	Potato
(j)	Matialu	Yam
(k)	Khara	Tall spinach
(l)	Kanta saga	Thorny spinach
(m)	Kosala	Spinach
(n)	Mula	Radish
(o)	Poi	Onctuous greens
(p)	Sorisa saga	Mustard greens
(q)	Chhachindra	Snake gourd
(r)	Jonhi	Luffa acutangula
(s)	Shimba	Country beans
(t)	Kadali	Plantain
(u)	Leutia sag	Amaranath
(v)	Sajana Chhuin	Drumstick
(w)	Bilati baigana	Tomato
(x)	Potala	
(y)	Kunduri	Creeper gourd
(z)	Beans	French beans

4. Fruits

(a)	Aamba	Mango
(b)	Lankamba	Casjew friot
(c)	Aata	Custard apple
(d)	Pijuli	Guava
(e)	Khajuri	Date
(f)	Kamala	Orange
(g)	Sapuri	Pine apple
(h)	Panasa	Jackfruit
(i)	Kadali	Banana
(j)	Talo	Palm fruit
(k)	Nadia	Coconut

(l)	Kendu	
(m)	Jamukoli	Blackberry
(n)	Papaya	Papaya
(o)	Barakoli	Berry
(p)	Tentuli	Tamarind

5. Spices

(a)	Piaja	Onion
(b)	Lasuna	Garlic
(c)	Kanchalanka	Green chilli
(d)	Sukhila lanka	Dry chilli
(e)	Dhania	Coriander
(f)	Sorisa	Mustard
(g)	Juani	Thymol
(h)	Mahuri	Aniseed
(i)	Ada	Ginger
(j)	Haldi	Turmeric
(k)	Luna	Salt
(l)	Labang	Cloves
(m)	Dalchini	Cinnamon
(n)	Alacicha	Cardamom
(o)	Methi	Tenugreek

6. Mushrooms

(a)	Uuihunka chhatu	Ant-hill mushroom
(b)	Balli chhatu	Sand mushroom
(c)	Nada chhatu	Straw mushroom
(d)	Baunsha chhatu	Bamboo mushroom
(e)	Salagachha chhatu	Sal-tree mushroom
(f)	Aambagachha chhatu	Mango-tree mushroom
(g)	Jammugacha chhatu	Black berry tree mushroom
(h)	Matti chhatu	Field mushroom
(i)	Karanjagachha chhatu	
(j)	Katha chhatu	Wood mushroom
(k)	Patra chhatu	Leaf mushroom

7. Oilseeds

(a)	Sorisa	Mustard
(b)	Tila	Niger

(c)	Rasi	Sesamum
(d)	Joda	Castor
(e)	Khasa	Linseed

8. Honey

(a) Machhia
(b) Baghua
(c) Pania
(d) Kharadinia
(e) Sheetadinia
(f) Baramasi

9. Meat and Fish

(a) Goat meat
(b) Lamb meat
(c) Deer meat
(d) Pork
(e) Beef
(f) Chicken
(g) Rabbit meat
(h) Reptile
(i) Birds
(j) Eggs
(k) All sorts of fish and
(l) Snakes

Methods of Cooking

The method of food preparation and cooking is an important factor in determining the level of nutrition intake of people. The absorbability of the essential food constituents in the diet depends on the method of cooking to a desired extent. Tribal people mostly take boiled, baked and parched food items. They always under cook, that is, they do not make any cooked food too soft. They eschew over-boiling and complete baking. They have a habit of eating some food items raw. They even eat fish and meat raw. They prefer below normal boiled meat. They love to masticate food items.

They sometimes peel off the vegetables, but usually cook them with their rinds. Ripe fruits are eaten after peeling of the outer covers. Before cooking food materials are not meticulously cleaned and washed. They believe that through washing essential food values are lost. They do not have any concept of vitamin. They, therefore, say that washing spoils the taste. They highly relish baked food, be it vegetable, meat or fish. They also consume viscera of animals and large fishes.

Social and Cultural Aspects of Epidemiology

Epidemiology is concerned with the distribution of diseases in space and the incidence of disease as influenced by natural and cultural environments. There is no contradiction of the fact that ecology and socio-cultural factors influence diseases. Social and cultural distinctions associated with variations in age, sex, ethnicity, class and community can have significant bearings on epidemiological phenomena. Sex and age differences have a correlation with the incidence of certain types of diseases.

Among non-literates and tradition-bound tribal people there are certain cultural habits, such as, bathing in the same pond or stream water alongwith their domestic animals, non-use of water for anal-washing after defecation, non-washing of menstrual fluid, non-washing of hand before eating food and non-washing of mouth after eating the principal meal of the day. A peculiar cultural practice is found among the Orissan tribes, that is, when a person is suffering from malaria and running high temperature, he/she is made to lie down under the sun. Their logic is that high temperature of the body would be neutralized by the heat of rays of the sun.

Social and cultural factors are casually connected with disease occurrences indirectly, when poverty is linked to malnutrition, and malnutrition induces a number of diseases among children, or directly, as in the case of some people using their own utensils for feeding the domestic animals, particularly pig, dog, cat and mongoose.

Social and cultural distinctions associated with differences in age, sex and occupation do have significant effects on epidemiological phenomena.

Age Differences

Due to lack of physiological resistance tribal children are susceptible to several diseases, such as, diarrhoea, dysentery, dyspepsia, common cold, fever, jaundice, scabies, ringworm, anaemia, etc. Death rate is relatively high among infants. The incidence of numerous acute infections is highest among children in general, but is more among tribal children. As people grow older they develop immunities that decrease their vulnerability of these diseases.

Sex Differences

Biological factors play a large part in sexual differences in mortality, with females having longer life expectancy. However, women frequently suffer from reproductive diseases, sustain ovary and breast ailments. Men on the other hand are affected by rural and cardiovascular diseases. More tribal women suffer from arthritis as they are frequently anaemic and always carry heavy loads on their head. Several tribal women, after child birth, suffer from gynac and obstetric problems.

Occupational Difference

There is a correlation between occupation and disease. Effects of occupation on disease have been an important aspects of epidemiology, because social aspects of pathology indicate that susceptibility to disease varies in accordance with the means of gaining a livelihood. Tribals who raise piggery suffer from worm infection. Likewise, tribal working in cement factories at Rajgangpur suffer from thoracic diseases.

Social Status and Ethnic Difference

Influence of social status and ethnic differences on disease occurrence has been established by several studies. This influence is significant in nutritional maladies and in infectious diseases, where occurrence is dependent on material conditions of life. Malnutrition is almost non-existence among the secular-sacerdetal functionaries of tribal communities as they are materially well off. Whereas the commoners mostly suffer from this malady. Infectious diseases occur more among the uneducated persons in tribal societies.

Difference in disease rates of ethnic groups have been an important problem in epidemiology. Occurrence of sickle cell anaemia has been investigated in this light, and inter group variations in its prevalence have been found in Orissa. Tribes belonging to Dravidian language family have reported positive, and their neighbouring tribes belonging to the Mundari Group have reported negative.

Cultural Correlates of Health and Sickness

Health, hygiene, sickness, diagnosis and disease-treatment comprise a vital sector of human society everywhere. In tribal India not much has been done in this important sector. And whatever little has been done, it is always from the view point of modern medical science. Modern allopathic treatment presupposes certain conditions which go along with it and follow it too. Such conditions are almost totally non-existence in tribal societies. However, all tribals, primitive or advanced, consider disease as pernicious and detrimental to normal life. It is certainly a departure, temporary or permanent, from the normal state of health.

Tribals do not consider any disease as the cause of neglect of body or its organs. They consider disease as an integral part of the life process. They believe disease causes both transient and intransient illness, and disease means unhappiness, fear, tragedy, expenditure, suffering and ultimately death. They assert that most diseases are caused by supernatural entities, but there are other factors too, such an environmental.

Etiology Illness

Tribals usually attributes (i) wrath or displeasure of supernatural entities as the cause of disease and sickness. One incurs the displeasure of ethereal beings for breach of appropriate rules of conduct, (ii) commitment of sins through breach of taboos, (iii) non-fulfilment of obligations towards masses, (iv) magico-religious or occultism as the other cause when sickness is believed to have been caused by the machinations (including evil eye and spirit intrusion) of witches and sorcerers, and (v) physical or environmental causes, which include accidents, venomous snake or insect-bite, attack by ferocious animals, eating of inappropriate food, contact with poisonous insects and plants, effect of changing weather and environmental factors.

Emic Classification of Diseases

Tribal people classify diseases as per the dictates of their culture.

1. Common or Frequent Diseases

(a) *Fever:* It causes body temperature. Sometimes, temperature is accompanied by body rigor or spasm. It alternates with fall of temperature and accompanied by perspiration and body pain and headache are common symptoms. The tendency of nausea persists, and the patient does not like to eat or drink anything. Long suffering causes swelling of face, abdomen and limbs.
Therapy: Magico-religious and administration of herbal medicine.

(b) *Fileria:* The patient sustains high temperature with rigor. Limbs swell and become tender. It causes weakness and constant headache.
Therapy: Magico-religious and administration of herbal medicines.

(c) *Common Headache:* Irresistible pain in the head. The whole head or any one side may ache.
Therapy: Magico religious and administration of herbal medicine.

(d) *Swelling of the body:* Loss of body weight, general weakness, complete loss of appetite, change of complexion and occasional nausea are the symptoms.

Therapy: Magico-religious and administration of herbal medicines.

(e) *Swelling of Innqual Lymph Glands:* Lymph glands swell. Body tempeature rises and headache is common.

Therapy: Magico-religious and administration of herbal medicine.

(f) *Nephrotic Syndrome:* Body swelling is accompanied by mild fever, herbal medicine and general weakness and complete loss of appetite occur.

Therapy: Magico-religious and administration of herbal medicine.

(g) *Colic pain:* It is a common disease and many people suffer from this ailment. The patient often experiences excruciating abdominal pain. General weakness develops and loss of appetite occurs. Some patients life long suffer and ultimately die of it.

Therapy: Magico-religious and administration of ethno-medicine.

(h) *Malnutrition:* It is extremely common. Its symptoms include dehydration, physical weakness, nausea, loose motion with nucus discharge, and abdominal pain.

Therapy: Magico-religious and administration of valia seed oil at the naval point.

(i) *Hookworm Infestation:* It is a common disease and many people suffer from this. One of its causes may be eating of raw meat and fish. Its symptoms include abdominal pain, loss of appetite and itching sensation.

Therapy: Application of ethno-medicine.

(j) *Roundworm Infestation:* It is a common disease and is believed to have been caused by witchcraft. Its symptoms include abdominal pain, fast appetite, physical fatigue and occasional body temperature.

Therapy: Magico-religious and administration of occult herbal medicine.

(k) *Amoebic Dysentery:* It is a common disease. Believed to be caused by inappropriate food, over-eating of chillies, summer heat and by occasional starvation. Its symptoms include pain in the abdomen, discharge of blood and mucus along with stool and mild body temperature.

Therapy: Administration of ethno-medicine by the Shaman.

(l) *Blood Dysentery:* It is caused by spirit-intrusion and by black magic. It is also caused by over-eating unhealthy food and chillies. Its symptoms include frequent motion of blood and mucus, body temperature and growing weakness leading to death.

Therapy: Spirit exoricism by the sorcerer, shaman administers ethno-medicine (barks of tamarind, mahua, black berry and piasala are boiled and residual water mixed with honey is given to the patient).

(m) *Jaundice:* Its cause is believed to be spirit-intrusion. Its symptoms include retina looking yellow, urine colour becoming yellow and body appearing bloodless. The patient runs slow temperature and experiences pain in the upper abdomen.

Therapy: The sorcerer exercises the spirit. The shaman administers ethnomedicine like juice of a creeper or groundseeds of custard apple.

(n) *Piles:* It is a non-contagious disease. It is believed to be caused by a malevolent spirit. Its symptoms include acute pain during defecation, discharge anal blood after defecation, loss of body weight and growing weakness.

Therapy: Exorcism of the spirit by the sorcerer, shaman prescribes a finger ring made out of the scale of the Baja/rakapta (scaly ant-eater raptile).

(o) *Diabetes:* It is caused by the wrath of supernatural entities. It is considered as a disease inducing syndrome. Its symptoms include frequent urination, fast appetite, quick thirst due to dehydration, perspiration, headache, pain in the limbs and anaemia.

Therapy: Black berry tree bark is boiled and the water is taken thrice a day.

(p) *Discharge of Blood with Urine:* Its cause is believed to be supernatural wrath. Some also believe that drinking of tube-well water also causes this disease. Hence those who suffer from this disease do not take tubewell water. Its symptoms include abdominal pain, mild body temperature, blood discharge alongwith urine and head reeling.

Therapy: The patient is administered juice of thalkudi *(consella asiatica)* and sugarcane juice.

(q) *Goiter:* Supernatural wrath is believed to be its cause. Some shamans also maintain that it is caused due to spirit intrusion. Its symptoms include swelling of thorax and pain in the swollen portion. Sometimes it bursts, which causes sudden death.

Therapy: Magico-religious rites performed by the shaman and he also prescribes herbal ethno-medicine. A paste is prepared out of the roots of three plants available in the forest (bajramuli, nardi and mustumir) of Koya area.

(r) *Lumbago:* It is caused due to malnutrition on the one hand and excess physical labour on the other. Its symptoms include pain in the waist region as well as in major joints of the body.

Therapy: The Shaman administered ethno-medicine prepared out of Karanja *(carisea carandas)* and Kendu *(diospyrus ambriyopeteris).*

(s) *Rheumatoid Arthritis:* The belief is that it is caused by spirit intrusion. If symptoms are swelling of body joints and decline of strength. The joints pain with little pressure on them; and thus the patient becomes immobile.

Therapy: Massaging of neem oil *(azadirachta indica)* on joints and application of red sandal wood paste over the joints.

(t) *Syphillis and Gonorrhoea:* It is believed that these are caused by the wrath of God. These are contagious and incurable. The symptoms include discharge of whitish fluid, and emission of foul smell from the genitals. Both vigina and penis become ulcerous.

Therapy: The Shaman performs a cathartic or purgative rite for the patient. The patient is advised to take juice of Capparis horrida, termenalia balerica and ambelica myrobalan. Besides the patient is advised to apply oil extracted from *Karanja* seeds *(carisea carendes).*

(u) *Hysteria:* It is believed that the disease is caused by spirit intrusion. Its symptoms include loss of skin sensitivity, and acute sensitivity to light. Partial paralysis of various parts of the body, impairment of hearing and inability to stand and walk. The patient experiences fouts of convulsims, tremor and vomiting.

Therapy: The sorcerer is engaged to perform a prophylactic rite for the exorcism of the spirit from the body of the victim.

Seasonal Diseases

Occurrences of certain diseases are tuned to specific seasons. Common diseases of the summer season are amoebic dysentery, malaria, chronic headache, lumbago, bacillary, dysentery and summer boils. The diseases of the rainy season are: diarrhoea, cold and cough, cold fever, bronchitis, maum and enlargement of tonsils. Common diseases of the winter season include scabies, ring worm, chicken pox and fever.

Tribal people conceptualize that some diseases are peculiar to man some others as peculiar to women. They consider physiological (sexual) immaturity as a male disease. Similarly, they consider inflammation of breast as an obstetrical disease and melancholia as a disease common to grown up girls.

Tribal people consider some diseases as child-specific, which occur in childhood. They believe that children are vulnerable to the inauspicious factor of evil eye. As a consequence of this factor children suffer from loss of appetite, vomiting, malnutrition, fever, diarrhoea and rickets. Tribal people make dichotomous distinctions between dieases, such as curable and incurable and hereditary and non-hereditary. They consider leprosy as incurable and tuberculosis, diabetes, fileria, colour blindness and epilepsy as hereditary. They too consider arthritis as old-age specific disease. This sort of knowledge is part of their cultural heritage.

Ethnomedical Specialists

When some sort of affiliation or sickness occurs, it may be ignored and tolerated or treated with or without the help of a specialist. Mostly remedy or treatment is sought from a native magico-medical practitioner. Amongst them there are specialists, such as diviner, ethno-medicine man, Shaman, midwife, masseur, and sorcerer. Therapists may have specialization in one type of skill or in more than one trade. Several years of training and apprenticeship is an integral attribute of a specialist. Besides, spiritual accreditation is a further attribute of indigenous medical roles.

In a tribal society there is a general lack of finer specialization of roles. Therefore, a particular functionary normaly combines in himself several functions, such as, divination, exorcism, medicine-prescription, performance of cathartic rites and shamanism. But there is no juxtaposition of the roles of shaman and sorcerer in one man. Shamans have multiple functions, and their services are always sought for. Their operations cover a wide range of activities, which include omen-reading, sooth-saying, divination for detection of the cause of suffering, exorcism, removal of the harmful effect of evil-eye, nullification of the influence of witchcraft or sorcery, propitiation of deities and manes, control or appeasement of malevolent spirits, preparation of magico-religious charms for clients, prescription and aministration of ethno-herbal medicines, cure of snakebites. All their activities centre round cure of diseases, amelioration of sufferings and removal of socio-personal maladies. They are always held in high esteem. Their conduct is never suspected or questioned as in the case of witches and sorcerers. He is regarded as a benefactor and friend of his society. He enjoys the confidence of his clientele.

Cultural Aspects of Therapeutics

Ethno-medicinal beliefs and practices are influenced by culture. The relationship between human sickness, treatment, healing-medicines and the rest of culture in a society is intimate. Concept of disease, classification of diseases, procedures of diagnosis and therapy are all influenced by culture. Indeed concepts of disease are cultural classification of illness. They do not, of course, cover the whole range of misfortune a community may face over a long period of time and in a general sense.

Studies, conducted among the Koya and Saora of Orissa, suggest that they make an emic classification of disease into eleven broad categories apart from the physical disabilities and deformities. The categories are: (1) common diseases, (2) Seasonal diseases, (3) Hereditary diseases, (4) Skin diseases, (5) Contagious diseases, (6) Dental diseases, (7) Mental diseases, (8) Child diseases, (9) Masculine diseases, (10) Feminine diseases, and (11)

Old age diseases.

Diagnosis of a disease is done through the identification of symptoms, which are culturally influenced. A grown up person reports the symptoms to the kins, and the shaman, whereas parents and kins decipher the symptoms of the disease of child. Though the symptoms of a disease are physical and mental, their comprehension is cultural.

Medicine men and shamans possess a comprehensive knowledge about the medicinal plants, herbs, tubers, roots, barks, leaves, flowers, seeds, fruits, birds, reptiles and animals in their environment from which they extract medicines. They have over the years, generation after generation, through personal experience, have established correlation between the properties of various ethno-medicinal elements and amelioration of particular diseases. Such knowledge is, of course, eco-culture specific. Therefore, it varies from tribe to tribe in details, but may not be in gross.

The following list provides an idea of ethno medicinal elements among the tribal communities:

	Oriya Term	*Botanical term*
1.	Anla	*emblica myrobalan*
2.	Bahada	*terminalia balerica*
3.	Horida	*caparis horrida*
4.	Saparkachu	*colacasia*
5.	Pippala	*ficus religiosa*
6.	Kendu	*dyospyros ebenum*
7.	Limba	*azadirachta indica*
8.	Sirisa	*albizzia lebbek*
9.	Dimiri	*ficus glomerata*
10.	Kaitha	*limonia acidissimo*
11.	Sal	*shorea robusta*
12.	Kusuma	*catharmus tinotorius*
13.	Sisu	*dalbergia latifolia*
14.	Baragacha	*ficus bengalensis*
15.	Tentuli	*tamarindus indica*
16.	Haladi	*carcuma domestica*
17.	Babul	*accasia arabica*
18.	Khaira	*accasia catecium*
19.	Baruna	*cratera religiosa*
20.	Mahula	*bassia latifolia*
21.	Haragaura	*balsam impatious balsamira*
22.	Simili	*bombax mallbericum*
23.	Gila	*gesalpinio bonducelia*
24.	Beto	*calamus viminalis*

25.	Polang	*callophylum inophyllum*
26.	Palasa	*lutee monospherma*
27.	Polanga	*alexandriam larvah*
28.	Panasa	*artocarpus*
29.	Jammu	*syzcium integrifolia lumini*
30.	Kaunria	*hebiscus annabinus.*
31.	Sunthi	*ginger dehydrate*
32.	Pippali	*piper longum*
33.	Raisorisa	*brassica compestris*
34.	Gaitri	*myristica fragrama*
35.	Kadamba	*antheephellus cadamber*
36.	Barkoli	*zyzyplus jujuba*
37.	Dubaghasa	*cynodam dactylon*
38.	Karmagacha	*nauclea parvifolin*
39.	Asoka	*araca indica*
40.	Chikku gachha	*plamneria acutifolia*
41.	Gulaich	*cedrela toona*
42.	Dhutura	*datura ferfuture*
43.	Jambila	*citrus aurantam*
44.	Aparajeeta	*cilitoria ternatia*
45.	Gargada	*coox lachrymajobs*
46.	Badabaunsa	*dendra calamus strictus*
47.	Kantabaunsa	*bambusa arundinacca*
48.	Bedu	*terminals tomentosa*
49.	Salapa	*caryotaurens*
50.	Bhalia	*kochilakhai*
51.	Thalkuni	*Contella asiatica*
52.	Kalamanga	*andrographis pamiculata*
53.	Nagakesara	*masua ferra*
54.	Karanja	*carisea carandus*
55.	Champa	*micholia champaca*
56.	Piaja	*allinumcepa*
57.	Rasuna	*allinum sibira*
58.	Neua	*annona reticulal*
59.	Aata	*annona squama*
60.	Jambila	*citrus aurantam*
61.	Juani	*carum capticum*
62.	Bakula	*mimusops elengi*

Modern Patent Medicines and Tribal Culture: Interface

Under the impact of state sponsored economic development programmes and processes of modernization traditional cultures of tribal communities have started changing. Ongoing literacy programmes, systems of education and general administration have increased the level of awareness of tribal communities to some extent, although the slogans "education for all, health care facilities for all, safe drinking water for all, communication facility to all, Panchayat headquarters, and more edible oil (raising of per capita consumption) for the country" still seem to be hollow. However, something has been achieved.

Primary Health Centre, dispensaries and small hospitals have been established in tribal areas or scheduled areas but often doctors and paramedical personnel are not there. Doctors rarely stay there because there is no scope for private practice. Under these pathetic conditions primary health care services do not reach the entire tribal population. Consequently quacks and medical mafias are indulging in drug-peddling and sale of spurious allopathic medicines and ampoules of distilled water. The situation is painful and appalling. Tribals are eager to use modern medicine for its quick results. Under these circumstances a new system be designed to cater to the needs of tribal people.

Medical science recognizes that there are three levels of treatment as ailments or sicknesses are classified into (i) minor, (ii) medium, and (iii) major depending on the gravity of suffering of a patient. Minor ailments can be attended to by trained health workers, the second category of sickness can be handled by general physicians, and the third category certainly requires the services of specialist physicians/surgeons. If the literate shaman, shamanies and tribal medicine men are imparted training in primary health care services, then they can serve the tribal people better and the present ugly scene can be obviated. This suggestion need be debuted and conclusion be arrived at.

REFERENCES

Ackernecht, Erwin H. 1942a. "Problems of Primitive Medicine", *Bulletin of the History of Medicine*, II: 503-521.

—. 1942b. "Primitive Medicines and Cultural Pattern", *Bulletin of the History of Medicine*, 12: 545-574.

Anderson, Odin W. 1958. "Infant Mortality and Social and Cultural Factors", in E.G. Jaco (ed.), *Patients, Physicians and Illness*. Glencoe, illinois: Free Press.

Behura, N.K. 1986. "The Paradigm of Koya Concept of Human Diseases," in *Banaja*, Bhubaneswar H.T.W. Department, Government of Orissa.

—. 1991. "Anthropology of Disease. Treatment and Cure," *Man and Life*, 17(1&2).

Francis, Thomas Jr. 1959. "The Epidemiological Appro'ach to Human Ecology," *The American Journal of Medical Science*, 237: 677-84.

Gladston, Iago. 1959. "Introduction", (pp-7-10) in I. Gladstone (ed.), *Medicine and Anthropology*, New York: International Universities Press.

Godelier, Maurice. 1978: *Perspectives in Marxist Anthropology*. Cambridge: Cambridge University Press.

King Stanley, H. 1963. "Social Psychological Factors in Illness", (pp. 99-121) in H.E. Freeman, S. Levine and L.G. Reader (eds.), *Handbook of Medical Sociology*. Englewood Cliffs, N.J.: Prentice Hall.

Lieban, R.W. 1973. "Medical Anthropology", in J.J. Honigmann (ed.), *Handbook of Social and Cultural Anthropology*. Chicago: Rand McNally and Company.

—. 1977. "The Field of Medical Anthropology", (pp. 13-31) in David Landy (ed.), *Culture, Disease and Healing*. New York: Macmillan Publication.

Mechanic, David. 1968. *Medical Sociology*, New York: Free Press and Macmillan.

Roemer, Milton, I. 1959. "Social Science and Organized Heal Service", *Human Organization*, 18: 75-79.

Rosen, George. 1963. "The Evolution of Social Medicine," (pp. 17-61) in H.E. Freeman, S. Levine and L.G. Reader (eds.) *op. cit.*

Scotach, Norman, 1960. "A Preliminary Report on the Relation of Socio-cultural Factors to Hypertension among the Zulu", *Annals of New York Academy of Sciences*, 84(17): 1000-1009.

—. 1953. "Medical Anthropology", (pp. 30-63) in B.J. Siege (ed.), *Biennial Review of Anthropology*. Stanford: Stanford University Press.

Suchman, Edward A. 1968. "Epidemiology", *International Encyclopaedia of Social Science*, 5: 97-101, New York: Free Press and Macmillan.

TWENTY

MALNUTRITION AND MORBIDITY PATTERNS
Case of Munda Women in the Urban Setting of Sambalpur, Orissa

BRAJA KISHORI MISHRA and
PRATIVA MANJARI TRIPATHY

Introduction

Women constitute a substantial proportion of population of a given society. The status of women, which reflects the type of society and culture they live in, is measured in terms of the level of their health, education, income, employment, rights as well as the role played by them in the family, community and in the society. The health status of the women which includes their physical, mental and social conditions in addition to their biological and physiological problems, is also affected by the prevailing norms and attitude of society (Park and Park, 1991).

Health is an obvious function of nutrition and in most of the underdeveloped areas in the world, food deficiency arises in a hostile environment. Added to malnutrition, there are also multiple illnesses resulting from infection and parasites that sap to an even greater extent the health and well-being of people (Rajyalakshmi, 1991). The reduced intake of essential nutrients during illness is likely to cause malnutrition. The indirect effects of malnutrition on the community are even more striking resulting in higher general death, maternal and infant mortality and higher rate of maternal morbidity and malnutrition with a lower expectation of life (ICSSR, 1975). Though malnutrition affects all segments of population, women and children appear to be more at risk. There is also the belief that the culturally determined social behaviour places the women and female child at a higher risk of malnutrition. Throughout their life cycle females receive less food and also of inferior quality than the males (Khan *et al.,* 1983); Gosh, 1985; Karkal and Pandey, 1989), for which women are at a higher risk of malnutrition.

Tribals constitute an important segment of the population of India, representing 7.6 per cent of the total population of the country. There is always a significant variation in the living and dietary habits of the tribal in comparison to non-tribal population. Over the past decades, a fundamental change seems to have occurred in the orientation of tribal research studies to generate baseline information on demographic, geographic, cultural, agricultural and socio-economic characteristics, which help to shed some light on the constraints to the development of the tribal communities. Malnutrition and morbidity pattern serve as the best index of health status of tribal communities and help in proper evaluation of the community health programmes as well as in detection and treatment of diseases related to nutrition (Rajyalakshmi, 1991).

Various studies on the health status of the Indian tribals indicate that the prevalence of diseases varies with the location, season, literacy, income levels and various other factors. The incidence of angular stomatitis, glossitis, night blindness, photophobia, malnutrition and non-nutritional disorders like scabies, dental caries, and malaria too are found to be high in the tribes of Andhra Pradesh, Central India, Maharashtra, Karnataka and Madhya Pradesh (NIN, 1973; Pingale, 1973; Pratap 1975; Gore *et al.*, 1977; Rajyalakshmi, 1991; Hanumantha Rao *et al.*, 1992 and 1993). Some other studies in India also indicate that unhygienic living condition of the tribals is the major cause of skin infection and gastric disorder (NIN, 1969; Sharma, 1971; NIN, 1973; Pingale, 1973; Ali, 1979).

Orissa is a small State of India, having a total population of about 31.6 million, out of which 22.2 per cent are Scheduled Tribes (1991 census). A review of literature reveals that no systematic study has been made on the health status of tribals of Orissa excepting the works of Sharma (1971) and Ali (1979). Munda is one of the 63 tribal communities inhabiting in the State of Orissa. An humble attempt has been made in this paper to study the health status of Munda women living within Municipality area of Sambalpur town. Incidence of malnutrition and morbidity pattern has been taken into consideration for the aforesaid purpose.

Study Area and Methodology

The survey was conducted during the last quarter of 1996 in Sambalpur. The town has a population of 131 thousands of which more than 11 thousand are Scheduled Tribe (Government of Orissa, 1995). Munda women of above 18 years of age were selected as the subjects of the study. Data were collected from 120 Munda women selected on the basis of simple random sampling.

A personal interview schedule was designed, pretested and administered for collection of general information on women. The clinical examination was performed to assess the level of health of women in relation to their food intake. Following Park and Park (1991:358) the women's hair, face, eyes, lips, tongue, teeth, gums, glands, skin and nails were observed and the abnormalities were recorded. To ascertain the morbidity pattern, some common diseases were selected and history about the incidence of illness from those specific diseases was recorded with the help of a schedule. The women were categorized into three groups on the basis of the frequency of illness from that particular disease during last year (one year prior to the conduct of field work). The three groups were "rarely ill" (who had suffered once for a maximum period of one week), "occasionally ill" (who had suffered for 2 to 3 times and each time for a period of one week or more) and "frequent ill" (who had suffered for 4 or more times from different diseases (as mentioned in our list) during the period concerned). The data on the occurrence of illness were analyzed in relation to few independent socio-economic variables and the results were compared with the other published documents on tribal communities of India.

Results and Discussion

Nutritional Deficiency and Age

Out of 15 women who had abnormal hairs, 26.6 per cent belonged to the age group of 25 to 29 (Table 20.1). Highest prevalence of vitamin 'A' deficiency indicated by night blindness was observed in the age group of 20 to 24 (24%). Signs of 'B' complex deficiency such as angular stomatitis and glossitis were prevalent in 20 to 23 per cent of the samples. The incidence of angular stomatitis was found to be more (30%) in the age group of 30 to 34 and the incidence of glossitis was found to be distributed evenly in all other age groups. 23.3 per cent and 40.8 per cent of respondents had abnormal teeth and dental caries respectively. Highest prevalence of dental caries was found in the age group of ≤ 19 (22.4%). Problems related to teeth were found to be higher (21%) in the age group 25 to 29. Abnormal gum was found in 57.5 per cent of the respondents out of which 45 per cent belonged to the age group ≤ 29 years. On the whole prevalence of goitre and skin abnormalities was found to be lower. Oedema was found in 1.7 per cent of the sample respondents. Of the 8 women who have brittle nails, 50 per cent belonged to the age group ≤ 29. Thus, it can be clearly observed from Table 27.1 that the prevalence of all the signs of nutritional deficiency was higher in younger age groups (≤ 35 years). As this is the peak period for the child-bearing and child rearing the prevalence of nutritional deficiency signs during this period is common, as the extra nutritional requirements are not adequately met.

TABLE 20.1: Prevalence of Nutritional Deficiency Signs among Munda Women according to Age Groups

Age group	N	CLINICAL SIGNS										
		Hair abnormal	Eyes night blindness	Lips Angular stomatitis	Tongue abnormal Glossitis	Teeth abnormal	Dental caries	Gums abnormal	Glands goitre	Skin abnormal	Nail abnormal	Oedma
≤ 19	24	—	4	—	4	4	11	10	—	—	3	1
			(16.0)		(17.4)	(14.3)	(22.4)	(14.5)			(37.5)	(50.0)
20–24	18	—	6	—	2	0	10	11	—	—	—	—
			(24.0)		(8.7)		(20.4)	(15.9)				
25–29	16	4	3	5	4	6	7	10	—	—	1	—
		(26.6)	(12.0)	(25.0)	(17.4)	(21.4)	(14.3)	(14.5)			(12.5)	
30–34	17	2	2	6	3	2	4	9	—	4	1	1
		(13.4)	(8.0)	(30.0)	(13.05)	(7.15)	(8.2)	(13.1)		(66.7)	(12.5)	(50.0)
35–39	10	3	1	4	3	4	6	8	—	2	1	—
		(20.0)	(4.0)	(20.0)	(13.05)	(14.3)	(12.2)	(11.6)		(33.5)	(12.5)	
40–44	8	—	—	3	—	3	3	5	1	—	—	—
				(15.0)		(10.7)	(6.15)	(72..0)	(100.0)			
45–49	9	1	2	2	1	2	1	7	—	—	—	—
		(6.6)	(8.0)	(10.0)	(4.3)	(7.15)	(2.0)	(10.2)				
50–54	8	3	3	—	3	4	4	5	—	—	—	—
		(20.0)	(12.05)		(13.05)	(14.3)	(8.2)	(7.2)				
≥ 55	10	2	4	—	3	3	3	4	—	—	2	—
		(13.4)	(16.0)		(13.05)	(10.7)	(6.15)	(5.8)			(25.0)	
Total	120	15	25	20	23	28	49	69	1	6	8	2
		(12.5)	(20.8)	(16.7)	(19.1)	(23.3)	(40.8)	(57.5)	(0.8)	(5.0)	(6.7)	(1.7)

Note: Figures in the parenthesis indicate percentage

Occupational Level and Nutritional Deficiency

Table 20.2 shows the percentage of prevalence of the signs of nutritional deficiency among the Munda women in terms of their occupational status. Of the 15 women who had abnormal hair, 86.7 per cent belonged to the employed women group. Vitamin 'A' deficiency signs were also observed more among the employed women (76%). Of the total women suffering from angular stomatitis and glossitis ('B' complex deficiency) 80 per cent and 74 per cent respectively belonged to the employed women group. Higher incidence of teeth abnormalities (78.6%) and dental caries (79.6%) was observed in case of employed women. Higher prevalence of gum abnormality was also found in employed women (78.3%).

Educational Level and Nutritional Deficiency

The percentage of prevalence of the signs of nutritional deficiency among the Munda women in relation to their educational status (Table 20.2) indicates a higher incidence of abnormal hair, vitamin 'A' deficiency, night blindness, vitamin 'B' complex deficiency affecting lips, tongue, teeth and gums among illiterate women. The women having education upto high school were found to have less incidence of the nutritional deficiency signs and symptoms. This might be due to proper selection and combination of the food stuffs in their diet because of their formal educational training.

Marital Status and Nutritional Deficiency

Of the total women who were suffering from nutritional deficiency signs, maximum belonged to the married group. 68 per cent of vitamin 'A' deficiency, 60 per cent of 'B' complex deficiency (angular stomatitis), 70 per cent of abnormal tongue, 64 per cent of abnormal teeth and 61 per cent of gum abnormality were observed among married women. The incidence of dental caries was also found to be more in case of unmarried women (Table 20.2).

Type of Family and Nutritional Deficiency

Table 20.3 indicates that the prevalence of nutritional deficiency signs, i.e. the incidence of vitamin 'A' deficiency (night blindness), and 'B' complex deficiency (abnormal lip, tongue, teeth, gum), were found to be higher in case of women of nuclear families than the women belonging to joint families.

TABLE 20.2: Percent Prevalence of Nutritional Deficiency Signs among Munda Women in relation to their Occupational Status, Educational Status and Marital Status

	N	CLINICAL SIGNS										
		Hair abnormal	Eyes night blindness	Lips Angular stomatitis	Tongue abnormal Glossitis	Teeth abnormal	Dental caries	Gums abnormal	Glands goitre	Skin abnormal	Nail abnormal	Oedma
Occupational Status												
Uncmp-	27	2	6	4	6	6	10	15	1	4	1	—
loyed		(13.3)	(24.0)	(20.0)	(26.0)	(21.4)	(20.4)	(21.7)	(100)	(66.7)	(12.5)	
Employed	93	13	19	16	17	22	39	54	—	2	7	2
		(86.7)	(76.0)	(80.0)	(74.0)	(78.6)	(79.6)	(78.3)		(33.3)	(87.5)	(100.0)
Educational Status												
Illiterate	43	9	13	7	7	17	10	24	1	4	4	1
		(60.0)	(52.0)	(35.0)	(30.4)	(60.7)	(20.4)	(34.8)	(100)	(66.7)	(50.0)	(50.0)
Primary	40	4	4	6	10	6	22	28	—	2	2	—
		(26.6)	(16.0)	(30.0)	(43.5)	(21.4)	(44.9)	(40.6)		(33.7)	(25.0)	
Medium	12	1	4	2	3	2	7	7			2	
		(6.7)	(16.0)	(10.0)	(13.05)	(7.1)	(14.3)	(10.1)	—	—	(25.0)	—
High School	25	1	4	5	3	3	10	10	—	—	—	1
and above		(6.7)	(16.0)	(25.0)	(13.05)	(10.8)	(20.4)	(14.5)				(50.0)
Marital Status												
Married	69	13	17	12	16	18	22	42	1	3	5	1
		(86.7)	(68.0)	(60.0)	(69.6)	(64.3)	(44.9)	(60.9)	(100)	(50.0)	(62.5)	(50.0)
Unmarried	51	2	8	8	7	10	27	27	—	3	3	1
		(13.3)	(32.0)	(40.0)	(30.4)	(35.7)	(55.1)	(39.1)		(50.0)	(37.5)	(50.0)
Total	120	15	25	20	23	28	49	69	1	6	8	2
		(12.5)	(20.8)	(16.7)	(19.1)	(23.3)	(40.8)	(57.5)	(0.8)	(5.0)	(6.7)	(1.7)

Note: Figures in the parenthesis indicate percentage.

Income Level and Nutritional Deficiency

The percentage of prevalence of nutritional deficiency sign among the Munda women in terms of per capita monthly income (Table 20.3) reveals that the women belonging to lower per capita income group were more susceptible to malnutrition and the prevalence of nutritional deficiency signs were observed to be more in that group. Higher incidence of vitamin 'A' deficiency (night blindness), vitamin 'B' deficiency (angular stomatitis) was observed in women belonging to ≤ Rs. 100 per capita monthly income. Only 8.7 per cent, 3.6 per cent, 1.5 per cent and 6.1 per cent of women belonging to the income group > Rs. 500 per capita per month, suffered from abnormal tongue, teeth, gum and dental caries respectively.

Thus the present survey reveals that prevalence of deficiency signs and symptoms was more in case of younger employed women, illiterate women and women who have lower per capita income. Rajyalakshmi (1991) observed that 70 per cent of the tribals of Andhra Pradesh suffered from the diseases related to eye and found it mostly to be non-nutritional in nature. Hanumantha Rao *et al.* (1992) observed highest prevalence of vitamin 'A' deficiency among the Maria Gonds school-age children of Maharashtra. They further noted a higher incidence of 'B' complex deficiency among the adults. Prevalence of goitre was found to be higher among adolescents in comparison to other age groups. The prevalence of all types of nutritional deficiency signs was observed to be higher among the females than of males in Maria Gond community (Hanumantha Rao *et al.* 1992). Observation of nutritional deficiency among the Jenukurubas of Karnataka reveals maximum prevalence of bitot spots, angular stomatisis in pre-school and school-age children. The prevalence of iodine deficiency (goitre) was found to be higher among the adolescents followed by the adults among Jenu Kurubas (Hanumantha Rao *et al.*, 1993).

Morbidity Pattern and Age

The morbidity pattern in terms of the age (Table 20.4a) reveals that, of the 26 women who suffered from frequent attack of pain and ache, 53.8 per cent belonged to the age group <35. Of the 12 cases of women who suffered from occasional attack of pain and ache, 66.7 per cent belonged to the age group < 35. The incidence of pain and ache was found to be more in younger age group which might be due to heavy work schedule of the young women. 21.7 and 57.5 per cent of women suffered from frequent and occasional attack of fever respectively. The frequency of attack from fever in older age group (> 35 years) was found to be higher (approximately 58%), but the occasional attack of fever was found to be more in younger age group, i.e. < 35 years

TABLE 20.3: Prevalence of Nutritional Deficiency Signs among Munda Women in relation to their Type of Family and Per-capita Per Month Income.

		CLINICAL SIGNS										
	N	Hair abnormal	Eyes night blindness	Lips Angular stomatitis	Tongue abnormal Glossitis	Teeth abnormal	Dental caries	Gums abnormal	Glands goitre	Skin abnormal	Nail abnormal	Oedma
Type of Family												
Joint	31	3	7	4	7	9	22	14	1	2	7	—
		(20.0)	(28.0)	(20.0)	(30.4)	(32.1)	(44.9)	(20.3)	(100)	(33.3)	(87.5)	
Nuclear	89	12	18	16	16	19	27	55	—	4	1	2
		(80.0)	(72.0)	(80.0)	(69.6)	(67.9)	(55.1)	(79.7)		(66.7)	(12.5)	(100.0)
Per Capita Income												
≤ 200	62	6	14	11	8	17	21	33	7	3	5	1
		(40.0)	(56.0)	(55.0)	(34.8)	(60.7)	(42.9)	(47.8)	(100)	(50.0)	(62.5)	(50.0)
> 200 – ≤ 500	51	8	10	8	13	10	25	35	—	3	3	1
		(53.3)	(40.0)	(40.0)	(56.5)	(35.7)	(51.0)	(50.7)		(50.0)	(37.5)	(50.0)
> 500 – ≤ 800	7	1	1	1	2	1	3	1	—	—	—	—
		(6.7)	(4.0)	(5.0)	(8.7)	(3.6)	(6.1)	(1.5)				
Total	120	15	25	20	23	28	49	69	1	6	8	2
		(12.5)	(20.8)	(16.7)	(19.1)	(23.3)	(40.8)	(57.5)	(0.8)	(5.0)	(6.7)	(1.7)

Note: Figures in the parenthesis indicate percentage.

(68.1%). 21.7 per cent of women suffered from occasional attack of diarrhoea, of which 65.4 per cent belonged to the age group <35. Of 36.7 per cent of women who suffered from occasional attack of malaria, 59 per cent were in the age group of <35. Only 3.3 per cent of women suffered from malaria frequently (Table 20.4a).

Digestive disorder was observed in 12 cases of the Munda women, out of which 9.2 per cent suffered from the same frequently. 54.5 per cent of women suffering from digestive disorder belonged to the younger age group (<35). 13.33 per cent of Munda women suffered from respiratory disorder, of which 12.5 per cent suffered from the same occasionally. Higher percentage of women of younger age group (<35) was found suffering from occasional attack of respiratory disorder (53.3%). Arthritis was present in 37.5 per cent of women. Only 3.3 per cent of women suffered from scabies (Table 20.4b).

Occupational Level and Morbidity Pattern

Problems like pain and ache, fever, diarrhoea, malaria, respiratory disorders, arthritis were found to be higher in case of employed women in comparison to the unemployed women (Table 20.5a and 20.5b). Of the 26 women who complained pain and ache, attack of fever and diarrhoea, about 80.8 per cent were employed. The occasional attack of malaria was also found to be higher in cases of employed women. Only 10 per cent and 13.3 per cent of the Munda women were found to be suffering from digestive disorder and respiratory infection respectively of which 50 per cent and 56 per cent were employed. The incidence of arthritis was also reported to be more in employed women. Though a large percentage of women were engaged in employment to supplement their family income they were found to be predisposed to a number of infections in comparison to unemployed women.

Educational Level and Morbidity Pattern

Incidence of all types of morbidity was found to be higher in case of illiterate women (Table 20.6a and 20.6b). Of the 21.7 per cent of women who suffered from frequent attack of pain and ache, 53.8 per cent belonged to illiterate group. Out of 21.7 per cent of women who frequently suffered from fever 46.2 per cent belonged to illiterate group. Out of 21.7 per cent of women who suffered from diarrhoea occasionally, 42.3 per cent belonged to illiterate group. It is interesting to note that of the 36.7 per cent of women who suffered from malaria occasionally, 27.3 per cent and 50 per cent belonged to the illiterate and upto primary education groups respectively (Table 20.6a). Around 64 per cent of women belonging to lower education groups (up to primary level) were found to be suffering from frequent attack of digestive

TABLE 20.4(a): Morbidity Pattern of the Munda Women according to their Age

Age Group	N	TYPE OF MORBIDITY											
		Pain and Ache			Fever			Diarrhoea			Malaria		
		F.A.	O.A.	R.A.	F.A.	O.A.	R.A.	F.A.	O.A.	R.A.	F.A.	O.A.	R.A.
≤ 19	24	6	2	16	2	18	4	—	5	19	1	8	15
		(23.1)	(16.7)	(19.5)	(7.7)	(26.1)	(16.0)		(19.2)	(20.4)	(25.0)	(18.2)	(20.8)
20–24	18	2	2	14	4	10	4	—	6	12	1	6	11
		(7.7)	(16.7)	(17.1)	(15.4)	(14.5)	(16.0)		(23.1)	(12.9)	(25.0)	(13.6)	(15.3)
25–29	16	3	1	12	1	10	5	—	2	14	—	4	12
		(11.5)	(8.3)	(14.6)	(3.85)	(14.5)	(20.0)		(7.7)	(15.1)		(9.1)	(16.7)
30–34	17	3	3	11	5	9	3	—	4	13	—	8	9
		(11.5)	(25.0)	(13.4)	(19.2)	(13.1)	(12.0)		(15.4)	(14.0)		(18.2)	(12.5)
35–39	10	2	1	7	1	7	2	1	1	8	—	6	4
		(7.7)	(8.3)	(8.5)	(3.85)	(10.1)	(8.0)	(100)	(3.9)	(8.6)		(13.6)	(5.6)
40–44	8	2	2	4	—	7	1	—	2	6	—	5	3
		(7.7)	(16.7)	(4.9)		(10.1)	(4.0)		(7.7)	(6.5)		(11.4)	(4.2)
45–49	9	5	—	4	5	1	3	—	1	8	—	3	6
		(19.2)		(4.9)	(19.2)	(1.4)	(12.0)		(3.8)	(8.6)		(6.8)	(8.3)
50–54	8	1	—	7	3	4	1	—	3	5	2	1	5
		(3.9)		(8.5)	(11.6)	(5.8)	(4.0)		(11.5)	(5.4)	(50.0)	(2.3)	(6.9)
≥ 55	10	2	1	7	5	3	2	—	2	8	—	3	7
		(7.7)	(8.3)	(8.5)	(19.2)	(4.3)	(8.0)		(7.7)	(8.6)		(6.8)	(9.7)
Total	120	26	12	82	26	69	25	1	26	93	4	44	72
		(21.7)	(10.0)	(68.3)	(21.7)	(57.5)	(20.8)	(0.8)	(21.7)	(77.5)	(3.3)	(36.7)	(60.0)

F.A. = Frequent Attack ; O.A. = Occasional Attack ; R.A. = Rare Attack

Note: Figures in the parenthesis indicate percentage.

TABLE 20.4(b): Morbidity Pattern among the Munda Women according to their Age

Age Group	N	TYPE OF MORBIDITY							
		Digestive Disorder			Respiratory Disorder			Arthritis	Scabies
		F.A.	O.A.	R.A.	F.A.	O.A.	R.A.	Present	Present
≤ 19	24	3	—	21	—	1	23	10	—
		(27.3)		(19.4)		(6.7)	(22.1)	(22.2)	
20–24	18	1	—	17	—	3	15	4	—
		(9.1)		(15.7)		(20.0)	(14.4)	(8.9)	
25–29	16	1	1	14	—	2	14	4	2
		(9.1)	(100)	(13.0)		(13.3)	(13.5)	(8.9)	(50.0)
30–34	17	1	—	16	—	2	15	4	1
		(9.1)		(14.8)		(13.3)	(14.4)	(8.9)	(25.0)
35–39	10	1	—	9	—	1	9	3	0
		(9.1)		(8.3)		(6.7)	(8.7)	(6.7)	
40–44	8	—	—	8	—	1	7	4	—
				(7.4)		(6.7)	(6.7)	(8.9)	
45–49	9	—	—	9	1	3	5	8	—
				(8.3)	(100)	(20.0)	(4.8)	(17.8)	
50–54	8	2	—	6	—	—	8	2	1
		(18.2)		(5.6)			(7.7)	(4.4)	(25.0)
≥ 55	10	2	—	8	—	2	8	6	—
		(18.2)		(7.4)		(13.3)	(7.7)	(13.3)	
Total	120	11	1	108	1	15	104	45	4
		(9.2)	(0.8)	(90.0)	(0.8)	(12.5)	(86.7)	(37.5)	(3.3)

F.A. = Frequent Attack ; O.A. = Occasional Attack ; R.A. = Rare Attack

Note: Figures in the parenthesis indicate percentage.

TABLE 20.5(a): Morbidity Pattern among the Munda Women in relation to their Occupational Status

Employment Status	N	TYPE OF MORBIDITY											
		Pain and Ache			Fever			Diarrhoea			Malaria		
		F.A.	O.A.	R.A.	F.A.	O.A.	R.A.	F.A.	O.A.	R.A.	F.A.	O.A.	R.A.
Employed	27	5	3	19	5	45	7	—	5	22	2	8	17
		(19.2)	(25.0)	(23.1)	(19.2)	(21.7)	(28.0)		(19.2)	(23.7)	(50.0)	(18.1)	(23.6)
Unemployed	93	21	9	63	21	54	18	1	21	71	2	36	55
		(80.8)	(75.0)	(76.9)	(80.8)	(78.3)	(72.0)	(100)	(80.8)	(76.3)	(50.0)	(81.9)	(76.4)
Total	120	26	12	82	26	69	25	1	26	93	4	44	72
		(21.7)	(10.0)	(68.3)	(21.7)	(57.5)	(20.8)	(0.8)	(21.7)	(77.5)	(3.3)	(36.7)	(60.0)

F.A. = Frequent Attack ; O.A. = Occasional Attack ; R.A. = Rare Attack

Note: Figures in the parenthesis indicate percentage.

TABLE 20.5(b): Morbidity Pattern among the Munda Women in relation to their Occupational Status

Employment Status	N	TYPE OF MORBIDITY									
		Digestive Disorder			Respiratory Disorder			Arthritis		Scabies	
		F.A.	O.A.	R.A.	F.A.	O.A.	R.A.	Present	Absent	Present	Absent
Employed	27	6	—	21	1	6	20	16	11	2	25
		(54.5)		(19.4)	(100)	(40.0)	(19.2)	(35.5)	(14.7)	(50.0)	(21.6)
Unemployed	93	5	1	87	—	9	84	29	64	2	91
		(45.5)	(100)	(80.6)		(60.0)	(80.8)	(64.5)	(85.3)	(50.0)	(78.4)
Total	120	11	1	108	1	15	104	45	75	4	116
		(9.2)	(0.8)	(90.0)	(0.8)	(12.5)	(86.7)	(37.5)	(62.5)	(3.3)	(96.7)

F.A. = Frequent Attack ; O.A. = Occasional Attack ; R.A. = Rare Attack

Note: Figures in the parenthesis indicate percentage.

disorder. Of the 16 women who suffered from respiratory disorders in the last one year, 43.8 per cent belonged to the illiterate group. Arthritis was reported in 49 per cent of women belonging to illiterate group (Table 20.6b).

Marital Status and Morbidity Pattern

Of the 21.7 per cent of women who suffered from pain and ache frequently, 57.7 per cent were found to be married (Table 20.7a). The incidence of fever was also observed to be higher in case of married women than that of unmarried women (57.7% married women suffered from occasional attack of fever). Occasional attack of diarrhoea and malaria was also found to be higher in married women (65.4% and 54.5%). Of the 37.5 per cent women who suffered from arthritis, 57.8 per cent were married. The incidence of scabies was very small (3.3%) in the total population (Table 20.7b).

Family Type of Morbidity Pattern

Pain/ache, fever, malaria, digestive disorders were reported to be higher in case of women from nuclear family background (Table 20.8a and 20.8b). Similarly women from nuclear families were reported to have higher incidence of occasional attack of fever (69%), diarrhoea (86.5%), malaria (90.9%), respiratory disorder (60%), arthritis (84.4%) and scabies (75%) (Table 20.8b).

Income Level and Morbidity Pattern

Of the 26 persons who suffered from frequent attack of pain and ache, 61.5 per cent were in the lower income group. Similarly, of the 95 persons who suffered from fever, 48.4 per cent were from the lower income group. Of 21.7 per cent women who suffered from diarrhoea occasionally (Table 20.9a), 53.8 per cent belonged to the lower income group. Similarly, of 48 persons who suffered from malaria either frequently or occasionally, only 2 per cent belonged to the higher income group whereas 45.8 and 52 per cent of women were from lower and middle-income groups respectively. Of the 12 women who suffered from digestive disorder, 72.7 per cent were from the lower income group. Of those women who occasionally suffered from respiratory disorders, 86.7 per cent were from the lower economic levels. The incidence of arthritis and scabies was also found to be more in case of lower income group in comparison with other income groups. Thus, in general, the morbidity rate was found to be more in case of women from lower economic group (Table 20.9b).

From the morbidity information, it is evident that fever, diarrhoea, malaria, arthritis were some of the major health problems found among the Munda

TABLE 20.6(a): Morbidity Pattern among the Munda Women in relation to their Educational Status

Educational status	N	Pain and Ache F.A.	Pain and Ache O.A.	Pain and Ache R.A.	Fever F.A.	Fever O.A.	Fever R.A.	Diarrhoea F.A.	Diarrhoea O.A.	Diarrhoea R.A.	Malaria F.A.	Malaria O.A.	Malaria R.A.
Illiterate	43	14 (53.8)	2 (16.7)	27 (32.9)	12 (46.2)	17 (24.65)	14 (56.0)	—	11 (42.3)	32 (34.4)	2 (50.0)	12 (27.3)	29 (40.3)
Upto Primary	40	5 (19.2)	7 (58.3)	28 (34.1)	9 (34.6)	29 (42.0)	2 (8.0)	1 (100.0)	6 (23.1)	33 (35.5)	1 (25.0)	22 (50.0)	17 (23.6)
Upto Middle School	12	2 (7.7)	—	10 (12.2)	3 (11.5)	6 (8.7)	3 (12.0)	—	2 (7.7)	10 (10.8)	—	2 (4.5)	10 (13.9)
Upto High School & Above	15	5 (19.3)	3 (25.0)	17 (20.8)	2 (7.7)	17 (24.65)	6 (24.0)	—	7 (26.9)	18 (19.4)	1 (25.0)	8 (18.2)	16 (22.2)
Total	120	26 (21.7)	12 (10:0)	82 (68.3)	26 (21.7)	69 (57.7)	25 (20.8)	1 (0.8)	26 (21.7)	93 (77.3)	4 (3.3)	44 (36.7)	72 (60.0)

F.A. = Frequent Attack ; O.A. = Occasional Attack ; R.A. = Rare Attack

Note: Figures in the parenthesis indicate percentage.

TABLE 20.6(b): Morbidity Pattern among the Munda Women in relation to their Educational Status

Educational Status	N	Digestive Disorder F.A.	Digestive Disorder O.A.	Digestive Disorder R.A.	Respiratory Disorder F.A.	Respiratory Disorder O.A.	Respiratory Disorder R.A.	Arthritis Present	Arthritis Absent	Scabies Present	Scabies Absent
Illiterate	43	2	1	40	—	7	36	22	21	2	41
		(18.1)	(100)	(37.0)		(46.7)	(34.6)	(48.9)	(28.0)	(50.0)	(35.3)
Upto Primary	40	5	—	35	—	3	37	18	22	1	39
		(45.65)		(32.4)		(20.0)	(35.6)	(40.0)	(29.3)	(25.0)	(33.6)
Upto middle School	12	—	—	12	1	2	10	1	11	—	12
				(11.1)	(100)	(13.3)	(9.6)	(2.2)	(14.7)		(10.3)
Upto High School and above	15	4	—	21	—	3	21	4	21	1	24
		(36.4)		(19.5)		(20.0)	(20.2)	(8.9)	(28.0)	(25.0)	(20.6)
Total	120	11	1	108	1	15	104	45	75	4	116
		(9.2)	(0.8)	(90.0)	(0.8)	(12.5)	(86.7)	(37.5)	(62.5)	(3.3)	(96.7)

F.A. = Frequent Attack ; O.A. = Occasional Attack ; R.A. = Rare Attack

Note: Figures in the parenthesis indicate percentage.

TABLE 20.7(a): Morbidity Pattern among the Munda Women in relation to their Marital Status

Marital Status	N	TYPE OF MORBIDITY: Pain and Ache			Fever			Diarrhoea			Malaria		
		F.A.	O.A.	R.A.	F.A.	O.A.	R.A.	F.A.	O.A.	R.A.	F.A.	O.A.	R.A.
Married	69	15	7	47	15	38	16	1	17	51	2	24	43
		(57.7)	(58.3)	(57.3)	(57.7)	(55.1)	(64.0)	(100)	(65.4)	(54.8)	(50.0)	(54.4)	(59.7)
Unmarried	51	11	5	35	11	31	9	—	9	42	2	20	29
		(42.3)	(41.7)	(42.7)	(42.3)	(44.9)	(36.0)		(34.6)	(45.2)	(50.0)	(45.6)	(40.3)
Total	120	26	12	82	26	69	25	1	26	93	4	44	72
		(21.7)	(10.0)	(68.3)	(21.7)	(57.5)	(20.8)	(0.8)	(21.7)	(77.5)	(3.3)	(36.7)	(60.0)

F.A. = Frequent Attack ; O.A. = Occasional Attack ; R.A. = Rare Attack

Note: Figures in the parenthesis indicate percentage.

TABLE 20.7(b): Morbidity Pattern among the Munda Women in relation to their Marital Status

Marital Status	N	TYPE OF MORBIDITY: Digestive Disorder			Respiratory Disorder			Arthritis		Scabies	
		F.A.	O.A.	R.A.	F.A.	O.A.	R.A.	Present	Absent	Present	Absent
Married	69	5	1	63	1	6	62	26	44	2	67
		(45.5)	(100)	(58.3)	(100)	(40.0)	(59.6)	(57.8)	(58.7)	(50.0)	(57.8)
Unmarried	51	6	—	45	—	9	42	19	31	2	49
		(54.5)		(41.7)		(60.0)	(40.4)	(42.2)	(41.3)	(50.0)	(42.2)
Total	120	11	1	108	1	15	104	45	75	4	116
		(9.2)	(0.8)	(90.0)	(0.8)	(12.5)	(86.7)	(37.5)	(62.5)	(3.3)	(96.7)

F.A. = Frequent Attack ; O.A. = Occasional Attack ; R.A. = Rare Attack

Note: Figures in the parenthesis indicate percentage.

TABLE 20.8(a): Morbidity Pattern among the Munda Women According to their Type of Family

Type of Family	N	Pain and Ache F.A.	Pain and Ache O.A.	Pain and Ache R.A.	Fever F.A.	Fever O.A.	Fever R.A.	Diarrhoea F.A.	Diarrhoea O.A.	Diarrhoea R.A.	Malaria F.A.	Malaria O.A.	Malaria R.A.
Extended	31	6	3	22	8	13	10	—	3	28	—	4	27
		(23.1)	(25.0)	(26.8)	(30.8)	(18.8)	(40.0)		(11.5)	(30.5)		(9.1)	(37.5)
Nuclear	89	20	9	60	18	56	15	1	23	65	4	40	45
		(76.9)	(75.0)	(73.2)	(69.2)	(81.2)	(60.0)	(100)	(88.5)	(69.5)	(100)	(90.9)	(62.5)
Total	120	26	12	82	26	69	25	1	26	93	4	44	72
		(21.7)	(10.0)	(68.3)	(21.7)	(57.5)	(20.8)	(0.8)	(21.7)	(77.5)	(3.3)	(36.7)	(60.0)

F.A. = Frequent Attack ; O.A. = Occasional Attack ; R.A. = Rare Attack

Note: Figures in the parenthesis indicate percentage

TABLE 20.8(b): Morbidity Pattern among the Munda Women According to their Type of Family

Type of Family	N	Digestive Disorder F.A.	Digestive Disorder O.A.	Digestive Disorder R.A.	Respiratory Disorder F.A.	Respiratory Disorder O.A.	Respiratory Disorder R.A.	Arthritis Present	Arthritis Absent	Scabies Present	Scabies Absent
Extended	31	2	—	29	1	6	26	7	24	1	30
		(18.2)		(26.9)	(100)	(40.0)	(25.0)	(15.6)	(32.0)	(25.0)	(25.9)
Nuclear	89	9	1	79	—	9	78	38	51	3	86
		(81.8)	(100)	(73.1)		(60.0)	(75.0)	(84.4)	(68.0)	(75.0)	(74.1)
Total	120	11	1	108	1	15	104	45	75	4	116
		(9.2)	(0.8)	(90.0)	(0.8)	(12.5)	(86.7)	(37.5)	(62.5)	(3.3)	(96.7)

F.A. = Frequent Attack ; O.A. = Occasional Attack ; R.A. = Rare Attack

Note: Figures in the parenthesis indicate percentage

TABLE 20.9(a): Morbidity Pattern among the Munda Women according to their Income Level

Per capita Income	N	Pain and Ache F.A.	Pain and Ache O.A.	Pain and Ache R.A.	Fever F.A.	Fever O.A.	Fever R.A.	Diarrhoea F.A.	Diarrhoea O.A.	Diarrhoea R.A.	Malaria F.A.	Malaria O.A.	Malaria R.A.
≤ 200	62	16	4	42	12	34	16	1	14	47	4	18	40
		(61.5)	(33.3)	(51.2)	(46.2)	(49.3)	(64.0)	(100)	(53.8)	(50.5)	(100)	(40.9)	(55.6)
> 200 – ≤ 500	51	9	8	32	19	31	6	—	11	40	—	25	26
		(34.6)	(66.7)	(41.5)	(53.8)	(44.9)	(24.0)		(42.3)	(43.0)		(56.8)	(36.1)
> 500 – ≤ 800	7	1	—	6	—	4	3	—	1	6	—	1	6
		(3.9)		(7.3)		(5.8)	(12.0)		(3.9)	(6.5)		(2.3)	(8.3)
Total	120	26	12	82	26	69	25	1	26	93	4	44	72
		(21.7)	(10.0)	(68.3)	(21.7)	(57.5)	(20.8)	(0.8)	(21.7)	(77.5)	(3.3)	(36.7)	(60.0)

F.A. = Frequent Attack ; O.A. = Occasional Attack ; R.A. = Rare Attack

Note: Figures in the parenthesis indicate percentage.

TABLE 20.9(b): Morbidity Pattern among the Munda Women according to their Income Level

Per Capita Income	N	Digestive Disorder F.A.	Digestive Disorder O.A.	Digestive Disorder R.A.	Respiratory Disorder F.A.	Respiratory Disorder O.A.	Respiratory Disorder R.A.	Arthritis Present	Arthritis Absent	Scabies Present	Scabies Absent
≤ 200	62	8	1	53	1	13	48	24	38	3	59
		(72.7)	(100)	(49.1)	(100)	(86.7)	(46.2)	(53.3)	(50.7)	(75.0)	(50.9)
> 200 – ≤ 500	51	3	—	48	—	1	49	20	31	1	50
		(27.3)		(44.4)		(6.7)	(47.1)	(44.4)	(41.3)	(25.0)	(43.1)
> 500 – ≤ 800	7	—	—	7	—	1	7	1	6	—	7
				(6.5)		(6.7)	(6.7)	(2.2)	(8.0)		(6.0)
Total	120	11	1	108	1	15	104	45	75	4	116
		(9.2)	(0.8)	(90.0)	(0.8)	(12.5)	(86.7)	(37.5)	(62.5)	(3.3)	(96.7)

F.A. = Frequent Attack ; O.A. = Occasional Attack ; R.A. = Rare Attack

Note: Figures in the parenthesis indicate percentage.

women followed by pain and ache, and respiratory infection. Earlier studies on various tribal groups in the country revealed that the incidence of scabies, infection, infestation and malnutrition is prevalent in tribal areas (NIN, 1969 and 1973; Sharma, 1971; Pingale, 1973; Gore *et al.,* 1977; Ali, 1979; Rajyalakshmi, 1991). International Institute for Population Science (1985) reported that out of 100 females 1.3 per cent, 7.9 per cent and 1.7 per cent suffered from pain and ache, fever and digestive disorders respectively. The incidence of malaria, tuberculosis, respiratory disorders and gynaecological diseases was found to be less in females of Orissa in general (NNMB, 1981). The relatively less incidence of scabies (3.3%), respiratory disorder (13.3%) and digestive disorder (10%) observed in our study might be due to the influence of urbanization and because of the better utilization of health care (prenatal and postnatal cares) services available in the Sambalpur town by our sample respondents.

Conclusion

There is always a significant variation in the living and dietary habits of tribals and non-tribal population. It was observed in our study that though the Munda women live in an urban complex having better health care facilities yet they suffer from a host of food deficiencies and infectious diseases. Since the effects of malnutrition and infections are synergistic, the combined effort of both health and nutrition personnel is essential to tackle these problems. Although the diseases can be cured through adequate and proper medical facilities, prevention is only possible by providing health and nutrition education through awareness programmes sponsored by the government and non-governmental agencies. This will help in maintaining the personal and environmental hygiene and in the proper selection, combination and consumption of varieties of low-cost food-stuffs. Besides, safe drinking water must be made available to prevent diarrhoea and dysentery.

It is important to note that information about the morbidity incidence obtained from the respondents give only an abstract of health problems of the area. To get a clear picture, a systematic epidemiological survey should be done. Reporting cases through health care systems and surveillance may also provide some indication of the relevant magnitude of disease incidence as well as the trends in controls and prevention (WHO, 1981).

REFERENCES

Ali. A. 1979. "Health and Genetic Problem of Khutia-konds of Burlubaru village, Phulabani district (Orissa)", *Adibasi* (XVIII): 56-62.

Ghosh, S. 1985. "Discrimination Begins at Birth", Paper prepared for the UNICEF Journalist, Workshop on the Female Child, New Delhi.

Gore, A.P., T. Shobha and M. Kulkarni. 1977. "Nutritional Status of Tribes in the Indravati River Basin," *Indian Journal of Nutrition and Dietetics,* 14: 167-171.

Government of Orissa. 1995. Statistical Outlines of Orissa. Bhubaneswar: Directorate of Economics and Statistics.

Hanumantha Rao, D., G.N.V. Brahman, K. Mallikhajuna Rao, Ch. Gal Reddy and N. Pralhad Rao. 1992. "Nutritional Status of Maria-Gonda-A Primitive Tribe of Maharashtra," *Indian Journal of Nutrition and Dietetics,* 29:61.66.

—. 1993. "Assessment of Nutritional Status of Jenu Kurubas-A Primitive Tribe of Karnatak," *Indian Journal of Nutrition and Dietetics,* 30:66-71.

International Institute for Population Science. 1985. Report on the Base Line Surveys on Fertility, Mortality and Related Factors in Orissa. Bhubaneswar: Department of Vital Statistics Directorate of Health Services.

Indian Council of Social Science Research. 1975. Status of Women in India. A Synopsis of Report of the National Committee on the Status of Women, New Delhi.

Karkal, M. and D. Pandey. 1989. *Studies on Women and Population: A Critique.* Bombay: Himalaya Publishing House.

Khan, M.E., S.K. Ghosh, Dastidar and R. Singh. 1983. "Nutrition and Health Practices among Rural Women—A Study of Uttar Pradesh, India," *Working Paper No. 31.* New Delhi: Operations Research Group.

National Institute of Nutrition. 1967. *Annual Report.* Indian Council of Medical Research, Hyderabad.

—. 1969. *Annual Report.* Indian Council of Medical Research, Hyderabad.

—. 1973. *Annual Report.* Indian Council of Medical Research, Hyderabad.

National Nutrition Monitoring Bureau. 1981. "Food and Nutrient Consumption Pattern in the Selected Districts of Different States, 1980," National Institute of Nutrition, Hyderabad: ICMR.

Park, J.E. and K. Park. 1991. *Preventive and Social Medicine.* Jabalpur: Banarasidas, Bharat.

Pingale, U. 1973. "Some Studies in Two Tribal Groups of Central India. Part I: Dietary intake and Nutritional Status." *Plant Foods for Man,* 1: 185-194.

Pratap, D.R. 1975. Tribes of Andhra Pradesh. World Telugu Conference Publication, Hyderabad: 1st World Telugu Conference Office.

Rajyalakshmi, P. 1991. *Tribal Food Habits.* New Delhi: Gian Publishing House.

Sharma, K. (eds.). 1971. *The Konds of Orissa: An Anthropometric Study,* New Delhi: Concept Publishing Company.

World Health Organization. 1981. Development of Indicators for Monitoring Progress towards Health for all by the year, 2000. Geneva, WHO.

TWENTY-ONE

INFANT MORTALITY AMONG THE KHARIA
Case of a Tribal Community of Orissa

S.S. GURU and RASHMI PRAMANIK

Of all types of mortality, infant mortality is most sensitive to socio-economic development and mobility. Therefore, for effective planning and implementation of any developmental programme, knowledge of infant/child mortality and their determinants are highly essential. This knowledge will help in the judicious use of the meagre inputs by different agencies of the government as well as the voluntary organizations in order to channelize the services in a balanced and equitable manner among the needy sections of the population. It has been established that there is a strong association among infant/child mortality, fertility level and acceptance of family planning practices (Mahadevan, 1979).

The United Nations' Population Report, 1983, indicates that every year round the world ten million infants do not survive to see their first birth day. As mortality is comparatively high in India and is likely to vary in different social and cultural groups within and between states, there is a need for understanding mortality in different parts of the country.

Tribal demography, hitherto has been a neglected area of study by demographers in India. No doubt, a few studies (mostly by anthropologists) have been carried out on fertility behaviour of a few selected tribal communities. However, many of these studies are based on very limited sample, which give less scope for wider generalization. Mortality studies among tribal are quite rare.

The present paper makes an humble attempt to examine the nature and extent of some socio-cultural factors on the incidence of infant death and survival among the Kharia. According to the 1971 census of India, western Orissa (comprising undivided districts of Sambalpur, Sundargarh, Bolangir and Kalahandi) accounts for approximately 82 per cent of the total Kharia population in the state which is 1,20,483. Available anthropological literature reveal that the Kharia exhibit a highly primitive form of economy and life-style in the central tribal belt of India.

A sample of 500 eligible couples were selected at random based upon a multi-staged sampling design. The study was focussed on live-births that occurred within a period of three years prior to the time of survey. Here an eligible couple is referred to one who had atleast one live birth during the reference period, i.e. not more than three years and not less than one year prior to the date of the survey. By administrating a pre-tested interview schedule relevant information were collected from the couples.

The level of infant mortality speaks of the state of the social and economic development of any population. Infant Mortality Rate (IMR) is widely accepted as the most crucial indicator of the Physical Quality of Life Index (PQLI) of a population (Morris and Alpin, 1982).

It is well known that educational and occupational status of parents, prenatal care and the technical ability of the delivery attendants are the major factors influencing infant mortality. Similarly, the cultural factors, viz. belief in fatalism, infant feeding practices, gender discrimination, etc. also influence infant mortality.

Education of the Mother

Education in general, and the female education in particular, works in various ways to influence child health. Mother's attitude and abilities to perform the role of a health agent in the family are of great importance. Education helps a woman to break away with the tradition which is considerably powerful among the tribal communities. Such a mother is likely to be more inclined to therapeutics for treatment of diseases. Moreover, educated mothers regard the utilization of modern health service facilities within their reach not as a boon but as a right (Caldwell, 1979). The single most crucial factor to bring down the level of infant mortality in Kerala may be attributed to higher female literacy in the state (Mahadevan, 1989).

We notice a sharp decline in infant deaths with advancement in maternal education. The illiterate mothers experienced the highest incidence of infant deaths. Again among the literates, the least incidence of infant death occurred to mothers with secondary and higher level of education. The differences observed in the incidence of infant deaths and survivals for differential level of mother's education are highly significant (at one per cent level) indicating an inverse relationship between the mother's education and infant mortality (Table 21.1).

The general notion among the tribal people is that home is the learning place for girls, where they have to learn household work in the company of their mothers and other elderly female members. Disinclination for co-education, demand for child labour, superstitions regarding female education

TABLE 21.1: Maternal Education and Infant Deaths—Survivals

Education of Mother	Infant Deaths	Infant Survivors	Total Births
Illiterate	131	268	399
	(32.83)	(67.17)	(100.00)
Primary (1-5)	12	45	57
	(21.05)	(78.95)	(100.00)
Secondary and Above (6+)	5	39	44
	(11.36)	(88.64)	(100.00)
Total	148	352	500
Chi-square	11.0147		
Level of Significance 1%			

Note: Figures in Parenthesis denote percentage.

and the distance of the school from home combine to contribute to higher female illiteracy among the Kharia.

Occupation of the Mother

More than the father's occupation, mother's occupation can be viewed as an explanatory variable, especially in a tribal situation, like the present sample, wherein one notices very high participation of female labour force compared to the non-tribal groups. Mother's work participation outside home, directly reduces the time spent for rearing the young. It particularly upsets the schedule of breast feeding. Studies in developing countries reveal that the health of infants who depend exclusively on breast feeding, may deteriorate if the mother is engaged in economic activities outside home (Sloan, 1971).

A look at the data on the differential influence of mother's occupation on the mortality and survival chances of infants suggest that highest number of infant deaths occurred to the mothers working as labourers outside home (34.37%) followed by non-workers (housewives). On the other hand mothers working as Class IV and other white collar jobs experienced the least incidence of infant deaths (17.39%). This association between mortality and survival chances of infants and the mothers occupation are significant (Table 21.2).

The differential level of female education, social stigma attached to women's participation in low category occupation like labourers may be attributed to the differences noticed in different categories of occupations.

Occupation of the Father

The occupation of the father generally determines the socio-economic status

TABLE 21.2: Maternal Occupation and Infant Mortality—Survivality

Occupation of Mother	Infant Deaths	Infant Survivors	Total Births
Non-worker (Housewife)	26 (23.42)	85 (76.85)	111 (100.00)
Wage Labourer	110 (34.37)	210 (65.63)	320 (100.00)
Class IV & Other employees	12 (17.39)	57 (82.61)	69 (100.00)
Total	148	352	500
Chi-square	10.4667		
Level of Significance 1%			

Note: Figures in Parenthesis denote percentage.

of any household since occupation is considered as a source of income. Occupational mobility among the Kharia, however is not significant. It only more or less reflects income.

It was observed that infant mortality was highest in the families of labourers (32.94%), followed by 26.73 per cent among the cultivators and petty businessmen. The lowest incidence of infant death (16.13%) was found among the Class IV employees. Thus, it is inferred that infant mortality is higher when the parents are in lower categories of occupation compared to the relatively higher ones (Table 21.3).

TABLE 21.3: Paternal Occupation and Infant Deaths—Survivals

Occupation of Father	Infant Deaths	Infant Survivors	Total Births
Labourer	111 (32.94)	226 (67.06)	337 (100.00)
Cultivators/Petty Businessmen	27 (26.73)	74 (73.27)	101 (100.00)
Class IV & Other employees	10 (16.13)	52 (83.87)	62 (100.00)
Total	148	352	500
Chi-square	7.5988		
Level of Significance 5%			

Note: Figures in Parenthesis denote percentage.

Socio-Economic Status of the Family

In order to examine the cumulative influence of income, educational attainment and occupational status of the parents (a couple is considered as one unit) on mortality and survival chances of infants, a composite index has been constructed and is trichotomized into low, moderate and high parental socio-economic status.

It was observed that couples with low socio-economic status experienced the highest incidence of infant deaths (33.53%). On the other hand, the least incidence of infant mortality occurred to couples with high socio-economic status. The Chi-square test (at one per cent level) confirms that the observed differences in infant survivals and mortality corresponding to the various levels of parental socio-economic status are highly significant. Hence, increase in parental socio-economic status leads to a reduction in infant mortality (Table 21.4).

TABLE 21.4: Parental Socio-economic Status (Index) and Infant Deaths—Survivals

Socio-economic Status Index	Infant Deaths	Infant Survivors	Total Births
Poor (Low)	113	224	337
	(33.53)	(66.47)	(100.00)
Moderate	26	77	103
	(25.24)	(74.76)	(100.00)
Good (High)	9	51	60
	(15.00)	(85.00)	(100.00)
Total	148	352	500
Chi-square	9.5728		
Level of Significance 1%			

Note: Figures in Parenthesis denote percentage.

The Family Structure

Family is universal and is the most simple and smallest form of human social grouping. The life style, food habits and decision-making are determined to a great extent by the structure of the family.

A look at the data on the structure of the family indicates that the nuclear family set-up is very common among the Kharia. It was observed that least incidence of infant deaths was recorded in nuclear families (21.98%), whereas the highest incidence of infant mortality occurred in joint families (34.96%). The corresponding figure for the joint-transitional family* is 28.85 per cent. The observed differences in the incidence of infant mortality and

* A joint-transitional family is one where the nuclear units live separately but perform certain socio-religious activities jointly.

TABLE 21.5: Family Structure and Infant Mortality—Survivality

Structure of Family	Infant Deaths	Infant Survivors	Total Births
Joint	93	173	266
	(34.96)	(65.04)	(100.00)
Joint-transitional	15	37	52
	(28.85)	(71.15)	(100.00)
Nuclear	40	142	182
	(21.98)	(78.02)	(100.00)
Total	148	352	500
Chi-square	8.7500		
Level of Significance 5%			

Note: Figures in Parenthesis denote percentage.

survivals corresponding to the family structure is also highly significant (at 5 per cent level) thereby indicating that joint family environment is not conducive to the safe growth of the infant (Table 21.5).

Though in the joint family, the presence of many members enhances the scope of child rearing than that of nuclear family, it was observed that in the sample population, female work participation outside home was much higher in joint family than that of nuclear family. Moreover, in a Kharia nuclear family the spouses enjoy greater freedom in family decision-making.

Fatalism

"Fatalism" is defined here as "the strong belief that all events are predetermined." Anthropological literature reveals that fatalism is very much pronounced among the tribes in India and the Kharias are no exception to it. They believe that children are the gift of God. The birth of a baby and its death during infancy or childhood are predetermined and are beyond human control.

The couples with strong faith in fatalism experienced the highest incidence of infant mortality (35.25%) whereas the least incidence of infant deaths occurred to the couples who do not believe in fatalism (15.91%). The Chi-square test confirms (at one per cent level) that the differences observed in the incidence of infant mortality and survivals corresponding to varied degrees of belief in fatalism on infant death are very significant (Table 21.6).

The Delivery Attendant

The type of delivery attendant is of immense importance in relation to survival

TABLE 21.6: Fatalism among Parents and Infant Mortality—Survivality

Extent of Faith	Infant Deaths	Infant Survivors	Total Births
High: Infant death is fully attributed to God's wrath and is not preventable at all.	104 (35.25)	191 (64.75)	295 (100.00)
Moderate: Infant Death is caused partially due to God's displeasure and is preventable to some extent	30 (25.64)	87 (74.36)	117 (100.00)
No Faith: Infant death is no doubt preventable and is not linked to God's displeasure	14 (15.91)	74 (84.09)	88 (100.00)
Total	148	352	500
Chi-square	13.3227		
Level of Significance 1%			

Note: Figures in Parenthesis denote percentage.

and mortality of infants in the sample population for the following reasons:

(a) Poor hygiene,
(b) Low rate of immunization of expectant mothers, and
(c) Unscientific methods practiced for deliveries at home (attended to by untrained traditional delivery attendants) including poor quality of materials used for cutting the umbilical cord and cleaning the mouth of the new born.

A significant difference between survival and mortality of infants corresponding to different types of delivery attendants was observed in the sample population. Very high incidence of infant mortality occurred among births attended to by indigenous untrained delivery attendants. A sharp decline in the incidence of infant deaths was noticed in case of home deliveries attended to by trained ANMs and *dais.* The hospitals deliveries recorded the least incidence of infant mortality. The chi-squares test confirms (at one per cent level) that the differences observed in the incidence of infant survivals and mortality corresponding to different types of delivery attendants are highly significant (Table 21.7). Thus, lesser the dependence on traditional untrained *dais,* the better is the chances of survival of the infants.

TABLE 21.7: Delivery Attendant and Infant Deaths—Survivals

Delivery Attendant	Infant Deaths	Infant Survivors	Total Births
Hospital Delivery	10	81	91
	(10.99)	(89.01)	(100.00)
Home delivery attended	33	145	178
to by ANM/ trained *Dais*	(18.54)	(81.46)	(100.00)
Home delivery attended to by	105	126	231
untrained *dais*/relatives	(45.45)	(54.55)	(100.00)
Total	148	352	500
Chi-square	48.1430		
Level of Significance 1%			

Note: Figures in Parenthesis denote percentage.

The Immediate Cause of Death

Our field observation revealed that information about the symptoms, conditions and duration of the diseases largely determined the cause of infant death in the sample population. Neo-natal deaths in our sample population exceeded the post-neonatal deaths. Tetanus was found to be the most preponderant

TABLE 21.8: Causes of Infant Death

Causes of Death	Neonatal Deaths	Post-neonatal Deaths	Infant Deaths
Tetanus	29	7	36
	(30.2)	(13.5)	(24.3)
Diarrhoea	8	17	25
	(8.3)	(32.7)	(16.9)
Other Gastro-intestinal	16	10	26
disorders	(16.7)	(19.2)	(17.6)
Respiratory diseases	11	8	19
	(11.5)	(15.4)	(12.8)
Prematurity Low	10	4	14
Birth-weight	(10.4)	(7.7)	(9.5)
Blue Baby	9	—	9
	(9.4)		(6.1)
Others*	13	6	19
	(13.5)	(11.5)	(12.8)
Total	96	52	148
	(100.00)	(100.00)	(100.00)

Note: Figures in Parenthesis denote percentage.

* Diseases like Jaundice, Pneumonia, Chickenpox are included in other category.

single and major cause of infant deaths. Water-borne diseases like diarrhoea and gastro-intestinal disorders and respiratory troubles were the major causes of post-neonatal mortality in the sample population (Table 21.8).

Conclusion

The causation of infant mortality is multivariate. Based upon our findings, a regular health education programme for the tribals is suggested to reduce the high incidence of infant mortality. Suitable approaches are to be evolved for promoting health education without interfering their socio-cultural value system. It is further suggested that health education be made a community programme rather than a mere governmental intervention. In this context the tribal chiefs and priests be taken into confidence and their influence over the community be utilized to ensure better communication between the subjects and the health educators. Human body physiology and etiology of diseases should be given priority under health education programme. Necessary care should be taken to provide some sustainable inputs to raise the health status of tribal people of our society. One of such inputs can be to educate the tribal female folk in health related matters.

REFERENCES

Caldwell, J.C. 1979. "Education as a Factor in Mortality Decline: An Examination of Nigerian Data", *Population Studies,* 33(3): 395-413.

Census of India 1971. Series 16, Orissa, Part V. *Special Tables on Scheduled Castes and Scheduled Tribes.* pp. 684-697.

Mahadevan, K. 1979. *Sociology of Fertility: Determinants of Fertility Differentials in South India.* New Delhi: Sterling Publishers.

—. 1989. *Population Dynamics in Indian States.* New Delhi: Mittal Publications.

Morris, David and B. Michella Me Alpin. 1982. *Measuring the Condition of India's Poor: The Physical Quality of Life Index.* New Delhi: Promilla.

Sloan, F. 1971. *Survival of Progeny in Developing Countries: Analysis of Evidence from Costa Rica, Mexico, East Pakistan and Pureto Rico.* Santa Monica Co. The Rand Corporation.

United Nations, 1983 Population Report.

TWENTY-TWO

MOTHER AND CHILD CARE AMONG SOME KHARIA COMMUNITIES IN SIMLIPAL AREA, ORISSA

RANJANA RAY, UJJAYINI BASU,
SUTAPA MUKHOPADHYAY, and SUTAPA GHOSH

Introduction

Before going into the problem of the Kharia communities an appraisal is made of the modern concept of mother and child care. Mother and child care begins much before the child is born. On the basis of this mother and child care is divided into three phases: antenatal, intranatal and postnatal care (Park, 1997).

Mother and Child Care

Antenatal Care

This involves regular check up of the general condition of the pregnant mother and of the proper growth of the foetus within according to the week of gestation. Besides this, if the condition is of high risk then special approach is taken. High risk women are those such as: older women pregnant for the first time, conditions of anaemia, women with twin pregnancies, previous history of abortion and complicated delivery. Health workers usually make home visits during the pregnancy. Major component of antenatal care is advice. Mother is more receptive to advice concerning herself and the baby. This is necessary because the baby takes all sorts of nourishment from the mother for its growth, both physical and mental (Jelliffe and Jelliffe, 1972). During this stage vital things like brain, bone, blood, etc. are formed in the baby (Shah and Shah, 1978). During this stage following measures are necessary:

(1) *Diet during pregnancy period:* 60,000 kilo calorie is necessary for the mother over and above normal metabolic requirements. During lactation mother requires 550 kilo calorie a day above the normal requisite nourishments. On an average a pregnant woman gains about 12 kms of weight during pregnancy. Studies indicate that average poor Indian woman gain about 6.5 kgs of weight during pregnancy (*I.C.M.R. Bulletin,* Dec. 1977). Thus a pregnant woman requires supplementary nutritive calorie.

(2) *Immunization:* Immunization for Titenus any time during pregnancy is a necessity. Preferably around twenty weeks of pregnancy first titenus vaccine should be given. The second one is given 4 to 6 weeks after the first vaccine. One month before the expected date of delivery the third dose is administered. Subsequent pregnancy needs only one booster dose. Immunization is very important for mother care.

(3) *Personal hygiene of the pregnant woman:* (a) Personal cleanliness is very important. A pregnant woman needs to take bath everyday and wear clean clothes. (b) Rest and sleep, at least two hours after mid-day meals, should be imposed. (c) Exercise is necessary but it consists of light out door work and absolute prohibition on heavy manual labour. (d) Oral hygiene is to be maintained.

(4) *Mother should report immediately in case of following warning signals:* (a) Swelling of feet, (b) headache, (c) blurring of vision, (d) bleeding and discharge from vagina.

(5) *Art of child care is to be taught. Mother craft education consists of the following:* (a) Nutrition, (b) education and advice on hygiene, (c) child bearing, (d) cooking, (e) family planning, and (f) family budget.

Government of India has launched a programme for the expecting woman by giving them 16 mg. of elemental iron and 5 gm. of folic acid daily through antenatal clinic, health centre and sub-centre to prevent anaemia in pregnancy.

Intranatal Care

Child birth is a normal physiological process but complication may arise since 80 per cent of India's population lives in rural areas. Most deliveries may have to take place at home with the help of a female health worker or mid wife *(dai)* or female relatives of the pregnant woman. For home delivery by mid-wife three things are necessary: (i) clean chord, (ii) clean hand, and

(iii) clean room. After the baby is born it should be immediately put to the breast and laid next to the mother.

Postnatal Care

Immediate care of mother and the new born is very important for prevention of complication of post partal period. Care is essential to the mother for rapid restoration to optimum health. Postnatal care includes teaching of mother about breast feeding, family planning and care of the new born. Contrary to popular belief, secretion of the breast, on the first two days of delivery, known as colostrum, should not be wasted and fed to the baby, as soon as possible after birth. Colostrum is rich in nutrient and immunoglobulins providing help to the baby to combat diseases. Further care includes the following:

(a) *Growth of the baby:* This is monitored by the growth chart which was first designed by David Morley and later modified by WHO. Growth chart is based on weight for age growth curve. Monitoring growth and nutrition of the baby is imperative until five years of age.
(b) *Immunization:* Universal immunization programme is launched by WHO and supported by Government of India. At birth the baby is immunized with one dose of B.C.G. (Basil Calmett Guerin) and OPV (Oral Polio Vaccine). Within 6 to 10 weeks another dose each of OPV and DPT (Diphtheria, Pertusis and Tetanus) is to be given.

Methodology

The present study is based on an empirical research on Kharia tribal population of Simlipal Research Forest area, Orissa. Standard anthropological field techniques were adopted for data collection. These were both verbal and non-verbal (Pleto and Pleto, 1978). Research methodologies involved structured interview and census survey, key informant interviews, and direct observations. Data were collected on several important aspects relevant to the present study, such as, age at marriage, age-specific fertility study, distribution of pregnant and lactating mothers, age-wise distribution of children, nutritional status of women and children and nature of mother and child care among Kharias. The study was conducted in three sample villages where Kharia people live. All of our sample population are hill Kharias (Roy and Roy, 1937; Vidyarthi and Upadhya, 1980).

The Sample Villages

Data on mother and her child were collected from three villages in Podagarh gram panchayat of Joshipur block in Mayurbhanj district, Orissa. The three villages are situated within the Simlipal Research Forest. The land is undulating in nature. It gradually rises and merges into the Simlipal range. The river Bhondon flows close to the villages and the Simlipal range stands a the background. The land is forested. The villages are situated on cleared ground by the side of the river. The river supplies water and aquatic products and other resources are gathered from the forest.

(1) *Podagarh Sahi:* It is situated on the western bank of the river Bhondon. It is about 14 km. away from Joshipur township. This is a multiethnic village. Along with the Kharia people, other tribal communities like Santal, Ho, Kol etc. live in the village.

(2) *Dhipa Sahi:* This is a monoethnic village and situated on a mound. That is why it is named as Dhipa Sahi. *Dhipa* meaning mound. This is about 13 kms. from Joshipur township.

(3) *Barajhilli Sahi:* Barajhilli Sahi is situated on the eastern bank of the river Bhondon, about 15 kms. away from Joshipur township. This is also a monoethnic village.

In Podagarh village 19 Kharia families reside. The total Kharia population of this village is 73. Out of this, the male population is 36 and the female population is 37. Five Kharia families live in Dhipa Sahi. The total population is 16, out of which 8 are male members and 8 are female members. Sixteen Kharia families inhabit the Barajhilli village. The total Kharia population of this Sahi is 58, the male and the female population are 32 and 26 respectively. The total Kharia population of the three villages is 147.

Table 22.1 shows the age-sex wise distribution of male and female population in the sample villages. The clustering is done at an interval of 10 years. Maximum number of individuals in the three villages belong to children category within 10 years of age. Male children are more in number compared to female children. Other age groupwise population are evenly distributed. There is a sharp decline in population from 41 years of age and above.

Special attention is given to children and women in the present study. Table 22.2 shows the age-sex wise distribution of children in the three villages. Two categories are made in this group; upto 6 years old, i.e. preschool stage, and from 6+ upto 12 years. Mention may be made of the children belonging to an age upto 1 year. This stage is for lactating babies. There are 8 children (4 males and 4 females) in the age group of one year. 16 (29.63%) male and 13 (24.07%) female children are found in the first group. The older children

TABLE 22.1: Showing Age-Sexwise Distribution of Kharia Population in the Three Villages

Age Group	Male		Female		Total	
	No.	%	No.	%	No.	%
0–10	26	17.68	19	12.92	45	30.60
11–20	11	7.48	14	9.52	25	17.00
21–30	11	7.48	16	10.88	27	18.36
31–40	16	10.88	11	7.48	27	18.36
41–50	7	4.76	5	3.40	12	8.16
51–60	5	3.40	4	2.74	9	6.14
60+	2	1.38	0	–	2	1.38
Total	78	53.06	69	46.94	147	100.00

category has 15 (27.78%) male and 10 (18.52%) female. Male-female ratio for both the infants and children is more or less the same.

Facilities in the Villlages

Health Care Facilities: Government of India has created health care facilities under the Integrated Child Development Scheme. Such centre known as *Anganbari* is located within a distance of about one km. from the villages. The cente provides basic health care facilities to the local mothers and children,

TABLE 22.2: Showing Age Sex-wise Distribution of Children at 6 Years Interval

Age Group	Male		Female		Total	
	No.	%	No.	%	No.	%
0–6	16	29.63	13	24.07	29	53.70
6+–12	15	27.78	10	18.52	25	46.30
Total	31	57.41	23	42.59	54	100.00

viz.. nutrition, immunization and non-formal education for preschool children. Cooked food is distributed free of cost to the pregnant mothers, new mothers, their babies and children upto 6 years of age. This is given in the morning around 11 a.m. at the centre. Usually the women are either in the field or in the forest during that time and miss the food.

For immunization the children are to be given B.C.G., T.T., D.P.T. injections. Pregnant mothers are to get iron tablets and T.T. Vaccines. On most cases due to non availability of the vaccines neither the mother nor the new born babies are immunized on time.

In case of ailments like prolonged fever, severe diarrhoea, etc. both the children and their mothers go to Joshipur Hospital which is 14 kms. away from the sample villages. It seems that at present they do not get much help from the indigenous medicine men because they do not reside nearby to their villages.

2. *Drinking Water:* The Kharia of the villages under study use the water of Bhodon river for drinking purpose they also use the same water for bathing and washing of utensils and clothes.

3. *Education:* Well-being of a child depends on several factors such as food and nutrition, health care system and education. There is only one schooi at Podagarh gram panchayat and it is up to the standard of class VI. For secondary education one has to go the village Durdura which is about 6 kms. away from the Podagarh village. The school at Durdura has provision of education up to class X level. Moreover, *Anganbari,* workers provide non-formal education to children.

The Kharia girls go to school up to the age of 7 or 8 years. Moreover, they cannot attend schools everyday, because whenever their mothers have job they stay back at home to take care of their younger brothers and sisters. The Kharia girls learn to do all sorts of domestic works when they reach the age of 8-9 years.

Grazing the goats is an important task for the children. School going among the Kharia children is a recent development. Kharias have started to send their children to school because their neighbours the Santals, Majhis and Mahatoes sent their children to the school. In the government aided school at Durdura every student gets mid-day meal of boiled rice and dal everyday. Free books are given to the students. Mid-day meal is also an attraction for the parents to send their children to school.

The Kharia

The Kharias have a wide distribution in eastern plateau region. The tribe is from a Mundari speaking stock. They belong to the Austro-Asiatic linguistic family (Risley and Crooke, 1869). As mentioned earlier the population under study belong to the group called Hill Kharia. They are found in small villages in the cleared ground in the forest. They live in small mud huts. They are sendentary people. At present they practice horticulture. Earlier they followed *jhum,* i.e. shifting method of cultivation. At present due to Forest Preservation Act this form of cultivation is prohibited. They keep kitchen garden adjacent to their home stead. In this they grow some inferior quality of rice, millet and lentils. They largely depend on forest product. Hill Kharias are medium statured people. Their skin colour vary between brown to light black. Nose is much depressed at the root, bridge is concave and eye slits are small. Often they show a tendency to form epicanthic fold. The face has a square appearance. The stronghold of Hill Kharias is in the Simlipal hill ranges of the Mayurbhanj District of Orissa. The elevation at which the Hill Kharias dwell is about 3,000 above the sea level (Roy and Roy, 1937).

Subsistence Pattern and Economy

The Kharia of Podagarh gram panchayat do not have any agricultural land of their own. Their occupation consists of collection of forest products and working as agricultural labour. These two types of pursuits provide them with cash. In addition to this, they produce some cereals, lentils and vegetables in their kitchen garden. Following is the detail of their occupation.

Collection of Forest Products

The main occupation of the Kharia is collection of honey, silk cocoon, lack and large red ants known locally as *kurkutti* or *koipoka*. They gather edible herbs, wild fruits, edible yams and tubers with digging sticks and hoes. The sal leaves and mahul kernels are collected during the summer months, i.e. from the end of March to the Middle of June. The other items are collected throughout the year. The Kharias sell the forest products at the local weekly market at Durdura. They also sell their products at Joshipur markets. Honey is sold at a price of Rs. 60 per kg., gum is sold for Rs. 8 per kg., and koipoka for Rs. 10 per kg. Besides these, they sell sal leaves, mahul and kusum in the summer season at the following price:

Sal leaves Rs. 80 per 1000 leaves

Mahul flower Rs. 6 per kg.

The Kusum oil processed by them is used as hair and body oil mainly. They sell the oil in the local market for Rs. 15 per kg.

Daily Labour

The next important occupation is daily labour. During winter almost all women go to the paddy field for harvesting. They work in the fields owned by the other people in exchange for wages. They reap paddy for Santhals, Mahatos and Majhis. The average distance of agricultural field is about 2 - 2½ kms. from their villages. All the able bodied women, including pregnant and lactating women, work in the field. Some women are found working at very advanced stage of pregnancy. They work for 7½ hours from the day break to dusk. At noon time they go home for mid-day meal. They stay at home for about 2 hours and again go back to the field around 3 p.m. Breast fed baby are often taken to the field during the work for feeding. An older child usually takes the baby. They reap the paddy before noon. After lunch they carry the sheaves to the threshing ground. At the end of the day they get their wages in terms of 4 *pana* (950 gms) of rice. Women are engaged in agricultural activities like harvesting, husking, winnowing and the storing of the grains. In summer season, i.e. in April and May, Kharia men go for hunting to the forest. Hunting is prohibited by the Reserve Forest Act. They enter into the forest very early in the morning at about 4 a.m. In a successful day, they may hunt a deer or a wild goat. However, they are severely beaten if caught red handed by the forest guards.

Income

They get cash by selling gum and forest resources. As wage labourers they also get direct cash payment. On the basis of the resource materials collected, consumed and sold by the Kharias under study, an estimation of average monthly income is made (Table 22.3).

TABLE 22.3: Showing Average Monthly Income of Kharias per Family.

	Items	Weekly Income (Rs.)	Monthly Income (Rs.)
1.	950 gm. rice x 4 days @ Rs. 7.60 per 950 gm.	30.40	121.60
2.	Gum (1 kg. = Rs. 8 x 4 kg. per week	32.00	128.00
3.	Other forest resources (per week) wood, kusum, koipoka, kendu etc.	25.00	100.00
4.	Leafy and green vegetables which are grown in their kitchen garden (per day Rs. 4)	28.00	112.00
5.	Daily labour (male) (4 days x Rs. 6)	24.00	96.00
	Total	139.40	557.60

Rice: This is mainly earned during the transplanting, weeding and the harvesting seasons. A woman usually gets work for four days a week. Accordingly calculation is made. 950 gms. of rice for four days @ Rs. 7.60 (per 950 gms.) gives about Rs. 30.40 for a week.

Gum: In a week about 4 kg. of gum may be collected. 1 kg. gum costs Rs. 8.

Other Forest Products: These include collection of wood, kusum, koipoka, etc. Usually a family earns about Rs. 25 in a week by selling these products. Income from the forest product is dependent on the season. There are other tribal groups who also depend on forest products; so competition is quite high.

Leafy and Green Vegetables from the Kitchen Garden: These are usually for their own consumption. The amount if calculated as Rs. 4 per day and Rs. 28 for one week. This is done on the basis of the quantity used by family per day calculation and its market value.

Daily Labour: This is kept as a separate item from rice because it is the women who get paid in rice for their work but the men are paid in cash. Men work in the agricultural field or they also work in the nearby Joshipur town. Their local wage rate is Rs. 6. At the most they get work for four days a week. Thus weekly income from this work is Rs. 24. They also keep live stock like goat and fowl. Sometimes they sell them at the rate of Rs. 100 for a goat and Rs. 40 for a fowl. The average monthly income of each Kharia family is Rs. 500 to Rs. 557.60.

They spend minimum for their clothes, i.e. on an average Rs. 50 per person per year. They hardly make any expenditure for medicine. Major part of income goes for food. The houses are built and maintained by the people. Material for house building are mud, wood and straw. The labour for the construction is usually not considered in the cost.

Women of the Village

For the study of Mother and Child care it is necessary to get an idea about the condition of women in the village. Of the 147 individuals under study 78 are male and 69 are female. Male female ratio is 0.885.

Age at Marriage

Among the Kharia marriage takes place after the attainment of puberty (Roy and Roy, 1957). They practise clan exogamy. Marriage is prohibited among near kins. From the present study it is found that women are married, when they are between 12 and 21 years of age. Table 22.4 shows the frequency distribution of the girls married at different ages. There is no spinster in the village. No woman remained unmarried after 21 years (Table 22.5). There is negligible surplus of males in the village.

TABLE 22.4 Showing Age-wise Distribution of Married Kharia Women.

Age at Marriage	No. of Women	
12–15	28	(65.12%)
16–19	11	(25.58%)
20–23	4	(9.30%)
Total	43	(100.00%)

TABLE 22.5: Showing Age-wise Distribution of Married and Unmarried Women.

Age Group	No. of Unmarried Women	No. of Married Women	Total
1–11	26 (37.68%)	—	26 (37.68)
12–22	—	10 (14.49%)	10(14.49%)
22 and above	—	33 (47.83%)	33 (47.83%)
Total	26 (37.68%)	43 (62.38%)	69 (100%)

Health Care

The health centre is located within one and half km of the village. Although they provide nutritive and immunization programme for the mothers at the three stages of mother care but the women of the village hardly have time to visit the centre at the stipulated time. They are busy either in the household work or in search for subsistence. Antenatal care is mostly in the traditional way as stipulated by older married relatives, mother or mother-in-law. Usually no extra care is taken by the mother for her own well-being. She engages herself in household and subsistence activities as she would have done before she was pregnant. As mentioned earlier they go for collection of forest products and work in the field even upto the very last stage of pregnancy. They are anaemic even to the untrained eyes of the field worker.

A health study was conducted on the basis of anthropometric measurements on mothers. In this case both expecting, lactating and women with older children are taken into consideration. Parameters, taken for this study are height, weight, midarm circumference and triceps skinfold. In the villages studied, the lower age limit for women becoming mature is 15 years of age. A total number of 37 women are there who have given birth. The anthropometric data on them indicate their health status (Table 22.6). The mean height is 147.52. cm. The height vary much among them (139cm –166.8 cm). The standard deviation is +6.33 cm. Mean weight is 33.81 kg. This vary between 30.5 cm and 46 cm. The standard deviation is +4.14 cm. The mean upper arm circumference is 21.2 cm; standard deviation is +1.69 cm. Comparison with standard (Jelliffee, 1966) suggests that on the basis of the above mentioned measurements, the women are undernourished (Table 22.6).

A further detailed study was made with an age grouping at 5 years interval (Table 22.7). Heightwise the younger women are shorter than the older women. The height of younger women within the age group 15-20 is 139.12 cm. on an average. The next young group of women belong to 21-25 years of age and have a mean height of 142.95 cm. Maximum height is found within the age group of 26-30 years (155.08 cm). All women above 30 have more or less similar height between 150 cm to 151 cm. The height in the

TABLE 22.6: Showing Anthropometric Measurements of the Mothers of Three Villages

No. of Mothers		Height		Weight		Upper Arm Circumference		Triceps Skinfold Measurement
37		Mean-147.52 cm Standard Deviation (SD) ± 6.3291		Mean -33.8 kg. Standard Deviation (SD) ± 4.1438		Mean -21.2 cm SD ± 1.6893		Mean - 6.1 cm. SD ± 1.3118
Range	Max.	Min	Max.	Min.	Max.	Min.	Max.	Min.
	139 cm	166.8 cm	30.5 kg	46 kg.	18 cm	26 cm	4 cm	9 cm

present study may not be of prime importance because the Kharia people as such are not very tall. The weight is taken in Kilogram. Women between the age of 15-20 years have a mean weight of 31.9 kg. 21-25 years age group have slightly more weight (34.9 kg.) Women belonging to age of 36-40 years shown maximum mean weight around 42 kg. Considering the height of the women, the weight is towards the leaner side. The standard weight of the Indian women is 45 kg (Mahadevan, 1986: 326).

The midarm circumference shows a lower mean value among the 15-20 years old women (19.04 cm). Women within the age group 26-40 have a higher mean for midarm circumference, i.e. 23.77 cm. The women belonging to the age groups 21-25 and 40 above have got maximum mean of 22.66 cm.

The mean triceps skinfold again is maximum for the age group 26-30 (7.33 cm). It is minimum for the age group 15-20 (4.8 cm). From the Table 28.7 it appears that women from the age group 26-30 are comparatively taller and fatter than that of the women from the younger and older age groups. This may be due to the natural condition of youths. In terms of the above measurements, it may be said that the Kharia women are not with robust health.

Food for Mother

There are taboo regarding the food intake of mothers. Consumption of milk is completely prohibited among the Kharias. They do not have any cattle. At the antenatal stage, egg is a taboo to the pregnant woman. They believe that egg contains the life of a chicken and if she eats an egg, her baby will die in her womb. All types of leafy vegetables are prohibited for the pregnant women. They take food twice daily. The food consists of mainly boiled rice. They do not throw away the water from the boiled rice. They take the rice with salt, chillies and vegetable curry. Red ant often adds to the delicacy, if they are found in the jungle. The vegetable usually consists of potato, brinjals, pumpkin and kundri. These are cooked with garlic, haldi paste, salt and few

TABLE 22.7: Showing Anthropometric Measurements of the Mothers of Three Villages according to Age Group

Age Group	No. of Mothers	Height in (Cm)	Weight in (Kg)	Midarm Cicumference	Triceps Skinfold in (mm)
15–20	5	Mean 139.12	Mean 31.9	Mean 19.04	Mean 4.8
		SD ±0.7025	SD±0.7348	SD±0.852	SD±0.748
21–5	8	Mean 142.95	Mean 34.9	Mean 21.87	Mean 5.62
		SD ± 2.3048	SD ±1.1842	SD ±0.780	SD ±0.737
26–30	9	Mean 155.08	Mean 40.3	Mean 23.77	Mean 7.33
		SD ±5.5666	SD ±1.5944	SD ±0.916	SD ±0.781
31–35	3	Mean 151.53	Mean 43.5	Mean 24.33	Mean 6.66
		SD ±0.4988	SD ±1.080	SD ±0.471	SD ±0.471
36–40	4	Mean 151.8	Mean 44.87	Mean 23.5	Mean 7.0
		SD ±1.5610	SD ±0.7395	SD ±0.5	SD ±0.707
41–45	3	Mean 151.8	Mean 42.6	Mean 22.66	Mean 5.33
		SD ±1.2832	SD ±0.9428	SD ±0.471	SD ±0.471
46–50	2	Mean 150.7	Mean 41.35	Mean 21.5	Mean 5.5
		SD ±1.4	SD ±0.15	SD ±0.5	SD ±0.5
51–55	2	Mean 151.2	Mean 41.5	Mean 22.5	Mean 4.5
		SD ±0.2	SD ±0.5	SD ±0.5	SD ±0.5
56–60	1	154.1	42	22	5
60+	0	0	0	0	0
Total	37				

drops of mustard oil. Women may take pulse soup as an added item at dinner. Pulses are not available daily. These are to be brought from the local market. Most of the vegetables are grown in the kitchen garden.

For postnatal period food taboo is mainly for meat, fish, egg, leafy vegetables, sweet and sour food. There is a belief that these food stuffs cause harm to the baby who is lactating.

At parturition the woman is kept in a separate compartment in the house. There the woman stays after birth for 21 days until ceremonial purification. They eat once and that food consists of boiled rice mixed with salt and garlic. She may consume leafy vegetable and light pulse soup with rice only after 3 months of the child birth. She cannot eat fish and meat for about a year after the child is born.

The nearby health centre provides facility for free immunization but none of the mothers studied had been completely immunized with the tet-vac. A few of them took one or two dose(s) according to their wish and the health workers' convenience. However, neither party was concerned with the completion of the immunization.

Child Birth

Usually child birth is taken as a natural phenomenon by the Kharias. The pregnent women continue with their normal life work until the labour pain is felt. A Kharia woman spends her major part of a day with household work as well as work related to subsistence of the family. At parturition the woman goes into that part of the room kept as a lying place. The midwife usually is a near relative or an older woman of the village. Besides the midwife and the female relations no one is allowed into the lying in compartment. The umbilical chord is cut off by a new blade (safety razor) by the woman who acts as a mid-wife. After birth, the chord is put into an earthen pot and plinthed under the mud floor of the labour compartment. The health workers are provided with a delivery kit consisting of safety razor, a piece of gauge and an antiseptic lotion for the naval chord. In the villages studied, only the new blade is used. Neither the gauge nor the antiseptic lotion is put to use. The naval chord of the child is smeared with boiled ghee. This they consider as an antiseptic measure.

Ceremonies after Child Birth

Excepting name giving to the baby, no ceremony is performed for twenty days after birth. On twenty-first day a ceremony known as *ekusia* is performed by the family on this day the child wears a new dress and the villagers are invited to a feast of boiled rice, pulse, vegetables and meat, if available.

Fertility Condition

Data are collected on the number of live birth, still birth and death at infancy. For convenience, mothers are grouped at 3 years interval. 37 mothers are present in the villages. From the present investigation it is found that a total number of 100 births have taken place during last 12 years. Out of these 89 are live birth, 7 still birth and 4 died at infancy. Between the age group of 37 and 40, there are 4 mothers and they have given birth 13 times and on an average they have given birth 3.2 times. Among the age group of 25-28, 11 women are found. They have given birth 37 times and on an average each woman has given birth 3.3 times. Crude birth rate is calculated on the basis of number of live births and midyear population. In the year 1997, 8 children were born (4 male and 4 female). The total population during July 1997 was 147. Death at infancy is quite less in number compared to live birth. Our data have been compared with corresponding figures relating to the rural/tribal population in India (Mahadevan, 1986).

Child Care

It is found that excepting some food taboos, not much of mother care is found among the Kharia women. The child after its birth is taken care by the *dai,* the midwife. The baby is bathed in tepid warm water and laid next to the mother and immediately put to the breast. The baby is breast fed upto 6 months of age. During this time no solid food or water is given to the baby. Mother takes care of the baby exclusively for the first 9 days. She is not allowed to come out of the lying in shed during these days. A fire is kept burning for 9 days near the baby. The ashes of the fire are buried on 9th day in the same place as the umbilical chord. On that day a name is given ceremonially to the baby. The mother and child are kept separated from the rest of the family members for 21 days. During this time they are not supposed to touch any cooked food.

Customarily, the Kharia couple set up their own household after marriage. The new mother takes care of her baby because her other female relations like, sister-in-law, mother-in-law, live in separate houses and they have their own household duties. In cases where the mother goes out for wage earning or performing extra-household then she keeps her baby in the custody of her mother-in-law or sister-in-law. The elder daughters also take care of their younger brothers and sisters when their mothers go out to work. A woman who has neither elder daughter nor mother-in-law and sister-in-law, keeps her baby in the custody of her neighbour's elderly girl usually of 7-8 years of age or with the old woman of the village. The child is taken to the mother at her working place for breast feeding. Usually this is done when the baby appears to be hungry.

Though mothers are very busy with household and out-door work, still they take care of their babies meticulously. They bath the babies, dress them and feed them regularly. They take special care of the children who are under three years of age and breast fed. When the children are old enough to take care of themselves, mother's duties is to give them meals in time and groom them with oil and comb their hair. They also take special care of their children during illness. Plenty of affection is conferred on the child by the parents. Generally each child remains breast fed until it reaches about three years of age. Very little solid food is given to children under the age of one year. They start on supplementary food when the baby is around 6 to 7 months. The main solid food items of the Kharia children are powdered boiled rice or rice gruel, biscuits, *muri,* i.e. puffed rice, boiled sweet potato *sujij* and *dalia.* After 2 years, the children eat everything, i.e. whatever is cooked for the adult members of the family. Consumption of fruits and green vegetables by the children mainly depends upon their availability. These include the hog-plum (amora), guava, jackfruit, sweet potatoes, leafy vegetables like matisag, kantamaris, modrunga, sajina and palang. Green vegetables like kundri, jonjora, korolloa, brinjal, pumpkin, papaya, chilly, tomato and legume are cooked and eaten according to the season.

For disease and sickness Kharias rely much on superstition and nature. If the child feels pain in its body, mother rubs its body with kusum oil. The child is given garlics to eat. At times garlic cloves are strung together and tied around the upper arm or neck of the child. In case of a breast fed baby having cold, the mother takes garlic with the belief that the medicinal value of garlic will pass from her to child through breast milk. Sometimes they put pastes of turmeric on the soft portion of the baby's head. They believe that with the paste the crown of the head will become hard and strong.

The children use pieces of neem sticks *(neem datan)* for brushing their teeth. They use mud from the river to clean their body in lieu of soap. Kusum oil is rubbed on the body and hair. They wash their bodies with soap, usually, lifebuoy, once in a week, if cash permits.

Most of the children, under 7 years, go naked during daytime. In winter months they wrap a piece of cloth around them tied at a knot round their neck, specially after dusk when it becomes chilly. During summer they are naked all time. Children above 7 years of age wear pieces, torn out of old *sarees* or *dhoties.* They may also wear a towel *(gamcha)* wrapped around their waists. For school the parents buy a dress for the child. This is the only dress that each child may own. Shoes are never worn by the children. The school boys are provided with shirt and a pair of shorts. Girls may get a frock.

Health Status of Children

Health status of the children are estimated on the basis of anthropometric measurements. Parameters considered are height, weight, skinfold and midarm circumference. The measurements are shown in the Tables 22.8 and 22.9. The Kharia children are not very well built. This may be due to the fact that Kharia are rather short statured people (Ray and Banerjee, 1994: 144). Study on nutrition of the group has shown that they are under nourished (Ray, *et al.*, 1997). In general the babies and children are of delicate structures, bones seem to jutt out, muscles are wasted skinfolds at upper arm and chest is very loose. They have large bellies. The children are malnourised. Most of the children (99%) suffer from sores, itches and skin diseases. This may be due to deficiency of Vitamin C. Most of them have anaemic look probably due to deficiency of iron.

TABLE 22.8: Showing Anthropometric Measurements of Boys

Age Group	No. of Males	Height (Cm)	Weight (Kg)	Mid Arm Circumference (Cm)
0–1	4	M – 63.6 cm	M – 5.5 kg.	M – 9.7 cm
		SD ± 1.1321	SD ± 0.4415	SD ± 0.4815
1–2	0	0	0	0
2–3	4	M – 86.1cm	M – 9.3 cm	M – 12.9 cm
		SD ± 0.6800	SD ± 0.4968	SD ± 0.4437
3–4	3	M – 94.2 cm	M –12.7 cm	M – 13.1 cm
		SD ± 0.5249	SD ± 0.2054	SD ± 0.0816
4–5	2	M – 103.5 cm	M – 15.2 cm	M – 14.2 cm
		SD ± 0.55	SD ± 0.05	SD ± 0.05
5–6	3	M – 110.5 cm	M – 17.7 cm	M – 15.1 cm
		SD ± 1.1897	SD ± 0.1699	SD ± 0.0816

TABLE 22.9: Showing Anthropometric Measurements of Girls

Age Group	No. of Females	Height (Cm)	Weight (Kg)	Mid Arm Circumference (Cm)
0–1	4	M – 62.1cm	M – 5.0cm	M – 9.2cm
		SD ± 0.4301	SD ± 0.4716	SD ± 0.6299
1–2	1	71.3	7.3	11.2
2–3	2	M – 79.1cm	M – 10.1cm	M – 12.0cm
		SD ± 0.4	SD ± 0.4	SD ± 0.15
3–4	1	95.0 cm	12.3 cm	13.1 cm
4–5	2	M – 100.5 cm	M – 14.1cm	M – 14.7 cm
		SD ± 0.55	SD ± 0.3	SD ± 0.1
5–6	3	M – 106.4cm	M – 15.8cm	M – 14.9 cm
		SD ± 0.4027	SD ± 0.2054	SD ± 0.05

Indications of the deficiency of proteins are observed from their rough skin and tanned (brown coloured) hair, though most of them use kusum oil for hair.

Anthropometric measurements of children such as height in cm, weight in kg, midarm circumference and skinfold are taken. Age independent anthropometric index of weight and height of preschool children is calculated. In the present case measurements upto the age of 6+ are taken. These have been compared with the charts for well nourished Indian children (Ghosh, 1985: 134-136). It appears from comparison of the computed data (Table

22.8) for boys with the standard that for height at 1 year age the mean value is about 10 cm less than standard. From second year onward the efficiency is less. The mean weight for babies upto 2 years of age deviates from standard for a well nourished child by about 4 kg. Later on the boys are still below the will nourished category but the difference is less marked on an average. Mid-arm circumference is below well nourished standard. Table 22.9 shows anthropometric measurements of girls of the village upto 6 years of age. All of the parameters point to the under nourished status of the girls. The age independent index of weight in kg and height in cm for preschool children, i.e. between 2 to 5 years of age is calculated (Ghai, 1990). The mean value is .83, a little below the normal category (0.88 - 0.97) but the index does not include them into the severely malnourished (0.79) category. The above mentioned anthropometric measurements indicate that Kharia children studied are not severely malnourished. The children get their nourishment from their mothers during lactating period. With the weaning and with the solid food consumption, their nutritional deficit starts as the major diet largely lacks in protein.

Conclusion

The present work is undertaken on a total population of 147 Kharias residing in three villages in the Simlipal Tiger Project Area of Mayurbhanj district of Orissa. The villages are at a distance of around 14 km. from the nearest township. Girls are married between 12 to 21 years of age. Birth rate is quite high among this group. Major subsistence economy consists of gathering of forest product and daily labour. Most of them keep a little kitchen garden.

Estimation shows that they live at a bare subsistence level. Forest do not supply them with plentiful resources. The villages do not have facilities like health care, pure drinking water and educational centres. Though at present the children are sent to the ICDS centre for non-formal education, the girl children are detained from going to school from the age of 4 or 5 years. They are supposed to learn the household work and take charge of the younger siblings, from a very young age. Children are well looked after by their mothers but in their own traditional way. There is hardly any special health care system for the pregnant women. There are some food taboos which deprives them of valuable nutrient. The lactating mother also is not given much by way of well balanced food. Main component of food is rice. Red ants supply them with occasional protein other than pulses. An insect's body again contains more carbohydrate than protein. Animal protein from hunting is almost absent. Babies remain largely breast fed for one year. They are completely weaned around 2/3 years of age. The health survey is based on anthropometric measurements carried on women and children. Parameters taken are height in cms, weight in kg., mid arm circumference in cms and skinfold measurements. Age independent anthropometric indices on weight and height are calculated. All the mean values of the age specific measurements are compared with the standards for Indian women and children. It is found that the health status is not within the well nourished condition but it is also not within the severely malnourished category. On the whole well being of a child among Kharias depends much on the affection, joint care of mother and female relatives, mainly on a traditional age old style. The health care as prescribed in the beginning is not followed by the people. Modern health-care system has not penetrated in an effective way among the hill Kharias residing in Simlipal forest area.

REFERENCES

Ghai, O.P. 1990. *Essential Peadiatrics*. New Delhi: Mehta Offset Works.

Ghosh, Shanti. 1985. *The Feeding and Care of Infants and Young Children*. New Delhi: Voluntary Health Association of India.

Jelliffe, D. and N. Jelliffe. 1972. *Mother and Child Care: Delivering the Services*. New Delhi: Twentieth Century Publication.

Mahadevan, K. 1986. (ed.). *Fertility and Mortality: Theory, Methodology and Empirical Issues*. New Delhi: Sage Publications.

Park, K. 1997. *Text Book of Preventive and Social Medicine*. Jabalpur: Banarasidas Banot.

Patel, S. 1993. *Tribal Families and Fertility at Cross Roads*. New Delhi: Mittal Publications.

Ray, Ranjana and J. Banerjee. 1994. "Anthropometric Study of Two Tribal Groups Living in Simlipal Forest Orissa", *Bulletin of the Department of Anthropology Dibrugarh University*, 22: 12-146.

Ray, Ranjana, J. Banerjee, A. K. Kundu and Ujjayani Basu. 1997. "A Study of Health Status of some Kharia and Mankria Women from Orissa", in Farida Ahmed and Ramendra Kumar Kar (eds.) *Health Studies in Anthropology. Department of Anthropology*, Dibrugarh University.

Roy, S.C. and R.C. Roy. 1937. *The Kharias*, Vol. I and II. Ranchi: Man in India.

Shah, P.M. and K. Shah. 1978. *Timely Health Care of Children and Mothers*. Bombay: Popular Prakashan.

Vidhyarthi, L.P. and V.S. Upadhyay 1980. *The Kharia, Then and Now—A Comparative Study of Hill, Dhelki and Dudh Kharia of the Central-eastern Region of India*. New Delhi: Concept Publishing Company.

NOTES ON CONTRIBUTORS

Ambasht, Nawal Kishore is a Professor and also the Member-Secretary of Education Research and Innovations Committee (ERIC), N.C.E.R.T., New Delhi. He participated in the East-West Centre Workshop on Cultural Aspects of Educational Leadership where he contributed to the development of a document on Ethnicity in Cross-Cultural Education. He has visited Hawaii, Alaska, Oregon and California for various academic purposes. He was selected for British Council Commonwealth Education Bursary award in 1979 meant for high level officers. He was attached to the University of Manchester to study non-formal education. Prof. Ambasht was sent on a foreign assignment to University of Sokoto, Nigeria by the Government of India during the period 1980-84. He served there with credit as Head of Education Extension Department of the Faculty of Education, member of the Senate and also worked on the Committee of Vice-Chancellors for the study of the future of the West African Education Council. He is a member of the Advisory Board of *Journal of Social Sciences.* Prof. Ambasht's major areas of interest are tribal education and non-formal education.

Mailing Address: Member-Secretary, ERIC
National Council of Educational Research and Training
Sri Aurobindo Marg,
New Delhi-110 016, India

Bagchi, T. obtained his Master's and doctoral degrees in Anthropology from Calcutta University. He served as Senior Research Fellow and Research Officer in the Department of Bio-chemistry and Nutrition and All India Institute of Hygiene and Public Health, Calcutta respectively between 1984 and 1988. He joined Anthropological Survey of India in 1988 and now holds the post of Assistant Keeper at the Western Regional Centre, Udaipur, Rajasthan, Dr. Bagchi has published a good number of articles in reputed journals and edited volumes. He is the author/co-editor of three books and an edited volume. He has carried out fieldwork among the tribal of West Bengal,

Bihar, Orissa, Gujarat and Rajasthan. Tribal Studies, development anthropology, museology are Dr. Bagchi's key research interest.

Mailing Address: Western Regional Centre
Anthropological Survey of India
Udaipur-313001
Rajasthan, India

Barik, Manas R. is a research scholar in the Department of Sociology, Sambalpur University. He has had a long exposure to fieldwork among the tribes of Orissa. His major research interests are tribal studies and gender issues.

Mailing Address: Department of Sociology
Sambalpur University
Sambalpur - 768 019
Orissa, India

Basu, Ujjayini is a registered research scholar under the University of Calcutta. She is working the supervision of Prof. Ranjana Ray for her Doctoral degree. She is a part time lecturer in Vivekananda College for Women, Calcutta.

Mailing Address: Dept of Anthropology
Calcutta University
35, Ballygunge Circular Road
Calcutta - 700 019
West Bengal
India

Behera, Deepak Kumar obtained his Master's degree (Gold Medalist) and Ph.D. from Sambalpur University, where he has been teaching anthropology since 1985. He has more than 50 research publications in reputed journals and edited volumes. Dr. Behera has also published one book and has edited six volumes. Of the six edited volumes, three are jointly with Prof.Georg Pfeffer of Institute of Ethnology of Free University of Berlin (Germany): two on tribal studies *(Contemporary Society: Tribal Studies,* Vol-I & Vol-II, 1997, Concept, New Delhi) and one on childhood matters *(Contemporary Society: Childhood and Complex Order,* 1996, Manak, New Delhi). Another volume edited by Dr. Behera is also on childhood matters *(Children and Childhood in Our Contemporary Societies,* 1998, Kamla-Raj Enterprises, New Delhi). Two other edited volumes on gender issues *(Gender and Society in India,* Vol-I &Vol-II, 1998, Manak, New Delhi) have been recently brought out by Dr.

Behera jointly with Prof. R. Indira of Mysore University. He has successfully completed half-a-dozen research projects funded by national bodies like UGC, ICSSR, Ministry of Welfare, National Literacy Mission Authorities, etc. He is a faculty member of the ongoing Shastri Indo Canadian project entitled "Empowering Women through Forestry: The Role of Indigenous Women...." Dr. Behera has participated in more than a dozen international conferences in Mexico, Germany, Belgium (twice), Sweden, Denmark, and USA, and has lectured at different universities and research institutes there. He was a UGC Visiting Fellow to Israel. Besides conducting research, he delivered a series of lectures in Tel Aviv University, Hebrew University and DCI, during his stay in Israel. Recently he went to South Africa as a Visiting Professor under an Agreement of Co-operation, signed between the Dept. of Anthropology, University of Orange Free State and Dept. of Anthropology, Sambalpur University. The agreement was signed under the initiatives of Dr. Behera, and Prof. Erasmus of the University of Orange Free State. Dr. Behera is the Editor of the international journal—*Journal of Social Sciences.* Recently Dr. Behera has been recently elected as a member of the Executive Board of International Union of Anthropological and Ethnological Sciences (IUAES) for the period 1998-2003. He is the youngest Indian in the long history of IUAES to get elected to the post. He has also been recently elected as Officer-at-Large of the International Sociological Association Research Committee-53—Sociology of Childhood for the session 1998-2002. He is a member of the International Advisory Board of the Journal—*Sociological Analysis* (North Carolina, USA) and also a member of the Editorial Board of Global Gutter Press (Cambridge, UK). Dr. Behera is a member of the core group of IUAES *Commission on Anthropology in Policy and Practice, Commission on Anthropological Dimension of Global Change* and *Commission on Urban Anthropology.* The first two commissions are affiliated to UNESCO through IUAES. Dr. Behera is now taking initiatives to create a new *Commission on Anthropology of Children and Childhood* in IUAES. The said commission is likely to be established by 2000 AD. Recently Dr. Behera chaired two different sessions, namely, *Resource Management through Indigenous Socio-cultural Practices* and *Children without Childhood in our Contemporary Society* at the 14th ICAES, held in Virginia, USA during July-August, 1998. Of the two, one was an officially sponsored session of the International Union of Anthropological and Ethnological Science *Commission on Anthropology in Policy and Practice.* Recently Dr. Behera also organized another session of ISA RC-53 on *Public Images of Childhood* (with Prof. Lucia Rabello de Castro of Brazil as the co-organizer) at the 14th World Sociology Congress, held in Montreal, Canada during July-August 1998. He has successfully guided three Ph.D. and twenty M.Phil scholars. Dr. Behera is the Director of the Institute of Evaluation, Research, Documentation and Training. His current interests in research are tribal studies, childhood matters, inter-ethnic relations and gender issues.

Mailing Address: Dr. Deepak Kumar Behera
Department of Anthropology
Sambalpur University
Jyoti Vihar, Burla
Sambalpur- 768 019
Orissa
India
Fax: ++91-(0) 663-404000/430158
email: <dkb@cal2.vsnl.net.in> or <dkb@vsnl.com>

Behura, N.K. is a retired Professor of Anthropology from Utkal University. Prof. Behura is a recipient of Rai Bahadur P.R. Chanda medal from the Asiatic Society of India in addition to a couple of Professional awards. Prof. Behura is the ex-President of Anthropology and Archaeology Section of Indian Science Congress Association. Fourteen scholars have been awarded with Ph.D. degrees in anthropology, sociology and home science under the supervision of Prof. Behura. He has also guided thirty M.Phil dissertations. He has published five books and ninety articles. He is a member of the Advisory Board of Journal of Social Sciences. The major areas of interest of Prof. Behura include development anthropology, linguistic anthropology, social systems and theoretical anthropology.

Mailing Address: A-147, Saheed Nagar
Bhubaneswar - 751 007
Orissa, India

Dash Sharma, P. obtained his M.Sc and Ph.D in Anthropology from the University of Delhi. At present he is the Professor of Physical Anthropology at Ranchi University. He has conducted extensive fieldwork among the tribes of North-East India (Assam, Manipur and Meghalaya) and in Chotanagpur plateau of Bihar. He is the founding father of Sarat Chandra Roy Institute of Anthropological Studies. Besides, he is the founder Editor of the Journal—*South Asian Anthropologist,* which is being published since 1980. He has received grants from World Wide Fund for Nature-India, for conducting studies on biodiversity conservation in Ranchi. Prof. Dash Sharma has published more than 80 research papers in the field of physical anthropology, bio-cultural anthropology and tribal development. He is the author of four books, covering aspects of ethnography, physical anthropology and human evolution. He has edited a book on the tribal situation in Chotanagpur. He organized an international symposium during the 11th ICAES held in

Vancouver in 1983. Prof. Dash Sharma has also organized five national level seminars at Ranchi University during 1989-97. He acted as a resource person in two World Bank funded projects on Tuberculosis and Malaria in the year 1996 and 1997. Prof. Dash Sharma delivered a series of lectures at Institute of Bangladesh studies at Rajshahi (Bangladesh) in March 1987. He is member of many learned societies in India and abroad. His current areas of interest include tribal development and biocultural anthropology.

Mailing Address: HI-98, Harmu Housing Colony
Ranchi - 834 012
Bihar, India

Erasmus, Piet A. is Professor and Head of the Department of Anthropology, University of Orange Free State, South Africa. He is a member of various scientific organizations and also serves as consulting editor of two scientific journals. He has published more than 20 research articles in addition to his contribution of a number of chapters to books. Prof. Erasmus has successfully drafted 13 research reports. He has presented a number of papers at national and international conferences. With his initiative the Department of Anthropology, Sambalpur University has entered into an agreement of co-operation with the Department of Anthropology, University of the Orange Free State. Under this agreement, there will be an exchange programme of scholars and faculty members of the two departments. He has done fieldwork and research among Thaba Nehu, Quaqwa, Bolshabelo and Managaung (Bloemfontein). He is a member of the Editorial Board of the *Journal of Social Sciences* which is being published from Delhi. His current interests in research are development studies and inter-ethnic relations.

Mailing Address: Department of Anthropology
University of Orange Free State
P.B. No. 339, Bloemfontein-9300
South Africa

Ghosh, Sutapa is a registered (UGC net qualified) research scholar of Calcutta University. She is working under the supervision of Prof. Ranjana Ray for her doctoral degree. She is a full time Lecturer in Anthropology in Sevabharati Mahavidyalaya, Kapagari, Midnapore, West Bengal

Mailing Address: Dept of Anthropology
Calcutta University
35, Ballygunge Circular Road

Calcutta - 700 019
West Bengal (India)

Guru, S.S. obtained his M.Sc, M.Phil and Ph.D. degrees in Anthropology from Sambalpur University. He also holds a diploma in Labour Laws and Personnel Management. He was the Associate Director of two Evolution Projects on Total Literacy Campaign, sponsored by National Literacy Mission Authority, New Delhi. Dr. Guru was a Lecturer in the Department of Anthropology and Tribal Studies, G.G. University, Bilaspur, M.P. He has got more than twelve years of post-graduate teaching experience. He has also successfully guided three M.Phil dissertations. Dr. Guru is the Associate Editor of three different volumes—*Contemporary Society: Tribal Studies* (Vol. I & II, New Delhi, Concept, 1997) and *Contemporary Society: Childhood and Complex Order* (New Delhi, Manak Pvt. Ltd., 1996). He is also an Associate Editor of the International Journal—*Journal of Social Sciences.* Dr. Guru has presented papers in different national seminars and conferences and published a number of research papers in various journals and edited volumes. His areas of interest include tribal demography, anthropology of children and childhood and women studies.

Mailing Address: Department of Anthropology
Sambalpur University
Sambalpur-768 019
Orissa, India

Mann, K. is a sociologist by profession. She has authored three books and published over two dozen papers mainly concerning tribal women. As a Research Associate of University Grants Commission and as Senior Fellow of Anthropological Survey of India, Dr. Mann has conducted fieldwork in various regions of the country. She has attended many seminars on the theme of her interest. Her area of special interest is tribal women.

Mailing Address: Department of Anthropology
University of Delhi
Delhi - 110 007, India

Mann, R.S. is a Professor of Social Anthropology in the Department of Anthropology, Delhi University. Prior to this, Prof. Mann was the Director of Anthropological Survey of India, Government of India. As such one finds in him a combination of empiricist and theorist. Prof. Mann has authored/edited fourteen books and over hundred articles in various Indian and foreign journals. He has participated in national and international seminars held in India and abroad. His specialization maps tribal ethnographies and theoretic concern.

Mailing Address: Department of Anthropology
University of Delhi
Delhi - 110 007 India

Mahapatra, L.K. is a retired Professor of Anthropology, Utkal University, Bhubaneswar. He was also the former Vice-Chancellor of Utkal University and Sambalpur University of Orissa. Prof. Mohapatra was a visiting Professor at Hamburg University and a visiting Fellow of the Ford Foundation, in Indonesia. Prof. Mohapatra was the former Director of Nabakrushna Chowdhury Centre for Development Studies, Bhubaneswar. He was also the consultant to UNESCO and World Bank in resettlement and rehabilitation (1985-87). Prof. Mohapatra was the recipient of Swami Pranabananda Award, R.P. Chand Centenary Memorial Medal. Currently Prof. Mohapatra is a member of International Commission on Anthropology in Policy and Practice, and International Commission on Anthropological Aspects of Global Environmental Change, both affiliated through International Union of Anthropological and Ethnological Science to UNESCO. He is also the president of Anthropological Society, Orissa and Association for Friendship and Cultural Cooperation with Indonesia. He is a member of the Advisory Board of *Journal of Social Sciences.* Prof. Mohapatra has published 125 articles in India and 27 abroad. He has also authored seven books including one published by UNESCO (1983).

Mailing Address: 16, Satyanagar
Bhubaneswar-751 007
Orissa, India

Mishra, Braja Kishori obtained her Master's (Gold Medalist) and Doctoral degrees in Home Science from Sambalpur University. At present she is Reader and Head of the Department of Home Science, Sambalpur University. She has got more than 18 years of post-graduate teaching and research experience. She has published a number of research articles in different journals of national repute. She has authored the book *Breast Feeding and Child Development* (Ashish Publishing House, New Delhi, 1993). Her areas of specialization are community nutrition, human development and family studies.

Mailing Address: Department of Home Science
Sambalpur University
Sambalpur -768 019
Orissa, India

Mukhopadhyay, Sutapa is a registered research scholar under University of Calcutta. She is working under the supervision of Prof. Ranjana Ray for her Doctoral degree.

She is a full time Lecturer in Vivekananda College for Women.

Mailing Address: Dept of Anthropology
Calcutta University
35, Ballygunge Circular Road
Calcutta - 700 019
West Bengal
India

Padhi, Itishree got her Master's degree (first class first) from Berhampur University and M.Phil (topper) and Doctoral degrees in Anthropology from Sambalpur University. At present she is a Lecturer in Anthropology in B.J.B. College, Bhubaneswar. She has to her credit one book entitled, *Role Conflict of Working Mothers in Teaching Profession.* and a number of research articles. She has participated in various national level conferences. Her current interest in research includes gender issue and development studies.

Mailing Address: Lecturer in Anthropology
3R-3/3 Kalpana Flat
Bhubaneswar - 14
Orissa, India

Pasayat, Chitrasen received his Master's, M.Phil and Doctoral degrees from Jawaharlal Nehru University, New Delhi. He was awarded U.G.C. Fellowship during 1985-90. Dr. Pasayat has done extensive research in tribal and rural areas of Western Orissa. The revised version of his Ph.D. thesis has already been published by Rawat Publishers, Jaipur. He has also to his credit more than twenty research articles. His current interests in research are folk culture, tribal studies and ethnicity.

Mailing Address: Dalei Para,
Sambalpur - 768 001
Orissa, India

Patel, Srikant is a Research Scholar in the Dept. of Anthropology, Sambalpur University. He is working on a development displacement issue for his doctoral degree. Mr. Patel has to his credit half a dozen publications in national and international journals. He has worked in a number of research projects funded by national bodies like ICSSR, NLMA, Ministry of Welfare, etc. He was a member of the external team for evaluating TLC in Rourkela city and Ganjam district. Mr. Patel has done intensive field work in different tribal pockets of Orissa. He is the Research Officer of the Institute for Evaluation, Research, Documentation and Training (INFERDT). Recently he presented a couple of papers in the 14th International Congress of Anthropological and Ethnological Sciences held in Virginia, USA during July-August, 1998. He is a member of the International Union of Anthropological and Ethnological Sciences (IUAES). Mr. Patel is also actively associated with the activities of the Commission on Anthropology in Policy and Practice that is affiliated to UNESCO through IUAES. His areas of research interests are development related displacement, tribal studies and gender issues.

Mailing Address: Mr. Srikant Patel,
Department of Anthropology,
Sambalpur University,
Sambalpur-768 019, Orissa, INDIA
Fax : ++91 663-404000
email: <srikantpatel@hotmail.com>

Pathy, Jaganath obtained his doctoral degree from Jawaharlal Nehru University, New Delhi. He is at present Professor of Sociology, South Gujarat University (Surat). For quite some time he was a faculty member of the Department of Anthropology and Sociology, Sambalpur University (Orissa). He has published four books and over eighty research articles. He was awarded U.G.C. (C.A) in Social Sciences, Indo-Canadian Fellowship and U.S. Fellowship. He is a member of the Advisory Board of the *Journal of Social Sciences.* Prof. Pathy's current interests in research are tribal studies, ethnicity, agrarian structure and development issues.

Mailing Address: Department of Sociology
South Gujarat University Campus
Udhna-Magdalla Road
Surat-7, Gujarat, India

Pathy, Suguna received M.A. (Sociology) degree from Saugar University and M.C.H. from Jawaharlal Nehru University. Her doctoral thesis is on tribal sociology. She teaches sociology of planning and development, industrial relations and labour movement in the Department of Sociology, South Gujarat University, Surat, Gujarat. She has published several articles in reputed journals and edited volumes. She is a member of various Professional Bodies and Advisory Boards. She has been awarded for Professional Competence from American Academy of Sciences, New York. She lectured in the Department of Humanities, Aleppo University, Syria, Faculty of Social Sciences, Allameh Tabatabaie University, Tehran, Iran and the Centre for Rural Development (Under the Ministry of Rural Development and Women Affairs), Isfaham, Iran. She is a member of the Advisory Board of *Journal of Social Sciences*. Her areas of interest are sociology of women, tribal studies and development.

Mailing Address: Department of Sociology
South Gujarat University Campus
Udhna-Magdalla Road
Surat-7, Gujarat, India

Patnaik, S.M. received his doctoral degree from the University of Delhi. At Present he is a Reader in the Department of Anthropology, University of Delhi. He has to his credit a number of publications in reputed journals and edited volumes. Dr. Patnaik has attended various conferences at national and international level. His current interest in research is development studies in the context of displacement and rehabilitation.

Mailing Address: Department of Anthropology
University of Delhi
Delhi - 110 007, India

Pfeffer, Georg is Professor of Ethnology at the Freie University of Berlin. He studied Ethnology, Sociology and History of Religions at Frieburg University, Germany where he obtained his doctoral degree in 1990. In 1971 he was appointed Assistant Professor at the South Asia Institute of University of Heidelberg where he was promoted to the position of an Associate Professor in 1979. During his career he has conducted fieldwork for several years in various parts of India and Pakistan and has learnt several Indian languages. Prof. Pfeffer has undertaken ten extended excursions to the tribes of middle India. In addition to his teaching and research obligations in Berlin he is an active member of several national and international academic societies and the co-editor of German Zeitschrift Fur Ethnologie. Prof. Pfeffer has number of research publications in reputed international journals. He has brought out three edited volumes jointly with Dr. D.K. Behera of Sambalpur University, Orissa, India. Of the three, two are on tribal studies and one is on childhood matters. He is a member of the Editorial Board of *Journal of Social Science*. Cults and kinship of Scheduled Tribes in Koraput and Phulbani districts of Orissa (India) are Prof. Pfeffer's key areas of interest.

Mailing Address: Institute Fur Ethnologie
Freie Universitat Berlin,
Drosselweg 1-3
14195 Berlin, Germany

Pramanik, Rashmi had her schooling in a public school in Kenya. She topped the merit list in Anthropology Honours under Sambalpur University. She has received a number of prizes in essay and debate competitions. Ms. Pramanik has presented a few papers in national level seminars and has also published some papers in national journals. Her current interest in research in anthropology of children and childhood.

Mailing Address: Department of Anthropology
Sambalpur University
Sambalpur - 786 019
Orissa, India

Prasad Rao, D.L. received his Master's degree in Political Science and Anthropology from Nagpur and Utkal Universities respectively. He got his Doctoral degree from Andhra University. He started his teaching profession from Andhra University in 1962 and retired as Professor from the same University in 1997. He has served as expert member of U.G.C. panels in sociology and anthropology. Prof. Prasad Rao was also the Chairman of Faculty of Arts, Andhra University. He is a member of the Advisory Board of *Journal of Social Sciences*. Prof. Prasad Rao's area of specialization is kinship and tribal studies.

Mailing Address: Department of Anthropology
Andhra University
Visakhapatnam - 530 003
A.P., India

Punalekar, S.P. received his Master's (Sociology) Ph.D. degrees from University of Bombay and South Gujarat University respectively. He received fellowships from University of Bombay and Sri Ram Centre for Industrial Research, New Delhi during his studies. He has worked in the department of Sociology, University of Bombay, Tata Institue of Social Sciences, Bombay and National Institute of Public Co-operation and Child Development, New Delhi. He was the Director of the C.S.S. from 1987-90. Prof. Punalekar is currently Senior Fellow in Centre for Social Studies, sponsored and financially supported by ICSSR, New Delhi, and the Education Department, Government of Gujarat. He has completed over 20 research studies under auspices of UNICEF, UNESCO, World Bank, APDC (Malaysia), etc. on themes like change and social transformation in rural India, urban slums and development, education among scheduled castes, caste and class violence, working class on small scale industry sector etc. Prof. Punalekar is a well-known figure in the Marathi as well as Gujarati Journalism circles. He was a visiting Professor at

Sardar Patel University, Shivaji University, Marathwada University, Bhim Rao Babasaheb Ambedkar University and Punjab University. He has served as a resource person in various Academic Staff Colleges in Maharashtra. He has visited Asia Pacific Development Centre (Malaysia) and University of Amsterdam (The Netherlands) in connection with the studies in poverty alleviation, IRDP assessment and street children in India. He was the President of the Gujarat Samajshastra Mandal Conference and Maharashtra Samajshastra Conference held in Vidyanagar and Wardha respectively. He is actively associated with Gujarat Forum for Women Studies of the MS University of Baroda and the Women's cell, Sardar Patel Institute of Public Administration, Ahmedabad. Prof. Punalekar has published over eighty papers in national and international journals. He has guided three Ph.D. scholars. Dalit Literature and dalit identity, legal and para legal institutes in tribal society, child labour, issues and policy questions are the areas in which Prof. Punalekar is presently working.

Mailing Address: Department of Social Studies
South Gujarat University
Udhna-Magdalla Road
Gujarat, India

Ray, Ranjana obtained her Doctoral degree from University of Calcutta. She is now a Professor of Anthropology in the same University. She has been in the teaching profession since 1974. Prof. Ray is the recipient of East West Center scholarship at the University of Hawaii during 1967-68. Recently she visited South Africa and delivered number of lectures in various research institutes and universities. She has published 55 papers in both international and national journals. She has also participated in a number of national and international seminars and conferences. Her areas of research interest are human adaptations, tribal studies, gender issues.

Mailing Address: Dept of Anthropology
Calcutta University
35, Ballygunge Circular Road
Calcutta - 700 019
West Bengal, India

Saraf, Samarendra is a retired Professor of Anthropology from Hari Singh Gour Vishwavidyalaya, Sagor. He has 40 years of research experience in the discipline. He was a gold medalist of University of Saugar for securing first class first position in the Master's degree in Anthropology in 1959. He was the recipient of the International Development Fellowship of the East-West

Centre, Honolulu, Hawaii in 1965. He was the co-chairperson of a session at the 9th ICAES held in Chicago in 1973. Prof. Saraf visited Germany and Czechoslovakia as UGC Visiting Fellow in 1985 and 1987 respectively. He was a Fellow of the Indian Institute of Advanced Study, Simla for the completion of his post-doctoral degree. He is now an Emeritus Fellow of UGC for the completion of his empirical study of the Hindu *tantrism*. He was the Director of the Academic Staff College of Dr. Hari Singh Gour Vishwavidyalaya, Sagor during 1989-92. Prof. Saraf has more than 100 research publications both in national and international journals and edited volume. He is the author of a book and co-editor of two volumes. His areas of special interest are anthropology of religion, communication and law, theoretical anthropology, applied anthropology and indology.

Mailing Address: Saraf Kutir
Laxmipur, Sagor 470 002
Madhya Pradesh, India

Singh, Gopal Shankar obtained his Master's and doctoral degrees from Banaras Hindu University and Jawaharlal Nehru University respectively. He has received a number of awards and has more than twenty research publications to his credit. Dr. Singh is member of various academic and institutional bodies. He has also successfully completed two research projects. At present Dr. Singh is actively engaged in his post-doctoral work. His current research interests include forest ecosystem, natural and rural resource management, biodiversity conservation, ecosystem management, etc.

Mailing Address: C/o Dr. Golab Singh
Sector-8, N-289, R.K. Puram
New Delhi - 110 022, India

Tripathy, Prativa M. received Master's and M.Phil degrees in Home Science from Sambalpur University. She worked as a Nutrition Demonstrator (I.C.D.S. Project) in a Nutrition Rehabilitation Centre, Fasimal, Sambalpur for a period of one year. Recently she completed a three months post-graduate certificate course in Nutrition (December 1997 to February 1998) at National Institute of Nutrition, Hyderabad. Ms. Tripathy has a few research publications to her credit. She is now working for her Ph.D. degree on "Health and Nutritional Status of Tribal Women: Comparative Study of the Rural and Urban Women".

Mailing Address: C/o Braja Kishori Mishra
Department of Home Science
Sambalpur University
Sambalpur-768019 Orissa, India

INDEX